Readings in Russian Civilization

Readings

VOLUME II

IMPERIAL RUSSIA, 1700–1917

in Russian Civilization

EDITED, WITH INTRODUCTORY NOTES, BY

THOMAS RIHA

SECOND EDITION, REVISED

THE UNIVERSITY OF CHICAGO PRESS

CHICAGO AND LONDON

ISBN: 0-226-71855-7 (paperbound)
Library of Congress Catalog Card Number: 69-14825

THE UNIVERSITY OF CHICAGO PRESS, CHICAGO 60637
The University of Chicago Press, Ltd., London

CONTENTS VOLUME II

*Items added in 2d edition.

CONTENTS VOLUME I

*Items added in 2d edition.

CONTENTS   VOLUME III

*Items added in 2d edition.

PREFACE TO THE SECOND EDITION

This new and enlarged version of *Readings in Russian Civilization* is the result of fairly extensive revisions. There are now 72 instead of 64 items; 20 of the selections are new. The first volume has undergone the least change with 3 new items, of which 2 appear in English for the first time. In the second volume there are 6 new items; all of them appear in English for the first time. The third volume has undergone the greatest revision, with 11 new items, of which 6 are newly translated from the Russian. It is the editor's hope that items left out in the new edition will not be sorely missed, and that the new selections will turn out to be useful and illuminating. The aim, throughout, has been to cover areas of knowledge and periods which had been neglected in the first edition, and to include topics which are important in the study of the Russian past and present.

The bibliographical headnotes have been enlarged, with the result that there are now approximately twice as many entries as in the old edition. New citations include not only works which have appeared since 1963, but also older books and articles which have come to the editor's attention.

The editor would like to thank several persons who have contributed to the improvement of the text. Some sixty professors answered a questionnaire sent out by the University of Chicago Press and suggested changes or improvements in the *Readings*. Most of these suggestions have been heeded, and the editor is grateful for this generous cooperation by his colleagues. Professor Josef Anderle should be singled out, since he offered particularly detailed comments and had been most helpful in the preparation of the first edition as well. Professors Richard Wortman and Richard Hellie suggested new documents and, in the case of Mr. Hellie, translated them as well. Howard Goldfinger, Sylvia Fain, and Walter Gleason helped with the translations.

Once again I should like to dedicate this new version of my work to my students at the University of Chicago and at the University of Colorado. They have made this enterprise not only a duty but also a pleasure.

BOULDER, COLORADO
JUNE, 1968

THOMAS RIHA

PREFACE TO THE FIRST EDITION

In selecting the readings for these volumes, I was guided by several considerations. The selection, first of all, was to be important for the period of Russian history under consideration. Second, it was to lend itself fairly easily to class analysis—if possible, by the discussion method. This meant that polemics were preferable to descriptions, though I could not, and indeed did not wish to, manage without the latter. The selection was to stimulate curiosity to the point where the reader would wish to pursue the subject further.

All things being equal, I tended to lean toward primary sources. Thus, of the final sixty-four items, forty-six, or 70 per cent, are of this nature. Nevertheless, this remains a book of readings, not a collection of documents. I did not want snips and pieces, no matter how important; each essay is intended to be of sufficient length to develop a point of view or an argument reasonably and sensitively. I wanted my selections to be readable; there is not all that much good writing in this often turgid field, and I made a deliberate attempt to hunt for those authors who took pride in their language and exposition.

At certain crucial points I made a deliberate effort to bring a Soviet point of view into play. This I found to be not only healthy for argument's sake but sometimes quite enlightening in its own right. I carried this principle into the bibliographies as well. These were intended to provide a few guideposts to those who might wish to investigate an individual problem. Paperback editions were indicated because they might lead to the building of small private libraries. One could, these days, build quite a respectable collection of paperbacks on Russia.

I tried to give each period of Russian history its due. The order of selections will be found to be approximately chronological, though in a few places items are grouped topically for the sake of convenience. Each volume concludes with a general assessment of the period where more than one point of view is presented. It was my hope that Russian civilization would thus be given certain stages and a definable shape. If the general contours turn out to be approximately accurate, my aim will have been achieved.

ACKNOWLEDGMENTS

My thanks are due, to begin with, to the College at the University of Chicago, which conceived of the Russian civilization course and gave it elbow room to develop. Donald Meiklejohn, Warner Wick, and Alan Simpson were sympathetic initiators and tolerant supervisors. For a colleague they provided Meyer Isenberg, whose warm participation was essential to the first years of the enterprise and who always reminded me of the aims of general education. Chicago's Russian specialists —Michael Cherniavsky, Leopold Haimson, Arcadius Kahan, and Hugh McLean— gave their time to make improvements in the selections. Richard Hellie, Jean Laves, and Marianna Tax Choldin acted as able assistants. Elizabeth Ireland and Wells Chamberlin first suggested publication. Michael Petrovich inspected the volumes and made valuable suggestions. Ruth Jensen piloted the manuscript through its many stages over three years and proved to be the ideal secretary. Last, but most important, my students at the University of Chicago supplied the curiosity and enthusiasm which is their valued hallmark. To them these three volumes are dedicated.

THOMAS RIHA

CHICAGO

18

RUSSIA UNDER PETER THE GREAT

By John Perry

Beginning in the fifteenth century and down to the present, Western technicians have gone to Russia in search of employment. Often they were hired by the government to help modernize the country. Peter the Great hired more of them than any previous ruler. Below is a passage from the account of one of them who served in Russia as a hydraulic engineer for fourteen years, 1698–1712. He had been hired by Peter during his historic embassy to London.

The work is filled with enthusiasm for the potential riches of Russia, respect for the labors of the great Tsar, and condemnation of the backwardness of Russia's population. Perry's rather disappointing experiences are representative. It should be remembered, too, that he was not entirely innocent in his dealings with the Russians. His book exerted a good deal of influence at the time of its appearance; Voltaire used it as a source for his own two-volume *History of the Russian Empire* (1759).

For a brief sketch of Perry, see Peter Putnam (ed.), *Seven Britons in Imperial Russia, 1698–1812*. Another account of Anglo-Russian encounters is M. S. Anderson, *Britain's Discovery of Russia, 1553–1815*. A contemporary of Perry, Charles Whitworth, wrote *Account of Russia As It Was in the Year 1710*. For a biography of Peter, see Vasily Kluchevsky, *Peter the Great* (paperback), and the much larger *Peter the Great* of Eugene Schuyler. For an analysis of the Soviet view of Peter's reforms, see Cyril Black, *Rewriting Russian History*. For nautical matters during this period, see Sir Cyprian Bridge, "History of the Russian Fleet during the Reign of Peter the Great," *Publications of the Navy Records Society* (London), Vol. XV (1899). Voltaire, who saw Peter in Paris during the second of the Emperor's visits to western Europe, wrote a *History of the Russian Empire under Peter the Great* which was commissioned by the Empress Elizabeth. The reader should also consult the *Memoirs* of Peter Henry Bruce, who served in Peter's armies from 1710 to 1724.

AN ACCOUNT OF RUSSIA, PARTICULARLY OF THOSE REMARKABLE THINGS DONE BY THE PRESENT TSAR

In the year 1698, his Tsarish Majesty being then in England, making his observations of our arts in building and equipping out our fleets, among several artificers etc. whom he was then pleased to entertain, I was recommended to him

From John Perry, *The State of Russia under the Present Tsar* (London, 1716), pp. 1–13.

by the then Lord Marquis of Carmarthen, Mr. Dummer (then Surveyor of the Navy), and some others, as a person capable of serving him on several occasions, relating to his new designs of establishing a fleet, making his rivers navigable, etc. After his Majesty had himself discoursed with me, particularly touching the making of a communication between the river Volga and the Don, I was taken into his service by his Ambassador Count Golovin, who agreed with me for the Salary of 300 pounds sterling per annum, to be paid me, with my travelling charges and subsistence money upon whatsoever service I should be employed; besides a farther reward to be given me to my satisfaction at the conclusion of any work I should finish.

Soon after my contract was made, the Tsar going from hence to Holland, took me along with him thither, and after I had made such observations as I had there an opportunity to do, I was sent directly to Moscow, with orders for my being immediately dispatched from thence into the province of Astrakhan, about a thousand versts (or Russ miles) beyond Moscow, to survey a work, which his Tsarish Majesty had before designed, and another person been employed upon for the making of the abovesaid communication for ships of war as well as trading vessels of burden, to pass between the Caspian and the Black Sea, by way of the said two great rivers, the Volga and the Don. The first of which rivers, after running between 3 and 4000 Russ miles through the Tsar's country, falls into the Caspian Sea; and the other, after running near half as far, falls into the Black Sea.

The distance of which communication between the said two rivers is about 140 Russ miles by way of two other small rivers, the one called the Lavla, which falls into the Don; the other the Kamishinka, which falls into the Volga; up-

on these small rivers sluices were to be placed to make them navigable, and a canal of near 4 Russ miles to be cut through the dry land where the said two small rivers come nearest together; which work, if finished, would be of very great advantage to the Tsar's country, especially in case of any war with the Turks or the Crimean Tatars, or with Persia or any of the countries bordering on the Caspian Sea. A draught of which intended communication, I laid down.

The said work was first begun by one Colonel Breckell, a German, who was a colonel in the Tsar's army, and who had the reputation of a very good engineer as to fortifications, and the like; but he very little understanding this business which he had taken upon him, and having unaccountably designed the canal, and the first sluice which he placed being blown up, that is having given way at the foundation, and the water taking its course underneath, at the first shutting of the gates, he therefore, upon his coming to Moscow the winter following, obtained a pass to be given as for one of his servants, whom he pretended to send for necessaries for the work, and himself went off with the said pass, and made his escape out of the country.

The Tsar had advice of this whilst he was in England and therefore he was pleased to send me immediately forward to examine whether the work was practicable or not. Accordingly I went and surveyed it the same year. His Majesty was pleased to order me to take it upon me, and to begin the canal in a new place, that I proposed as more practicable for it.

Upon which work I was employed three summers successively, having demanded 30,000 men for it, but never had half that number, and the last year not 10,000 men given me, nor the necessary artificers and materials that were wanting, sufficiently provided. Of which I every winter, at my return to Moscow, gave a list into the Tsar's own hand, setting forth the necessity of being better supplied with what was wanting. But the Tsar having about this time lost the battle of Narva, and the war with Sweden being like to continue, which required more immediate supplies of men and money; in the latter end of the year 1701 I received orders to let that work stand still. I was sent to do another work, at Voronezh. And Prince Alexei Golitsyn, who had the government of the province of Astrakhan, where the work was situated, was displaced by the Tsar from his command, for his having discouraged the work, and not having supplied me with the necessary men and materials; for which the said prince ever after became my irreconcilable enemy, and by his interest (being allied to the greatest families) influenced the next lord, under whose command I afterwards served, very much to my prejudice.

Besides the general dislike which most of the old boyars had to all new undertakings which the Tsar, by the advice of strangers, engaged in, beyond what his predecessors ever had attempted to do, one occasion which made the Lord Golitsyn particularly dissatisfied with the said work, was this: after the aforesaid Breckell had unskillfully fixed his first sluice, which upon the first trial of the waters gave way, fearing the dangerous consequence that might fall upon him in an arbitrary government, deserted as aforesaid, and afterwards writ a letter of complaint to the Tsar against the said Lord Golitsyn, alleging that he had not been supplied with necessaries for the work, and particularly complained of the ill usage that he had received from the said Lord, who was then an enemy to the work, and who had struck him with his cane, and threatened to hang him. This happened whilst the Tsar was

abroad; and the Tsar having accused the said Lord, on his coming home, as not having discharged the trust that was reposed in him, he thereupon became irreconcilable to the work, and made reflections upon it, as a thing impossible to be done by the hands of men. He represented it as burdensome to the country by the number of men that were employed in it, and used all his endeavors to have had it given over as impracticable, declaring it as his opinion that God had made the rivers to go one way, and that it was presumption in man to think to turn them another.

As soon as I arrived in Moscow, by order as aforementioned, I petitioned for my salary that was then due to me, and which I was in hopes to have received, having as yet not been paid a penny of it, but only my subsistence money.

At this time my Lord Apraxin (whom the Tsar had a little before sent to supervise the said work, and who had then the chief inspection of building the Tsar's Navy, and is since made Lord High Admiral) was pleased to discourse me concerning his Majesty's ships at Voronezh, which being built of green timber, were in a very short time so decayed that they were ready to sink in the river. I told his lordship that there was a method which I believed might be put in practice upon that river, or somewhere near it, without careening, or the least straining of the ships, to place them upon the dry land to be refitted by damming up the course of the river . . . which his lordship told me would be a very acceptable service. Assuring me that I should be better assisted with men and materials than I had been with Prince Golitsyn; and that he would not only justly pay me my wages but that he would be my Patron, and help me to all my arrears which I then petitioned for, as soon as I had done this work which would be of great use to the Tsar in establishing his navy designed against the Turks.

Accordingly, in the year 1702 I was sent down to Voronezh, and pitched upon a place at the mouth of the river, which I found most proper for raising the water to the height that was required . . . which in little more than 16 months I performed to satisfaction, and the first time that the sluices were shut, I placed 16 ships (some of them of 50 guns) upon the land, to be refitted, fitting upright upon blocks as in our dry docks in England. . . .

But although this work was performed to their full satisfaction, yet when I demanded my salary and arrears that was due to me I was again farther put off by the said Lord Apraxin, until I had done another work which I was ordered to do on the same river and that then I should not fail of having all my money together given me.

The Tsar at the time when the aforesaid work was finished came himself to Voronezh, and gave directions for repairing his said ships that sat upon the land; and was then farther pleased to command me to survey the river, whether by the fixing of another large sluice higher up upon the Voronezh, the same could be made navigable the whole way from the city, for ships of 80 guns (such as he intended to build) to be launched and come down into the river Don at any time of the year.

Accordingly when I had surveyed and made my report to his Majesty that the same was practicable, he was pleased to command me to take it in hand, which I began in 1704. And the year following I finished the same to satisfaction, as I was commanded. . . .

When this last work at Voronezh was also finished to satisfaction, I again moved my Lord Apraxin for my wages, but I found the honor of his word and promises made to me, was but little regarded. For I was again put off as before, and was as far from receiving my money as ever. . . . However, after performing each of the said works, his Lordship, to keep me in some temper, gave me a small present to the value of about 250 pounds sterling.

The fixing of sluices that are to bear but little weight of water, for the making rivers and streams navigable for small vessels for inland carriage, where the floods are not great, is easy and practiced everywhere, but I do not know of any river that has before been made navigable for ships of near so great dimensions. And the ground where I was obliged to place the last sluice being extremely bad, when I came to dig below the surface of the river, I met with such extraordinary force of springs that all the pumps that could be placed could not discharge the water . . . which obliged me to let the works stand still six weeks, till I had made an engine on purpose for throwing out the water, which wrought night and day for several months together, and would easily discharge ten or twelve tons of water in a minute. The Tsar happening to come again to Voronezh, when I was obliged to use this engine, he came several times to see it work with several of his lords with him, and was extremely pleased with it, it being an improvement of an engine which I first made at Portsmouth dock above 23 years since. . . .

Whilst I was doing this last work at Voronezh . . . a person was ordered to make a new kind of docks on the river Voronezh for building his Majesty's 80-gun ships, with chests fixed to the bottom of them, to float them down the Don and over the bar at Azov, being from the mouth of the river Voronezh (as the stream runs) above 1000 Russ miles. . . .

It being then in winter, and his Majesty, upon the arrival of a courier from Poland, going suddenly from thence, he was pleased the night before he went to leave orders with my Lord Apraxin in writing for my making some particular observations at the coming down of the floods, and that my opinion, together with his three master ship-builders (which were two English and one Rus) should be taken, touching the place to be pitched upon for the building of the said docks. But quite different from my opinion a place was chosen for it, and the work was resolved to be carried on in a sandy foundation, and by a method that was no way proper for it; I therefore verbally urged to my Lord Apraxin the ill consequences . . . that upon the coming down of the floods the foundation of the work would blow up, and perhaps destroy the ships when they were half built (as it afterwards happened). But his Lordship thinking me perhaps only desirous to advance my own opinion . . . and adhering also to the persuasion of the Tsar's aforesaid Rus builder and another person of the same nation who had their private interest in it, having a small village in the place that was marked out for the said work, for which they were to have a much better given them in the room of it: I found his Lordship did not mind my words. . . .

19

LOMONOSOV EXCERPTS

By Boris Menshutkin

Mikhail Lomonosov (1711–65) was certainly one of the greatest Russians of all time. "Historian, rhetoretician, mechanician, chemist, mineralogist, artist and poet, he scrutinized and fathomed everything," Pushkin said of him. Today Moscow University, the greatest educational institution of the Soviet Union, is named after him. Excerpts from a biography of this man of genius will illustrate his many talents. The author was a leading Russian chemist who devoted much of his life to the study of Lomonosov's heritage.

For another biography of Lomonosov, see B. Kudryavtsev's *The Life and Work of M. V. Lomonosov*. There is an interesting article by Chapin Huntington, "M. Lomonosov and Benjamin Franklin," *Russian Review*, XVIII, 294–306. On Lomonosov as a literary figure, see Boris Unbegaun's "Russian Grammars before Lomonosov," *Oxford Slavonic Papers*, VII, 98–116. For a sample of Lomonosov's poetry, see Leo Wiener's *Anthology of Russian Literature*, Vol. I. For Lomonosov's place in the Russian eighteenth century, see Hans Rogger, *National Consciousness in Eighteenth Century Russia*. The first volume of *Science is Russian Culture* by Alexander Vucinich covers the eighteenth century. See also Luce Lengevin, "Lomonosov and the Science of His Day," *Impact of Science on Society*, XIII, No. 2 (1963), 93–120; L. Maistrov, "Lomonosov, Father of Russian Mathematics," *Soviet Review*, March, 1962; and Philip Pomper, "Lomonosov and the Discovery of the Law of the Conservation of Matter in Chemical Transformations," *Ambix*, X, (1962).

The topography of Lomonosov's native land deserves brief mention. Eighty kilometers from Archangel, just where the Northern Dvina flows into the White Sea, the river branches out into a number of arms which form many islands and islets. Each of these arms has its own name, such as Kholmogorka, Rovdogorka, Bystrokurka, and so on, as has every island. On one of these islands, ten kilometers from where the Northern Dvina begins to split into branches, is situated the city of Kholmogory. Facing it to the east, on the river Kholmogorka, is Kurostrov. There, in the beginning of the eighteenth century, were as many as twenty villages, settled almost exclusively by coast dwellers and encircling the highland center of Kurostrov. In one of these, the village of Denisovka, lived

Reprinted from B. Menshutkin, *Russia's Lomonosov* (Princeton, N.J.: Princeton University Press, 1952), pp. 11–24, 73–75, 81, 84–89, 134–40, 186–91. Used by permission of Princeton University Press. Copyright, 1952, by Princeton University Press.

Vasily Dorofeyev Lomonosov, the father of the future scholar and academician.

Vasily Dorofeyev was a typical coast dweller of his time and one of the most well-to-do and enterprising. He owned several ships and traded on the Murmansk shore, but often, in quest of profit, penetrated far into the Arctic Ocean. A pioneer among the coast folk, he was the first to build a new ship there and rig it in the European manner. It was a galiot of considerable size named the *Sea Gull*. Ownership of such vessels enabled him to engage in the transport of government supplies and private goods from Archangel to Pustozersk, Solovky, Kola, and on the river Mezen and along the shore of Lapland. At that time he owned a considerable amount of land. Thus he was able to accumulate substantial wealth. This is indicated by the fact that the Dmitrievsky stone church at Kurostrov was built chiefly with money which he contributed.

Vasily Dorofeyev's only son, Mikhailo Vasilyevich, was born in 1711 to his wife by his first marriage, Yelena Ivanovna Sivkovka, daughter of the deacon of the village of Nikolayevsk Matigory. The exact day of his birth is unknown, but accepted opinion sets it as the eighth of November. The education of young Lomonosov differed in no way from that given to other coastland children. Until the age of ten he remained in the village. Then his father began to take him out on business every year so that he might be trained from youth to assume the responsibilities which would be his when his father grew old. These voyages continued until Lomonosov was almost nineteen years old. During these years he made himself thoroughly conversant with the life of the coast dwellers, learned about shipbuilding and the manufacture of salt and other coastal products, and became acquainted with the most diverse areas of north Russia.

Even then Lomonosov, the future scholar, revealed himself. Everywhere he made careful observations, noticed all the details of his surroundings, and retained exact recollections of what he saw. Although it is known that he could not have traveled in the northern seas after 1730, here, for example, is what he writes in one of his letters of 1761: "The Lapps are distinguished both by poor growth and weakness because they rarely eat bread and meat, feeding almost exclusively on fish. I, being then fourteen, towered above and outweighed strong Lapps of thirty. Even though they are always sunburned in summer and do not know either rouge or white paint, when I chanced to see them naked I was surprised at their whiteness, in which they surpass the freshest codfish, their chief daily food."

During the winter Lomonosov spent with his books all the time he had free from business duties. From his early years he had studied reading and writing with Ivan Shubny, his neighbor in the village, and later probably studied with the deacon of the village church, S. N. Sabelnikov. I. I. Lepekhin writes: "Even as a twelve-year-old boy he loved to read the Psalms and services in church and, in accordance with the custom here, the Lives of the Saints as printed in the Prologues. In this he was very clever and endowed with a profound memory. When he had read some biography or discourse, after the chanting he would recite it accurately in shortened form to the old men sitting in the refectory." Undoubtedly in these youthful years, Lomonosov became much occupied with religious matters because of the influences of ecclesiastical and other religious books—the only ones he had at his disposal. Another influence was that of the religious dissenters and Old Believers, who were very numerous at that time in the Northern Dvina region and were naturally very much preoccupied with discussions on the "true faith. . . ."

However, as far as we are able to judge, the attraction of religion did not last long. About 1725 Lomonosov was able to obtain his first nonreligious books from one of the villagers, Christofor Dudin. These were the *Slavic Grammar* of Smotritsky and Magnitsky's *Arithmetic*. Smotritsky's *Grammar* went through a series of editions in the seventeenth century and was considered at the time the best book of its type. Grammar, defined as "the well-known art of teaching how to read and write well," was a broader subject than it now is. The *Grammar* was provided with a prosody in which were explained the rules "of the meter or quantitative measure of the composition of verses." The *Arithmetic* of Magnitsky, published in Moscow in 1703, was "for the sake of instruction of wisdom-loving boys and girls." It represented not only what we would now consider a book on arithmetic, but also a popularly expounded collection of all sorts of exact and natural sciences: geometry, physics, geography, astronomy, and so on. All of this information was so presented as to apply to the Russian life of this time, and in such a way that the reader could understand everything without a teacher if only he were industrious and zealous. Magnitsky's point of view was expressed in the maxim, "the faculty of speech and writing should be drilled in the knowledge and glorification of God."

These two books probably also had a decisive significance in directing Lomonosov's intellectual activity toward the exact sciences. But it was not easy for him to pursue them. His father married again in 1725, for the third time, to Irina Semyonovna Korelskaya of Nikolayevsk Matigory. This second stepmother was not well disposed toward

Lomonosov. As he himself writes: "Although I had a father who was a good man by nature, though brought up in the utmost ignorance, I had a wicked and jealous stepmother who tried in every way to arouse anger in my father. She made out that I was always idly sitting at my books so that I was constantly obliged to read and study what I could in solitary and desolate places, and to suffer cold and hunger."

Later, people who knew (Lomonosov's closest relatives at that time were serving in the Archangel customhouse) explained to him that in order to study science it was indispensable, first of all, to learn the Latin language, through which at that time all scholars communicated, in which scientific books were written almost exclusively, and by means of which all teaching was conducted. But it was impossible for Lomonosov to study this language in his native land. Although a Slavo-Latin School was founded in Kholmogory in 1723 by the Archbishop Varnava, as a general rule peasants subjected to a poll tax, as was Lomonosov, were not admitted.

Oppressive family tyranny, constant outbursts by the second stepmother against the "ne'er-do-well" Lomonosov, brought him to a decision to leave his family and try to obtain elsewhere by his own efforts the knowledge and education he desired. Quite naturally his thoughts settled on Moscow, the center of the cultural life of the day, where it would be easiest to realize his ambition. As already pointed out, the active trade relations of the Northern Dvina region with the capital of the time, then only beginning to yield its supremacy to the young St. Petersburg, naturally resulted in the constant presence there of many coast dwellers. They had lived there a long time, knew the city well, and had their offices and shops there. The clerks of these shops were sent as escorts of the long winter wagon trains of goods. Undoubtedly Lomonosov was able to learn from them all that interested him.

He realized his aims at the end of the year 1730. We have documentary evidence on the subject, for in the record of the Kurostrov district is the following memorandum: "In 1730, on the seventh day of November, Mikhailo Vasilyev Lomonosov was allowed to go to Moscow and to the sea until the month of September of the following year, 1731, and Ivan Banev signed the guarantee of payment of his poll tax."

Further on, another statement, which is provided by Lomonosov himself, will be adduced as to the circumstances of his departure from Denisovka. He interrupted his journey for a few days at the Antonievo-Siisky monastery, where he served temporarily as psalm reader. From there he set out directly with one of the numerous caravans which was hastening to make use of the established sledge route to deliver goods to Moscow. Lomonosov arrived in Moscow in the middle of January. He stayed with a fellow villager, the clerk Pyatukhin, and immediately petitioned for admission to one of the Moscow schools. At first he tried to settle in the accounting school (the school of navigation, according to other sources). But at the end of January he submitted to Archimandrite Herman of the Zaikonospassky monastery a petition for admission to the Moscow Slavo-Graeco-Latin Academy connected with the monastery.

In order to be enrolled, Lomonosov concealed his peasant origin in the examination and represented himself to be the son of a nobleman of Kholmogory. In a decree of the synod of July 7, 1723, an order had been promulgated "to dismiss and henceforth not to admit people belonging to estate owners and the sons of peasants, as well as the stupid and the malignant." Evidently they did not demand an immediate presentation of full proof of Lomonosov's noble origin and admitted him to the academy.

A higher institution of learning in the early eighteenth century had little in common with what we are now accustomed to understand by that appellation. The Slavo-Graeco-Latin Academy, founded in 1684, consisted of eight classes: four lower ones (grammar, syntax); two middle classes (poetry, rhetoric) and two higher (philosophy, religion). The instruction in the lower classes was concentrated chiefly on the study of Latin, learned so thoroughly that at the end of the fourth year the students could read and write it, and on the study of the Slavonic language. In addition, they had to know geography, history, the catechism, and arithmetic. In the middle classes, the students were already obliged to speak Latin. The students' scholarship was entrusted to auditors chosen from the most diligent pupils, and then later to teachers. General recitations were conducted on Saturdays, when the lazy were subjected to floggings.

The middle classes, poetry and rhetoric, were for a time devoted to prosody, composition, and eloquence, and then to the chief subject, theology: the older classes also were given up to religion and philosophy. Once they had progressed into the upper classes, the pupils were made "students" and finished the course as "learned theologians." Thus the academy was, essentially, a specialized theological faculty.

Lomonosov's position in the academy was a fairly difficult one, and only his unquenchable thirst for learning enabled him to endure the severe environment in which he was obliged to study. In one of his letters he describes his life in the academy in the following terms: "When studying in the Spassky School I was subjected on all sides to powerful influences, which in those years were almost irresistible, hindering me from knowledge. On the one hand, my father, having no other children than myself, said that I, being the only one, had abandoned him and had abandoned all the fortune (measured by local conditions) which he had amassed for me by bloody sweat and which, after his death, others would plunder. On the other hand there was inexpressible poverty: since I had only an altyn (three kopeks) a day for wages, I could not have more for food each day than a half a kopek's worth of bread and half a kopek's worth of kvas, and the rest for paper, shoes, and other necessities. In such a manner I lived for five years and never abandoned learning. On the one hand they wrote that, knowing my father's means, the good people at home set their daughters' caps for me—they had proposed even while I was yet there. On the other hand, the schoolboys, little children, used to cry out and point at me with their fingers, 'Look, what a blockhead to be studying Latin at twenty!' "

Lomonosov's astounding talents were not slow in making themselves felt. He went through the first three classes in one year, during which he applied himself especially to Latin. At the end of a year he could compose Latin poems of moderate length. However, he obviously could not find in the academy what he so yearned for, the exact sciences. The longer he remained there and the more he developed, the less it satisfied him; he felt no inclination toward those scholastic and theological sciences which alone made up the curriculum. This spiritual dissatisfaction, together with the impossibilty of approaching the goals he had projected and his extremely difficult material circumstances (the state scholarship was only an altyn a day—and outside presents amounted

barely to a few rubles a year) compelled him to search for a chance to change his position. Such an opportunity came in 1734.

Early in the eighteenth century the expansion of Russian dominions to the southeast was in progress. In 1734 the government equipped an expedition under the leadership of I. K. Kirillov and Colonel Tevkelev to secure the eastern frontier definitely. With this in view it was proposed to found a new city (the present Orenburg) in order both to enter into trade relations as actively as possible with the inhabitants of the province and to spread Orthodoxy among them. To realize the latter aim, an indispensable member of the expedition, in addition to "officers, artillerymen, engineers, naval officers, and other people of varied ranks," had to be a learned priest of the Slavo-Graeco-Latin Academy; hence all the "learned" priests in Moscow at the time received an invitation to join the expedition. Not one of them, however, was favorably disposed toward leaving the capital to go into the hinterland, and all declined the opportunity. Thereupon Kirillov appealed to the archimandrite of the Zaikonospassky monastery with the proposal that one of the students of the older classes be ordained as a priest. Lomonosov turned out to be the one who was willing.

Again at the "candidate's table" of the Slavo-Graeco-Latin Academy, Lomonosov was subjected to a detailed cross-examination on his origin, since at that time they were very strict on the point that only those possessing legal qualifications should be made priests. This time, on September 4, 1734, "he said in the questioning that his father was the priest Vasily Dorofeyev of the Church of the Presentation of the Most Holy Mother of God in Kholmogory, and that he, Mikhailo, had lived with his father and had never lived elsewhere, had not enlisted as a dragoon or a soldier or in the service of Her Imperial Majesty, had not been sent into exile with the carpenters; that he had been correctly recorded as the real son of his father and was exempt from taxes. He had separated from his father to go to Moscow in the first days of December 1730. Having arrived in Moscow in the month of January 1731, he was enrolled in the above-mentioned academy, where he had since remained, and had progressed as far as rhetoric in his studies. He, Mikhailo, being still unmarried, was only twenty-three years old. . . . He had no heresy, sickness, deafness, or injury in any member. He could write cursively. And in case he had spoken falsely, then his priestly rank should be taken from him, he should be shaven, and be sent into cruel servitude in a distant monastery.

"To this examination the student of the Moscow Slavo-Graeco-Latin Academy, Mikhailo Lomonosov, has set his hand. . . ."

Quite as would be expected after Lomonosov's real origin was discovered, any possibility of his promotion to the priesthood or of his participation in the Orenburg expedition fell through. Expulsion from the academy was threatened him, but it did not take place, evidently because he enjoyed the good will of all the persons in authority. That much is clear not only from the fact that the inquiry remained without harmful consequences for him, but also that, in answer to a special petition from Lomonosov, the archimandrite ordered him to Kiev after (in December 1734) he had entered the class in philosophy. He was to stay there a year to complete his education in the Kiev Ecclesiastical Academy, then considered the foremost of the Russian educational institutions. In Kiev, however, Lomonosov found

nothing that was not theological and, thoroughly dissatisfied, returned to Moscow before the year elapsed to finish his education there.

But Lomonosov was not to become a learned cleric. At the end of 1735 an extraordinary event occurred which severed immediately his connection with the Slavo-Graeco-Latin Academy and fully satisfied all his aspirations in a way which he had probably never dreamed. His stay in the academy was fruitful in that, besides providing Latin and other studies, it enabled him to make up to some degree what he lacked —a general education—and logic and philosophy contributed to that clarity of thinking and exposition which is manifest in all his scientific works.

The cause of the unexpected change in Lomonosov's position lay in St. Petersburg at the Academy of Sciences, which had been founded some years before and with which he was inseparably connected from that time until his death. The Academy of Sciences owed its origin to Peter the Great, who discussed the possibility of founding it with the famous philosopher Leibnitz as early as 1711–16. However, not until 1720 did Peter take steps to realize his plans, concerning which he wrote to Leibnitz's closest colleague, the philosopher Christian von Wolf, whom he knew personally. . . .

Those few years in the life of the academy during which Peter I and Catherine I reigned were the years of its flowering. But when Peter II ascended the throne the capital was moved back to Moscow and the academy fell upon evil days. For years at a time it received no grants of money and was obliged to carry on its numerous institutions— printing office, type foundry, graver's plant, workshop for making precision instruments, and the like—as best it could by running into debt. Since the academy had no officially ratified statutes, all power in it belonged to the chancellery, of which the director (and librarian) was Johann Daniel Schumacher, the actual head of the entire academy. The gymnasium and university also declined during this period, since many families had moved to Moscow in the wake of the court. In 1734 I. A. Korff was appointed chief director of the Academy of Sciences. He was an energetic man who had done everything he could to better the condition of the academy. In order to fill up the gymnasium and the university, he petitioned the senate in 1735 to issue a decree requiring that students with sufficient preparation to listen to the professors' lectures be sent from the monasteries and the schools of Russia to the gymnasium of the academy.

The senate issued a decree in conformity with this petition, and among other things the rector of the Zaikonospassky academy was instructed to choose and send to St. Petersburg twenty students in the eminent sciences. However, they found only twelve in all of such students, since the best scholars were quickly snatched up from the senior classes by the hospital and other institutions. These students, "in our opinion by no means of the least keenness of mind," as the archimandrite wrote, were outfitted for the road. The best of all of them was Mikhailo Lomonosov. They left Moscow on December 23, 1735, and arrived in St. Petersburg on New Year's Day, 1736; they were enrolled at once as students of the University of St. Petersburg and immediately began their studies. Thus was the opportunity to study the exact sciences presented to Lomonosov.

However, this was little in comparison with what awaited him in the very near future. A great exploring expedition from the academy was then at work in

Siberia. The foremost representatives of the natural sciences were members of the expedition, but there was no chemist who was also acquainted with metallurgy and mining. No foreigners of this type were available, at least not any who wished to travel to Russia. Therefore, on the advice of one of the well-known metallurgists of Germany, I. Henckel of Freiburg, Baron Korff, the chief director of the academy, decided to send him three students best prepared to study chemistry and metallurgy. The academy selected three Muscovites, Lomonosov, Vinogradov, and the son of the mining councillor, Reiser. When the elder Reiser learned of this, like a practical man he pointed out to Baron Korff the necessity of acquainting the chosen students in at least an elementary way with those theoretical studies on which metallurgy and mining are based: mathematics, mechanics, physics, philosophy, and chemistry. This intelligent suggestion was adopted and, having changed its original decision, the academy resolved to send the students to Marburg to learn the elements of the necessary basic sciences. They were to go to Professor Christian Wolf, who gave his consent to their instruction in the University of Marburg. . . .

II

Soon after his return from abroad, Lomonosov had already won renown as a poet who fulfilled excellently the obligation of presenting festival odes—odes on the occasion of the birthdays, name-days, and the accession to the throne of ruling personages. His reputation became established as a poet who was always ready to present specimens of his art. For this reason he was sometimes given extra commissions by the court, for which he had to lay aside all other business.

When in the year 1750 the Russian

theater and plays written exclusively by Russian authors came into fashion, it was decided by the authorities to make up for the paucity of the repertoire of the time with tragedies by Lomonosov. And here we find a note of September 29, 1750, in the journal of the chancellery of the Academy of Sciences; "On this date the Lord President of the Academy announced an oral ukase from Her Imperial Majesty by which it was ordered him, the Lord President: that professors Tredyakovsky and Lomonosov should compose tragedies and report thereon to them in the chancellery." Lomonosov applied himself forthwith to the commission: in the notebook of his first tragedy, *Tamira and Selim,* stands the inscription: "Begun on September 29 after dinner." He finished it in four weeks, and on November 1 the academy directed that six hundred copies be printed at once. Since a new edition was required as early as January 1751, the tragedy evidently pleased the contemporary public. . . .

Another of Lomonosov's noteworthy achievements was his contribution to the founding of the University of Moscow. In his incessant labors for the propagation of education in Russia, he often pointed out to Count Ivan Shuvalov that it was necessary to found a university in Moscow, and on principles as liberal as possible. Shuvalov, in the fulfillment of this noble project, constantly asked advice of Lomonosov, who drew up detailed notes for him. According to Lomonosov's view, the plan of the university should be broad enough so that in the future, when the university had developed, there should be an adequate staff of professors, although at first it would only be possible to invite a part of them. Thus there would be left a sum of money free to use on auxiliary institutes, and above all on a library. Therefore it was proposed that the number of professors should not be less than twelve; three on the medical faculty, three on the faculty of jurisprudence, and six on the philosophical faculty.

In all probability, the elaborately conceived project which was presented by Shuvalov to the senate also belonged to Lomonosov. All necessary legal steps were taken without delay, and the university was formally opened by Shuvalov on January 12, 1755, St. Tatiana's day. Unquestionably, Lomonosov was the real founder of the oldest Russian university, although evidently he took no part in the opening itself. The first professors of the new university were several of his students. One of the first books published by the printing house founded in connection with the University of Moscow was the second edition of a collection of Lomonosov's works, printed by the order of Shuvalov. (The first volume appeared in 1757; the second in 1759.) This showed how highly he esteemed Lomonosov. . . .

In 1756 Lomonosov came into free possession of six burned-out places on the right bank of the Moika canal, not far from the present Pochtamsky bridge, with the stipulation that within five years he build a stone house on the site. Lomonosov set about building at once, and erected a stone house of moderate size, with a laboratory and a flight of wide steps, where he always dined in summer and entertained his fellow countrymen from the seacoast, who never failed to visit him when they are arrived in St. Petersburg with their wares. He moved into his own house in 1757.

During this period of Lomonosov's scientific activity his electrical experiments were of outstanding significance. In North America, about the middle of the eighteenth century, Benjamin Franklin was actively studying the nature and properties of electricity. His experiments led him to realize the truth of the idea expressed by many before him that thunderclouds are electrically charged and that there is in them the same kind of electricity as that generated by machines or produced in the Leyden jar, which was discovered about 1745. Franklin proposed to decide the question as to whether clouds were electrified in this manner: A man standing isolated on a high spot would hold a piece of iron which had been drawn to a sharp point. If, when pointed directly at the overhanging cloud, the iron became electrified, that would be proof of the presence of electricity in the cloud. Franklin himself did not perform this experiment, but the French physicist Dalibard set up near Paris an iron pole forty feet high, partly insulated by a wooden support. When on May 10, 1752, a thundercloud came over this pole, it was electrified so strongly that it discharged sparks four centimeters in length. In June of the same year (1752) Franklin, knowing nothing of Dalibard's experiments, released a silk kite below a cloud. A metal point was made fast to the kite, and to the point was tied a hemp rope by which the kite was held. On the lower end of the rope was attached a key, and to the key a silk string, which insulated the whole system. When the rope became wet with rain, sparks could be drawn from the key. In this manner it was proved that clouds are electrified and that lightning is an electric spark.

People in St. Petersburg learned very soon of Franklin's experiments, and one of the academicians, G. V. Richmann, who had long worked on electricity, repeated them and inserted a description of them in the *St. Petersburg News.* . . .

In the next year, 1753, Richmann continued his experiments and submitted accounts of them to the *St. Petersburg News.* Lomonosov, as Richmann's closest friend, also took part in them,

and both prepared to speak on electricity in the formal session of the academy. During a session of the academy conference on July 26 of that year, Richmann observed that a thundercloud was coming close, and hastened to his home, which was on the corner of the fifth line and Grand Avenue on Vailyevsky Island. He wanted to show the electrical phenomena to the master of engraving at the academy, Sokolov, in order to have a drawing made. Sokolov tells what happened later thus: "When the professor had looked at the electric indicator he judged that the thunder was still far off and believed that there was no immediate danger; however, when it came very close, there might be danger. Shortly after that the professor, who was standing a foot away from the iron rod, looked at the indicator again; just then a palish blue ball of fire, as big as a fist, came out of the rod without any contact whatsoever. It went right to the forehead of the professor, who in that instant fell back without uttering a sound onto a box standing behind him. At the very same moment followed a bang like the discharge of a small cannon, whereat the master of engraving fell to the ground and felt several blows on his back. It was later discovered that they came from the wire, which was torn to pieces and which left burned stripes on his caftan from shoulder to skirt."

Lomonosov described this event in a letter to Shuvalov in such beautiful clear language that it ought to be quoted.

"Gracious sir, Ivan Ivanovich, you will consider what I am now writing to your excellency a marvel, since the dead do not write. I still do not know—at least I doubt whether I am alive or dead. I see that Professor Richmann was killed by thunder under circumstances precisely like those under which I was working at the very same time. On the

26th of this July at one o'clock in the afternoon, a thundercloud came up from the north. The thunder was remarkable for its force, without a drop of rain. Looking at the thunder machine which had been set up, I saw not the slightest indication of the presence of electricity. However, while they were putting the food on the table, I obtained extraordinary electric sparks from the wire. My wife and others approached and they as well as I repeatedly touched the wire and the rod suspended from it, for the reason that I wished to have witnesses see the various colors of fire about which the departed Professor Richmann used to argue with me. Suddenly it thundererd most violently at the exact time that I was holding my hand to the metal, and sparks crackled. All fled away from me, and my wife implored that I go away. Curiousity kept me there two or three minutes more, until they told me that the soup was getting cold. But by that time the force of electricity greatly subsided. I had sat at table only a few minutes when the man servant of the departed Richmann suddenly opened the door, all in tears and out of breath from fear. I thought that some one had beaten him as he was on the way to me, but he said, with difficulty, that the professor had been injured by thunder. Going to his home with the greatest possible speed my strength allowed, I arrived to see him lying lifeless. His poor widow and her mother were just as pale as he. The death which I so narrowly escaped and his pale corpse, the thought of our friendship, the weeping of his wife, his children, and his household, affected me so deeply that I could say nothing and give no answer to the great number of people who had assembled as I looked at that person with whom I had sat in conference an hour ago and discussed our future public convocation. The first blow from the suspended ruler with the thread fell on his head, where a cherry-red spot was visible on his forehead; but the electric force of the thunder had passed out of his feet into the floor boards. His feet and fingers were blue and his shoe torn but not burned through. We tried to restore the movement of the blood in him, since he was still warm; however, his head was injured and there was no further hope. And thus he verified, by a lamentable experiment, the fact that it is possible to draw off the electric force of thunder; this must be by directing it, however, onto an iron staff which should stand in an empty place where the thunder can strike as much as it wishes. Nonetheless, Mr. Richmann died a splendid death, fulfilling a duty of his profession. His memory will never die; but his poor widow, his mother-in-law, and his five-year-old son, who has shown much promise, and his two daughters, one about two years old and the other about six months, weep both for him and for their own great misfortune. Therefore, your excellency, I implore you as a true lover and patron of science to be their gracious helper in order that the poor widow of the estimable professor shall have sustenance until her death, and that she may educate the little son of Richmann to be such a lover of the sciences as was his father. Richmann's salary was 860 rubles; most gracious sir, obtain this pension for the poor widow or for her children until death! The Lord God will reward you for this good deed, and I would esteem it more than if it were for myself. Furthermore, in order that this incident should not be publicly interpreted to the detriment of the growth of the sciences, I most humbly beg you to have pity upon science and upon your excellency's very humble servant, Mikhail Lomonosov, who is now in tears. . . ."

III

Lomonosov managed the gymnasium and the university connected with the Academy of Sciences until his death. He built a dormitory for the students, and did everything he could to make certain that the money apportioned for the maintenance of the gymnasium students would be paid on time (each received thirty-six rubles a year); he took care that the number of students should also equal the quota of forty; and, in 1759, he established rules for them, some excerpts of which are interesting. It was recommended "to apply the utmost diligence to the sciences and not to heed any other inclination"; to get along politely with the teachers, not to quarrel, not to prevent others from studying, not to use "words base and vulgar" in conversation. "When someone is reciting a lesson in response to a question of the teacher and does not know it thoroughly, the comrade sitting near him should not whisper advice to him and thus encourage his sloth. An abettor of this kind is subject to just the same punishment as the one who does not know." Cleanliness should be observed "not only in irreproachable work but also at table, and in caring for books, bed, and clothes." Sloth is of all things most harmful to students "and on that account should be overcome in every way by obedience, temperance, watchfulness, and patience." It was necessary to guard against "low, bad company, which might soon lead to a do-nothing and idle life as well as truancy from school."

Regardless of these excellent rules, the students undoubtedly led a hard life, and we frequently find descriptions of flights from the institution by students in which even teachers took part. Thus, having fled in December 1762, the student Morozov and the teacher Golovin were in hiding more than a month with counterfeit passports. Before escaping, Morozov stole the uniform cloak of another student, Kosov. For these misdemeanors Morozov was forced to serve in the army in 1763. In general, thefts also were frequent among the students even though severe punishment was prescribed for this; thus it was ordered that the student Arsenyev, convicted of drunkenness and thievery, should be expelled and "have severe punishment by rods inflicted on him in front of all the students and gymnasts, and should be sent, with an explanatory note, to the War Collegium [Ministry] to be conscripted as a soldier."

The gymnasium was located at that time in a rented building which had fallen into complete disrepair. In the winter the dough froze in the kneading trough in the kitchen and the ink froze in the rooms. Broken panes in classroom windows were patched with paper. The manner in which lessons proceeded is described thus in the report of the inspector: "The teachers in winter give lectures while dressed in fur coats, moving back and forth in the classroom, but the students, not equipped with warm clothes and not having the freedom to rise from their places, shiver, whereby arises an obstruction all through the body and the mange and scurvy set in; because of these illnesses they are obliged to give up attendance at classes. Thus it is not remarkable if the progress of the students is not in proportion to the effort of the teachers." . . .

The department of geography, of which Lomonosov became the head in 1757, was founded at the Academy of Sciences "for the study of matters which pertain to Russian geography," and its chief task was the preparation of accurate maps of Russia, constantly checking and revising them by means of new information coming into the department. The department consisted of professors and instructors with students working under their direction. In 1745 this department brought out an atlas of Russia, the maps of which later proved to be inaccurate in many respects. For twelve years previous to 1757 nothing had been done to correct them, and when Lomonosov entered upon his duties he decided first of all to undertake the preparation of maps as nearly exact as possible. To this end a questionnaire of thirty points was drawn up. These points were carefully examined in sessions of the conference, and later, toward the end of 1759 and 1760, the questionnaire was sent through the senate to all towns for an early reply. The questions related to "the size of the cities, the number of stone and wooden houses, on what river or lake they stand, when the fairs take place, what sort of businesses and crafts there are, what sort of workshops, factories, mills, arable land, and forests; on which hand, looking downstream the hilly [bluff] side of the river lies, where the landing places are, when the rivers open up and when they freeze over; at what distance the neighboring towns are situated; where there are notable and high mountains; what kinds of grain are sown more than others and which ones yield best," and a series of other economic problems. If there are any plans or records in the town, copies of them should be sent. The *Kammerkollegia* (Government department with functions of a finance ministry) was asked to furnish the number of souls in each village so that the large ones should not be omitted and the small recorded and the proportion thus be lost. Information on the monasteries and churches was requested of the holy synod. Appropriations for travel and subsidiary expenses were obtained from the senate for two geographical expeditions to "determine the longitude and latitude of important places, by means of astronomical obser-

vations." These expeditions, however, were not equipped in spite of all Lomonosov's attempts. During his life, likewise, the replies to the questionnaire that were received were not put to use, and the undertaking, which he had set up on such a large scale, thus failed to yield results—certainly, not without the help of his enemies. . . .

IV

Today we value Lomonosov primarily as an outstanding philosopher and thinker. While still a student, he divined the basic theme of investigation which was most of all to further the development of physics and chemistry: the study of the minute particles of which all bodies are composed and of their properties. Connecting all phenomena with the properties of the particles which make up matter, he himself came to some remarkable conclusions and foretold the general conditions and paths of the development of both physics and chemistry down to our time. In many other sciences, too, he expressed extremely important ideas which were not proved to be correct until many years later. His many-sided genius made itself felt everywhere, and in everything he was years, decades, or a century ahead of his time.

A consequence of this was that he could not bring his remarkably vast projects to actual completion. The stage of development of the sciences in the middle eighteenth century by no means corresponded to the lofty demands which Lomonosov made upon them. There was neither the requisite apparatus nor even hints as to the method of those researches which he wished to undertake. He did what he could himself—he invented a multitude of new apparatus, a multitude of methods which were new for the time—but of course he could not accomplish everything alone. If information had been preserved for us of all the new devices and instruments which were constantly born in his head and ordered to be built by the workmen of the academy and later by his own craftsmen, then we should have an amazing gallery of Lomonosov's inventions.

A second consequence was the fact that almost none of his contemporaries, even the academicians, could understand what he did or appreciate it at its true value. That, we are barely able to do today, after a century and a half or more. Not grasping the significance of his work in chemistry and physics, they thought it not worth special attention. During Lomonosov's life, so far as we can judge, there was only one man who appreciated him fully, who understood all the significance of what he did, who was initiated into all the details of his scientific thought. This was the famous mathematician, Academician Leonhard Euler, and I think it necessary to devote a few words here to their relations, which undoubtedly exercised no small influence on the development of Lomonosov's creative activity in science.

Leonhard Euler, a member of the Academy of Sciences since 1727, probably saw Lomonosov when the latter was a student of the university in the academy in 1736. Then, we know that Euler on May 4, 1739, read Lomonosov's dissertation which was sent from Marburg, and that he left St. Petersburg three days before Lomonosov returned from abroad. We know also that Euler returned to St. Petersburg a year after Lomonosov died, in 1766, and remained there until his own death, September 7, 1783. Thus after 1736 they could not have seen each other. Their correspondence began at the beginning of 1748, after Euler had sent to the academy very good reports on Lomonosov's first dissertations. Later he asked that Lomonosov be urged to write a work in compe-

tition for the prize offered by the Berlin Academy of Sciences in 1749 on the subject, *The Production and Composition of Saltpeter*. (This Lomonosov did, but he did not receive the prize.) . . .

Lomonosov constantly united with his love for the sciences the urge to propagate them as widely as possible among the Russian people. This was yet another trait of his character which Pushkin fully discerned. "Lomonosov was a great man," he says. "Between Peter I and Catherine II he was the only original champion of the Enlightenment. He founded the first university; rather, he himself was our first university." We have seen many times what steps Lomonosov took toward this end and we must accord him his just due; very few people can take credit for such a feat as the founding of a university. And although Lomonosov took no part in the work of the University of Moscow after its foundation, he did not cease to devote attention to events taking place there. It was not for nothing that his works were printed at the press of the University of Moscow from 1757 to 1759. . . .

But the propagation of learning was one component part of Lomonosov's vastly broader plan by which he sought to promote the welfare of the entire Russian people. Indispensable to that end were profound economic reconstructions in the way of life prevailing in his time and he intended to write—and probably wrote—a series of letters and reports on these themes. They have not come down to us, and we must assume that G. G. Orlov confiscated them immediately from among the papers Lomonosov left. Only a letter to Shuvalov concerning the increase of the Russian population has been preserved, but it discloses Lomonosov's basic points of view as a statesman. This over-all national scale of his activity became especially marked in the last five years of his life, when he had attained the highest degree of fame and influence and when his voice was undoubtedly listened to. "How joyful to work for the welfare of society," he says in the ode dedicated to Count Shuvalov, the inventor of new types of cannon (1760).

How correct is his opinion of his own verse as a diversion in comparison with matters dealing with the welfare of the whole nation! And yet the great majority of his contemporaries saw him only as a poet, a philologist, an orator, the founder of the Russian language. These services, of course, were tremendous, the more so as they were in the last analysis evident to all and were preserved *in toto* for posterity. Lomonosov himself confessed that his scientific innovations would have no immediate propagators among the Russians; that his efforts to do everything possible to ameliorate the condition of the people, his efforts to raise the level of culture, for the propagation of enlightenment, would find no response in the ruling class. He realized that his beloved mosaics and the glass factory, on the development of which he had expended so much strength and energy, putting forth all his genius, would cease to exist after him. All this he expressed on his death bed to Academician Stählin: "Friend, I see that I must die and I look on death peacefully and indifferently. I regret only that I was un-able to bring to completion everything I undertook for the benefit of my country, for the increase of learning, and for the greater glory of the academy, and that now, at the end of my life, I realize that all of my good intentions will van-ish with me."

But if Lomonosov had been able to foresee the future, he would not have given way to such somber reflections, for the projects which he began were realized sooner or later. Already during the reign of Catherine II far-reaching reforms took place for the expansion of education. The end of the eighteenth century saw the foundation of the School of Mines (now the Mining Institute) and the Academy of Medicine and Surgery, while the universities of Kharkov, Kazan, and St. Petersburg were founded at the beginning of the nineteenth century. Parallel to these, there quickly developed a network of elementary and secondary schools.

In surveying Lomonosov's scientific activity, which he always considered by far the most important aspect of his work, we have already had occasion to point out the close connection of the development of chemistry from 1790 to 1800 with those quantitative methods of research which he constantly advanced and applied. His physical chemistry was revived more than a century after his death, and in a very short time came to luxuriant flower.

20

CATHERINE THE GREAT'S
"INSTRUCTIONS"   EXCERPTS

Catherine II was the only intellectual ever to sit on the Russian throne. Before she issued her *Instructions,* of which parts appear below, she had consulted the works of the great legal authorities—Montesquieu, Beccaria, and Blackstone—from whom she borrowed liberally. The sentiments expressed in her document are quite noble, but little came of them in practice. Voltaire, who took them at face value, declared the document "the finest monument of the century." Within four years of its appearance (1767), it was published in twenty-four foreign versions. France forbade the entry of the document, which was considered too radical, and later the Russian emperor Paul forbade its circulation within Russia.

The Memoirs of Catherine the Great (paperback), edited by Dominique Maroger, are a source of prime importance. *The Memoirs of Princess Dashkow* relate the views of a close associate of the Empress. *The Correspondence of Catherine the Great,* edited by G. Ilchester, describes her contacts with Europe's foremost minds. William Tooke's *View of the Russian Empire during the Reign of Catherine the Second* (3 vols.) is an account by a contemporary visitor. *An Account of Russia in 1767* by George Macartney was written by the British ambassador to Catherine's Court. Some five hundred pages of diplomatic reports by British envoys covering the years 1762–69 are printed, in the original English, in Volume XII of the *Sbornik Russkogo Istoricheskogo Obshchestva.* "Beccaria in Russia," by T. Cizova, *Slavonic and East European Review,* 1962, describes the great Italian jurist who influenced Catherine. Basil Dmytryshyn analyzes "The Economic Content of the 1767 Nakaz of Catherine II," in the *American Slavic and East European Review* for 1960. Soviet work on Catherine is summarized by Leo Yaresh in "The Age of Catherine II," *Research Program on the USSR,* LXXVI (1965), 30–42. Perhaps the best monograph on Catherine is still G. P. Gooch, *Catherine the Great and Other Studies.*

THE INSTRUCTIONS TO THE COMMISSIONERS FOR COMPOSING A NEW CODE OF LAWS

1. The Christian Law teaches us to do mutual Good to one another, as much as possibly we can.

2. Laying this down as a fundamental Rule prescribed by that Religion, which has taken, or ought to take Root in the Hearts of the whole People; we cannot but suppose, that every honest Man in the Community is, or will be, desirous of seeing his native Country at the very

From W. Reddaway (ed.), *Documents of Catherine the Great* (Cambridge University Press, 1931), pp. 215–16, 249, 257–58, 293–94. Used by permission of the publisher.

Summit of Happiness, Glory, Safety, and Tranquillity.

3. And that every Individual Citizen in particular must wish to see himself protected by Laws, which should not distress him in his Circumstances, but, on the Contrary, should defend him from all Attempts of others, that are repugnant to this fundamental Rule.

4. In order therefore to proceed to a speedy Execution of what *We* expect from such a general Wish, *We*, fixing the Foundation upon the above first-mentioned Rule, ought to begin with an Inquiry into the natural Situation of this Empire.

5. For those Laws have the greatest Conformity with Nature, whose particular Regulations are best adapted to the Situation and Circumstances of the People, for whom they are instituted. . . .

6. Russia is an European State.

7. This is clearly demonstrated by the following Observations: The Alterations which *Peter the Great* undertook in Russia succeeded with the greater Ease, because the Manners, which prevailed at that Time, and had been introduced amongst us by a Mixture of different Nations, and the Conquest of foreign Territories, were quite unsuitable to the Climate. *Peter the First*, by introducing the Manners and Customs of Europe among the European People in his Dominions, found at that Time such Means as even he himself was not sanguine enough to expect.

8. The Possessions of the Russian Empire extend upon the terrestrial Globe to 32 Degrees of Latitude, and to 165 of Longitude.

9. The Sovereign is absolute; for there is no other Authority but that which centers in his single Person, that can act with a Vigour proportionate to the Extent of such a vast Dominion.

10. The Extent of the Dominion requires an absolute Power to be vested in that Person who rules over it. It is expedient so to be, that the quick Dispatch of Affairs, sent from distant Parts, might make ample Amends for the Delay occasioned by the great Distance of the Places.

11. Every other Form of Government whatsoever would not only have been prejudicial to Russia, but would even have proved its entire Ruin.

12. Another Reason is: That it is better to be subject to the Laws under one Master, than to be subservient to many.

13. What is the true End of Monarchy? Not to deprive People of their natural Liberty; but to correct their Actions, in order to attain the *supreme Good.* . . .

210. Proofs from Fact demonstrate to us, that the frequent Use of capital Punishment never mended the Morals of a People. Therefore, if *I* prove the *Death* of a Citizen to be neither *useful* nor *necessary to Society in general, I* shall confute *those* who *rise up against* Humanity. *I* repeat here, *to Society in general;* because the Death of a Citizen can *only* be useful and necessary in *one* Case; which is, when, though he be *deprived* of Liberty, yet has *such Power* by his *Connections,* as may *enable* him to raise Disturbances dangerous to the publick Peace. This Case can happen only, when a People either loses, or recovers their Liberty; or in a Time of Anarchy, when the *Disorders* themselves hold the *Place* of Laws. But in a Reign of Peace and Tranquillity, under a Government established with the united Wishes of a whole People; in a State well fortified against external Enemies, and protected within by strong Supports; that is, by its own internal Strength and virtuous Sentiments rooted in the Minds of the Citizens; and where the whole Power is lodged in the Hands of a Monarch; in such a State, there can be *no* Necessity for *taking away the Life*

of a Citizen. The twenty Years Reign of the Empress ELIZABETH PETROVNA gives the Fathers of the People a more illustrious Example for imitation than a Reign of the most shining Conquests.

211. It is not the *Excess* of Severity, nor the *Destruction* of the human Species, that produces a powerful Effect in the Hearts of the Citizens, but the *continued Duration* of the Punishment.

212. The Death of a Malefactor is not so efficacious a Method of deterring from Wickedness, as the *Example continually remaining* of a Man, who is deprived of his Liberty for *this End*, that he might *repair*, during a Life of *Labour*, the *Injury* he has done to the Community. The Terror of Death, excited by the Imagination, may be more strong, but has not Force enough to resist that *Oblivion*, so natural to Mankind. It is a general Rule, that rapid and violent Impressions on the human Mind, *disturb* and *give Pain*, but do not *operate* long upon the *Memory*. . . .

264. *Of the Propagation of the human Species in a State.*

265. Russia is not only *greatly* deficient in the *number* of her Inhabitants; but at the same Time, extends her Dominion over *immense* Tracts of Land; which are neither peopled nor improved. And therefore, in a Country so circumstanced, *too much* Encouragement can never be given to the *Propagation* of the human Species.

266. The Peasants generally have twelve, fifteen, and even twenty Children by one Marriage; but it rarely happens, that one *Fourth* of these ever attains to the *Age* of Maturity. There must therefore be some Fault, either in their Nourriture, in their Way of Living, or Method of Education, which occasions this *prodigious* Loss, and disappoints the *Hopes* of the Empire. How flourishing would the State of this Empire be, if we could but ward off, or pre-

vent this fatal Evil by proper Regulations!

267. You must add to *this*, that two Hundred Years are now elapsed, since a *Disease* unknown to our Ancestors was imported from America, and *hurried* on the Destruction of the human Race. This Disease spreads *wide* its *mournful* and *destructive* Effects in *many* of our Provinces. The utmost Care ought to be taken of the Health of the Citizens. It would be highly prudent, therefore, to stop the Progress of this Disease by the Laws.

268. Those of Moses may serve here for an Example. LEVITIC. chap. xiii.

269. It seems too, that the Method of exacting their Revenues, *newly* invented by the Lords, diminishes both the *Inhabitants*, and the *Spirit of Agriculture* in Russia. Almost all the Villages are *heavily* taxed. The Lords, who seldom or never *reside* in their Villages, lay an Impost on every Head of one, two, and even five Rubles, without the least Regard to the *Means* by which their Peasants may be able to *raise* this Money.

270. It is highly necessary that the Law should prescribe a Rule to the Lords, for a more judicious Method of raising their Revenues; and oblige them to levy *such* a Tax, as *tends least* to separate the Peasant from his House and Family; this would be the Means by which Agriculture would become more extensive, and Population be more increased in the Empire.

271. Even now some Husbandmen do not see their Houses for fifteen Years together, and yet pay the tax annually to their respective Lords; which they procure in Towns at a vast Distance from their Families, and wander over the whole Empire for that Purpose.

272. The more happily a People live under a government, the more easily the Number of the Inhabitants increases. . . .

519. It is certain, that a *high* Opin-

ion of the *Glory* and *Power* of the Sovereign, would *increase* the *Strength* of his Administration; but a *good Opinion* of *his Love of Justice, will increase it at least as much.*

520. All this will never please those Flatterers, who are daily instilling this pernicious Maxim into all the Sovereigns on Earth, *That their People are created for them only.* But *We* think, and esteem it *Our* Glory to declare, "That *We* are created for *Our* People; and, for this Reason, *We* are obliged to Speak of Things just as they ought to be. For God forbid! That, after this Legislation is finished, any Nation on Earth should be more just; and, consequently, should flourish more than Russia; otherwise the Intention of *Our* Laws would be totally frustrated; an Unhappiness *which I do not wish to survive.*

521. All the Examples and Customs of different Nations, which are introduced in this Work, ought to produce no other Effect, than to co-operate in the Choice of those Means, which may render the People of Russia, humanly speaking, the *most happy* in themselves of any People upon Earth.

522. Nothing more remains now for the Commission to do, but to compare every Part of the Laws with the Rules of these Instructions.

CONCLUSION

523. *Perhaps some Persons may object, after perusing these Instructions, that they will not be intelligible to every one. To this it may be answered: It is true, they will not be readily understood by every Person, after one slight Perusal only; but every Person may comprehend these Instructions, if he reads them with Care and Attention, and selects occasionally such Articles as may serve to direct him, as a Rule, in whatever he undertakes. These Instructions ought to be frequently perused, to render them more familiar: And every one may be firmly assured, that they will certainly be understood; because,*

524. Assiduity *and* Care *will* conquer *every Difficulty; as, on the Contrary,* Indolence *and* Carelessness *will* deter *from every laudable Attempt.*

525. *To render this difficult Affair more easy; these Instructions are to be read over once, at the Beginning of every Month, in the Commission for composing the New Code of Laws, and in all the subordinate Committees, which depend upon it; particularly the respective Chapters and Articles intrusted to their Care, till the Conclusion of the Commission.*

526. *But as no perfect Work was ever yet composed by Man; therefore, if the Commissioners should discover, as they proceed, that any Rule for some particular Regulation has been omitted, they have Leave, in such a Case, to report it to Us, and to ask for a Supplement.*

The Original signed with Her Imperial Majesty's *own Hand, thus,*

CATHERINE.

Moscow, July 30.
1767.

21

THE LEGISLATIVE COMMISSION OF 1767

By Sergei Solov'ev

"The assembly of the deputies," wrote the English diplomat Henry Shirley to the Foreign Office from Moscow on August 13, 1767, "is become at present the great favourite occupation of the Empress, and excludes, at least in appearance, all other business from her Cabinet. The Russians think and talk of nothing else . . . and it would be the most useless attempt to endeavour to persuade them that this assembly is far from being a check to the despotic power of their Sovereign. A man, however, who will consider with attention their manner of proceeding, what they are permitted to deliberate upon, and how far they are allowed to extend their reformations, and will compare it with what is practised in those countries blest with a mixt Government, will soon perceive that this is nothing more than a certain number of men sent by every province of the Empire, and by those Nations under the protection of Russia, to be in some respect the Empress' councillors in the drawing up the laws of this country. . . ."

Additional reports by British diplomats on the Commission are in Volume XII of the *Sbornik Russkogo Istoricheskogo Obshchestva*, pages 304–7, 326–31, and 357–61. Volume V of Vasily Kliuchevsky's *History of Russia* has an account of the Commission; there is an essay on the institution in Maxim Kovalevsky's *Russian Political Institutions*. The economic views of the deputies are analyzed at great length in *A History of Russian Economic Thought*, edited by John Letiche, which is a Soviet textbook translated into English. Marc Raeff's *Origins of the Russian Intelligentsia* (paperback) refers fairly often to the Commission; his article "State and Nobility in the Ideology of M. M. Shcherbatov," *American Slavic and East European Review*, October, 1960, discusses one of the figures quoted below. K. Papmehl writes on "Civil Liberties in the Records of the Great Commission," *Slavonic and East European Review*, June 1964. Sergei Solov'ev, who was a great Russian historian of the second half of the nineteenth century, is discussed in Anatole Mazour's *Modern Russian Historiography*.

For studies of the Russian nobility in the eighteenth century see Paul Dukes, *Catherine the Great and the Russian Nobility*; a chapter in *The European Nobility in the Eighteenth Century* (paperback), edited by Albert Goodwin; and Marc Raeff, "Home, School and Service in the Life of the 18th Century Russian Nobleman," *Slavonic and East European Review*, June, 1962.

Translated by Walter Gleason from S. Solov'ev, *Istoriia Rossii s Drevneishikh Vremen,* XIV (Moscow, 1965), 75, 77–78, 79–80, 83, 87–88, 89, 92, 95, 104–6, 119.

Catherine wanted to hear the frank opinions of the various classes of the Russian people, to acquaint herself, in the contemporary idiom, with the "mood" of the population among whom she wanted to spread the principles of contemporary thought; she wanted to become familiar with the views of the population in order to explore the soil before the planting, to discover what was possible to accomplish, to what the people would respond, and what was as yet impossible to undertake. Her interests in this case were practical; our interest, as her heirs, is no less, it is historical. The representatives of the various classes were gathered together for the joint discussion of affairs of the highest interest. This was an assembly of various estates, and we must, therefore, expect from each a desire to define their relations toward the other classes to their own advantage, especially as each deputy received instructions in that sense from his electors, and considered it to be his duty to justify their confidence. As for the noble class, it was divided into two parts, the old nobility, and men of the newly ennobled families. . . .

And thus the Assembly heard voices against the law of Peter the Great whereby those attaining certain ranks were thereby ennobled. It was the turn of the deputy of the Yaroslav nobility, Prince Mikhail Shcherbatov, soon to draw the attention of the meeting upon himself by his erudition, the literary polish of his speeches, and the ardor with which he delivered them. One of his opponents made the following comment about him: "I noticed that in his opinions Prince Shcherbatov very rarely bases himself on former laws, but supports his views by the most reasonable arguments, with which he was richly favored by God." Shcherbatov said: "The circumstances of the times and various developments

forced Peter the Great to create, in the interests of our own welfare, situations which now, because of the change in customs, are not only useless, but might become harmful. The aforementioned laws contain the principle by which anyone rising to officer rank is considered a noble, and his children are automatically entered on the nobility rolls. In the circumstances of Peter's times such privileges for those rising to officer rank were necessary in order to force the nobles to enter service; but now, when it is evident that the Russian nobility, through its singular love of the fatherland, of glory, and because of its zeal toward its monarchs is sufficiently inclined toward both service and the sciences, it would seem that the law equating this class with anyone who, by any method, attains officer rank, should be abolished. . . ."

Other deputies repeated the same thoughts, supplementing them with details. Ignat'ev, deputy of the Rzhevo–Volodimir nobility, said: "Many of the lower clerks, burghers, and others of the same type, holding governmental and general-officer rank, and serving in various official posts, buy large villages, multiply factories and plants, and thus limit the ancient nobility's ability to purchase villages. When a nobleman, engaged in farming and earning his keep by his own labor, wishes to buy a neighboring village at a moderate price, he finds that individuals not of the nobility, having large sums of money, raise their price by three or more times, and acquire the villages for themselves. In this way the noble, deprived of the means of increasing his own estate, falls into difficulties and his villages fall into decay. It is my opinion that those who have achieved high rank in the service and are not of noble origin should be banned from the enjoyment of noble status and the right to buy villages. Some of them may say: if they are not permitted to enjoy the nobility's status and the right to buy villages how will they earn their sustenance when they retire from the service and no longer receive salaries? To this one must answer that the same money with which they buy villages could be lent out, and, receiving a percentage on their capital, they could use it as if it were income from the villages. . . ."

The deputy of the Mikhailov nobility, Semen Naryshkin, attempted to define what differences, in his opinion, had to be established between the officers' corps and the nobility. Promotion to officers' rank serves as a reward for good behavior in lower ranks, while elevation into the nobility is a reward for exceptional service to the fatherland. Naryshkin also expressed the nobility's attitudes toward the possession of peasants: "We consider the dignity of the noble as something sacrosanct, separating him from the rest. It gives him and his descendants the right to own others, and to look after their well-being." But defenders of Peter the Great's legislation did not yield and one of them, the deputy of the city of Ruza, Smirnov, proposed to limit the inheritance of the nobility: "Since rank is received not through inheritance, but through services to the fatherland, and since it dies together with the person holding it, I propose that, so as not to enable heirs to enjoy the fruits of someone else's labor, so as not to promote passivity in the acquisition of rank through individual effort, so that those who deserve rewards not hope to receive the ranks earned by their forefathers, in order to strengthen the zeal for service in the descendants, to oppose despondency, negligence, and despair, and to encourage persons of the very lowest position

toward the achievement of the highest level of honor, noble status and its privileges not be heritable, but that everyone attempt to attain it by merit. . . ."

The ancient nobility, aroused against the easy attainment of noble status by people of low birth, stressed their own superior education and higher learning. But the means of giving their own children such an education was not always accessible to all of them, and they petitioned for the establishment of schools. . . . The nobility of Kostroma in their instructions to their deputy petitioned: "Many poor nobles are unable not only to educate and train their children in the sciences necessary to a nobleman, but on account of dire poverty they are not even able to take the children to distant state schools, so that the children grow up in ignorance and laziness, and not only become incapable of service, but do not have the faintest idea of the conduct of a nobleman. In order to maintain the usefulness of such people for the state, schools and seminaries should be established in the provincial and district cities for their education and training in literacy and the basics of mathematics and foreign languages, and especially for their decent upbringing. . . ."

The nobility demanded that the right to own peasants be reserved to themselves; the merchants demanded the exclusive right to trade. Alexei Popov, deputy of the Rybinsk merchants, said: "Instead of the expected improvement we perceive with deepest distress from the opinions given in the Commission by the many distinguished deputies that greater burdens are in store for Russian merchants, as if they were quite unessential to the state. Instead of confirming the decrees of Emperor Peter the Great bestowing upon the merchants their rights and liberties, and strictly forbidding persons of any other calling to conduct trade, through which the merchants could achieve the greatest prosperity, the afore-mentioned distinguished deputies pro-pose injuries to the merchants, asking that the well-born nobility, and the peas-ants as well, be allowed to enjoy the mer-chants' privileges. These distinguished deputies insist that merchants be forbid-den to own factories and mining estab-lishments. To justify such moves they say that the maintenance by the merchants of the factories and plants is not useful to society, and that it would be much more useful to leave the possession of these to nobles who have retired and are living in the villages. To this they add that peasants who have brought their products into the city should have the right to sell them retail. Should all this be confirmed the merchants would in-evitably fall into ruin, and with them commerce also might come to a com-plete halt. For although peasants and people of no rank are as yet forbidden by law to trade, the merchants, in spite of this, put up with many injuries and hindrances from them. What will hap-pen when everyone will be permitted to trade? . . ."

Apropos of these arguments, the dep-uty of the College of Commerce Mezheni-nov expressed a curious opinion: "Sev-eral distinguished deputies have argued as to whether nobles and merchants should own factories and plants, and whether such commerce would not bring disrepute to the calling of a noble. It would seem that discussion on this point is completely unnecessary. Let each look out for his own well-being, and in this way no one will be ashamed of anything, provided that one does not hinder the other. It would be best of all if nobles would found factories of the type which do not yet exist in Russia. But in this respect our Russian people are like birds, who, finding a piece of bread, fight over

it until it crumbles into pieces, is mixed with sand and dirt, and completely lost. Not more than twenty years ago the nobles, having realized that a substantial profit could be made on sailing cloth, and not thinking that a great many such fac-tories had already been built, so that sailmakers hardly knew what to do with their cloth, also began to build fac-tories of this kind, and did not realize their error until they were entirely ruined. . . ."

The demand for the improvement of law courts was recurrent in the petitions of the state, or black, peasants. The peas-ants of the Kazan district wrote: "We, as a people mute and ignorant of the laws, selling everything we own, hire lawyers for the prosecution of our law-suits, but these deceive and betray both parties; in addition, these suits require many witnesses, a great deal of informa-tion is demanded, and due to this the suit is drawn out, the petitioner and the defendant are ruined, and reach the point where they cannot pay the govern-ment's fee, nor even feed themselves. . . ."

As should have been expected, vehe-ment complaints as to the state of law enforcement were heard in the Commis-sion. The nobles charged that complaints against ecclesiastics must be lodged with the diocesan authority, against manufac-turers with the College of Manufacturing, against mine-owners with the College of Mines, against merchants with the city authorities, against mailmen with the Post Office; should it not be ordered that everyone be judged equally in all law courts? When complaining in law suits about "impious extortion and cursed usury," should it not be ordered that the officials concerned, the secretaries and state servitors, in all cases swear an oath that they have not taken a bribe; those guilty of venality, no matter how small the bribe, should be subject to the death penalty. Lermontov, deputy of the Galician nobles, spoke against the College of Justice: "From the innumerable quantity of business in the aforementioned College, rare is the petitioner who can receive, without incurring substantial loss, satisfaction in the time allowed by law. It is known to everyone in this assembly that in the College of Justice slanderers derive great advantage from the delay of suits. They draw out the time, and lead the petitioners to the point of exhaustion and complete ruin. It also happens that the College, having held up a case a long time, refers it for decision to another judicial organ. . . ."

We have seen how the author of the "Instruction" forcefully opposed tortures, and how earlier her restrictions were introduced by decrees, but in the instructions to deputies from their electors we meet requests for the abolition of these innovations, these restrictions. Thus, in the instructions of the Vereisk district nobility it is said: "Will it not be permitted to judge arrested criminals and thieves by the former laws for greater fear and a final elimination of crimes? Without torture crime cannot be rooted out; criminals must be frightened. Many thieves, caught with the stolen object, confess only to that particular theft, and previous robberies are concealed." . . .

The Suzdal nobility complained about the elimination of the death penalty and the limitations on the use of torture, for "some people, when they do not see murder punished by torture and execution commit crimes more freely, and peasants murder their lords; for this reason, cruel outrages, robberies, plunderings, and larceny of this type seem to be on the increase." . . .

Catherine had the right to be dissatisfied with certain individual developments, but she could not help admitting that the general goal for which she had created the Commission, had been achieved. "The Legislative Commission," she said in one of her notes, "having met, gave me insight and information about the entire empire with which we have to deal and about which we should care. It gathered all the laws and analyzed the materials, and would have done more of this had not the Turkish war begun. Then the deputies were dispersed, and the military went into the army. The *Instruction* to the Commission introduced a unity of rules and discussion unparalleled in the past. Many began to judge colors as colors and not as blind men judge colors. At least they came to know the will of the law-giver, and acted in harmony with it."

22

A JOURNEY FROM ST. PETERSBURG
TO MOSCOW   EXCERPTS

By Alexander Radishchev

Radishchev (1749–1802) is often called the father of the Russian intelligentsia. Dedicating his work to a friend, he wrote: "I looked about me—my heart was troubled by the sufferings of humanity." His famous book, suppressed by the censor unitl 1905, is today a Soviet classic. He was the first to raise his voice on behalf of causes which generations of the intelligentsia after him continued to plead. Like *Uncle Tom's Cabin*, the *Journey* is an abolitionist tract. It was translated into English by the late Leo Wiener of Harvard; we reproduce excerpts from the edition of Roderick Page Thaler.

There are several biographies of Radishchev: *Alexander Radishchev: The First Russian Humanist*, by Boris Evgeniev; *The First Russian Radical*, by David Lang; *A Russian Philosophe*, by Allen McConnell; and *The Philosophical Ideas of Alexander Radishchev* by Jesse Clardy. The Soviets view the man as the first Russian revolutionary; see John Letiche (ed.), *History of Russian Economic Thought*, pp. 549–646, for an extended Soviet analysis; see also Allen McConnell, "Soviet Images of Radishchev's Journey from St. Petersburg to Moscow," *Slavic and East European Journal*, Spring, 1963. Two studies of Russian thought which examine Radishchev are Vasily Zenkovsky's *A History of Russian Philosophy*, Vol. I, and Stuart Tompkins' *The Russian Mind from Peter the Great through the Enlightenment*. See also Roderick Thaler, "Radishchev, Britain and America," *Harvard Slavic Studies*, Vol. IV, and a chapter on Radishchev in Max Laserson's *The American Impact on Russia* (paperback).

Aleksandr Nikolaevich Radishchev was born in Moscow on August 20/31, 1749, three days after Goethe, six years after Jefferson, ten years before the younger Pitt. Until he was eight years old, he lived on his father's estate at Verkhnee Oblyazovo in what was then Saratov province (now in Penza *oblast'*), some three hundred miles north of present-day Stalingrad, two hundred miles south of Kazan', and one hundred miles west of the Volga River. His father was a well-educated landed gentleman who seems to have been liked and trusted both by his own peasants and by the gentry of his district. His peasants protected him during the Pugachev Rebellion, when many peasants were only too happy to murder their proprietors. In

Reprinted by permission of the publishers from A. Radishchev, *A Journey from St. Petersburg to Moscow* (Cambridge, Mass.: Harvard University Press, 1958), pp. 4–7, 9–19, 46–48, 158–60, 164–71, 187–90, 201–10, 239–41, 248–49. Copyright 1958, by The President and Fellows of Harvard College.

1787 he was elected marshall of the gentry of his district, Kuznetsk, in Saratov province.

From 1757 to 1762, between the ages of eight and thirteen, Radishchev lived in Moscow with his mother's relatives, the Argamakov family. The head of the Argamakov family was the curator of the newly founded Moscow University, and their home was always full of teachers and students. From 1762 to 1766 Radishchev was in the Corps des Pages in St. Petersburg, where he may have acquired some of his intense dislike for the Court Service. He was in St. Petersburg in 1765 when Mikhaylo Vasil'evich Lomonosov, the Russian Benjamin Franklin, died there. Lomonosov, a very different sort of man from most of those at court, embodied many of the qualities Radishchev most admired, and to him Radishchev devoted the last chapter of his *Journey*.

In 1766 Radishchev was one of twelve Russians sent by the government to study at the University of Leipzig. Among his fellow students at Leipzig were Aleksey Mikhaylovich Kutuzov, to whom the *Journey* was dedicated; Pyotr Ivanovich Chelishchev, who figures prominently in the *Journey*; Matvey Kirilovich Rubanovsky, whose niece Radishchev later married; Fyodor Vasil'evich Ushakov, whose biography Radishchev later wrote, telling particularly about their years at the University; and Goethe. Like Goethe, Radishchev particularly enjoyed Professor Christian Furchtegott Gellert's lectures on poetry and rhetoric, and Professor Ernst Platner's lectures in philosophy and physiology. The Russian students had been sent "to study the Latin, German, French, and. if possible, Slavonic languages, . . . moral philosophy, history, but particularly natural and international law, as well as the law of the Roman Empire. Each one is free to study the other sciences as he wishes." Accordingly Radishchev studied many of the French philosophers, not only Montesquieu, Voltaire, and Rousseau, but the now less well-known Bayle, Fénelon, Helvétius, Mably, and Raynal.

In 1771 Radishchev returned to Russia and entered the Civil Service as a clerk of the Senate. He was transferred to the Military Service, to the staff of General Bruce, in 1773. In this same year, when he was twenty-four, he published his first book: a translation, with introduction and notes, of Mably's *Observations sur l'histoire de la Grèce*. What I have seen of this translation is a very fair rendering of the original, not slavishly literal, but certainly close to Mably's meaning. Perhaps the most striking passage in the work is one in which Radishchev renders Mably's word "despotisme" by the Russian word "samoderzhavstvo," which means "autocracy." The Russian government at this time, and down to 1917, officially called itself an autocracy. In one of his numerous notes, Radishchev comments at length on this word. "Autocracy," he says, "is the state of affairs most repugnant to human nature. . . . The injustice of the sovereign gives the people, who are his judges, the same or an even greater right over him than the law gives him to judge criminals. The sovereign is the first citizen of the people's commonwealth."

In 1775, the war with Turkey won and the Pugachev Rebellion suppressed, Radishchev received his honorable discharge with the rank of second major. He married Anna Vasil'evna Rubanovskaya, with whom he was very happy until her death in 1783. In 1777 their first child, Vasily, was born, and Radishchev went back into the Civil Service, in the Department of Commerce. He had a successful career in the Service, was promoted in 1780, 1782, 1784, and finally, in 1790, became Chief of the St. Petersburg Custom House. He won honor as well as rank, being made a Knight of the Order of St. Vladimir in 1785.

When he resigned from the Service in 1775, Radishchev made a journey from St. Petersburg to Verkhnee Oblyazovo to ask his parents' blessing for his marriage. On the way, he traveled through some of the country ravaged by the Pugachev Rebellion in the past two years. When he reached home, he was told how his father's peasants had helped his father hide out safely in the woods and had disguised his younger brothers and sisters as peasant children while Pugachev's men were near their estate. But he also heard of things that had happened to many another landlord, less enlightened and less generous to the peasants than his father. In the *Journey* Radishchev, referring more than once to the Pugachev Rebellion, warns his fellow serf-owners, in vivid and striking language, that a far worse and more terrible rebellion awaits them. Only by prompt and substantial reforms —above all, by freeing the serfs—can they hope to avert revolution. . . .

Radishchev worked at the *Journey* intermittently over the course of ten years, beginning part of it as early as 1780. One of his own footnotes, which refers to the death of the Austrian Emperor Joseph II, must have been written after February 20, 1790. Part of the chapter "Podberez'e" was written no later than 1782, while another chapter, "Torzhok," contains a reference to "the late Frederick II, King of Prussia," who died in 1786. There are only two brief references to the French Revolution, which in any case was only in its early stages by the time the *Journey* was published, in May 1790. Russia had been at war with Turkey since 1787 and with Sweden since 1788, a fact which should be kept in mind when reading Radishchev's ac-

count of a sale of serfs as recruits for the army, and his particular rejoicing at Russian victories over the Turks in earlier wars.

Much the greater part of his book, however, was written by 1788. It would have been better for Radishchev had he published it then, before the French Revolution had gotten under way at all. It had not yet gone very far by 1790, but it had gone far enough to frighten Catherine II, to make her expect to see its poisonous, subversive contagion everywhere. "The purpose of this book," she wrote in her Notes on the *Journey*, "is clear on every page: its author, infected and full of the French madness, is trying in every possible way to break down respect for authority and for the authorities, to stir up in the people indignation against their superiors and against the government." In one of his two brief references to the French Revolution, Radishchev had simply listed Mirabeau, along with Demosthenes, Cicero, Pitt, Burke, and Fox, as a great orator to whom Lomonosov was comparable. The Empress was furious at Radishchev's "praise of Mirabeau, who deserves not once but many times over to be hanged. . . ."

At the end of the book was the usual imprimatur, the statement that it was printed "With the permission of the Department of Public Morals." The Empress, noting this, said: "This is probably a lie, or else carelessness." It was actually carelessness. Radishchev had submitted the manuscript to the censor, who had cut out substantial parts of it. But Radishchev had nevertheless printed it all, on his own press. He then submitted the whole thing to the police, who gave it their official stamp of approval without reading it again. It never occurred to them that anyone would dare to print anything they had cut out.

Radishchev had printed the *Journey*

anonymously, but it was a very simple matter for the Empress to discover who had written it. Frank, straightforward, outspoken, Radishchev had none of the instincts of a revolutionary. In 1789 he had dedicated his *Life of Fyodor Vasil'evich Ushakov* to Aleksey Mikhaylovich Kutuzov, whom he addressed as "my best beloved friend." In 1790 he dedicated the *Journey* "To A.M.K., My Best Beloved Friend," using exactly the same words. He went on to say: "Everything my mind and heart may wish to produce shall be dedicated to you, my comrade." Radishchev and Kutuzov were both well known in St. Petersburg, and Catherine herself had sent them off as comrades to the University of Leipzig. They had been good friends ever since. If this were not enough, the author of the *Journey* calls himself an inhabitant of St. Petersburg and later speaks of walking down the customs pier and looking at the ships, with more than a mere layman's knowledge of the ships and their cargoes. It was earlier in this very year 1790 that the Empress had made Radishchev Chief of the St. Petersburg Custom House. If it be objected that an editor with nothing else to do might notice such details in a book, but that an Empress with two wars to fight and a fair-sized country to govern would hardly have time, the editor must ruefully reply that the Empress found time to write ten closely printed pages of notes on the *Journey,* and that she noticed some things in it which he had missed.

The Empress's private secretary, Aleksandr Vasil'evich Khrapovitsky, noted in his diary that "She was graciously pleased to say that he [Radishchev] was a rebel, worse than Pugachev." On June 30/July 11, 1790, Radishchev was arrested and imprisoned in the Fortress of St. Peter and St. Paul. On July 24/August 4, he was condemned to death. Ten days later, Russia and Sweden made

peace in the Treaty of Verela. In honor of the peace, the Empress, on September 4/15, mercifully commuted Radishchev's sentence to banishment for ten years to Ilimsk in eastern Siberia, some three hundred miles north of Irkutsk and forty-five hundred miles east of St. Petersburg. She also deprived him of his status as a member of the gentry, of his rank in the service, and of his order of knighthood. But she did not confiscate his property, and she permitted him to travel without wearing fetters, after the first day. . . .

Less than a month after the commutation of Radishchev's sentence, Count Semyon Romanovich Vorontsov, the Russian ambassador to England, wrote a letter to his brother, Count Aleksandr Romanovich Vorontsov, President of the Commerce Collegium, Radishchev's superior officer in the service and lifelong friend. The ambassador wrote from Richmond, England, on October 1/12, 1790: "The condemnation of poor Radishchev hurts me deeply. What a sentence and what a commutation for a mere blunder! What will they do for a crime or for a real revolt? Ten years of Siberia is worse than death for a man who has children from whom he must part, or whom he will deprive of an education and a chance to enter the service if he takes them with him. It makes one shudder." But now, in time of trouble, Radishchev was very fortunate in his family and friends. His brother, a government official in Archangel, took care of his two elder sons. His deceased wife's sister, Elizaveta Vasil'evna Rubanovskaya, took care of his youngest son and his only daughter, and with them followed him into exile. In 1791 she married him, and they had three children in Siberia: two girls and a boy. Count Aleksandr Vorontsov proved to be a faithful friend, sending money, books, and news, and using his influence to make things easier for the exile. It was Vorontsov who prevailed upon the Empress to allow Radishchev to travel to Siberia unfettered, and who persuaded the governor of Ilimsk to let Radishchev go off on long walks and hunting trips. . . .

Fortunately for Radishchev, the Empress Catherine II died, November 6/17, 1796. Her son and successor, the Emperor Paul, had been treated abominably by his mother and hated everything that she had done. Accordingly, on November 23/December 4, 1796, Paul issued an Imperial rescript permitting Radishchev to leave Siberia and to live on his estate in European Russia, where his "conduct and correspondence" would be "under observation" by the governor of the province. Radishchev therefore went to live on his estate of Nemtsovo, near Maloyaroslavets in Kaluga province, some seventy-five miles southwest of Moscow, where he arrived in June 1797. His wife had died on the way back from Siberia, but in January 1798 Radishchev and all his children—four sons and three daughters—set off for Verkhnee Oblyazovo to see his parents. He stayed with them for a whole year, returned to Nemtsovo in 1799, and remained there until 1801. . . .

The Emperor Paul was assassinated on March 11/23, 1801. Four days later, the Emperor Alexander I freed Radishchev from being "under observation" and restored to him his status as one of the gentry, his rank in the service, and his order of knighthood. On August 6/18, 1801, on the recommendation of Count Aleksandr Vorontsov, Radishchev was appointed a member of the Commission on Revision of the Laws. Four years earlier, the Emperor Paul, at his coronation, had issued one new law of whose purpose Radishchev had heartily approved. On April 5/16, 1797, Paul had forbidden that peasants be required to work more than three days a week on their master's land. Radishchev, in the *Journey,* had particularly attacked landlords who required their peasants to give all their time to work on their master's land and allowed them no time to work their own. Now Radishchev hoped that under the reputedly more liberal Emperor Alexander I it would be possible to take further steps to protect the peasants. . . .

Two statements made by Radishchev as a member of the Commission have been preserved. The Commission debated at length the question of recommending a change in the law regulating the compensation to be paid to a serf-owner whose serf had been unintentionally killed. The Commission, including Radishchev, finally recommended a substantial increase in the amount of compensation. But Radishchev also sent to the Senate his own supplementary "minority report," in which he said that if a serf were killed, money should be paid, not to his owner, but to his parents, wife, or children. Although he approved of the increase in compensation, he wrote that "the value of human blood cannot be measured in terms of money." Again, Radishchev disagreed with the rest of the Commission as to the proper methods of trying persons accused of blasphemy, acts of rebellion, murder, robbery, and other capital offenses. The Commission recommended that the law should remain as it was, and specifically, that such accused persons should neither be permitted to challenge their judges nor be given a list of the charges against them. Radishchev, in a dissenting opinion worthy of Holmes or Brandeis, held that in every such trial the accused should be allowed to choose someone to defend him, and that if he could find no one, the court itself must provide someone to defend him; that the accused should have the right to challenge his judges; and that no one should be condemned to death by less than a two-thirds majority of the judges. . . .

In short, Radishchev had very high hopes for reform, but he was deeply discouraged and depressed by the attitude of the other members of the Commission, especially the chairman. Count Zavadovsky. One of the best Russian authorities on Radishchev, Professor Borozdin, accepted as "very probably correct" Pushkin's account of Radishchev's death. Pushkin said that the Emperor Alexander I ordered Radishchev

to set forth his ideas on certain questions of government. Poor Radishchev, carried away by the subject, . . . remembered the old days and, in a project presented to the government, revealed his old opinions. Count Z[avadovsky] was astonished at the youthfulness of his gray hairs and said to him in friendly reproof: "Eh, Aleksandr Nikolaevich, do you still want to talk the same old nonsense? Or didn't you have enough of Siberia?" In these words Radishchev saw a threat. Distressed and terrified, he went home, remembered the friend of his youth, the student at Leipzig [probably Fyodor Vasil'evich Ushakov] who had first suggested to him the thought of suicide . . . and took poison. He had foreseen his end long before and had prophesied it himself!

The *Journey* is full of Radishchev's view of suicide. In one place he advised his sons: "If there is no refuge left on earth for your virtue, if, driven to extremes, you find no sanctuary from oppression, then remember that you are a man, call to mind your greatness, and seize the crown of bliss which they are trying to take from you. Die. As a legacy I leave you the words of the dying Cato." When he had committed suicide, Cato had said: "Now I am my own master." And so, on September 12/24, 1802, Radishchev became his own master. . . .

A JOURNEY FROM ST. PETERS-BURG TO MOSCOW

LYUBANI

I suppose it is all the same to you whether I traveled in winter or in summer. Maybe both in winter and in summer. It is not unusual for travelers to set out in sleighs and to return in carriages. In summer. The corduroy road tortured my body; I climbed out of the carriage and went on foot. While I had been lying back in the carriage, my thoughts had turned to the immeasurable vastness of the world. By spiritually leaving the earth I thought I might more easily bear the jolting of the carriage. But spiritual exercises do not always distract us from our physical selves; and so, to save my body, I got out and walked. A few steps from the road I saw a peasant ploughing a field. The weather was hot. I looked at my watch. It was twenty minutes before one. I had set out on Saturday. It was now Sunday. The ploughing peasant, of course, belonged to a landed proprietor, who would not let him pay a commutation tax [*obrok*]. The peasant was ploughing very carefully. The field, of course, was not part of his master's land. He turned the plough with astonishing ease.

"God help you," I said, walking up to the ploughman, who, without stopping, was finishing the furrow he had started. "God help you," I repeated.

"Thank you, sir," the ploughman said to me, shaking the earth off the ploughshare and transferring it to a new furrow.

"You must be a Dissenter, since you plough on a Sunday."

"No, sir, I make the true sign of the cross," he said, showing me the three fingers together. "And God is merciful and does not bid us starve to death, so long as we have strength and a family."

"Have you no time to work during the week, then, and can you not have any rest on Sundays, in the hottest part of the day, at that?"

"In a week, sir, there are six days, and we go six times a week to work on the master's fields; in the evening, if the weather is good, we haul to the master's house the hay that is left in the woods; and on holidays the women and girls go walking in the woods, looking for mushrooms and berries. God grant," he continued, making the sign of the cross, "that it rains this evening. If you have peasants of your own, sir, they are praying to God for the same thing."

"My friend, I have no peasants, and so nobody curses me. Do you have a large family?"

"Three sons and three daughters. The eldest is nine years old."

"But how do you manage to get food enough, if you have only the holidays free?"

"Not only the holidays: the nights are ours, too. If a fellow isn't lazy, he won't starve to death. You see, one horse is resting; and when this one gets tired, I'll take the other; so the work gets done."

"Do you work the same way for your master?"

"No, Sir, it would be a sin to work the same way. On his fields there are a hundred hands for one mouth, while I have two for seven mouths: you can figure it out for yourself. No matter how hard you work for the master, no one will thank you for it. The master will not pay our head tax; but, though he doesn't pay it, he doesn't demand one sheep, one ·hen, or any linen or butter the less. The peasants are much better off where the landlord lets them pay a commutation tax without the interference of the steward. It is true that sometimes even good masters take more than three rubles a man; but even that's bet-

ter than having to work on the master's fields. Nowadays it's getting to be the custom to let villages to tenants, as they call it. But we call it putting our heads in a noose. A landless tenant skins us peasants alive; even the best ones don't leave us any time for ourselves. In the winter he won't let us do any carting of goods and won't let us go into town to work; all our work has to be for him, because he pays our head tax. It is an invention of the Devil to turn your peasants over to work for a stranger. You can make a complaint against a bad steward, but to whom can you complain against a bad tenant?"

"My friend, you are mistaken; the laws forbid them to torture people."

"Torture? That's true; but all the same, sir, you would not want to be in my hide." Meanwhile the ploughman hitched up the other horse to the plough and bade me goodbye as he began a new furrow.

The words of this peasant awakened in me a multitude of thoughts. I thought especially of the inequality of treatment within the peasant class. I compared the crown peasants with the manorial peasants. They both live in villages; but the former pay a fixed sum, while the latter must be prepared to pay whatever their master demands. The former are judged by their equals; the latter are dead to the law, except, perhaps, in criminal cases. A member of society becomes known to the government protecting him, only when he breaks the social bonds, when he becomes a criminal! This thought made my blood boil.

Tremble, cruelhearted landlord! on the brow of each of your peasants I see your condemnation written. . . .

VYSHNY VOLOCHOK

. . . The story of a certain landed proprietor proves that man for the sake of his personal advantage forgets humanity towards his fellow man, and that to find an example of hard-heartedness we need not go to far-off countries nor seek miracles through thrice-nine lands; they take place before our eyes in our own country.

A certain man who, as they say in the vernacular, did not make his mark in the government service, or who did not wish to make it there, left the capital, acquired a small village of one or two hundred souls, and determined to make his living by agriculture. He did not apply himself to the plough but intended most vigorously to make all possible use of the natural strength of his peasants by applying them to the cultivation of the land. To this end he thought it the surest method to make his peasants resemble tools that have neither will nor impulse; and to a certain extent he actually made them like the soldiers of the present time who are commanded in a mass, who move to battle in a mass, and who count for nothing when acting singly. To attain his end he took away from his peasants the small allotment of plough land and the hay meadows which noblemen usually give them for their bare maintenance, as a recompense for all the forced labor which they demand from them. In a word, this nobleman forced all his peasants and their wives and children to work every day of the year for him. Lest they should starve, he doled out to them a definite quantity of bread, known by the name of monthly doles. Those who had no families received no doles, but dined according to the Lacedaemonian custom, together, at the manor, receiving thin cabbage soup on meat days, and on fast days bread and kvas, to fill their stomachs. If there was any real meat, it was only in Easter Week.

These serfs also received clothing befitting their condition. Their winter boots, that is, bast shoes, they made for themselves; leggings they received from their master; while in summer they went barefooted. Naturally these serfs had no cows, horses, ewes, or rams. Their master did not withhold from these serfs the permission, but the means to have them. Whoever was a little better off and ate sparingly, kept a few chickens, which the master sometimes took for himself, paying for them as he pleased.

With such an arrangement it is not surprising that agriculture in Mr. So-and-So's village was in a flourishing condition. Where the crops were a failure elsewhere, his grain showed a fourfold return; when others had a good crop, his grain had a tenfold return or better. In a short time he added to his two hundred souls another two hundred as victims of his greed, and, proceeding with them just as with the first, he increased his holdings year after year, thus multiplying the number of those groaning in his fields. Now he counts them by the thousand and is praised as a famous agriculturist.

Barbarian! You do not deserve to bear the name of citizen. What good does it do the country that every year a few thousand more bushels of grain are grown, if those who produce it are valued on a par with the ox whose job it is to break the heavy furrow? Or do we think our citizens happy because our granaries are full and their stomachs empty? Or because one man blesses the government, rather than thousands? The wealth of this bloodsucker does not belong to him. It has been acquired by robbery and deserves severe punishment according to law. Yet there are people who, looking at the rich fields of this hangman, cite him as an example of perfection in agriculture. And you wish to be called merciful, and you bear the name of guardians of the public good! Instead of encouraging such violence, which you regard as the source of the country's wealth, direct your humane vengeance against this enemy of society. Destroy the tools of his agriculture, burn his barns, silos, and granaries, and scatter their ashes over the fields where he practiced his tortures; stigmatize him as a robber of the people, so that everyone who sees him may not only despise him but shun his approach to avoid infection from his example.

TORZHOK

... Everyone in our country is now permitted to own and operate a printing press, and the time has passed when they were afraid to grant this permission to private individuals, and when, because in free printing offices false statements might be printed, they renounced the general good and this useful institution. Now anybody may have the tools of printing, but that which may be printed is still under watch and ward. The censorship has become the nursemaid of reason, wit, imagination, of everything great and enlightened. But where there are nurses, there are babies and leading strings, which often lead to crooked legs; where there are guardians, there are minors and immature minds unable to take care of themselves. If there are always to be nurses and guardians, then the child will walk with leading strings for a long time and will grow up to be a cripple. . . .

Having recognized the usefulness of printing, the government has made it open to all; having further recognized that control of thought might invalidate its good intention in granting freedom to set up presses, it turned over the censorship or inspection of printed works to the Department of Public Morals. Its duty in this matter can only be the prohibition of the sale of objectionable works. But even this censorship is superfluous. A single stupid official in the De-

partment of Public Morals may do the greatest harm to enlightenment and may for years hold back the progress of reason: he may prohibit a useful discovery, a new idea, and may rob everyone of something great. Here is an example on a small scale. A translation of a novel is brought to the Department of Public Morals for its imprimatur. The translator, following the author, in speaking of love calls it "the tricky god." The censor in uniform and in the fullness of piety strikes out the expression, saying, "It is improper to call a divinity tricky." He who does not understand should not interfere. If you want fresh air, remove the smoky brazier; if you want light, remove that which obscures it; if you do not want the child to be timid, throw the rod out of the school. In a house where whips and sticks are in fashion, the servants are drunkards, thieves, and worse.[1]

Let anyone print anything that enters his head. If anyone finds himself insulted in print, let him get his redress at law. I am not speaking in jest. Words are not always deeds, thoughts are not crimes. These are the rules in the *Instruction for a New Code of Laws*. But an offense in words or in print is always an offense. Under the law no one is allowed to libel another, and everyone has the right to bring suit. But if one tells the truth about another, that cannot, according to the law, be considered a libel. What harm can there be if books

---

[1] They tell of a censor of this sort who would not permit any works to be published in which God was mentioned, saying, "I have no business with Him." If in any work the popular customs of this or that foreign country were criticized, he considered this inadmissible, saying, "Russia has a treaty of friendship with that country." If a prince or count was mentioned anywhere, he did not permit that to be printed, saying, "That is a personal allusion, for we have princes and counts among our distinguished personages."

are printed without a police stamp? Not only will there be no harm; there will be an advantage, an advantage from the first to the last, from the least to the greatest, from the Tsar to the last citizen. . . .

The dissenters from the revealed religion have so far done more harm in Russia than those who do not acknowledge the existence of God, the atheists. There are not many of the latter among us, because few among us are concerned about metaphysics. The atheist errs in metaphysics; the dissenter in crossing himself with only two fingers. Dissenters or *raskol'niki* is our name for all those Russians who in any manner depart from the common doctrine of the Greek Church. There are many of them in Russia; hence they are allowed to hold divine services. But why should not every aberration be permited to be out in the open? The more open it is, the quicker it will break down. Persecutions have only made martyrs; cruelty has been the support of the Christian religion itself. The consequences of schisms are sometimes harmful. Prohibit them. They are propagated by example. Destroy the example. A printed book will not cause a *raskol'nik* to throw himself into the fire, but a moving example will. To prohibit foolishness is to encourage it. Give it free rein; everyone will see what is foolish and what is wise. What is prohibited is coveted. We are all Eve's children.

But in prohibiting freedom of the press, timid governments are not afraid of blasphemy, but of criticism of themselves. He who in moments of madness does not spare God, will not in moments of lucidity and reason spare unjust power. He who does not fear the thunders of the Almighty laughs at the gallows. Hence freedom of thought is terrifying to governments. The freethinker who has been stirred to his depths will

stretch forth his audacious but mighty and fearless arm against the idol of power, will tear off its mask and veil, and lay bare its true character. Everyone will see its feet of clay; everyone will withdraw the support which he had given it; power will return to its source; the idol will fall. But if power is not seated in the fog of contending opinions, if its throne is founded on sincerity and true love of the common weal, will it not rather be strengthened when its foundation is revealed? And will not the true lover be loved more truly? Mutuality is a natural sentiment, and this instinct is deeply implanted in our nature. A solid and firm building needs only its own foundation; it has no need of supports and buttresses. Only when it is weakened by old age does it have need of lateral support. Let the government be honest and its leaders free from hypocrisy; then all the spittle and vomit will return their stench upon him who has belched them forth; but the truth will always remain pure and immaculate. He whose words incite to revolt (in deference to the government, let us so denominate all firm utterances which are based on truth but opposed to the ruling powers) is just as much a fool as he who blasphemes God. Let the government proceed on its appointed path; then it will not be troubled by the empty sound of calumny, even as the Lord of Hosts is not disturbed by blasphemy. But woe to it if in its lust for power it offends against truth. Then even a thought shakes its foundations; a word of truth will destroy it; a manly act will scatter it to the winds.

A personal attack, if it is unjustly offensive, is a libel. A personal attack which states the truth is as admissible as truth itself. If a blinded judge judges unjustly, and a defender of innocence publicizes his unjust decision and shows up his wiles and injustice, that will be a personal attack, but one that is permissible; if he calls him a venal, false, stupid judge, that is a personal attack, but it is admissible. But if he begins to call him dirty names and slanders him with offensive words such as one hears in the marketplace, that is a personal attack, but it is offensive and inadmissible. But it is not the business of the government to defend the judge, even though he may have been criticized unjustly. Not the judge, but the *person* offended, should appear as plaintiff in this case. Let the judge justify himself, before the world and before those who appointed him, by his deeds alone.[2] Thus one must judge of a personal attack. It deserves punishment, but in print it will do more good than harm. If everything were in order, if decisions were always rendered in accordance with the law, if the law were founded on truth, and all oppression were barred then perhaps, and only then, a personal attack might be injurious to the state. . . .

I will close with this: the censorship of what is printed belongs properly to society, which gives the author a laurel wreath or uses his sheets for wrapping paper. Just so, it is the public that gives its approval to a theatrical production, and not the director of the theater. Similarly the censor can give neither glory

nor dishonor to the publication of a work. The curtain rises, and everyone eagerly watches the performance. If they like it, they applaud; if not, they stamp and hiss. Leave what is stupid to the judgment of public opinion; stupidity will find a thousand censors. The most vigilant police cannot check worthless ideas as well as a disgusted public. They will be heard just once; then they will die, never to rise again. But once we have recognized the uselessness of the censorship, or, rather, its harmfulness in the realm of knowledge, we must also recognize the vast and boundless usefulness of freedom of the press. . . .

MEDNOE

. . . Twice every week the whole Russian Empire is notified that N.N. or B.B. is unable or unwilling to pay what he has borrowed or taken or what is demanded of him. The borrowed money has been spent in gambling, traveling, carousing, eating, drinking, etc.—or has been given away, lost in fire or water, or N.N. or B.B. has in some other way gone into debt or incurred an obligation. Whatever the circumstances, the same story is published in the newspapers. It runs like this: "At ten o'clock this morning, by order of the County Court, or the Municipal Magistrate, will be sold at public auction the real estate of Captain G., Retired, viz., a house located in—— Ward, No.——, and with its six souls, male and female. The sale will take place at said house. Interested parties may examine the property before the auction."

There are always a lot of customers for a bargain. The day and hour of the auction have come. Prospective buyers are gathering. In the hall where it is to take place, those who are condemned to be sold stand immovable. An old man, seventy-five years of age, leaning on an

---

[2] Mr. Dickinson, who took part in the recent revolution in America and thus achieved fame, and later became President of Pennsylvania, did not disdain to do battle with those who attacked him. The most heinous accusations against him were published. The first officer of the state went into the arena, published his defense, justified himself, overthrew the contentions of his opponents, and put them to shame. . . . This is an example worth imitating, of the way one ought to take revenge when publicly attacked by another in print. If one rages against the printed word, one only leads others to conclude that what is printed is true, and that he who seeks revenge is precisely such a man as he is described in print.

elmwood cane, is anxious to find out into whose hands fate will deliver him, and who will close his eyes. He had been with his master's father in the Crimean Campaign, under Field Marshal Munnich. In the Battle of Frankfurt he had carried his wounded master on his shoulders from the field. On returning home he had become the tutor of his young master. In childhood he had saved him from drowning, for, jumping after him into the river into which he had fallen from a ferry, he had saved him at the risk of his own life. In youth he had ransomed him from prison, whither he had been cast for debts incurred while he was a subaltern of the Guards. The old woman, his wife, is eighty years of age. She had been the wet-nurse of the young master's mother; later she became his nurse and had the supervision of the house up to the very hour when she was brought out to this auction. During all the time of her service she had never wasted anything belonging to her masters, had never considered her personal advantage, never lied, and if she had ever annoyed them, she had done so by her scrupulous honesty. The forty-year-old woman is a widow, the young master's wet-nurse. To this very day she feels a certain tenderness for him. Her blood flows in his veins. She is his second mother, and he owes his life more to her than to his natural mother. The latter had conceived him in lust and did not take care of him in his childhood. His nurses had really brought him up. They part from him as from a son. The eighteen-year-old girl is her daughter and the old man's granddaughter. Beast, monster, outcast among men! Look at her, look at her crimson cheeks, at the tears flowing from her beautiful eyes. When you could neither ensnare her innocence with enticements and promises nor shake her steadfastness with threats and punishments, did

you not finally use deception, and, having married her to the companion of your abominations, did you not in his guise enjoy the pleasures she scorned to share with you? She discovered your deception. Her bridegroom did not touch her couch again, and since you were thus deprived of the object of your lust, you employed force. Four evildoers, your henchmen, holding her arms and legs—let us not go on with this. On her brow is sorrow, in her eyes despair. She is holding a little one, the lamentable fruit of deception or violence, but the living image of his lascivious father. Having given birth to him, she forgot his father's beastliness and her heart began to feel a tenderness for him. But now she fears that she may fall into the hands of another like his father. The little one—. Thy son, barbarian, thy blood! Or do you think that where there was no church rite, there was no obligation? Or do you think that a blessing given at your command by a hired preacher of the word of God has established their union? Or do you think that a forced wedding in God's temple can be called marriage? The Almighty hates compulsion; He rejoices at the wishes of the heart. They alone are pure. Oh, how many acts of adultery and violation are committed among us in the name of the Father of joys and the Comforter of sorrows, in the presence of His witnesses, who are unworthy of their calling! The lad of twenty-five, her wedded husband, the companion and intimate of his master. Savagery and vengeance are in his eyes. He repents the service he did his master. In his pocket is a knife; he clutches it firmly; it is not difficult to guess his thought—. A hopeless fancy! You will become the property of another. The master's hand, constantly raised over his slave's head, will bend your neck to his every pleasure. Hunger, cold, heat, punishment, everything will be against you. Noble thoughts are foreign to your mind. You do not know how to die. You will bow down and be a slave in spirit as in estate. And if you should try to offer resistance, you would die a languishing death in fetters. There is no judge between you. If your tormentor does not wish to punish you himself, he will become your accuser. He will hand you over to the governmental justice. Justice! Where the accused has almost no chance to justify himself! Let us pass by the other unfortunates who have been brought out for sale. . . .

GORODNYA

As I drove into this village, my ears were assailed not by the melody of verse, but by a heart-rending lament of women, children, and old men. Getting out of my carriage, I sent it on to the post station, for I was curious to learn the cause of the disturbance I had noticed in the street.

Going up to one group of people, I learned that a levy of recruits was the cause of the sobs and tears of the people crowded together there. From many villages, both crown and manorial, those who were to be drafted into the army had come together here.

In one group an old woman fifty years of age, holding the head of a lad of twenty, was sobbing. "My dear child, to whose care are you committing me? To whom will you entrust the home of your parents? Our fields will be overgrown with grass, our hut with moss. I, your poor old mother, will have to wander about begging. Who will warm my decrepit body when it is cold, who will protect it from the heat? Who will give me food and drink? But all that does not weigh so heavily upon my heart as this: who will close my eyes when I die? Who will receive my maternal blessing?

Who will return my body to our common mother, the moist earth? Who will come to remember me at my grave? Your warm tears will not fall upon it; I shall not have that consolation."

Near the old woman stood a grown-up girl. She, too, was sobbing. "Farewell, friend of my heart; farewell, my shining sun. I, your betrothed, will never know comfort or joy again. My friends will not envy me. The sun will not rise for me in joy. You are leaving me to pine away, neither a widow nor a wedded wife. If our inhuman village elders had only let us get married, if you, my darling, could have slept but one short night on my white breast. Perhaps God would have taken pity on me and given me a little son to comfort me."

The lad said to them: "Stop weeping, stop rending my heart. Our Sovereign calls us to service. The lot fell on me. It is the will of God. Those not fated to die will live. Perhaps I will come home to you with the regiment. I may even win rank and honors. Dear Mother, do not grieve. Take care of my Praskov'yushka." This recruit was drafted from an Economic village.[3]

From another group standing nearby I heard altogether different words. Amidst them I saw a man of about thirty, of medium size, standing erect and looking happily at the people around him.

"The Lord has heard my prayers," he said. "The tears of an unfortunate man have reached the Comforter of all men. Now I shall at least know that my lot may depend on my own good or bad behavior. Heretofore it depended on the arbitrary whims of a woman. I am con-

[3] A village of serfs, formerly belonging to a monastery. Since the secularization of monastic lands by Peter III in 1762 these villages belonged to the state and were administered by the Economic College.

soled by the thought that hereafter I shall not be flogged without a fair trial!"

Having gathered from what he said that he was a manorial serf, I was curious to learn the cause of his unusual joy. To my question he replied: "Dear sir, if a gallows were placed on one side of you and a deep river ran on the other, and you, standing between these two perils, could not possibly escape going either to the right or to the left, into the noose or into the water, which would you choose? Which would sense and impulse make you prefer? I think everyone would rather jump into the river, in the hope of escaping from peril by swimming to the other shore. No one would willingly investigate the strength of the noose by putting his neck into it. This was my situation. A soldier's life is a hard one, but better than the noose. Even that would be all right, if that were the end, but to die a lingering death under the cudgel, under the cat-o'-nine-tails, in chains, in a dungeon, naked, barefooted, hungry, thirsty, under constant abuse—my lord, although you look upon your peasants as your property, often less regarded than cattle, yet, unfortunately, they are not without feeling. You appear to be surprised to hear such words from the lips of a peasant; but why, when you hear them, are you not surprised at the cruelty of your brothers, the noblemen?"

And in very truth I had not expected such words from a man dressed in a gray caftan and with his head shaven. But wishing to satisfy my curiosity, I asked him to tell me how, being of such a low estate, he had arrived at ideas which are frequently lacking in men improperly said to be nobly born.

"If it will not tire you to hear my story, I will tell you: I was born in slavery, the son of my master's former valet. How happy I am to think that they will never again call me Van'ka or any other offensive name, that they will never again call me like a dog by whistling. My old master, a kindhearted, reasonable, and virtuous man, who often lamented the fate of his slaves, wanted, on account of my father's long service, to do something special for me; so he gave me the same education as his son. There was hardly any difference between us, except that the cloth of his coat was perhaps better. Whatever they taught the young master, they taught me, too; our instruction was exactly the same, and I can say without boasting that in many things I did better than my young master.

" 'Vanyusha,' the old master said to mé, 'your happiness depends entirely on you. You have more of an inclination for learning and morality than my son. He will be rich by inheritance and will know no want, while you have known it from birth. So try to be worthy of the pains I have taken for you.' When my young master was in his seventeenth year, he and I were sent to travel abroad with a tutor, who was told to look upon me as a traveling companion, not a servant. As he sent me away, my old master said to me: 'I hope that you will return to give me and your parents joy. You are a slave within the borders of this country, but beyond them you are free. When you return, you will not find fetters imposed upon you because of your birth.' We were away for five years and then returned to Russia, my young master happy at the thought of seeing his father, and I, I must confess, flattering myself that I would obtain what I had been promised. My heart was atremble as I again entered the borders of my country. And indeed my foreboding was not false. In Riga my young master received the news of his father's death. He was deeply moved by it; I was thrown into despair. For all my efforts to win his friendship and confidence had been in vain. Not only did he not love me, but—perhaps from envy, as is characteristic of small souls—he hated me.

"Observing the anxiety produced in me by the death of his father, he told me he would not forget the promise that had been made to me, if I would be worthy of it. It was the first time he had ventured to tell me so, for, having received control of his property through the death of his father, he had dismissed his tutor in Riga, paying him liberally for his labors. I must do justice to my former master: he has many good qualities, but timidity of spirit and thoughtlessness obscure them.

"A week after our arrival in Moscow, my master fell in love with a pretty girl, but one who with her bodily beauty combined a very ugly soul and a hard and cruel heart. Brought up in the conceit of her station, she respected only external show, rank and wealth. In two months she became my master's wife, and I became her slave. Until then I had not experienced any change in my condition and had lived in my master's house as his companion. Although he never gave me any orders, I generally anticipated his wishes, as I was aware of his power and of my position. Scarcely had the young mistress crossed the threshold of the house, in which she was determined to rule, before I was made aware of my hard lot. On the first evening after the wedding and all next day, when I was introduced to her by her husband as his companion, she was occupied with the usual cares of a bride; but in the evening, when a fairly large company came to the table and sat down to the first supper with the newly married pair, and I sat down in my usual place at the lower end of the table, the new mistress said to her husband in a fairly loud voice that if he wished her to sit at the table with the guests, he

must not permit any serfs to sit there. He looked at me and, at her instance, sent word to me that I should leave the table and eat my supper in my room. Imagine how deeply this humiliation hurt me! I suppressed the tears that came to my eyes, and withdrew. I did not dare to make my appearance the next day. They brought me my dinner and supper without saying anything to me. And so it went on succeeding days. One afternoon, a week after the wedding, the new mistress inspected the house, and, after apportioning the duties and living quarters to all the servants, entered my rooms also. They had been furnished for me by my old master. I was not at home. I will not repeat what she said there, to ridicule me, but when I returned home they gave me her order, whereby I was sent down to a corner on the ground floor with the unmarried servants, where my bed and my trunk, with my clothes and linens, had already been placed; all my other things she had left in my former rooms, in which she installed her serving maids.

"What took place in my soul when I heard this is easier to feel, if you can, than to describe. But so as not to detain you with superfluous details: my mistress, after taking control of the house and finding that I had no aptitude for service, made me a lackey and decked me out in livery. The least, imaginary remissness in my duties led to my ears being boxed, beatings, and the cat-o'-nine-tails. O, my lord, it would have been better if I had never been born! How many times did I complain against my dead benefactor for having fostered a responsive soul in me. It would have been better for me if I had grown up in ignorance and had never learned that I am a man, equal to all others. Long, long ago I would have freed myself from my hateful life, if I had not been held back by the prohibition of our Supreme Judge. I determined to bear my lot patiently. And I endured not only bodily wounds, but also those which she inflicted upon my soul. But I almost broke my vow and cut short the miserable remains of my woeful life as a result of a new blow to my soul.

"A nephew of my mistress, a youngster of eighteen years, a sergeant of the Guards, educated in the fashion of Moscow dandies, became enamored of a chambermaid of his aunt's, and, having quickly won her ready favors, made her a mother. Although he was usually quite unconcerned in his amours, in this case he was somewhat embarrassed. For his aunt, having learned about the affair, forbade the chambermaid her presence, and gently scolded her nephew. She intended, after the fashion of benevolent mistresses, to punish the one whom she had formerly favored by marrying her off to one of the stable boys. But since they were all married already, and since, for the honor of the house, there had to be a husband for the pregnant woman, she selected me as the worst of all the servants. In the presence of her husband, my mistress informed me of this as though it were a special favor. I could not stand this abuse any longer. 'Inhuman woman!' I cried. 'You have the power to torment me and to wound my body; you say the laws give you the right to do this. I hardly believe it, but I know full well that no one can be forced to marry.' She listened to my words in ominous silence. Then I turned to her husband and said: 'Ungrateful son of a generous father, you have forgotten his last will and testament, you have forgotten your own promise; but do not drive to despair a soul nobler than yours! Beware!' I could say no more, because, by command of my mistress, I was taken to the stable and whipped mercilessly with the cat-o'-nine-tails. The next day I could hardly get up out of bed from the beat-

ing; but I was brought before my mistress again. 'I will forgive you your impudence of yesterday,' she said; 'marry my Mavrushka; she begs you to, and I want to do this for her, because I love her even in her transgression.' 'You heard my answer yesterday,' I said; 'I have no other. I will only add that I will complain to the authorities against you for compelling me to do what you have no right to.' 'Then it's time for you to become a soldier!' my mistress screamed in a fury.—A traveler who has lost his way in a terrible desert will rejoice less when he finds it again than I did when I heard these words. 'Take him to be a soldier!' she repeated, and the next day it was done. Fool! She thought that being made a soldier would be a punishment for me, as it is for the peasants. For me it was a joy, and as soon as they had shaved my forehead, I felt like a new man. My strength was restored. My mind and spirit began to revive. O hope, sweet solace of the unfortunate, remain with me!" A heavy tear, but not a tear of grief and despair, fell from his eyes. I pressed him to my heart. His countenance was radiant with new joy. "All is not yet lost," he said; "you arm my soul against sorrow by making me feel that my misery is not endless."

From this unfortunate man I went to a group in which I saw three men fettered in the strongest irons. "It is amazing," I said to myself as I looked at these prisoners, "now they are downcast, weary, timid, and they not only do not want to become soldiers, but the greatest severity is required to force them into that status; but as soon as they become accustomed to the execution of their hard duty, they grow alert and spirited, and even look with scorn upon their former condition." I asked one of the bystanders who, to judge from his uniform, was a government clerk: "No doubt you have put them in such heavy fetters because you are afraid they will run away?"

"You guessed it. They belonged to a landed proprietor who needed money for a new carriage and got it by selling them to crown peasants, to be levied into the army."

I.—"My friend, you are mistaken. Crown peasants can't purchase their brothers."

He.—"It isn't done in the form of a sale. Having by agreement received the money, the master sets these unfortunates free; they are presumed to be 'voluntarily' registered as crown peasants of the commune which paid the money for them; and the commune, by common consent, sends them to be soldiers. They are now being taken with their emancipation papers to be registered in our commune."

Free men, who have committed no crime, are fettered, and sold like cattle! O laws! Your wisdom frequently resides only in your style! Is this not an open mockery? And, what is worse, a mockery of the sacred name of liberty. Oh, if the slaves weighted down with fetters, raging in their despair, would, with the iron that bars their freedom, crush our heads, the heads of their inhuman masters, and redden their fields with our blood! What would the country lose by that? Soon great men would arise from among them, to take the place of the murdered generation; but they would be of another mind and without the right to oppress others. This is no dream; my vision penetrates the dense curtain of time that veils the future from our eyes. I look through the space of a whole century. I left the crowd in disgust.

But the fettered prisoners are free now. If they had any fortitude, they could put to naught the oppressive intentions of their tyrants. Let us go back to them.—"My friends," I said to the captives, these prisoners of war in their own country, "do you know that if you

do not freely wish to enter the army, no one can now compel you to do so?"

"Stop making fun of poor wretches, sir. Even without your jesting, it was hard enough for us to part, one from his poor old father, another from his little sisters, a third from his young wife. We know that our master sold us as recruits for a thousand rubles."

"If you did not know it before, you must know now that it is against the law to sell men as recruits, that peasants cannot legally buy men, that your master has set you free, and that the purchasers intend to register you in their commune, as though of your own free will."

"O, sir, if that is really so, we do thank you. When they line us up for muster, we will all say that we do not want to become soldiers and that we are free men."

"Add to it that your master sold you at a time when such a sale was not legal, and that they are delivering you up as recruits in violation of the law."[4] One can easily imagine the joy that lighted up the faces of these unfortunates. Leaping up from their places and vigorously shaking their fetters, they seemed to be testing their strength, as though they would shake them off. But this conversation could have gotten me into serious trouble, for the recruiting officers, having heard what I said, rushed toward me in violent anger, and said, "Sir, don't meddle with other people's business, and get away while the getting's good!" When I resisted, they pushed me so violently that I was forced to leave this crowd as fast as I could. . . .

THE EMPRESS CATHERINE II'S NOTES ON THE *JOURNEY*

[The starred pages here refer to the pages of Radishchev's original edition of the *Journey*.]

---

[4] During the time of a levying of recruits, it was illegal to make any contract for the sale of serfs.

No. 1

This book was printed in 1790 without mention of the printing press and without any visible permission at the beginning, although at the end it says: "With the permission of the Department of Public Morals." This is probably a lie, or else carelessness. The purpose of this book is clear on every page: its author, infected and full of the French madness, is trying in every possible way to break down respect for authority and for the authorities, to stir up in the people indignation aganst their superiors and against the government.

He is probably a Martinist or something similar. He has learning enough, and has read many books. He has a melancholy temperament and sees everything in a very somber light; consequently he takes a bilious black and yellow view of things.

He has imagination enough, and he is audacious in his writing. . . .

The author is maliciously inclined on page *60. This is particularly evident from the following pages. Pages *72, *73. They show clearly enough the purpose for which this whole book was written. It is a safe bet that the author's motive in writing it was this, that *he does not have entrée to the palace.* Maybe he had it once and lost it, but since he does not have it now but does have an evil and consequently ungrateful heart, he is struggling for it now with his pen. On page *75. Our babbler, is timid. If he stood closer to the sovereign, he would pipe a different tune. We have seen a lot of such humbugs, especially among the Schismatics. The firmer their hearts, the more they change when the time comes.

I do not know how great the lust for power is in other rulers; in me it is not great.

Page *76. The fledglings teach the mother bird. *Malice* is in the malicious; I have none of it.

"The murder called war": What do they want, to be left defenseless to fall captive to the Turks and Tatars, or to be conquered by the Swedes?

In criticizing the poor execution of our commands, they are accusing themselves.

Pages *77, *78 are written with a seditious purpose, and the care taken in rooting out an evil is criticized adversely. . . .

Page *81 is full of abuse, invective, and evil-minded interpretation of things. This villainy continues through the following pages: *82, *83, *84, and *85. But withal they were unable to censure the intentions, and so were obliged to turn to their fulfillment; hence they are criticizing society, and not the Sovereign's good heart or intentions. . . .

Page *88. He refers to "information: what I have had the good luck to learn." I think that information was picked up in Leipzig; hence the suspicion falls on Messrs. Radischev and Chelishchev, the more so since they are said to have established a printing press in their house.

Pages *92, *93, *94, *95, *96, *97 preach the doctrines of the Martinists and other theosophists.

Page *98 is so indecent that it cannot even be mentioned.

*99, *100, *101. Speaking of Novgorod, of its free government, and of Tsar Ioann Vasil'evich's cruelty to it, he does not say anything about the cause of this punishment, which was that, having accepted the union, Novgorod had surrendered to the Polish Republic; consequently the Tsar punished the apostates and traitors, in which, to tell the truth, he did not keep within bounds.

*102. The author cries: "But what right did he have to rage against them? What right did he have to take Novgorod for himself?" Answer: the old right of sovereignty and the law of Novgorod and of all Russia and of the whole world, which punishes rebels, and apostates from the Church. But the question is raised here only to deny monarchical rights, and should therefore be left without an answer.

On *103. The questions brought up here are the ones over which France is now being ruined.

No. 5

Tell the author that I have read his book from cover to cover, and that in the course of reading it I have come to wonder whether I may in some way have offended him. For I do not want to judge him without hearing him, although he judges sovereigns without hearing their justification. . . .

*410, *411, *412, *413, *414, *415, *416 continue to describe the miserable condition of the peasants.

On *418 begins the eulogy on Lomonosov, which continues to the end of the book. This contains praise of Mirabeau, who deserves not once but many times over to be hanged. Here the Empress Elizabeth Petrovna is treated with disrespect. Here it is evident that the author

is not a true Christian. And it seems probable that he has appointed himself the leader, whether by this book or by other means, in snatching the scepters from the hands of monarchs; but, since one man alone could not do this, and since there are indications that he has a few accomplices, he should be questioned on this matter, as well as on his real intentions. And, since he himself writes that he loves the truth, he should be asked to say how the matter stood. If, however, he does not write the truth, I shall be compelled to seek evidence, and things will be worse for him than before.

On *453 the author promises a continuation of this book "on our return journey." Where is this work? Was it begun, and where is it?

Of the line "With the permission of the Department of Public Morals" I will say that it is a deceitful and contemptible act to add anything to a book after the permission has been signed. It must be determined how many copies were published and where they are.

23

MEMOIR ON ANCIENT
AND MODERN RUSSIA   EXCERPTS

By Nicholas Karamzin

Born into a middling gentry family near Samara, Karamzin (1766–1826) first made a name with his *Letters of a Russian Traveller* (1792-96), one of the best pieces of Russian prose of the period. A short story in the sentimental style, *Poor Liza* (1792), brought him fame overnight. In 1803 he was appointed Historiographer of the Russian Empire. His multivolume *History of the Russian State* achieved great popularity in his lifetime.

His *Memoir*, presented to Alexander I in 1811, was a conservative's attempt to stem the tide of change in the Russian government. It was a debate with the reformer Speransky, though the latter is not mentioned by name. Though the *Memoir* had no practical effect, it is of interest as a sample of the thinking of an important segment of literate Russia.

The book is in three parts: a survey of Russian history to 1800; a consideration of several aspects of Alexander's regime; and Karamzin's recommendations for action. Sections of the last two parts are reproduced here in the translation of Professor Richard Pipes of Harvard.

Karamzin's *Letters of a Russian Traveller* is available in an English translation. Professor Pipes's Introduction to the *Memoir* is an excellent biography of the man; the same author has written "Karamzin's Concept of Monarchy," *Harvard Slavic Studies*, IV, 35–58. See also R. McGrew's "Notes on the Princely Role in Karamzin's *History of the Russian State*," *American Slavic and East European Review*, XVIII, 12–24, and Horace Dewey, "Sentimentalism in the Historical Writings of N. Karamzin," *American Contributions to the Fourth International Congress of Slavicists* (Moscow, 1958). There is a chapter on Karamzin in Anatole Mazour, *Modern Russian Historiography*. Marc Raeff's *Michael Speransky* is a study of the man whom Karamzin was attacking. Speransky also appears in Leo Tolstoy's *War and Peace*, Vol. II, Part III, chap. 18. See also A. Cross, "Karamzin and England," *Slavonic and East European Review*, December, 1964, and his "Karamzin Studies," *ibid.*, January, 1967. Henry Nebel has written *Karamzin: A Russian Sentimentalist*.

THE REIGN OF ALEXANDER I

So far I have spoken of bygone reigns, now I shall turn to the present reign, addressing myself to my conscience and to my sovereign, to the best of my understanding. What entitles me to do so? My love for the fatherland and for the

Reprinted by permission of the publishers from R. Pipes (ed.), *Karamzin's Memoir on Ancient and Modern Russia* (Cambridge, Mass.: Harvard University Press, 1959), pp. 138–40, 149–56, 158–67, 192–95, 200–204. Copyright 1959, by The President and Fellows of Harvard College.

monarch, and some knowledge culled from the chronicles of the world and from conversations with great men, that is, from their works. What do I want? To test in good faith Alexander's magnanimity, and to say what I consider just, and what history some day shall confirm.

Two schools of thought predominated at the time of Alexander's accession. Some urged that Alexander, to his eternal glory, take steps to bridle the unlimited autocracy which had had such disastrous consequences in the reign of his father. Others, dubious of the practical value of such an undertaking, wanted him only to restore the ruined system of Catherine, which appeared so happy and sound in comparison with Paul's. In point of fact, can one limit autocracy in Russia without, at the same time, emasculating the tsar's authority, salutary for the country, and if so, how? Superficial minds lose no time and answer: "Yes, one can. All one has to do is to establish the supremacy of law over all, including the monarch." But whom shall we entrust with the authority over the inviolability of this law? The Senate? The Council? Who will sit in these institutions? Will they be officials selected by the sovereign or by the country? In the former event they will be an assembly of the tsar's sycophants; in the latter they will want to argue with the tsar over authority—I see an aristocracy, not a monarchy. Furthermore, what will the senators do should the monarch violate the law? Will they expostulate with His Majesty? And should he have a good laugh at them, will they declare him a criminal? Will they incite the people? . . . Every good Russian heart shudders at this frightful prospect. Two political authorities in one state are like two dreadful lions in one cage, ready to tear each other apart; and yet law without authority is nothing. Autocracy has founded and resuscitated Russia. Any change in her political constitution has led in the past and must lead in the future to her perdition, for she consists of very many and very different parts, each of which has its own special civic needs; what save unlimited monarchy can produce in such a machine the required unity of action? If Alexander, inspired by generous hatred for the abuses of autocracy, should lift a pen and prescribe himself laws other than those of God and of his conscience, then the true, virtuous citizen of Russia would presume to stop his hand, and to say: "Sire! you exceed the limits of your authority. Russia, taught by long disasters, vested before the holy altar the power of autocracy in your ancestor, asking him that he rule her supremely, indivisibly. This covenant is the foundation of your authority, you have no other. You may do everything, but you may not limit your authority by law!" But let us assume that Alexander actually prescribes royal authority some kind of statute based on the principles of public good, and sanctions it by a sacred oath. Would such an oath be capable of restraining Alexander's successors unless it were strengthened with other means, means which in Russia are either unfeasible or dangerous? No, let us be done with schoolboy sophistries, and affirm that there is only one true method for a sovereign to make certain that his successors do not abuse their authority: let him rule virtuously, let him accustom his subjects to goodness! In this manner he will engender salutary customs, principles, and public opinions which will keep future sovereigns within the bounds of legitimate authority far more efficiently than all the ephemeral forms. How? By inspiring them with a fear of arousing universal hatred with a contrary system of government. It may be safe occasionally for one tyrant to follow another, but it is never safe for him to follow a wise king! "The sweet repels us from the bitter," said Vladimir's legates after becoming acquainted with European religions.

Russia was then unanimous in its high esteem of the young monarch's qualities. He has now ruled for ten years, and there is no reason to change this opinion. I will go further: there is general agreement that no monarch perhaps ever exceeded Alexander in his love for and dedication to the public good, that none was as impervious to the lustre of his office, or as capable of retaining simple human virtues on the throne. But here I need spiritual fortitude to speak the truth. Russia is seething with dissatisfaction. Complaints are heard in the palaces and in the cottages; the people lack confidence as well as enthusiasm for the government, and condemn strongly its aims and policies. An amazing political occurrence! Usually, the successor of a cruel monarch easily wins for himself general acceptance when he softens the political régime. How then shall we explain this woeful condition of public opinion among a people who have been calmed by Alexander's gentleness, whom he had freed from the threat of unjust persecution by the Secret Chancery and Siberian exile, and to whom he has given the freedom to enjoy all the pleasures permissible in civil societies? By the unfortunate situation in Europe, and by what I consider to be important mistakes of the Government. For, alas, it is possible with good intentions to err in the choice of means. Let us see. . . .

POLITICAL INSTITUTIONS

Alexander, inspired with love for the common good, and with the best intentions, took counsel, and, in accord with the ideas of Field Marshal Münnich and the political system of foreign countries, established ministries. To begin with, let us call attention to the excessive haste with which this move was made. The ministries were created and set in motion before the ministers had been provided with an Instruction, that is, with a dependable, clear guide to help them carry out their important duties! Let us next inquire into their utility. Ministerial bureaus have replaced colleges. Where work had been carried out by eminent officials such as a president and several assessors, men with long training and with a strong sense of responsibility for their whole office, we came to see insignificant officials, such as directors, filing clerks, desk heads, who, shielded by the minister, operated with utter impunity. It may be countered that the minister did everything and answered for everything; but in fact only ambition has no bounds. Human capacity and ability are quite narrowly circumscribed. For example, was the Minister of the Interior, who appropriated for himself nearly all of Russia, capable of gaining a good insight into the endless stream of papers flowing through his office? Could he understand at all subjects of such diversity? [As a consequence of his inability to do so] committees began to mushroom; they were like a parody of the ministries, and demonstrated the latter's inability to provide an effective government. At last the government realized the excessive complexity of the Ministry of the Interior . . . and what did it do? It added a new ministry, one whose structure was as complex and incomprehensible to Russians. What? Wardship comes under the Ministry of the Police? And medicines too? Etc., etc. . . . This ministry is either a mere department of the Ministry of the Interior, or it has been misnamed. And can this second reorganization be said to have enhanced the government's reputation for wisdom? First it acts, and then it says: "Sorry, we have made a mistake; this matter belongs not to this but to that ministry." Such subjects must be the first thought over, for otherwise people lose confidence in the firmness of laws.

In the second place, the ministers, having emerged upon the ruins of the colleges (since the isolated colleges of War and of Admiralty are of no significance in this order), wedged themselves between the sovereign and the people, eclipsing the Senate, and divesting it of its power and greatness. And although the ministers are subordinate to the Senate insofar as they must submit reports to it, yet by being able to say: "I had the pleasure to report to His Majesty!" they can silence the Senators, with the result that so far this alleged responsibility has proven but a meaningless ritual. Edicts and laws submitted by the ministers and approved by the sovereign are communicated to the Senate only for promulgation. From this it follows that Russia is governed by ministers, that is, that within his own department every minister may act at will. We ask: who deserves more confidence: a single minister, or an assembly of most eminent statesmen, which we have to come to regard as the supreme government, the principal instrument of royal power? True, the ministers constitute a Committee which is to approve every new establishment before its confirmation by the monarch. But does not this Committee resemble a council of six or seven different nationals, each of whom speaks his own language, and cannot understand the others? Must the Minister of the Navy grasp the subtleties of juridical science, on the principles of political economy and trade, and so forth? What is even more important is that every minister needs complaisant colleagues to satisfy his own needs, and therefore

tends to acquire the habit of complaisance himself.

"Patience," reply the royal counselors, "we shall yet devise a method of curbing ministerial authority"—and they issue the act establishing the Council.

Catherine II, too, had a council following the precept that two heads are better than one. What mortal can do without advice where important matters are involved? Sovereigns need it most of all. In questions of war and peace, which call for an unequivocal *yes* or *no*, Catherine took the advice of certain select lords. This was her council, one essentially *secret*, that is, special, the empress' own. She did not transform it into a formal state council because she did not want to destroy Peter's Senate, which, as we have shown, cannot exist alongside another supreme governing institution. What is to be gained from debasing the Senate in order to elevate another organ of government? If the Senators are unworthy of royal trust, they need only to be replaced. The Senate cannot govern as long as the Council, acting in lieu of it, reviews affairs formally and also in its own name, and, to boot, issues laws jointly with the sovereign. Nowadays, royal decrees read: "having considered the Council's opinion. . . ." Thus, the Senate is left out? What is it then? Will it stay as a mere court of law? . . . We shall see, because we have been instructed to stand by for more supplementary state statutes, reforms of the Senate, gubernii, etc. "A monarchy," writes Montesquieu, "must have a repository of laws." The points we have raised here cannot be materially affected by the impending changes: the Council will either perform the functions of the Senate, or it will serve as its moiety, its department. All this is playing with names and forms, it is to ascribe to them a significance which objects alone possess. I congratulate the person who invented this new formula or preamble to laws: "Having considered the Council's opinion"—but the Russian sovereign will take wisdom under consideration wherever he happens to find it: in his own mind, in books, in the judgment of his best subjects. In an autocracy laws need no confirmation save the signature of the sovereign; the totality of power is his. The Council, the Senate, the committees and ministers are nothing more than the agencies by means of which this authority operates, they are the sovereign's proxies—where he himself acts, they are not consulted. The expression: "le conseil d'état entendu" is meaningless to a Russian; let the French, rightly or not, use it! . . . True, in Russia it also used to be written: "The sovereign commanded, and the Boyars concurred," but this legal formula had been for some time a sort of requiem for the defunct boyar aristocracy. Shall we revive the form when both the thing and the form itself have long ago been destroyed?

The Council, it is said, will curb the ministers. The emperor is going to submit to the Council for its consideration the most important ministerial proposals. In the meanwhile, however, the ministers will continue to govern the country in the sovereign's name. The Council does not intercede in the normal course of events, because it is consulted only on extraordinary occasions, and yet it is this everyday course of political activity which determines whether our time is blessed or cursed.

Only those laws are salutary which had for long been desired by the best minds of the country, and of which, so to say, the people have had a premonition, insofar as they represent the readiest remedy for an acknowledged evil. The establishment of the ministries and the Council was not anticipated by anyone. The least the authors of this reform

might have done was to have explained the advantages of these new institutions. I read and see nothing but dry forms. They draw lines for my eyes, leaving my mind undisturbed. Russians are told: "So far it has been thus—now it will be different." Why? This they fail to say. Whenever Peter the Great carried out important political reforms, he used to give the nation an account; take a look at his Church Statutes, in which he opens to you his whole heart, in which he reveals to you all the motives, all the causes as well as aims of this statute. On the whole, Russia's new legislators are distinguished more for the art of clerkship than for that of statesmanship. They issue a project of Ministerial Instruction. What could be more important or interesting? Here, no doubt, one can find defined the competence, purpose, method, and obligations of every minister? . . . But nothing of the kind! A few words are tossed out on the principal matter, and everything else consists of secretarial trivia: they tell how ministerial departments are to correspond with each other, how papers are to come and go, how the sovereign is to open and close his rescripts! Montesquieu suggests the symptoms which indicate the rise and decline of empires—the author of this project provides with similar airs the criteria with which to gauge the success or failure of a chancery. I sincerely acclaim his knowledge of this matter, but I condemn the following resolution: "If the sovereign issues an edict which is contrary to the judgment of the minister, then the minister is free not to countersign it." It follows that in an autocratic state the minister has the legal right to advise the public that in his opinion an edict is harmful? The minister is the monarch's arm, and nothing else! the arm does not judge the head. The minister affixes his signature to Personal Imperial

Edicts not for the benefit of the public but for the emperor, as assurance that they are written, word for word, as he has commanded. Such mistakes in fundamental political conceptions are scarcely excusable. In defining an important ministerial responsibility the author writes: "The minister is tried in two instances; when he oversteps the bounds of his authority, or when he fails to make use of the means at his disposal to forestall harm." But where are these bounds of authority and these means defined? One should first make the law, and then speak of punishing the offender. And can this notorious ministerial responsibility really be a subject of trial in a Russian solemn court? Who selects the ministers? The sovereign. Let him then reward with his favor those who deserve it, and dismiss those who do not, without ado, quietly and discreetly. A bad minister is the sovereign's mistake; such mistakes ought to be corrected, but in secret, so that the nation retains trust in the personal choices of the tsars.

This is the light in which our good Russians view the new political institutions; realizing how unripe these institutions are they long for the old order. In the brilliant reign of Catherine II, when we had a Senate, colleges, and a Procurator-General, our affairs made satisfactory progress. Prudent legislators of the past, when compelled to introduce changes into the political systems, tried to depart as little as possible from the old. "If you have no choice but to alter the number of officials and their authority," says the sage Machiavelli, "then, for the sake of the people, do at least keep their titles unchanged." We do quite the opposite; leaving the thing itself unchanged, we invent titles, and contrive different methods to produce the same effect! An evil to which we have grown accustomed bothers us much less than a new evil, while new

benefits do not wholly inspire confidence. The reforms accomplished so far give us no reason to believe that future reforms will prove useful; we anticipate them more with dread than with hope, for it is dangerous to tamper with ancient political structures. Russia, after all, has been in existence for a thousand years, and not as a savage horde, but as a great state. Yet we are being constantly told of new institutions and of new laws, as if we had just emerged from the dark American forests! We require more preservative than creative wisdom. Peter's excesses in imitating foreign powers are justly condemned by history, but are they not worse yet in our own time? Where, in what European country, do the people prosper, where does justice flourish, where does good order prevail, where are hearts content and minds at rest? In France? It is true, they have a Conseil d'État, Secrétaire d'État, Sénat conservateur, Ministres de l'Intérieur, de la Justice, des Finances, de l'Instruction publique, de la Police, des Cultes; it is equally true that Russia of Catherine II had neither these institutions nor these officials. Yet where do we find a civil society fulfilling its true mission—in the Russia of Catherine II, or in the France of Napoleon? Where do we find more arbitrary power and absolutist whim? Where are the affairs of state handled with greater legality and order? We perceive in Alexander's beautiful soul a fervent desire to institute in Russia the rule of law. He could have attained this aim more readily, and made it more difficult for his successors to deviate from the lawful order, had he left the old institutions intact but imbued them, so to say, with a constant zeal to serve the public interest. It is far easier to change new things than old ones. Alexander's successors are much more likely to be impressed with the power which is heightened in the Senate than that which is attributed to the present Council. Novelties breed novelties, and encourage despotic licentiousness.

Let us say once and let us say again that one of the main reasons for the dissatisfaction of Russians with the present government is its excessive fondness for political changes, changes which shake the foundations of the empire, and the advantages of which are still an open question.

EDUCATION

The intentions of Alexander demonstrate consistently his desire to promote the public good. Abhorring the senseless principle which holds that the tranquillity of the sovereign entails the ignorance of his subjects, he has spent millions to found universities, gymnasia, and schools. . . . Alas, these measures turn out to cause greater loss to the treasury than they bring benefit to the fatherland. The professors have been invited before there were students to hear them, and though many of these scholars are prominent, few are really useful; for the students, being but poorly acquainted with Latin, are unable to understand these foreign instructors, and are so few in number that the latter lose all desire to appear in class. The trouble is that we have built our universities on the German model, forgetting that conditions in Russia are different. At Leipzig or Göttingen a professor need only to appear on the platform for the lecture hall to fill with an audience. In Russia there are no lovers of higher learning. The gentry perform service, while the merchants care only to obtain a thorough knowledge of mathematics or of foreign languages for purposes of trade. How many young men in Germany study to become lawyers, judges, pastors, professors! Russian scribes and judges, on the other hand, have no need to know

Roman laws. Our priests are given an education of sorts at the seminaries, and proceed no further. As for the academic profession, its rewards are yet so unfamiliar in Russia, that it will be a long time before parents will decide to prepare their sons for it. Instead of the sixty professors whom we had called from Germany to Moscow and the other cities, I would have invited twenty at most, but I would have spared no expense to increase the number of government scholarships at the gymnasia; needy families, enrolling their sons there, would bless the sovereign's generosity, and thus, poverty aided by charity, would produce in Russia in a decade or two a profession of scholars. I dare say no other method can be as effective in bringing this undertaking to a successful conclusion. The constructing and purchasing of buildings for universities, the founding of libraries, cabinets, and scholarly societies, and the calling of famous astronomers and philologists from abroad—all this is throwing dust in the eyes. What subjects are not being taught today even at such places as Kharkov and Kazan! And this at a time when it takes the utmost effort to find in Moscow a teacher of Russian, when it is virtually impossible to find in the whole country a hundred men who know thoroughly the rules of orthography, when we lack a decent grammar, when imperial decrees make improper use of words; the important Bank Act, for instance, says: "to give money without time limit," instead of *"a perpetuite,"* *"without repayment,"* and the Manifesto on Commercial Tariffs speaks of *"shortening* the importation of merchandise," etc., etc. Let us also call attention to certain strange features of this new educational system. The best professors, who should devote their time to science, are busy furnishing candles and firewood to the university! Their economic responsibilities comprise also the upkeep of the one hundred or more schools which are subordinated to the University Council. In addition, the professors are required annually to travel around the provinces to inspect schools. How much wasted money and effort! Previously, the economy of the university was entrusted to the care of a special university chancery, and properly so. Let the superintendent of schools inspect the district schools in his province once every three years, but it is absurd as well as pathetic to see these poor professors being shaken up and down in *kibitkis* on their annual peregrinations! They can learn the condition of every gymnasium or school from the latter's reports, without ever stepping outside the Council: well-attended schools are good, poorly attended schools are bad, and bad schools are almost always the result of one and the same cause, namely, poor teachers. Why not appoint good ones? Are there none? Or are they in short supply? . . . What is responsible for this? The inactivity of the local Pedagogical Institute (I speak only of the one in Moscow, with which I am acquainted). Professorial jaunts will not remedy this shortcoming. Altogether, so far the Ministry of so-called Education in Russia has done nothing but slumber, as if it were unaware of its importance and wanting a course of action, waking up from time to time only to demand of the sovereign money, distinctions, and medals.

Having done much to promote in Russia the cause of learning, and noting with displeasure the gentry's lack of interest in university studies, the government resolved to make academic pursuits mandatory, and issued the ill-advised Examination Act. Henceforth, no one is to be promoted to the rank of Counselor of State or Collegiate Assessor without a certificate of studies. In the past, functionaries of the most enlightened states had been required to know only what was essential to their work: the engineer, engineering, the judge, law, and so on. But in Russia, the official presiding in the Civil Court must know Homer and Theocritus, the Senate Secretary—the properties of oxygen and all the gases, the Deputy Governor—Pythagorean geometry, the superintendent of a lunatic asylum—Roman law, or else they will end their days as Collegiate or Titular Counselors. Neither forty years of state service nor important accomplishments exempt one from the obligation of having to learn things which are entirely alien and useless for Russians. Never before had love of knowledge led to an act so contrary to the spirit of knowledge! It is amusing that the author of the Instruction which commands everyone to master rhetoric, should himself be guilty of grammatical errors! . . . But let us leave alone the ridiculous, and turn to the harmful prospects of this act. Heretofore, the gentry and the other classes of Russia sought in the service either distinctions or emoluments. The former motive is harmless; the latter dangerous, since inadequate salaries expose covetous men to all the temptations of graft. Under conditions now in force, what can provide a Titular or Collegiate Counselor with an inducement for service in case he happens to be ignorant of physics, statistics, or the other sciences? The better, i.e., ambitious officials, will retire; the inferior, i.e., greedy ones will remain in the service to fleece the living and the dead. Instances of this are occurring already. Instead of enacting this new decree, one need only have enforced the provisions of the University Act, which requires young men, prior to entry into the service, to show proof of studies. From beginners one may ask anything, but it is unfair to confront an old official with new conditions of service; he has turned gray on his job, relying on the rules of honor, and hoping some day to obtain the rank of Counselor of State, promised him by law—and now you violate this state contract. Moreover, instead of general knowledge, every man should be required to know only that which is necessary for the service to which he wants to devote himself. Examine the lower officials of the College of Foreign Affairs in statistics, history, geography, diplomacy, and languages; others only in their native tongue and in Russian law, and not in Roman law, which is of no use to us; others yet in geometry in case they aspire to becoming surveyors, etc. To seek the superfluous is as bad as to reject the necessary.

SERFDOM AND THE PROBLEM OF EMANCIPATION

The Examination Act was everywhere greeted with sarcastic ridicule. The act to which I want to turn next has offended many and gladdened no one, although the sovereign, when he issued it, was inspired by the most sacred humanitarianism. We have heard of monstrous landowners who engaged in an inhuman traffic with people. Having purchased a village, these men picked the peasants fit for military service, and then sold them without land. Let us assume that there still are such beasts today. Trade of this kind should then be outlawed by a strict decree, containing a proviso that the estates of the unworthy landowners engaging in it are to be placed under guardianship. The enforcement of such a law could be entrusted to the governors. Instead of doing this, the government outlaws the sale and purchase of recruits. In the past, the better farmer toiled gladly for ten, twenty years in order to accumulate 700 or 800 rubles with which to pur-

chase a recruit, so as to keep his family intact. Now he has lost his most powerful incentive to engage in beneficent hard work and stay sober. Of what use is wealth to a parent if it cannot save his beloved son? Yes, inn-keepers rejoice, but the heads of families weep. The state must have its recruits—it is better to draw them from miserable than from happy people, for the latter are incomparably worse off in the army than they were before. I would like to ask whether the peasants of a tyrannical landlord—one whose greed is such that he would be capable of selling them as recruits—prosper from the prohibition of such sales? If anything, their lot may be less miserable in the regiments! But as for the landowners of modest means, they have now lost an opportunity of ridding themselves of unsatisfactory peasants or household serfs, to their own and to society's benefit; under the old system the lazy intemperate peasant would mend his ways in the strict military school, while the diligent, sober one would remain behind the plow. Moreover, the example itself exercised a salutary effect, and other peasants swore off the bottle knowing the master's rights to sell them as recruits. What means has a petty landowner nowadays with which to frighten his dissolute peasants when it is not his turn to furnish recruits? The cane? Backbreaking labor? Is it not more useful to have them frightened of the cane in the ranks of the military company? One may argue that our soldiers have improved as a result of this decree, but have they indeed? I inquired of generals—they have not noticed it. At any rate; it is true that the village peasants have deteriorated. The father of three or even two sons readies in good time one of them for the draft, and keeps him unmarried; the son, knowing what awaits him, drinks, because good behavior will not save him from military service. The legislator should view things from a variety of angles and not merely from one; or else, extirpating one evil, he may occasion yet greater evil.

Thus we are told that the present government had the intention of emancipating proprietary serfs. One must know the origins of this bondage. In Russia in the ninth, tenth, and eleventh centuries the only bondmen were the *kholopy*, i.e., either foreigners captured in war or purchased, or criminals deprived by law of citizenship, together with their descendants. But rich men, disposing of a multitude of *kholopy*, populated their lands with them, and in this manner arose the first serf villages in the modern sense of the word. Furthermore, proprietors also admitted into servitude free peasants on terms which more or less constrained the latter's natural and civil liberties; some of these peasants, upon receipt of land from the proprietor, committed themselves and the children to serve him forever. This was the second source of slavery in the countryside. Other peasants—and they constituted the majority—rented land from the owners in return for a payment consisting only of money or a set quantity of cereals, while retaining the right to move on elsewhere after the expiration of a fixed period of time. These free movements, however, had their drawbacks, for great lords and wealthy men lured free peasants away from weak landlords, and the latter, left with deserted fields, were unable to meet their state obligations. Tsar Boris was the first to deprive all peasants of this freedom to move from place to place, that is, he bound them to their masters. Such was the beginning of general bondage. This law was changed, limited, and made subject to exceptions; it was tried in courts for many years; at last it attained to full force, and the ancient distinction

between serfs and *kholopy* disappeared entirely. It follows: (1) that the present-day proprietary serfs were never landowners; that is, they never had land of their own, which is the lawful, inalienable property of the gentry; (2) that the serfs who are descended of the *kholopy* are also the lawful property of the gentry and cannot be personally emancipated without the landlords' receiving some special compensation; (3) that only the free peasants who were bound to their masters by Godunov may, in justice, demand their previous freedom; but since (4), we do not know which of them are descended of the *kholopy*, and which of free men, the legislator faces no mean task when he tries to untie this Gordian knot, unless he is bold enough to cut through it by proclaiming all to be equally free: the descendants of war captives, purchased, lawful slaves, as well as the descendants of enserfed peasants, the former being freed by virtue of the law of nature, and the latter by virtue of the power of the autocratic monarch to abrogate the statutes of his predecessors. I do not want to pursue this controversy further, but I should like to point out that as far as the state is concerned, natural law yields to civil law, and that the prudent autocrat abrogates only those laws which have become harmful or inadequate, and which can be replaced by superior ones.

What does the emancipation of serfs in Russia entail? That they be allowed to live where they wish, that their masters be deprived of all authority over them, and that they come exclusively under the authority of the state. Very well. But these emancipated peasants will have no land, which—this is incontrovertible—belongs to the gentry. They will, therefore, either stay on with their present landlords, paying them quitrent, cultivating their fields, delivering bread where necessary—in a word, continuing to serve them as before; or else, dissatisfied with the terms, they move to another, less exacting, landlord. In the first case, is it not likely that the masters, relying on man's natural love for his native soil, will impose on the peasants the most onerous terms? Previously they had spared them, seeing in the serfs their own property, but now the greedy among them will try to exact from the peasants all that is physically possible. The landlords will draw up a contract, the tiller will renege—and there will be lawsuits, eternal lawsuits! In the second case, with the peasant now here, now there, won't the treasury suffer losses in the collection of the soul-tax and other revenues? Will not agriculture suffer as well? Will not many fields lie fallow, and many granaries stay empty? After all, the bread on our markets comes, for the most part, not from the free farmers but from the gentry. And here is one more evil consequence of emancipation: the peasants, no longer subjected to seignorial justice from which there is no appeal and which is free of charge, will take to fighting each other and litigating in the city—what ruin! ... Freed from the surveillance of the masters who dispose of their own *zemskaia isprava*, or police, which is much more active than all the Land Courts, the peasants will take to drinking and villainy— what a gold mine for taverns and corrupt police officials, but what a blow to morals and to the security of the state! In short, at the present time, the gentry, dispersed throughout the realm, assist the monarch in the preservation of peace and order; by divesting them of this supervisory authority, he would, like Atlas, take all of Russia upon his shoulders. Could he bear it? A collapse would be frightful. The primary obligation of the monarch is to safeguard the internal and external unity of the state; benefiting estates and individuals comes second. Alexander wishes to improve the lot of the peasants by granting them freedom; but what if this freedom should harm the state? And will the peasants be happier, freed from their masters' authority, but handed over to their own vices, to tax farmers, and to unscrupulous judges? There can be no question that the serfs of a sensible landlord, one who contents himself with a moderate quitrent, or with labor on a *desiatina* of plowland for each household, are happier than state peasants, for they have in him a vigilant protector and defender. Is it not better quietly to take measures to bridle cruel landlords? These men are known to the governors. If the latter faithfully fulfill their obligations, such landlords will promptly become a thing of the past; and unless Russia has wise and honest governors, the free peasants will not prosper either. I do not know whether Godunov did well in depriving the peasants of their freedom since the conditions of that time are not fully known. But I do know that this is not the time to return it to them. Then they had the habits of free men—today they have the habits of slaves. It seems to me that from the point of view of political stability it is safer to enslave men than to give them freedom prematurely. Freedom demands preparation through moral improvement—and who would call our system of wine-farming and the dreadful prevalence of drunkenness a sound preparation for freedom? In conclusion, we have this to say to the good monarch: "Sire! history will not reproach you for the evil which you have inherited (assuming that serfdom actually is an unequivocal evil), but you will answer before God, conscience, and posterity for every harmful consequence of your own statutes."

I do not condemn Alexander's law permitting villages to gain their freedom with their masters' permission. But are many of them sufficiently rich to avail themselves of it? Will there be many prepared to surrender all they have in return for freedom? The serfs of humane landlords are content with their lot; those who serve bad landlords are impoverished—the situation of both categories renders this law ineffectual.

THE IMPORTANCE OF FINDING PROPER MEN FOR GOVERNMENT SERVICE

The main trouble with the legislators of the present reign is their excessive reverence for political forms. This weakness accounts for the invention of various ministries, the founding of the Council, and so forth. The work itself is performed no better—it is merely performed in offices and by officials of a different designation. Let us follow a different principle, and say that what matters are not forms, but men. Retain the ministries and the Council: they will prove useful as long as they are staffed throughout with wise and honest men. Thus, our first good wish is: may God favor Alexander in the successful choice of men! The greatness of the internal policies of Peter was due to his ability to make such choices, and not to the establishment of the Senate or the colleges. This monarch was passionately fond of able men. He looked for them in monastic cells and in dark ship cabins: there he found Feofan and Ostermann, men celebrated in our political history. Alexander is faced with different circumstances and endowed with different spiritual qualities of modesty and serenity from Peter, who went everywhere alone, spoke to everyone, listened to everyone, and ventured to assess the quality of a person from a single word, a single glance. But let the rule remain the same; *seek men!* Let him who enjoys the sovereign's confidence spot such men even from afar, and appoint them to the very highest positions. Appointments must be made strictly according to ability not only in republics, but also in monarchies. Some men are gradually led, others are lifted to great heights by the omnipotent arm of the monarch; the law of gradual progress holds for most, but not for all men. A person endowed with a ministerial mind must not end up as a head clerk or secretary. Rank depreciates not from the rapidity of promotion, but from the stupidity or disrepute of the dignitaries who hold it; and as for the envy which a meritorious person provokes, it dissipates quickly. You do not form a useful ministry by composing an instruction, but by preparing good ministers. Although it is true that their proposals are examined by the Council, yet what assurance have you of the wisdom of its members? Over-all wisdom comes only of individual wisdom. In short, what we need now above all, is men!

But these men are needed not only for the ministries and Council, but also and particularly for the office of governor. Russia consists not of Petersburg and not of Moscow, but of fifty or more subdivisions know as gubernii. If all goes well there, then the ministers and the Council can rest on their laurels; and it will go well there if you find in Russia fifty wise and conscientious individuals to devote themselves zealously to the well-being of the half million Russians entrusted to each of them, to curb the rapacious greed of minor officials and cruel landlords, to re-establish justice, pacify the land-tillers, encourage merchants and industry, and to protect the interests of the exchequer and the nation. If the governors cannot or will not accomplish these things, they are badly chosen; if they lack the means to do so, then the structure of gubernatorial authority is unsound. (1) What manner of men are most contemporary governors? Men without talent, who allow their secretaries to profit from all kinds of wickedness, or men without conscience, who derive profit from wickedness themselves. One need not leave Moscow to be aware that the head of a certain province is a fool, and has been one for a long time! While in another he is a thief, and has been one for a long time! . . . The land buzzes with rumor, but the ministers either do not know it, or do not want to know it! What is the use of your new ministerial institutions? Why do you write laws— for posterity? Men, not documents, govern. (2) In the past, the governor was subordinated only to the Senate; now, he must, in addition, deal with various ministers. How much bother and writing! And, worst of all, many branches of the provincial administration are outside his competence, such as schools, imperial domains, state forests, highways, waterways, and the mail. What a great diversity ond profusion! In consequence of this arrangement, the gubernia has not one chief, but many, some of whom reside in Petersburg and some in Moscow. Such a system of government is in violent conflict with our ancient, truly monarchic system, in which unity and forcefulness of power was attained by having it concentrated in the hands of the viceroy. Each gubernia represents Russia in microcosm. We want the whole country to be governed by a single authority, and its constituent parts by many. We fear abuses in the central government, but do they not exist in the local government? As a large house cannot be run in an orderly fashion unless it has a steward who accounts for everything to the master, so the gubernii will be put in order only when we terminate the regime which permits so many officials to function independently of the gover-

nors who answer to the sovereign for the tranquillity of the country, and do so to a far greater extent than all the ministers, counselors, and Senators living in St. Petersburg. Is this one consideration not proof enough that we must raise the dignity of the governor's office by endowing it with universal respect? Model your governors on the viceroys of Catherine; give them the dignity of senators, and reconcile their authority with that of the ministers, whose true function should be merely to serve as secretaries of the sovereign in the various branches of government—and then all you will need to know is how to choose men!

THE ROLE OF THE GENTRY IN THE RUSSIAN SYSTEM

Autocracy is the Palladium of Russia; on its integrity depends Russia's happiness. But from this it does not follow that the sovereign, in whose hands rests the plenitude of power, should degrade the gentry, who are as ancient as Russia herself. The gentry were never anything except a brotherhood of outstanding men serving the grand princes or tsars. It is bad when a servant obtains mastery over a weak lord, but a prudent lord respects his choice servants, and considers their honor his own. The rights of the well-born are not something apart from monarchical authority—they are its principal and indispensable instrumentality by means of which the body politic is kept in motion. Montesquieu said: "point de Monarque—point de noblesse; point de noblesse; point de Monarque!" The gentry are a hereditary estate. Some people must be trained to fulfill certain obligations so as to maintain order and provide the monarch with a source whence to draw the servants of the state. The people labor, the merchants trade, and the gentry serve, for which they are rewarded with distinctions and benefits, respect and comfort. Personal changeable ranks cannot replace the hereditary, permanent nobility, and, necessary as they are to mark grades in the state service, in a sound monarchy they must not be allowed to encroach upon the fundamental rights of the nobility, or to acquire its privileges. Noble status should not depend on rank, but rank on noble status; that is, the attainment of certain ranks should be made unconditionally dependent on the candidate's being a gentleman, a practice we have failed to observe from the time of Peter the Great, an officer being *ipso facto* a nobleman. Superior talent, which is not related to class origin must not be barred from higher office—but let the sovereign knight a person before bestowing upon him high rank, and let him do so with some solemn ceremony, on the whole seldom, and with utmost selectivity. The advantages of such a practice are evident: (1) Frequent promotion of commoners to the rank of minister, lord, or general must be accompanied by a grant of wealth, which the aureole of eminent office requires. This drains the treasury. . . . The gentry, on the other hand, having inherited wealth, can manage even in the higher posts without financial assistance from the treasury. (2) The gentry feel offended when they find the steps of the throne occupied by men of low birth, where, since the days of old, they had been accustomed to see dignified boyars. This is unobjectionable when these men are distinguished by uncommon and sublime talents; but if they are men of ordinary ability, then it is better that their positions be given to gentlemen. (3) The mind and heart are furnished by nature, but they are formed by upbringing. A gentleman, favored by fortune, is accustomed from birth to feel self-respect, to love the fatherland and the sovereign for the advantages of his birth-right, and to be powerfully attracted to distinctions which his ancestors have earned and he himself will earn by his own accomplishments. These attitudes and feelings imbue him with that nobility of spirit which, among other things, was the reason for the institution of the hereditary nobility. It is an important excellence which the natural gifts of a commoner can but seldom supplant, because a commoner, dreading scorn even when he enjoys an eminent status, usually dislikes the gentry, and hopes with personal arrogance to make others forget his base origin. Virtue is rare. You must seek in the world common rather than superior souls. It is not my opinion, but that of all deep-thinking statesmen, that a monarchy is buttressed by firmly established rights of the wellborn. Thus, I wish that Alexander would make it a rule to enhance the dignity of the gentry, whose splendor may be called a reflection of the tsar's aureole. This aim is to be attained not only by means of state charters, but also by those, so to say, innocent, effortless signs of consideration, which are so effective in an autocracy. For instance, why should the emperor not appear occasionally at solemn assemblies of the nobility as their chairman, and not in the uniform of a guards officer, but in that of a nobleman? This would be far more effective than eloquent letters and wordy assurances of royal esteem for the society of the wellborn. But the most effective method of elevating the gentry would be a law admitting every nobleman into military service in the rank of an officer, conditional only on his knowing well the essentials of mathematics and of Russian. Limit the payment of wages to recruits—and all the wellborn, in accord with the interests of the monarchy founded on conquests, shall take to swords instead of the penholders with which the rich and poor alike among them equip their sons to serve in chanceries, archives, and courts, much to the detriment of the state; for at present the gentry feel a revulsion to the barracks where their youths, sharing with common soldiers menial work as well as menial amusement, may suffer corruption of health and morals. Indeed, what is there among things necessary for the service that one cannot learn in an officer's rank? And it is much pleasanter for a noble to acquire learning at this rank than as a noncommissioned officer. Were this done, our armies would profit from the influx of young, well-educated nobles, who now waste away as court clerks. The guards would remain an exception—in the guards only would nobles begin service as noncommissioned officers. But in the guards, too, a sergeant of gentle birth should be distinguished from the son of a soldier. Military discipline which does not help us win victories can and ought to be relaxed. Severity in trifles destroys the zeal for work. Keep the warriors busy with games or guard parades, but not to the point of exhaustion. Work on the soul even more than on the body. The heroes of the guard parade turn into cowards on the battlefield; how many examples have we known! In Catherine's time, officers sometimes went about in evening clothes, but they went bravely into battle as well. The French are no pedants, and win. We saw the Prussian heroes!

THE ROLE OF THE CLERGY

As with the gentry, so with the clergy: its usefulness to the state is proportionate to the general respect which it enjoys among the people. I do not propose to re-establish the Patriarchate, but I should like to see the Synod have a more important body of members and sphere of action. I wish it consisted entirely of archbishops, and that it met in joint sessions with the Senate on important occasions when the state issues new fundamental laws in order to hear them read, to accept them into their repositiones of law, and to promulgate them —of course, without any contradiction. Efforts are being made right now to increase the number of clerical schools, but it would be better yet to pass a law which would prohibit the investiture of eighteen-year-old pupils, and introduce a strict examination as a prerequisite of every investiture whatsoever; also one which would insist that bishops show greater concern for the morals of the parishioners, employing for this purpose the sensible and efficacious means furnished them by the Synod, and conceived as well by Peter the Great. The character of these important spiritual dignitaries is always a good indicator of a people's moral condition. Good governors are not enough. Russia also needs good priests. Having both we shall require nothing more, and envy no one in Europe.

24

THE DECEMBRISTS
EXTRACTS FROM DOCUMENTS

The Decembrist uprising in 1825 is sometimes called the first Russian revolution. Though unsuccessful, it lived on in the minds of those who would some day overthrow the autocracy forever. Our selections will suggest some of the thoughts, plans, and programs of those who wanted to reorganize Russia along more democratic lines. The statements are taken from the testimony of several Decembrist leaders before the investigation commission charged by Nicholas I to reveal the causes and nature of the conspiracy designed to topple his throne.

The Decembrist Movement (paperback), edited by Marc Raeff, has additional documents on the topic. Mikhail Zetlin's *The Decembrists* is a portrait of the men and their venture. Marc Raeff's *Michael Speransky* has an account of their trial. Constantin de Grunwald's *Nicholas I* is a biography of the monarch against whom the movement was directed. Franco Venturi's *Roots of Revolution* (paperback) begins with the Decembrists. Sergei Utechin's *Russian Political Thought* (paperback) considers them also. There are chapters on the Decembrists in Thomas Masaryk's *The Spirit of Russia*; Stuart Tompkins' *The Russian Mind*; Avram Yarmolinsky's *The Road to Revolution* (paperback); Max Laserson's *The American Impact on Russia* (paperback); and Sidney Monas' *The Third Section*. See also two articles on Pestel: "The Character of Pestel's Thought," by Arthur Adams, in the *American Slavic and East European Review*, Vol. XXII, and "Pavel Pestel: The Beginnings of Jacobin Thought in Russia," in the *International Review of Social History*, Vol. III (1958). There is a Soviet study by V. Tarasova, "The Decembrist Nikolai Turgenev and the Struggle against Slavery in the USA," *Soviet Studies in History*, Summer, 1964.

EXTRACTS FROM PESTEL'S TESTIMONY

QUESTION 6: How did the revolutionary ideas gradually develop and become implanted in men's minds? Who first conceived these ideas and continued to preach and spread them throughout the State?

ANSWER 6: This question is very difficult to answer, for it must go beyond the realm of discussion about the secret Society. However, in order to fulfill the demand of the Committee I shall try so far as I can explain it.

From A. Mazour, *The First Russian Revolution* (Berkeley: University of California Press, 1937), pp. 273–85. Footnotes have been omitted. Used by permission of the publisher.

295

Political books are in the hands of everyone; political science is taught and political news spread everywhere. These teach all to discuss the activities and conduct of the Government, to praise one thing and assail another. A survey of the events of 1812, 1813, 1814, and 1815, likewise of the preceding and following periods, will show how many thrones were toppled over, how many others were established, how many kingdoms were destroyed, and how many new ones were created; how many Sovereigns were expelled, how many returned or were invited to return and were then again driven out; how many revolutions were accomplished; how many *coup d'états* carried out—all these events familiarized the minds of men with the idea of revolutions, with their possibilities, and with the favorable occasions on which to execute them. Besides that, every century has its peculiar characteristic: ours is marked by revolutionary ideas. From one end of Europe to the other the same thing is observed, from Portugal to Russia, without the exception of a single state, not even England or Turkey, those two opposites. The same spectacle is presented also in the whole of America. The spirit of reform causes mental fermentation [*faire bouillir les esprits*]. Here are the causes, I think, which gave rise to revolutionary ideas and which have implanted them in the minds of people. As to the cause of the spread of the spirit of reform through the country, it could not be ascribed to the Society, for the organization was still too small to have any popular influence.

EXTRACT FROM A LETTER OF KAKHOVSKY TO GENERAL LEVASHEV

Your Excellency,
Dear Sir!

The uprising of December 14 is a result of causes related above. I see, Your Excellency, that the Committee established by His Majesty is making a great effort to discover all the members of the secret Society. But the government will not derive any notable benefit from that. We were not trained within the Society but were already ready to work when we joined it. The origin and the root of the Society one must seek in the spirit of the time and in our state of mind. I know a few belonging to the secret Society but am inclined to think the membership is not very large. Among my many acquaintances who do not adhere to secret societies very few are opposed to my opinions. Frankly I state that among thousands of young men there are hardly a hundred who do not passionately long for freedom. These youths, striving with pure and strong love for the welfare of their Fatherland, toward true enlightenment, are growing mature.

The people have conceived a sacred truth—that they do not exist for governments, but that governments must be organized for them. This is the cause of struggle in all countries; peoples, after tasting the sweetness of enlightenment and freedom, strive toward them; and governments, surrounded by millions of bayonets, make efforts to repel these peoples back into the darkness of ignorance. But all these efforts will prove in vain; impressions once received can never be erased. Liberty, that torch of intellect and warmth of life, was always and everywhere the attribute of peoples emerged from primitive ignorance. We are unable to live like our ancestors, like barbarians or slaves.

But even our ancestors, though less educated, enjoyed civil liberty. During the time of Tsar Aleksei Mikhailovich the National Assembly, including representatives of various classes of the people, still functioned and participated in important affairs of the State. In his reign five such Assemblies were summoned. Peter I, who killed everything national in the State, also stamped out our feeble liberty. This liberty disappeared outwardly but lived within the hearts of true citizens; its advancement was slow in our country. Wise Catherine II expanded it a little; Her Majesty inquired from the Petersburg Free Economic Society concerning the value and consequences of the emancipation of peasants in Russia. This great beneficial thought lived in the heart of the Empress, whom the people loved. Who among Russians of her day and time could have read her INSTRUCTION without emotion? The INSTRUCTION alone redeems all the shortcomings of that time, characteristic of that century.

Emperor Alexander promised us much; he, it could be said, enormously stirred the minds of the people toward the sacred rights of humanity. Later he changed his principles and intentions. The people became frightened, but the seed had sprouted and the roots grew deep. So rich with various revolutions are the latter half of the past century and the events of our own time that we have no need to refer to distant ones. We are witnesses of great events. The discovery of the New World and the United States, by virtue of its form of government, have forced Europe into rivalry with her. The United States will shine as an example even to distant generations. The name of Washington, the friend and benefactor of the people, will pass from generation to generation; the memory of his devotion to the welfare of the Fatherland will stir the hearts of citizens. In France the revolution which began so auspiciously turned, alas, at the end from a lawful into a criminal one. However, not the people but the court intrigues and politics were responsible

for that. The revolution in France shook all the thrones of Europe and had a greater influence upon the governments and peoples than the establishment of the United States.

The dominance of Napoleon and the war of 1813 and 1814 united all the European nations, summoned by their monarchs and fired by the call to freedom and citizenship. By what means were countless sums collected among citizens? What guided the armies? They preached freedom to us in Manifestoes, Appeals, and in Orders! We were lured and, kindly by nature, we believed, sparing neither blood nor property. Napoleon was overthrown! The Bourbons were called back to the throne of France and, submitting to circumstances, gave that brave, magnanimous nation a constitution, pledging themselves to forget the past. The Monarchs united into a Holy Alliance; congresses sprang into existence, informing the nations that they were assembled to reconcile all classes and introduce political freedom. But the aim of these congresses was soon revealed; the nations learned how greatly they had been deceived. The Monarchs thought only of how to retain their unlimited power, to support their shattered thrones, and to extinguish the last spark of freedom and enlightenment.

Offended nations began to demand what belonged to them and had been promised to them—chains and prisons became their lot! Crowns transgressed their pledges, the constitution of France was violated at its very base. Manuel, the representative of the people, was dragged from the Chamber of Deputies by gendarmes! Freedom of the press was restricted, the army of France, against its own will, was sent to destroy the lawful liberty of Spain. Forgetting the oath given by Louis XVIII, Charles X compensates *émigrés* and for that purpose burdens the people with new taxes.

The government interferes with the election of deputies, and in the last elections, among the deputies only thirty-three persons were not in the service and payment of the King, the rest being sold to the Ministers. The firm, courageous Spanish people at the cost of blood rose for the liberty of their country, saved the King, the Monarchy, and the honor of the Fatherland; of their own volition the people themselves received Ferdinand as King. The King took the oath to safeguard the rights of the people. As early as the year 1812, Alexander I recognized the constitution of Spain.

Then the Alliance itself assisted France by sending her troops, and thus aided in dishonoring her army in the invasion of Spain. Ferdinand, arrested in Cadiz, was sentenced to death. He summoned Riego, swore to be once more loyal to the constitution and to expel the French troops from his territory, and begged Riego to spare his life. Honest men are apt to be trustful. Riego gave guaranty to the Cortes for the King, and he was freed. And what was the first step of Ferdinand? By his order Riego was seized, arrested, poisoned and, half-alive, that saint-martyr hero who renounced the throne offered to him, friend of the people, savior of the King's life, by the King's order is now taken through the streets of Madrid in the shameful wagon pulled by a donkey, and is hanged like a criminal. What an act! Whose heart would not shudder at it? Instead of the promised liberty the nations of Europe found themselves oppressed and their educational facilities curtailed. The prisons of Piedmont, Sardinia, Naples, and, in general, of the whole of Italy and Germany were filled with chained citizens. The lot of the people became so oppressive that they began to regret the past and to bless the memory of Napoleon the conqueror!

These are the incidents which enlightened their minds and made them realize that it was impossible to make agreements with Sovereigns. . . .

The story told to Your Excellency that, in the uprising of December 14 the rebels were shouting "Long live the Constitution!" and that the people were asking "What is Constitution, the wife of His Highness the Grand Duke?" is not true. It is an amusing invention. We knew too well the meaning of a constitution and we had a word that would equally stir the hearts of all classes— LIBERTY!

* * *

The events of December are calamitous for us and, of course, must be distressing to the Emperor. Yet the events of this date should be fortunate for His Imperial Highness. After all, it was necessary sometime for the Society to begin its activities, but hardly could it have been so precipitate as in this instance. I swear to God, I wish the kind Sovereign prosperity! May God aid him in healing the wounds of our Fatherland and to become a friend and benefactor of the people. . . .

Most obedient and devoted servant of Your Excellency.

PETER KAKHOVSKY

1826
February, 24th day

EXTRACT FROM A LETTER OF
A. BESTUZHEV TO
NICHOLAS I

Your Imperial Highness!

Convinced that You, Sovereign, love the truth, I dare to lay before You the historical development of free thinking in Russia and in general of many ideas which constitute the moral and political basis of the events of December 14. I shall speak in full frankness, without concealing evil, without even softening expressions, for the duty of a loyal subject is to tell his Monarch the truth without any embellishment. I commence.

The beginning of the reign of Emperor Alexander was marked with bright hopes for Russia's prosperity. The gentry had recuperated, the merchant class did not object to giving credit, the army served without making trouble, scholars studied what they wished, all spoke what they thought, and everyone expected better days. Unfortunately, circumstances prevented the realization of these hopes, which aged without their fulfillment. The unsuccessful, expensive war of 1807 and others disorganized our finances, though we had not yet realized it when preparing for the national war of 1812. Finally, Napoleon invaded Russia and then only, for the first time, did the Russian people become aware of their power; only then awakened in all our hearts a feeling of independence, at first political and finally national. That is the beginning of free thinking in Russia. The government itself spoke such words as "Liberty, Emancipation!" It had itself sown the idea of abuses resulting from the unlimited power of Napoleon, and the appeal of the Russian Monarch resounded on the banks of the Rhine and the Seine. The war was still on when the soldiers, upon their return home, for the first time disseminated grumbling among the masses. "We shed blood," they would say, "and then we are again forced to sweat under feudal obligations. We freed the Fatherland from the tyrant, and now we ourselves are tyrannized over by the ruling class." The army, from generals to privates, upon its return, did nothing but discuss how good it is in foreign lands. A comparison with their own country naturally brought up the question, Why should it not be so in our own land?

At first, as long as they talked without being hindered, it was lost in the air, for thinking is like gunpowder, only dangerous when pressed. Many cherished the hope that the Emperor would grant a constitution, as he himself had stated at the opening of the Legislative Assembly in Warsaw, and the attempt of some generals to free their serfs encouraged that sentiment. But after 1817 everything changed. Those who saw evil or who wished improvement, thanks to the mass of spies were forced to whisper about it, and this was the beginning of the secret societies. Oppression by the government of deserving officers irritated men's minds. Then the military men began to talk: "Did we free Europe in order to be ourselves placed in chains? Did we grant a constitution to France in order that we dare not talk about it, and did we buy at the price of blood priority among nations in order that we might be humiliated at home?" The destructive policy toward schools and the persecution of education forced us in utter despair to begin considering some important measures. And since the grumbling of the people, caused by exhaustion and the abuses of national and civil administrations, threatened bloody revolution, the Societies intended to prevent a greater evil by a lesser one and began their activities at the first opportunity. . . .

You, Sovereign, probably already know how we, inspired by such a situation in Russia and seeing the elements ready for change, decided to bring about a *coup d'état.* . . . Here are the plans we had for the future. We thought of creating a Senate of the oldest and wisest Russian men of the present administration, for we thought that power and ambition would always have their attraction. Then we thought of having a Chamber of Deputies composed of national representatives. . . . For enlightenment of the lower classes we wished everywhere to establish Lancasterian schools. And in order to bring about

moral improvement we thought of raising the standard of the clergy by granting to them a means of livelihood. Elimination of nearly all duties, freedom
from distillation and road improvement
for the state, encouragement of agriculture and general protection of industry
would result in satisfying the peasants.
Assurance and stability would attract to
Russia many resourceful foreigners. Factories would increase with the demand
for commodities, while competition
would stimulate improvement, which
rises along with the prosperity of the
people, for the need of commodities for
life and luxury is constant. . . .

Most devoted servant of
Your Imperial Highness,
ALEXANDER BESTUZHEV

[no date]

EXTRACT FROM A LETTER OF V. STEINGEL TO NICHOLAS I

. . . No matter how many members
there may be found of the secret Society
or those who had only known of it; no
matter how many may be deprived of
freedom on account of it, there still remain a great many people who share
those ideas and sentiments. Russia is
already so educated that even shopkeepers read newspapers and newspapers report what is said in the Chamber of
Deputies in Paris. Is not the first thought
to occur in everyone's mind, "Why cannot we discuss our rights?" The greater
number of professors, literary men, and
journalists have to adhere wholeheartedly to those who wish a constitutional
government, for freedom of the press is
to their personal advantage. So do book-
sellers and merchants. Finally, all those
who were in foreign countries, and some
who were educated there, and all those

who served or serve now in the Guard
hold the same opinions. Who of the
young men, even somewhat educated,
have not read and have not been fasci-
nated with the works of Pushkin, which
breathe freedom? Who has not cited the
fables of Denis Davydov, such as his
"Head and Feet"? Perhaps among those
who have the fortune to surround Your
Honor, there are such. Sovereign! In
order to eradicate free thinking, there is
no other means than to destroy an entire generation, born and educated in
the last reign. But if this is impossible,
there remains one thing—to win hearts
by kindness and attract minds by decisive and evident means toward the future prosperity of the state.

Most devoted,
BARON VLADIMIR IVANOV STEINGEL

January 11th day
1826

EXTRACT FROM A LETTER OF A. YAKUBOVICH TO NICHOLAS I

Your Highness!

. . . In describing the condition of
Russia I did not reproach the authorities, but pointed out the source of present-day evils and those which threaten
us in the distant future. Sovereign! The
antiquated structure of the state administration demands important changes.
The Empire, in the little over a hundred
years since it emerged from the darkness of crude ignorance, has undergone
every quarter of a century complete
changes in the formation of ideas and
in moral demands. Grant equal advantages to Your soldiers by lowering the
term of military service; by decisive
legislative measures and strict execution make everyone fulfill his duties,
spread the light of science and education, give liberty to commercial activities, and the restless or the *Carbonari*

will vanish like darkness in the face of the sun. You will be the benefactor and savior of the Fatherland from many calamities, and the love of Your grateful fifty-two million subjects will only be the beginning of Your immortal glory.

Devoted subject of Your
Imperial Highness,
ALEXANDER YAKUBOVICH

1825, December 28
Peter and Paul Fortress
Cell No. 3

THE OATH FOR MEMBERS WHO ENTER THE UNITED SLAVS

Upon joining the United Slavs for the liberation of myself from tyranny and for the restoration of freedom, which is so precious to the human race, I solemnly pledge on these arms brotherly love, which is to me divine and from which I expect the fulfillment of all my desires. I swear to be always virtuous, always loyal to our aim, and to observe the deepest secrecy. Hell itself with all its horrors will not be able to compel me to reveal to the tyrants my friends and their aims. I swear that only when a man proves undoubted desire to become a participant, will my tongue reveal the Society; I swear, to the last drop of my blood, to my last breath, to assist you, my friends, from this sacred moment. Special activity will be my first virtue, and mutual love and aid my sacred duty. I swear that nothing in the world will be able to move me. With sword in hand I shall attain the aim designated by us. I will pass through a thousand deaths, a thousand obstacles—I will pass through, and dedicate my last breath to freedom and the fraternal union of the noble Slavs. Should I violate this oath, then let remorse be the first vengeance for my hideous offense, let the point of this sword turn against my heart and fill

it with hellish torment; let the moment of my life that is injurious to my friends, be the last one; let my existence be transformed into a chain of unheard misery from the fatal moment that I forget my pledge. May I see all that is dear to my heart perish by this weapon and in horrible suffering, and this weapon, reaching me, the criminal, cover my body with wounds and cast infamy upon me; and the accumulated burden of physical and moral evil shall impress on my forehead the sign of a monstrous son of Nature.

A MANIFESTO, DRAWN BY "DICTATOR" TRUBETSKOI ON THE EVE OF DECEMBER 14, 1825

The Manifesto of the Senate should proclaim:

(1) abolition of the former government;

(2) establishment of a Provisional Government until a permanent one is decided upon by representatives;

(3) freedom of the press, hence abolition of censorship;

(4) religious tolerance to all faiths;

(5) abolition of the right to own men;

(6) equality of all classes before the law and therefore abolition of military courts and all sorts of judicial commissions from which all cases proceed to civil courts;

(7) announcement of rights for every citizen to occupy himself with whatever he wishes and therefore—nobleman, merchant, middle-class man, peasant— all to have equal right to enter military, civil, or clerical service, trade wholesale or retail, paying established taxes for such trade; to acquire all kinds of property such as land, or houses in villages and cities; make all kinds of contracts among themselves, or summon each other for trial;

(8) cancellation of poll tax and arrears;

(9) abolition of monopolies on salt and alcohol; permission for free distillation and for the procuring of salt with payment of tax according to the respective amounts of salt and alcohol produced;

(10) abolition of recruiting and military colonies. . . .

The Provisional Government is instructed to:

(1) equalize all classes;

(2) form all local, Community, County, Gubernia, and Regional administrations;

(3) form a National Guard;

(4) form a judicial branch with a jury;

(5) equalize recruiting obligations among all classes;

(6) abolish a permanent army;

(7) establish a form of election of representatives to the Lower Chamber which will have to ratify the future of Government.

AN APPEAL

The Lord took pity on Russia and sent death to our tyrant. Christ said: "You shall not be slaves of men, for you were redeemed by my blood." The world did not listen to this sacred command and fell into misery. But our suffering moved the Lord, and today He is sending us freedom and salvation. Brethren! Let us repent of our long servility and swear: let there be a sole Tsar in Heaven and on Earth, Jesus Christ.

25

APOLOGY OF A MADMAN   EXCERPTS

By Peter Chaadaev

Chaadaev (1794–1856) was the grandson of the eighteenth-century historian Prince Mikhail Shcherbatov. In 1811 he became an officer and served in the campaigns against Napoleon. He was involved in the societies which led to the Decembrist uprisings but left Russia in 1823. Upon his return in 1826 he was arrested and interrogated, but released. He settled in Moscow where he remained till his death, one of the most prominent thinkers of his generation. He was a member of no camp, though he must be considered a Westernizer. Because of his admiration for Catholicism, however, he believed in a different order from that desired by most Westernizers.

His literary heritage comprises eight essays and a large number of letters, all in French, the language in which he felt most comfortable. Only one essay, "A Philosophical Letter," was published during his lifetime, in 1836. Herzen described it as "a shot that rang out in a dark night; it forced all to awaken." While all literate Russia discussed the essay, the Moscow *Telescope,* which had printed it, was suppressed, its editor N. I. Nadezhdin exiled, and the censor who had passed it dismissed. Chaadaev was declared insane by order of Nicholas I and put under police supervision. For a year he had to endure daily visits by a physician and a policeman. His next essay was entitled "Apology of a Madman"; reprinted below is an excerpt entitled "The Legacy of Peter the Great." The first two excerpts are taken from his letters.

For a text of additional "Philosophical Letters" of Chaadaev see *Tri-Quarterly,* Spring, 1965, and Volume I of *Russian Philosophy,* edited by James Edie *et al.* Eugene Moskoff has written *The Russian Philosopher Chaadaev.* There are chapters on the man in *The Spirit of Russia* by Thomas Masaryk and in Richard Hare's *Pioneers of Russian Social Thought* (paperback). See also Alexander Koyre, "Chaadaev and the Slavophils," *Slavonic and East European Review,* March, 1927, and Janko Lavrin, "Chaadaev and the West," *Russian Review,* 1963. Raymond McNally has written several articles on the man: "Chaadaev's Evaluation of Peter the Great," *Slavic Review,* 1964; "Chaadaev's Evaluation of the Western Christian Churches," *Slavonic and East European Review,* June, 1964; "The Significance of Chaadaev's Weltanschaung," *Russian Review,* October, 1964; "The Books in Chaadaev's Libraries," *Jahrbücher für Geschichte Osteuropas,* Vol. XIV (1966); and "Chaadaev versus Khomiakov," *Journal of the History of Ideas,* 1966.

From Hans Kohn (ed.), *The Mind of Modern Russia* (New Brunswick, N.J.: Rutgers University Press, 1955), pp. 38–57. Copyright 1955 by The Trustees of Rutgers College in New Jersey.

RUSSIA AND THE WORLD

From "Letters on the Philosophy of History," 1829–31

One of the most deplorable things in our strange civilization is that we still have to discover the truths, often very trivial ones, which other, even less advanced peoples discovered long ago. We have never moved in concert with other peoples; we do not belong to any of the great families of mankind. We are not part of the Occident, nor are we part of the Orient; and we don't have the traditions of the one or of the other. Since we are placed somewhat outside of the times, the universal education of mankind has not reached us. . . .

All peoples undergo a time of violent agitation, of passionate restlessness, of action without thought. At that time men wander around in the world like bodies without a soul. It is the age of the great emotions, of the large undertakings, of the grand passions of the people. People then move vehemently, without any apparent aim, but not without profit for posterity. All societies pass through these periods, and from them receive their most vivid reminiscences, their miracles, their poetry, and all their most powerful and most fruitful ideas: these reminiscences are the necessary bases of societies. Otherwise the societies would not have any fond memories to cling to; the dust of their earth would be their only tie. The most interesting epoch in the history of mankind is that of the adolescence of the nations, for that is the moment when their faculties develop rapidly, a moment which lingers in their memories and serves as a lesson once they are mature. Over here we have nothing like it. The sad history of our youth consists of a brutal barbarism, then a coarse superstition, and after that a foreign, savage, and degrading domination of the spirit which was later inherited by the national power. We have not known an age of exuberant activity and of the exalted play of moral forces among the people as others have. The period in our social life which corresponds to this moment was characterized by a dull and dreary existence, without vigor or energy, which was enlivened only by abuse and softened only by servitude. There are no charming recollections and no gracious images in our memory, no lasting lessons in our national tradition. If you look over all the centuries in which we have lived and over all the territory which we cover, you will not find a single fond memory, or one venerable monument which forcefully speaks of bygone times or retraces them in a vivid or picturesque manner. We live in the most narrow present, without a past or a future, in the midst of a flat calm. And if at times we strive for something, it is not with the hope and desire for the common good, but with the childish frivolity of the baby who stands up and stretches out his hand to grasp the rattle which his nurse is holding. . . .

The peoples of Europe have a common physiognomy, a family resemblance. Despite their general division into Latins and Teutons, into southerners and northerners, it is plain to anyone who has studied their history that there is a common bond which unites them into one group. You know that not too long ago all of Europe considered itself to be Christian, and this term had its place in public law. Besides this general character, each of these peoples has its own character, but all that is only history and tradition. It is the ideological patrimony inherited by these peoples. There each individual is in full possession of his rights, and without hardship or work he gathers these notions which have been scattered throughout society, and profits from them. Draw the parallel yourself and see how we can profit from this interchange of elementary ideas, and use them, for better or for worse, as a guide for life. Note that this is not a question of studying, of lectures, or of anything literary or scientific, but simply of a relation between minds; of the ideas which take hold of a child in his crib, which are surrounding him when he plays, which his mother whispers to him in her caresses; of that which in the form of various sentiments penetrates the marrow of his bones, the very air he breathes, and which already permeates his soul before he enters the world and society. Do you want to know what these ideas are? They are the concepts of duty, justice, law and order. They are derived from the same events which have shaped society; they are the integral elements of the social world in these countries.

This is the atmosphere prevailing in the Occident. It is more than history, it is more than psychology; it is the physiology of the European man. What do you have to put in its place over here? I don't know whether one can deduce anything absolute from what we have just said, or whether one can derive strict principles from it. But it is easy to see how this strange situation of a people which cannot link its thought to any progressive system of ideas that slowly evolve one from the other within a society, of a people which has participated in the general intellectual movement of other nations only by blind, superficial, and often clumsy imitation, must be a strong influence on each individual within that people. . . .

God forbid! I certainly do not claim that we have all the vices and that Europe has all the virtues. But I do say that one has to judge a people by studying the general spiritual attitude which is at the base of its existence, and only this spirit can help it to attain a more perfect moral state or an infinite devel-

opment, and not this or that trait in its character.

The masses are subject to certain forces at the summit of society. They do not think for themselves; but among them there is a certain number of thinkers who do think for themselves, and thus provide an impetus to the collective intelligence of the nation and make it move onward. While the small number meditates, the rest feel, and the general movement takes place. This is true for all the peoples of the earth with the exception of a few brutal races whose only human attribute is their face. The primitive peoples of Europe, the Celts, the Scandinavians, and the Germans, had their druids, their scalds, and their bards; all were powerful thinkers in their own way. Look at the people of North America who are being destroyed by the materialistic civilization of the United States: among them are men of great depth.

Now, I ask you, where are our sages, where are our thinkers? Which one of us ever thought, which one of us is thinking today? And yet we are situated between the great divisions of the world, between the Orient and the Occident, one elbow leaning on China and the other one on Germany. Therefore, we should be able to combine the two principles of an intelligent being, imagination and reason, and incorporate the histories of the whole globe into our own. However, that is not the role assigned to us by Providence. Far from it, she doesn't seem to have concerned herself with us at all. Having deprived the hearts of our people of her beneficent influence, she has left us completely to ourselves; she did not want to bother with us, and she did not want to teach us anything. The experience of the ages means nothing to us; we have not profited from the generations and centuries which came before us. From looking at us it seems as though the moral law of mankind has been revoked especially for us. Alone of all the peoples in the world, we have not given anything to the world, and we have not learned anything from the world. We have not added a single idea to the pool of human ideas. We have contributed nothing to the progress of the human spirit, we have disfigured it. From the first moment of our social existence we have not created anything for the common good of man. Not a single useful thought has grown in the sterile soil of our fatherland; no great truth has been brought forth in our midst. We did not take the trouble to devise anything for ourselves, and we have only borrowed deceptive appearances and useless luxuries from the devices of others.

A strange fact! Even in the all-inclusive scientific world, our history is not connected with anything, doesn't explain anything, doesn't prove anything. If the hordes of barbarians who convulsed the world had not crossed the country in which we live before swooping down on the Occident, we could hardly have filled one chapter of world history. In order to be noticed we had to expand from the Bering Straits to the Oder. Once, a great man wanted to civilize us, and, in order to give us a taste of the lights, he threw us the mantle of civilization; we picked up the mantle, but we did not touch civilization. Another time, a great prince, in associating us with his glorious mission, led us to victory from one end of Europe to the other; when we returned from this triumphal march across the most civilized countries of the world, we brought back only ideas and aspirations which resulted in an immense calamity, one that set us back half a century. There is something in our blood which repels all true progress. Finally, we have only lived, and we still only live, in order to give a great lesson to a remote posterity which will understand it; today, despite all the talk, our intellectual achievements are *nihil*. I cannot help but admire this astonishing blank and this solitude in our social existence. It contains the seeds of an inconceivable destiny, and doubtlessly also man's share of that destiny, as does everything which happens in the moral sphere. Let us ask history: she is the one who explains the peoples.

What did we do during the struggle between the energetic barbarism of the northern peoples and religion's high ideals, a struggle out of which rose the edifice of modern civilization? Driven by a fatal destiny, we searched unhappy Byzantium for the moral code which was to educate us, and thus we incurred that people's utter contempt. Shortly before that, an ambitious spirit [Photius] had led this family away from universal brotherhood; thus we adopted an idea which had been disfigured by human passion. At that time everything in Europe was animated by the vital principle of unity. Everything was derived from it, and everything converged on it. The whole intellectual movement of the time tended to bring about the unity of human thought, and all activity originated in this driving need to arrive at a universal idea, which is the essence of modern times. Strangers to this marvelous principle, we became a prey to conquest. Once we were freed from the yoke of the foreigner, we could have profited from the ideas which had blossomed forth during that time among our Occidental brothers, if we had not been separated from the common family. Instead we fell under a harsher servitude, one which was sanctified by the fact of our deliverance.

How many bright lights had already burst forth in the Europe of that day to dispel the darkness which had seemed to cover it! Most of the knowledge on which humanity prides itself today had already been foreshadowed in men's minds; the character of society had already been fixed; and, by turning back to pagan antiquity, the Christian world had rediscovered the forms of beauty that it still lacked. Relegated in our schism, we heard nothing of what was happening in Europe. We had no dealings with the great event taking place in the world. The distinguished qualities which religion has bestowed on modern peoples have made them, in the eyes of sound reason, as superior to the ancient peoples as the latter were to the Hottentots or the Laplanders. These new forces have enriched the human mind; these principles have made submission to an unarmed authority as gentle as it was brutal before. Nothing of all that took place over here. Despite the fact that we were called Christians, we did not budge when Christianity, leaving the generations behind it, advanced along the path which its divine Founder had indicated in the most majestic manner. While the world entirely rebuilt itself, we built nothing; we stayed in our thatched hovels. In one word, the new fortunes of mankind did not touch us. Christians, the fruit of Christianity did not ripen for us. . . .

In the end you will ask me: aren't we Christians, and can one become civilized only in the way Europe was? Unquestionably we are Christians; aren't the Abyssinians Christians as well? Certainly one can be civilized in a different manner than Europe was: haven't the Japanese been civilized, even more so than the Russians, if we are to believe one of our compatriots? Do you believe that the Christianity of the Abyssinians or the civilization of the Japanese will bring about that order of things of which I just spoke, or that they constitute the ultimate goal of the human race? Do

you believe that these absurd aberrations from the divine and human truths will make heaven come down to earth? . . .

All the nations of Europe held hands while advancing through the centuries. Today, no matter how many divergent paths they try to take, they always find themselves together. One does not have to study history in order to understand the family development of these peoples. Just read Tasso, and you will see them all bowing down before the walls of Jerusalem. Remember that for fifteen centuries they spoke to God in the same language, lived under a single moral authority, and had the same belief. Remember that for fifteen centuries, each year, on the same day, at the same hour, with the same words, they all together raised their voices towards the Supreme Being, to extol his glory. A wonderful concert, a thousand times more sublime than all the harmonies of the physical world! Moreover, since that sphere where the Europeans live, the only one where the human race can fulfill its final destiny, is the result of the influence that religion had on them, it is clear that up to now our lack of faith or the insufficiency of our dogmas has kept us out of this universal movement, in which the social ideal of Christianity has been formulated and developed. We have thus been thrown into that category of peoples who will profit only indirectly from Christianity's influence, and at a much later date. Therefore, we must try to revive our faith in every possible way and give ourselves a truly Christian enthusiasm, since it is Christianity which is responsible for everything over there. That is what I meant when I said that this education of the human race has to begin once more for our benefit. . . .

Fundamentally, we Russians have nothing in common with Homer, the Greeks, the Romans, and the Germans;

all that is completely foreign to us. But what do you want! We have to speak Europe's language. Our exotic civilization rests so much on Europe's that even though we do not have its ideas, we have no other language but hers; hence we are forced to speak it. If the small number of mental habits, traditions, and memories we have do not link us to any people of this earth, if, in effect, we do not belong to any of these systems of the moral universe, we still, because of our social superficialities, belong to the Occidental world. This link, which in truth is very feeble, which does not unite us so closely to Europe as is commonly thought, and which fails to let every part of our being feel the great movement taking place over there, still makes our future destiny dependent on this European society. Therefore, the more we try to amalgamate with it, the better off we shall be. . . .

Certainly we cannot remain in our desert much longer. Let us do all we can to prepare the way for our descendants. We are unable to bequeath them that which we do not have—beliefs, reason molded by time, a strong personality, opinions well-developed in the course of a long intellectual life that has been animated, active, and fruitful in its results—but let us at least bequeath them a few ideas which, even though we did not find them ourselves, will at least have a traditional element in them, if transmitted from one generation to the next. By this very fact they will have a certain power and a certain profundity which our own ideas did not have. We shall thus be worthy of posterity, and we shall not have inhabited this earth uselessly.

RUSSIA'S INTERCOURSE WITH EUROPE

From Letters to A. I. Turgenev, 1833 and 1835

Here, my friend, is a letter for the illustrious Schelling which I ask you to forward to him. The idea of writing to him came to me from something you once said about him in one of your letters to her ladyship, your cousin. The letter is open, read it, and you will see what it is about. Since I talked about you in it, I wanted it to reach him through you. It would give me great pleasure if, when you send it to him, you could let him know that I understand German; because I am anxious for him to write to me (if he does me that honor) in the language in which he so often revived my friend Plato, and in which he transformed science into a combination of poetry and geometry, and by now perhaps into religion. And heavens! It is time that all this became one thing. . . .

Please don't be offended, but I prefer your French letters to your Russian ones. There is more free rein in your French letters, you are more yourself. Moreover, you are good when you are completely yourself. . . . Besides, you are essentially a European. You know that I know something about it. You should really wear the garb of a Frenchman. . . .

Like all peoples, we too are galloping today, in our own way if you like, but we are speeding, that is certain. I am sure that in a little while the great ideas, once they have reached us, will find it easier to realize themselves in our midst and to incarnate themselves in our individuals than anywhere else, because here they will find no deep-rooted prejudices, no old habits, no obstinate routines to fight. It seems to me that the European thinker should not be totally indifferent to the present fate of his meditations among us. . . .

What? You live in Rome and don't understand it after all that we have told and retold each other about it! For once, understand that it is not a city like all the others, a heap of stones and of people; it is an idea, it is an immense fact. One should not look at it from the top of the Capitol or from the gallery of St. Peter, but from that intellectual summit which brings so much delight when one treads on its sacred soil. Rome will then be completely transfigured right before your eyes. You will see the large shadows by which these monuments project their prodigious teachings over the whole surface of the earth, and you will hear a powerful voice resound from this silent body and tell you ineffable mysteries. You will know that Rome is the link between ancient times and new times, because it is absolutely necessary that there be one spot on earth to which, at times, every man can turn in order to rediscover materially and physiologically all the memories of the human race, something sensible, tangible, in which the thought of the ages is summed up in a visible manner—and that spot is Rome. Then these prophetic ruins will tell you all the fates of the world; their tale will be a whole philosophy of history for you, a whole doctrine, and more than that, a living revelation. . . . But the Pope, the Pope! Well, isn't the Pope another idea, a completely abstract thing? Look at the figure of that old man, carried on his litter, under his canopy, always in the same manner for thousands of years, as though it were nothing. Seriously, where is the man in all that? Isn't he an all-powerful symbol of time, not of that time which passes but of the time which does not move, through which everything else passes but which itself remains motionless, and in which and by which everything happens? Tell me, don't you absolutely want a single intellectual monument on the earth, one which lasts? Don't you need something more in the way of human achievement than the pyramid of granite which knows how to fight the law of death, but nothing else?

That great play which is put on by the peoples of Europe, and which we attend as cold and impassive spectators, makes me think of that little play by Mr. Zagoskin whose title is *The Dissatisfied*, which is to be given here and will be attended by a cold and impassive audience. The dissatisfied! Do you understand the malice of that title? What I don't understand is where the author found the characters for his drama. Thank God, here one sees only perfectly happy and satisfied people. A foolish well-being and a stupid satisfaction with ourselves, those are our outstanding traits at the present time; it is remarkable that at the moment when all that the Christian peoples inherited from paganism, the blind and excited nationalism which makes them each other's enemies, is fading away, and when all the civilized nations are beginning to give up their self-complacency, we take it upon ourselves idiotically to contemplate our imaginary perfections. . . .

Take any epoch you like in the history of the Occidental peoples, compare it to the year we are in now [1835], and you will see that we do not embrace the same principle of civilization that those peoples do. You will find that those nations have always lived an animated, intelligent, and fruitful life; that they were handed an idea at the very beginning, and that it is the pursuit of that idea and its development which make up their history; and finally that they have always created, invented, and discovered. Tell me, what idea are we developing? What did we discover, invent, or create? It is not a question of running after them; it is a question of an honest appraisal of ourselves, of looking at ourselves as we are, to cast away the lies and to take up the truth. After that we shall advance, and we shall advance more rapidly than the others because we have come after them, because we have all their experience and all the work of the centuries which precede us. The people in Europe are strangely mistaken about us. There is Mr. Jouffroy, who tells us that we are destined to civilize Asia. That is all very well; but, I beg you, ask him what Asian peoples have we civilized? Apparently the mastodons and the other fossilized populations of Siberia. As far as I know, they are the only races we have pulled out of obscurity, and that thanks only to Pallas and Fischer. Some Europeans persist in handing us the Orient; with the instinct of a kind of European nationalism they drive us back to the Orient so as not to meet us any longer in the Occident. Let us not be taken in by their involuntary artifice; let us discover our future by ourselves, and let us not ask the others what we should do. It is evident that the Orient belongs to the masters of the sea; we are much farther away from it than the English, and we no longer live in an age when all Oriental revolutions come from the middle of Asia. The new charter of the India Company will henceforth be the true civilizing element of Asia. On the contrary, it is Europe to whom we shall teach an infinity of things which she could not conceive without us. Don't laugh: you know that this is my profound conviction. The day will come when we shall take our place in the middle of intellectual Europe, as we have already done in the middle of political Europe; and we shall be more powerful, then, by our intelligence than we are today by our material forces. That is the logical result of our long solitude: great things have always come from the desert.

THE LEGACY OF PETER THE GREAT
From "Apology of a Madman," 1837

For three hundred years Russia has aspired to consort with Occidental Europe; for three hundred years she has taken her most serious ideas, her most fruitful teachings, and her most vivid delights from there. For over a century Russia has done better than that. One hundred and fifty years ago the greatest of our kings—the one who supposedly began a new era, and to whom, it is said, we owe our greatness, our glory, and all the goods which we own today—disavowed the old Russia in the face of the whole world. He swept away all our institutions with his powerful breath; he dug an abyss between our past and our present, and into it he threw pell-mell all our traditions. He himself went to the Occidental countries and made himself the smallest of men, and he came back to us so much the greater; he prostrated himself before the Occident, and he arose as our master and our ruler. He introduced Occidental idioms into our language; he called his new capital by an Occidental name; he rejected his hereditary title and took an Occidental title; finally, he almost gave up his own name, and more than once he signed his sovereign decrees with an Occidental name.

Since that time our eyes have been constantly turned towards the countries of the Occident; we did nothing more, so to speak, than to breathe in the emanations which reached us from there, and to nourish ourselves on them. We must admit that our princes almost always took us by the hand, almost always took the country in tow, and the country never had a hand in it; they themselves prescribed to us the customs, the language, and the clothing of the Occident. We learned to spell the names of the things in Occidental books. Our own history was taught to us by one of the Occidental countries. We translated the whole literature of the Occident, we learned it by heart, and we adorned ourselves with its tattered garment. And finally, we were happy to resemble the Occident, and proud when it consented to count us as one of its own.

We have to agree, it was beautiful, this creation of Peter the Great, this powerful thought that set us on the road we were to travel with so much fanfare. It was a profound wisdom which told us: That civilization over there is the fruit of so much labor; the sciences and the arts have cost so much sweat to so many generations! All that can be yours if you cast away your superstitions, if you repudiate your prejudices, if you are not jealous of your barbaric past, if you do not boast of your centuries of ignorance, if you direct your ambition to appropriating the works of all the peoples and the riches acquired by the human spirit in all latitudes of the globe. And it is not merely for his own nation that this great man worked. These men of Providence are always sent for the good of mankind as a whole. At first one people claims them, and later they are absorbed by the human race, like those great rivers which first fertilize the countryside and then pay their tribute to the waters of the ocean. Was the spectacle which he presented to the universe upon leaving his throne and his country to go into hiding among the last ranks of civilized society anything else but the renewed effort of the genius of this man to free himself from the narrow confines of his fatherland and to establish himself in the great sphere of humanity?

That was the lesson we were supposed to learn. In effect we have profited from it, and to this very day we have walked along the path which the great emperor traced for us. Our immense development is nothing more than the realization of that superb program. Never was a people less infatuated with itself than the Russian people, such as it has been shaped by Peter the Great, and never has a people been more successful and more glorious in its progress. The high intelligence of this extraordinary man guessed exactly the point of our departure on the highway of civilization and the intellectual movement of the world. He saw that lacking a fundamental historical idea, we should be unable to build our future on that important foundation. He understood very well that all we could do was to train ourselves, like the peoples of the Occident, to cut across the chaos of national prejudices, across the narrow paths of local ideas, and out of the rusty rut of native customs; that we had to raise ourselves, by one spontaneous outburst of our internal powers, by an energetic effort of the national conscience, to the destiny which has been reserved for us. Thus he freed us from previous history which encumbers ancient societies and impedes their progress; he opened our minds to all the great and beautiful ideas which are prevalent among men; he handed us the whole Occident, such as the centuries have fashioned it, and gave us all its history for our history, and all its future for our future.

Do you believe that if he had found in his country a rich and fertile history, living traditions, and deep-rooted institutions, he would have hesitated to pour them into a new mold? Do you not believe that faced with a strongly outlined and pronounced nationality, his founding spirit would have demanded that that nationality itself become the necessary instrument for the regeneration of his country? On the other hand, would the country have suffered being robbed of its past and a new one, a European one, being put in its place? But that was not the case. Peter the Great found only a blank page when he came to power, and with a strong hand he wrote on it the words *Europe* and *Occident:* from that time on we were part of Europe and of the Occident.

Don't be mistaken about it: no matter how enormous the genius of this man and the energy of his will, his work was possible only in the heart of a nation whose past history did not imperiously lay down the road it had to follow, whose traditions did not have the power to create its future, whose memories could be erased with impunity by an audacious legislator. We were so obedient to the voice of a prince who led us to a new life because our previous existence apparently did not give us any legitimate grounds for resistance. The most marked trait of our historical physiognomy is the absence of spontaneity in our social development. Look carefully, and you will see that each important fact in our history is a fact that was forced on us; almost every new idea is an imported idea. But there is nothing in this point of view which should give offense to the national sentiment; it is a truth and has to be accepted. Just as there are great men in history, so there are great nations which cannot be explained by the normal laws of reason, for they are mysteriously decreed by the supreme logic of Providence. That is our case; but once more, the national honor has nothing to do with all this.

The history of a people is more than a succession of facts, it is a series of connected ideas. That precisely is the history we do not have. We have to learn to get along without it, and not to vilify the persons who first noticed our lack. From time to time, in their various searches, our fanatic Slavophils exhume objects of general interest for our museums and our libraries; but I believe it is permissible to doubt that these Slavophils will ever be able to extract something from our historic soil which can fill the void in our souls or condense the vagueness of our spirit. Look at Europe in the Middle Ages: there were no events which were not absolutely necessary in one way or another and which have not left some deep traces in the heart of mankind. And why? Because there, behind each event, you will find an idea, because medieval history is the history of modern thought which tries to incarnate itself in art, in science, in the life of men, and in society. Moreover, how many furrows of the mind have been plowed by this history! . . .

The world has always been divided into two parts, the Orient and Occident. This is not merely a geographical division, it is another order of things derived from the very nature of the intelligent being—Orient and Occident are two principles which correspond to two dynamic forces of nature; they are two ideas which embrace the whole human organism. . . .

The Orient was first, and it spread waves of light all over the earth from the heart of its solitary meditations; then came the Occident, which, by its immense activity, its quick word, its sharp analysis, took possession of its tasks, finished what the Orient had begun, and finally enveloped it in its vast embrace. But in the Orient, the docile minds, who were prostrated before the authority of time, exhausted themselves in their absolute submission to a venerated principle, and one day, imprisoned in their immovable syntheses, they fell asleep, without any inkling of the new fates in store for them; whereas in the Occident the minds proudly and freely advanced, bowing only to the authority of reason and of God, stopping only before the unknown, with their eyes always fixed on the unlimited future. And you know that they are still advancing, and you also know that since the time of Peter the Great we believe that we are advancing with them.

But here comes another new school.

It no longer wants the Occident; it wants to destroy the work of Peter the Great and again follow the desert road.

Forgetting what the Occident has done for us, ungrateful towards the great man who civilized us, towards the Europe which taught us, this school repudiates both Europe and the great man; and in its hasty ardor, this newborn patriotism already proclaims that we are the cherished children of the Orient. Why, it asks, do we have to look for lights among the peoples of the Occident? Don't we have in our midst the germs of an infinitely better social order than Europe has? Why don't we leave it to time? Left to ourselves, to our lucid reason, to the fertile principle which is hidden in the depth of our powerful nature, and above all to our saintly religion, we shall soon go beyond those peoples who are a prey to errors and to lies. For what should we envy the Occident? Its religious wars, its Pope, its chivalry, its Inquisition? Truly beautiful things! Is the Occident the native land of science and of all deep things? It is the Orient, as is well known. Let us then withdraw to the Orient, which we touch everywhere and from which erstwhile we derived our beliefs, our laws, and our virtues, all that made us the most powerful people in the world. The old Orient is fading away: well, aren't we its natural heirs? Henceforth it is among us that these wonderful traditions will perpetuate themselves, that all these great and mysterious truths, with whose safekeeping we were entrusted from the very beginning, will realize themselves. Now you understand whence came the storm which beat down upon me the other day, and you see how a real revolution is taking place in our midst and in our national thought. It is a passionate reaction against the Enlightenment and the ideas of the Occident, against that enlightenment and those ideas which made us what we are, and of which even this reaction, this movement which today drives us to act against them, is the result. But this time the impetus does not come from above. On the contrary, it is said that in the upper regions of society the memory of our royal reformer has never been more venerated than it is today. The initiative, then, has been entirely in the hands of the country. Whither will this first result of the emancipated reason of the nation lead us? God only knows! If one truly loves one's country, it is impossible not to be painfully affected by this apostasy on the part of our most highly developed minds towards the things which brought us our glory and our greatness; and I believe that it is the duty of a good citizen to do his best to analyze this strange phenomenon.

We are situated to the east of Europe; that is a positive fact, but it does not mean that we have ever been a part of the East. The history of the Orient has nothing in common with the history of our country. As we have just seen, the history of the Orient contains a fertile idea which, in its time, brought about an immense development of the mind, which accomplished its mission with a stupendous force, but which is no longer fated to produce anything new on the face of the earth. . . .

Believe me, I cherish my country more than any of you. I strive for its glory. I know how to appreciate the eminent qualities of my nation. But it is also true that the patriotic feeling which animates me is not exactly the same as the one whose shouts have upset my quiet existence, shouts which have again launched my boat—which had run aground at the foot of the Cross—on the ocean of human miseries. I have not learned to love my country with my eyes closed, my head bowed, and my mouth shut. I think that one can be useful to one's country only if one sees it clearly; I believe that the age of blind loves has passed, and that nowadays one owes one's country the truth. I love my country in the way that Peter the Great taught me to love it. I confess that I do not feel that smug patriotism, that lazy patriotism, which manages to make everything beautiful, which falls asleep on its illusions, and with which unfortunately many of our good souls are afflicted today. I believe that if we have come after the others, it is so that we can do better than the others; it is so that we may not fall into their faults, their errors, and their superstitions. . . . I believe that we are in a fortunate position, provided that we know how to appreciate it. It is a wonderful privilege to be able to contemplate and judge the world from the height of independent thought, free from unrestrained passions and petty interests which elsewhere disturb man's view and pervert his judgment. More is to come: I am firmly convinced that we are called on to resolve most of the social problems, to perfect most of the ideas which have come up in the old societies, and to decide most of the weighty questions concerning the human race. I have often said it, and I like to repeat it: in a way we are appointed, by the very nature of things, to serve as a real jury for the many suits which are being argued before the great tribunals of the human spirit and of human society.

26

LETTER TO GOGOL

By Vissarion Belinsky

In 1847 Nikolai Gogol (1809–52), whose *Dead Souls* and *The Inspector General* had been hailed by Belinsky (1811–48) as a crusade "against all that is bad in Russia," published his *Selected Passages from a Correspondence with Friends,* a defense of serfdom and autocracy, of Orthodoxy and mysticism. Belinsky could not but criticize this attempt to glorify all that he hated. Surprised at the vehement attacks which met his book, Gogol wrote: "I cannot understand how it happened that I have aroused the anger of all Russians." It was then that Berlinsky wrote the letter, printed below, of which Alexander Herzen said: "It is a work of genius—and, I believe, his testament as well." Belinsky's death a few months later saved him from official persecution. In 1849 Dostoevski was condemned to death for "having circulated the letter of the journalist Belinsky full of insolent expressions against the Orthodox Church and the Emperor." The sentence was commuted to penal servitude at the last moment.

Despite government reprisals, the letter circulated in many copies. After much travel through Russia the Slavophile Ivan Aksakov wrote his father: "There is not a high school teacher in the Russian provinces who does not know Belinsky's 'Letter to Gogol' by heart."

For a biography of Belinsky, see Herbert Bowman's *Vissarion Belinsky.* For Belinsky's place in the history of the intelligentsia, see a series of articles by Isaiah Berlin, "A Marvellous Decade," *Encounter,* June, November, and December, 1955, and May, 1956; the third instalment is devoted to Belinsky. See also H. Cloutier, "Belinsky, Advocate of Liberty," *Russian Review,* VIII, 20–33. For a Soviet view, see Z. Smirnova, *The Socio-Political Views of Belinsky,* and E. Kresky's article, "Soviet Scholarship on Belinsky," *American Slavic and East European Review,* VII, 269–75. See also Ralph Matlaw's paperback anthology, *Belinsky, Chernyshevsky and Dobroliubov.* There are chapters on Belinsky and the so-called "democratic criticism" in George Lukacs, *Studies in European Realism,* as well as in *Studies in Rebellion* by Evgenii Lampert, and *The Positive Hero in Russian Literature* by Rufus Mathewson. There are three paperback biographies of Gogol, by Vladimir Nabokov, Vsevolod Setchkarev, and Janko Lavrin, all entitled *Nikolai Gogol.*

You are only partly right in regarding my article as that of an angered man:

From V. Belinsky, *Selected Philosophical Works* (Moscow, 1956), pp. 536–46.

that epithet is too mild and inadequate to express the state to which I was reduced on reading your book. And you are entirely wrong in ascribing that state to your indeed none too flattering references to the admirers of your talent. No, there was a more important reason for this. One could suffer an outraged sense of self-esteem, and I would have had sense enough to let the matter pass in silence were that the whole gist of the matter; but one cannot suffer an outraged sense of truth and human dignity; one cannot keep silent when lies and immorality are preached as truth and virtue under the guise of religion and the protection of the knout.

Yes, I loved you with all the passion with which a man, bound by ties of blood to his native country, can love its hope, its honour, its glory, one of the great leaders on its path of consciousness, development and progress. And you had sound reason for at least momentarily losing your equanimity when you forfeited that love. I say that not because I believe my love to be an adequate reward for a great talent, but because I do not represent a single person in this respect but a multitude of men, most of whom neither you nor I have ever set eyes on, and who, in their turn, have never set eyes on you. I find myself at a loss to give you an adequate idea of the indignation which your book has aroused in all noble hearts, and of the wild shouts of joy which were set up on its appearance by all your enemies—both the non-literary—the Chichikovs, the Nozdrevs and the mayors[1] . . . and by the literary, whose names are well known to you. You see yourself that even those people who are of one mind with your book have disowned it. Even if it had been written as a result of deep

and sincere conviction it could not have created any other impression on the public than the one it did. And it is nobody's fault but your own if everyone (except the few who must be seen and known in order not to derive pleasure from their approval) received it as an ingenious but all too unceremonious artifice for achieving a sheerly earthly aim by celestial means. Nor is that in any way surprising; what is surprising is that you find it surprising. I believe that is so because your profound knowledge of Russia is only that of an artist, but not of a thinker, whose role you have so ineffectually tried to play in your fantastic book. Not that you are not a thinker, but that you have been accustomed for so many years to look at Russia from your *beautiful far-away*,[2] and who does not know that there is nothing easier than seeing things from a distance the way we want to see them; for in that *beautiful far-away* you live a life that is entirely alien to it, you live in and within yourself or within a circle of the same mentality as your own which is powerless to resist your influence on it. Therefore you failed to realize that Russia sees her salvation not in mysticism, nor asceticism, nor pietism, but in the successes of civilization, enlightenment and humanity. What she needs is not sermons (she has heard enough of them!) or prayers (she has repeated them too often!), but the awakening in the people of a sense of their human dignity lost for so many centuries amid the dirt and refuse; she needs rights and laws conforming not with the preaching of the church but with common sense and justice, and their strictest possible observance. Instead of which she presents the dire spectacle of a country where men traffic

---

[1] Chichikov and Nozdrev: characters in Gogol's *Dead Souls*; The Mayor: one of the characters of his *The Inspector-General*.

[2] Gogol went abroad in 1836 where, with short trips to Russia, he lived for many years.

in men, without even having the excuse so insidiously exploited by the American plantation owners who claim that the Negro is not a man; a country where people call themselves not by names but by sobriquets, such as Vanka, Vaska, Steshka, Palashka; a country where there are not only no guarantees for individuality, honour and property, but even no police order, and where there is nothing but vast corporations of official thieves and robbers of various descriptions. The most vital national problems in Russia today are the abolition of serfdom and corporal punishments and the strictest possible observance of at least those laws which already exist. This is even realized by the government itself (which is well aware of how the landowners treat their peasants and how many of the former are annually done away with by the latter), as is proven by its timid and abortive half-measures for the relief of the white Negroes and the comical substitution of the single-lash knout by a cat-o'-three-tails.[3]

Such are the problems which prey on the mind of Russia in her apathetic slumber! And at such a time a great writer, whose beautifully artistic and deeply truthful works have so powerfully contributed towards Russia's awareness of herself, enabling her as they did to take a look at herself as though in a mirror—comes out with a book in which he teaches the barbarian landowner in the name of Christ and Church to make still greater profits out of the peasants and to abuse them still more. . . . And you would expect me not to become indignant? . . . Why, if you had made an attempt on my life I could not have hated you more than I do for these disgraceful lines. . . . And after this, you expect people to believe the sincerity of your book's intent! No! Had you really been inspired by the truth of Christ and not by the teaching of the Devil you would certainly have written something entirely different in your new book. You would have told the landowner that since his peasants are his brethren in Christ, and since a brother cannot be a slave to his brother, he should either give them their freedom, or, at least, allow them to enjoy the fruits of their own labour to their greatest possible benefit, realizing as he does, in the depths of his own conscience the false relationship in which he stands towards them.

And the expression: *"Oh you unwashed snout, you!"* From what Nozdrev and Sobakevich[4] did you overhear this, to give to the world as a great discovery for the edification and benefit of the muzhiks, whose only reason for not washing is that they have let themselves be persuaded by their masters that they are not human beings? And your conception of the national Russian system of trial and punishment, whose ideal you have found in the foolish saying that both the guilty and innocent should be flogged alike? That, indeed, is often the case with us, though more often than not it is the man who is in the right who takes the punishment, unless he can ransom himself, and for such occasions another proverb says: *guiltlessly guilty!* And such a book is supposed to have been the result of an arduous inner process, a lofty spiritual enlightenment! Impossible! Either you are ill—and you must hasten to take a cure, or . . . I am afraid to put my thought into words! . . .

Proponent of the knout, apostle of ignorance, champion of obscurantism and Stygian darkness, panegyrist of Tatar morals—what are you about! Look

[3] The knout with a single lash used as an instrument of punishment was replaced by the cat-o'-three-tails in the Russian criminal code of 1845.

[4] Sobakevich—another figure from *Dead Souls.*

beneath your feet—you are standing on the brink of an abyss! . . . That you base such teaching on the Orthodox Church I can understand: it has always served as the prop of the knout and the servant of despotism; but why have you mixed Christ up in this? What in common have you found between Him and any church, least of all the Orthodox Church? He was the first to bring to people the teaching of freedom, equality and brotherhood and set the seal of truth to that teaching by martyrdom. And this teaching was men's *salvation* only until it became organized in the Church and took the principle of Orthodoxy for its foundation. The Church, on the other hand, was a hierarchy, consequently a champion of inequality, a flatterer of authority, an enemy and persecutor of brotherhood among men—and so it has remained to this day. But the meaning of Christ's message has been revealed by the philosophical movement of the preceding century. And that is why a man like Voltaire who stamped out the fires of fanaticism and ignorance in Europe by ridicule, is, of course, more the son of Christ, flesh of his flesh and bone of his bone, than all your priests, bishops, metropolitans and patriarchs—Eastern or Western. Do you mean to say you do not know it! It is not even a novelty now to a schoolboy. . . . Hence, can it be that you, the author of *Inspector-General* and *Dead Souls*, have in all sincerity, from the bottom of your heart, sung a hymn to the nefarious Russian clergy which you rank immeasurably higher than the Catholic clergy? Let us assume that you do not know that the latter had once been something, while the former had never been anything but a servant and slave of the secular powers; but do you really mean to say you do not know that our clergy is held in universal contempt by Russian society and the Russian people? Of whom do the Russian people relate obscene stories? Of the priest, the priest's wife, the priest's daughter and the priest's farm hand. Does not the priest in Russia represent for all Russians the embodiment of gluttony, avarice, servility and shamelessness? Do you mean to say that you do not know all this? Strange! According to you the Russian people is the most religious in the world. That is a lie! The basis of religiousness is pietism, reverence, fear of God. Whereas the Russian man utters the name of the Lord while scratching himself somewhere. He says of the icon: *if it isn't good for praying it's good for covering the pots.*

Take a closer look and you will see that it is by nature a profoundly atheistic people. It still retains a good deal of superstition, but not a trace of religousness. Superstition passes with the advances of civilization, but religiousness often keeps company with them too; we have a living example of this in France, where even today there are many sincere Catholics among enlightened and educated men, and where many people who have rejected Christianity still cling stubbornly to some sort of god. The Russian people is different; mystic exaltation is not in its nature; it has too much common sense, a too lucid and positive mind, and therein, perhaps, lies the vastness of its historic destinies in the future. Religiousness with it has not even taken root among the clergy, since a few isolated and exclusive personalities distinguished for such cold ascetic reflectiveness prove nothing. But the majority of our clergy has always been distinguished for their fat bellies, scholastic pedantry and savage ignorance. It is a shame to accuse it of religious intolerance and fanaticism; rather could it be praised for an exemplary indifference in matters of faith. Religiousness with us appeared only among the schismatic sects who formed such a contrast in spirit to the mass of the people and were so insignificant before it numerically. . . .

You, as far as I can see, do not properly understand the Russian public. Its character is determined by the condition of Russian society in which fresh forces are seething and struggling for expression, but weighed down by heavy oppression and finding no outlet, they induce merely dejection, weariness and apathy. Only literature, despite the Tatar censorship, shows signs of life and progressive movement. That is why the title of writer is held in such esteem among us, that is why literary success is easy among us even for a writer of small talent. The title of poet and writer has long since eclipsed the tinsel of epaulettes and gaudy uniforms. And that especially explains why every so-called liberal tendency, however poor in talent, is rewarded by universal notice, and why the popularity of great talents which sincerely or insincerely give themselves to the service of orthodoxy, autocracy and nationality declines so quickly. A striking example is Pushkin, who had merely to write two or three verses in a loyal strain and don the *kammerjunker*'s livery to suddenly forfeit the popular affection! And you are greatly mistaken if you believe in all earnest that your book has come to grief not because of its bad trend, but because of the harsh truths alleged to have been expressed by you about all and everybody. Assuming you could think that of the writing fraternity, but then how do you account for the public? Did you tell it less bitter home truths less harshly and with less truth and talent in *Inspector-General* and *Dead Souls?*

Indeed the old school was worked up to a furious pitch of anger against you, but *Inspector-General* and *Dead Souls* were not affected by it, whereas your latest book has been an utter and disgraceful failure. And here the public is right, for it looks upon Russian writers as its only leaders, defenders, and saviours against Russian autocracy, orthodoxy and nationality, and therefore, while always prepared to forgive a writer a bad book, will never forgive him a pernicious book. This shows how much fresh and healthy intuition, albeit still in embryo, is latent in our society, and this likewise proves that it has a future. If you love Russia rejoice with me at the failure of your book! . . .

I would tell you, not without a certain feeling of self-satisfaction, that I believe I know the Russian public a little. Your book alarmed me by the possibility of its exercising a bad influence on the government and the censorship, but not on the public. When it was rumoured in St. Petersburg that the government intended to publish your book in many thousands of copies and to sell it at an extremely low price my friends grew despondent; but I told them there and then that the book, despite everything, would have no success and that it would soon be forgotten. In fact it is now better remembered for the articles which have been written about it than for the book itself. Yes, the Russian has a deep, **though still underdeveloped, instinct for truth.** . . .

Were I to give free rein to my feelings this letter would probably grow into a voluminous notebook. I never thought of writing you on this subject though I longed to do so and though you gave all and sundry printed permission to write you without ceremony with an eye to the truth alone. Were I in Russia I would not be able to do it, for the local "Shpekins" open other people's letters not merely for their own pleasure but as a matter of official duty, for the sake of informing. This summer incipient consumption has driven me abroad [and

Nekrasov has forwarded me your letter to Salzbrunn which I am leaving today with Annenkov for Paris via Frankfort-on-Main].[5] The unexpected receipt of your letter has enabled me to unburden my soul of what has accumulated there against you on account of your book. I cannot express myself by halves, I cannot prevaricate; it is not in my nature. Let you or time itself prove to me that I am mistaken in my conclusions. I shall be the first to rejoice in it, but

I shall not repent what I have told you. This is not a question of your or my personality, it concerns a matter which is of greater importance than myself or even you; it is a matter which concerns the truth, Russian society, Russia. And this is my last concluding word: if you have had the misfortune of disowning with proud humility your truly great works, you should now disown with sincere humility your last book, and atone for the dire sin of its publication by new creations which would be reminiscent of your old ones.

Salzbrunn,
July 15, 1847

[5] The words in brackets were omitted by Herzen in *The Polar Star* to avoid implicating Annenkov and Nekrasov, who might have been persecuted by the Russian secret police.

27

YOUNG MOSCOW

By Alexander Herzen

Herzen (1812–70) enrolled in Moscow University in 1829. There he met most of the men he describes in the following pages. Entering government service, he aspired to become a model official. But he became convinced that the Russia of Nicholas I was no place to fulfil this dream. Twice he was sentenced to exile in remote provinces for entertaining "dangerous ideas." When his father died in 1846, he found himself wealthy and left Russia the following year, never to return. He spent the rest of his life in western Europe, primarily in Paris and London. He was the first Russian to be recognized as an equal by European intellectuals. He made friends with Michelet, Hugo, Proudhon, Mazzini, Garibaldi, and Carlyle. His London home became the center of opposition to the Russian government. There he began to publish the Russian journals *The Polar Star* (from 1855) and *The Bell* (from 1857). The latter became very influential in Russia, whence it was smuggled in thousands of copies and read even by the Emperor. In London Herzen also began his remarkable autobiography, from which our excerpt is taken. In the words of Sir Isaiah Berlin he was "a kind of Russian Voltaire of the mid-nineteenth century." "Young Moscow" belongs to the fourth part of the memoirs and first appeared in *The Polar Star* in 1855 and 1862.

The autobiography is available in two translations entitled *The Memoirs* or *My Past and Thoughts*. Other works of Herzen in English include *From the Other Shore* and *The Russian People and Socialism* (in paperback). For a biography see Martin Malia, *Alexander Herzen and the Birth of Russian Socialism*. Also of interest is E. H. Carr, *The Romantic Exiles* (in paperback). Of Sir Isaiah Berlin's essays, "The Marvellous Decade," *Encounter*, June, November, December, 1955, and May, 1956, the last is devoted to Herzen. For a Soviet view, see G. Teriaev's *Herzen*. See also Edward Brown, "The Circle of Stankevich," *American Slavic and East European Review*, XVI, 349–68, and his "Stankevich and Belinsky," in *American Contributions to the Fourth International Congress of Slavicists* (Moscow, 1958). For more information on Stankevich, see Edmund Kostka, "At the Roots of Russian Westernism: N. V. Stankevich and His Circle," *Slavic and East European Studies*, VI, 158–76. There is a small monograph, *Stankevich and His Moscow Circle, 1830–1840*, by Edward J. Brown. Franco Venturi's *Roots of Revolution* (paperback) has two chapters on Herzen.

From A. Herzen, *Selected Philosophical Works* (Moscow, 1956), pp. 525–45.

I regard Belinsky as one of the most remarkable figures of Nicholas' time. After the liberalism which had somehow survived 1825 in Polevoy, after the lugubrious article of Chaadayev,[1] Belinsky appeared on the scene with his caustic criticism, engendered by suffering, and his passionate interest in every question. In a series of critical articles he touched, in season and out of season, upon everything, everywhere true to his hatred of authority and often rising to poetic inspiration. The book he reviewed usually served him as a starting-point—he abandoned it half-way and grappled hold of some other problem. The line "That's what kindred are" in *Onegin*[2] was enough for him to summon family life before the judgement seat and to pick family relations to pieces down to the last shred. Who does not remember his articles on *The Tarantass*, Turgenev's *Parasha*, Derzhavin, Mochalov, and *Hamlet*? How true he remains to his principles, what intrepid consistency he shows! How adroit he is in steering clear of the sandbanks of the censorship, and what boldness he displays in his attacks on the aristocracy of literature, on the writers of the upper three grades, these high officials of literature who are always ready to defeat an opponent if not by fair means then by foul, if not by debate then by informing the police. Belinsky scourged them mercilessly, goading the petty vanity of the stilted mediocre authors of eclogues, promoters of learning, benevolence, and sentimentality; he derided their most cherished ideas, the poetical dreams fostered by their flaccid brains, their naïveté, hidden under a St. Anna ribbon.[3]

[1] The reference is to "A philosophical letter to a lady" by Peter Chaadayev; Nikolai Polevoi, editor of the *Moscow Telegraph* (1825–34), a journal of liberal views.

[2] Alexander Pushkin's *Eugene Onegin*, a novel in verse.

How they hated him for it!

The Slavophils date their official existence from the war upon Belinsky. It was he who taunted them into wearing the *murmolka* and the *zipun*.[4] It will be recalled that Belinsky had formerly written in *Otechestvennye Zapiski*, while Kireyevsky entitled his excellent journal *Evropeets*; these titles prove best of all that at first there were merely shades of opinion and not differences of parties.[5]

Belinsky's essays were awaited with feverish impatience by the younger generation of Petersburg and Moscow beginning with the 25th of every month. Half a dozen times the students would drop in at the coffee-house to ask whether the *Otechestvennye Zapiski* had been received; the heavy volume was snatched from hand to hand. "Is there an article by Belinsky?" And if there was, it was devoured with feverish interest, with laughter, with disputes . . . and three or four cults or *reputations* were no more.

Skobelev, the governor of the Fortress of Peter and Paul, might well say in jest to Belinsky when he met him in Nevsky Prospect: "When are you coming to us? I have a nice warm litle cell all ready reserved for you." . . .

Worried financially by unscrupulous literary agents, morally fettered by the censorship, surrounded in Petersburg by people little sympathetic to him, and

[3] The Order of St. Anne—a high government decoration, bestowed for valuable service to the crown.

[4] *Murmolka*: a cap; *zipun*: a homespun coat. The Slavophiles wore the cap and the coat to indicate their preference for native Russian dress as against Western clothing.

[5] *Otechestvennye Zapiski* (Notes of the Fatherland)—a journal of the Westerners; *Evropeets* (The European), edited by Kireyevsky, a Slavophile journal. Herzen draws attention to the fact that the titles, if taken to describe the views of the editors, would be quite misleading.

consumed by a disease to which the Baltic climate was fatal, he became more and more irritable. He shunned outsiders, was savagely shy, and sometimes spent weeks together in gloomy inactivity. Then the publishers sent note after note demanding copy, and the enslaved writer, grinding his teeth, took up his pen and wrote those biting articles throbbing with indignation, those indictments which so impressed their readers.

Often, utterly exhausted, he would come to us to rest, and lie on the floor playing with our two-year-old child for hours together. While we were only the three of us things went swimmingly, but if there came a ring at the door, his face began working all over and he would look about him uneasily, searching for his hat; though he often remained out of Slavic weakness. Then a word, an observation that went against his grain would lead to the most curious scenes and disputes. . . .

Once in Passion Week he went to dine with a writer and Lenten dishes were served. "Is it long," he asked, "since you have grown so devout?" "We eat Lenten fare," answered the writer, "simply for the sake of the servants." *"For the sake of the servants?"* said Belinsky, and he turned pale. "For the sake of the servants?" he repeated and rose. "Where are your servants? I'll tell them that they are deceived, any open vice is better and more *humane* than this contempt for the weak and uneducated, this hypocrisy in support of ignorance. And do you imagine that you are free people? You are to be bracketed with all the tsars and priests and slave-owners. Good-bye, I don't eat Lenten fare for the edification of others, I have no *servants!*"

Among the Russians who had become inveterate Germans, there was one in-structor of our university who had lately arrived from Berlin; he was a good-natured man in blue spectacles, stiff and decorous; he had deranged and enfeebled his brains with philosophy and philology, and there he stopped for ever. A doctrinaire and to some extent a pedant, he was fond of holding forth in edifying style. Once at a literary evening in the house of that novelist who observed the Lent for the sake of his servants, this gentleman was preaching some sort of twaddle, *honnête et moderée.* Belinsky was lying on a couch in the corner and as I passed him he took me by the flap of my coat and said "Do you hear the rubbish that monster is talking? My tongue has been itching to answer him, but my chest hurts and there are such a lot of people. Be a father to me, make a fool of him somehow, squash him, crush him with a gibe, you can do it better—come, there's a good soul."

I laughed and told Belinsky that he was setting me on him like he might a bulldog on a rat. I scarcely knew the man and had hardly heard what he had said.

Towards the end of the evening, the gentleman in blue spectacles, after abusing Koltsov for having abandoned the national costume, suddenly began talking of Chaadayev's famous letter and concluded his commonplace remarks, uttered in that academic tone which of itself provokes derision, with the following words: "Anyway, I consider his action mean, contemptible. I have no respect for such a man."

There was in the room only one man closely associated with Chaadayev, and that was I. I shall have a great deal to say about Chaadeyev later on; I always liked and respected him and was liked by him; I thought it was unseemly to let this outrageous remark pass unchallenged. I asked him dryly whether he supposed that Chaadayev had written his letter insincerely or from ulterior motives.

"Not at all," answered the gentleman.

An unpleasant conversation followed; I mentioned that the epithets "mean and contemptible" *were* mean and contemptible when applied to a man who had boldly expressed his opinion and had suffered for it. He talked to me of integrity of the nation, of the unity of the fatherland, of the crime of destroying that unity, of sacred things that must not be touched.

All at once Belinsky interfered. He leapt up from his sofa, came up to me as white as a sheet and, slapping me on the shoulder, said: "Here you have them, they have spoken out—the inquisitors, the censors—keeping thought in leading-strings . . ." and so on and so forth. He was in a towering rage and interspersed grave words with deadly sarcasms: "Why are we so sensitive, pray? People are flogged, yet we don't resent it, sent to Siberia, yet we don't resent it, but here Chaadayev, you see, has insulted the national honour—how dared he?—to talk is impudence, a flunkey must never speak! Why is it that in more civilized countries where one would expect national susceptibilities to be more developed than in Kostroma and Kaluga words are not resented?"

"In civilized countries," replied the gentleman in blue spectacles with inimitable self-complacency, "there are prisons in which they confine the insane creatures who insult what the whole people respect—and a good thing too."

Belinsky seemed to tower above us— he was terrible, great at that moment. Folding his arms over his sick chest, and looking straight at his opponent, he answered in a hollow voice: "And in still more civilized countries there is a guillotine for those who think that a good thing."

Saying this, he sank exhausted in an easy chair and ceased speaking. At the word "guillotine" our host turned pale, the guests were uneasy and silence fell. The learned gentleman was annihilated, but it is just at such moments that human vanity goes out of hand. Turgenev advises that, when a man has gone to such lengths in argument that he is himself frightened, he should move his tongue ten times round the inside of his mouth before uttering another word.

Our opponent, unaware of this homely advice, feebly continued talking through his hat, addressing the rest of the company rather than Belinsky. "In spite of your intolerance," he said at last, "I am certain that you would agree with me. . . ."

"No," answered Belinsky, "whatever you might say I shall never agree with anything!"

Everyone laughed and went in to supper. The learned gentleman picked up his hat and left.

Suffering and privation soon completely undermined Belinsky's sickly constitution. His face, particularly the muscles about his lips, and the gloomily fixed look in his eyes testified equally to the intense working of his spirit and the rapid dissolution of his body.

I saw him for the last time in Paris in the autumn of 1847; he was in a very bad way, afraid of speaking aloud, and only occasionally his old energy revived and its ebbing fires glowed brightly. It was at such a moment that he wrote his letter to Gogol.

The news of the revolution of February found him still alive; he died taking its glow for the flush of the rising dawn.

* * *

Thirty years ago, the Russia of the *future* existed exclusively among a few boys, hardly more than children, so small and inconspicuous that there was room for them under the heels of the jackboots of the autocracy—yet in them la'y the heritage of December 14, the heritage of a purely national Russia, as well as of the learning of all humanity. This new life struggled on like the grass sprouting at the mouth of the still smouldering crater.

In the very maw of the monster these children, so unlike other children, grew, developed and began to live a different life. Weak, insignificant, unsupported, and persecuted by everybody, they might have easily perished, leaving no trace, but they *survived*, or, if they died on their way, all did not die with them. They were the rudimentary cells, the embryos of history, barely perceptible and barely existing—like all embryos.

Little by little, groups of them were formed. Those elements which had traits in common gathered round their centres: then the groups repelled one another. This splitting up gave them breadth of vision and many-sidedness in their development; after developing to the end, that is, to the extreme, the branches united again by whatever names they may be called—Stankevich's circle, the Slavophils, or our own circle.

The leading characteristic of them all was a profound feeling of aversion for official Russia, for their environment, and at the same time the urge to escape out of it—and, in some of them, a vehement desire to change the contemporary state of affairs.

The objection that these circles, unnoticed both from above and from below, formed an exceptional, a casual, a disconnected phenomenon, that the education of the young people was for the most part exotic, alien, and that they rather express the translation of French and German ideas into Russian than anything of their own, seems to us quite groundless.

Possibly about the turn of the last century there was in the aristocracy a sprinkling of Russian foreigners who had sundered all ties with the national life; but they had neither practical interests, nor environment sharing their convictions, nor a literature of their own. They died out barren. Victims of the divorce from the people brought about by Tsar Peter, they remained eccentric and whimsical, not merely superfluous but undeserving of pity. The war of 1812 put an end to them—the old generation lived on, but none of the younger developed in that direction. To bracket with them men of the stamp of Chaadayev would be the greatest mistake.

Protest, denunciation, hatred for one's country, has a completely different significance from indifferent aloofness. Byron, lashing at English life, fleeing from England as from the plague, remained a typical Englishman. Heine, trying, out of exasperation at the loathsome political state of Germany, to become French, remained a genuine German. The highest protest against Judaism—Christianity—is permeated with the spirit of Judaism. The separation of the states of North America from England could lead to war and hatred, but it could not make the Americans un-English. . . .

If the aristocrats of the past century, who consistently ignored everything Russian, remained in reality incredibly more Russian than the house-serfs remained peasants, it is even more impossible that the younger generation could have lost their Russian character because they studied science and philosophy in French and German books. A section of our Moscow Slavs reached the point of ultra-Slavism with Hegel in their hands.

The very circles of which I am speaking sprang into existence in natural response to a deep inner need of the Russian life of that period.

We have spoken many times of the stagnation that followed the crisis of 1825. The moral level of society sank, development was interrupted, everything progressive and energetic was effaced. Those who remained—frightened, weak, distracted—were petty and shallow; the worthless generation of Alexander occupied the foremost place. As time went on they changed into cringing officials, lost the savage poetry of revelry and aristocratic ways together with every shadow of independent dignity; they served assiduously, they made the grade, but they never became high dignitaries in the full sense of the word. Their day was over.

Under this great world of society, the great world of the people maintained an indifferent silence; nothing was changed for them—their plight was bad, indeed, but not worse than before—the new blows were not intended for their scourged backs. *Their time had not yet come.* It was between this roof and this foundation that our children were the first to raise their heads—perhaps because they did not suspect how dangerous it was; anyway, by means of these children, Russia, stunned and stupefied, began to come to life again.

What impressed them was the complete contradiction of the *words* they were taught with the *realities* of life around them. Their teachers, their books, their university spoke one language which was intelligible to heart and mind. Their father and mother, their relations, and all their surroundings spoke other things with which neither mind nor heart was in agreement, but with which the powers that be and pecuniary interests were in accord. Nowhere did this contradiction between education and real life reach such proportions as among the nobility of Russia. The uncouth German student with

his round cap covering a seventh part of his head, with his world-shaking sallies, is far nearer to the German *Spiessbürger* than is supposed, while the French *collégien*, thin with vanity and emulation, is already *en herbe l'homme raisonnable, qui exploite sa position.*

The number of educated people amongst us has always been extremely small; but those who were educated have always received an education, not perhaps very thorough, but fairly general and humane: it humanized them all. But a *human* being was just what the bureaucratic hierarchy or the successful maintenance of the landowning regime did not require. The young man had either to dehumanize himself—and the greater number did so—or to stop short and ask himself: "But is it absolutely essential to go into the service? Is it really a good thing to be a landowner?" After that for some, the weaker and more impatient, there followed the idle existence of a cornet on the retired list, the sloth of the country, the dressing-gown, eccentricities, cards, wine, etc.; for others a time of ordeal and inner travail. They could not live in complete moral disharmony, nor could they be satisfied with a negative attitude of withdrawal; awakened thought demanded an outlet. The various solutions of these questions, all equally harassing for the young generation, determined their distribution into various circles.

Thus, for instance, our little circle was formed in the university and found Sungurov's circle already in existence. His, like ours, was concerned rather with politics than with learning. Stankevich's circle, which came into existence at the same time, was equally near and equally remote from both. It followed another path, and its interests were purely theoretical.

Between 1830 and 1840 our convictions were too youthful, too ardent and passionate, not to be exclusive. We could feel a cold respect for Stankevich's circle, but we could not come into closer contact with it. They traced philosophical systems, were absorbed in self-analysis, and found peace in a luxurious pantheism from which Christianity was not excluded. The stuff of our dreams was woven out of ways of organizing a new league in Russia on the pattern of the Decembrists and we looked upon knowledge as merely a means. The government did its best to strengthen us in our revolutionary tendencies.

In 1834 the whole of Sungurov's circle was sent into exile and—vanished.

In 1835 we were exiled. Five years later we came back, hardened by our experience. The dreams of youth had become the irrevocable determinaton of maturity. That was the heydey of Stankevich's circle. Stankevich himself I did not find in Moscow—he was in Germany; but it was just at that moment that Belinsky's articles were beginning to attract universal attention.

On our return we measured our strength with them. The battle was an unequal one for both sides; origins, weapons, and language—all were different. After fruitless skirmishes we saw that it was our turn now to undertake serious study and we too set to work upon Hegel and the German philosophy. When we had made a sufficient study of it, it became evident that there was no ground for dispute between us and Stankevich's circle.

The latter was inevitably bound to break up. It had done its bit—and had done it most brilliantly; its influence on the whole of literature and academic teaching was immense—one need but recall the names of Belinsky and Granovsky; Koltsov was formed in it; Botkin, Katkov, and others belonged to it.[6] But it could not remain an exclusive circle without lapsing into German doc-

trinairism—men who were alive and Russian had no leanings that way.

In addition to Stankevich's circle, there was another one, formed during our exile, and, like us, it was at swords' points with Stankevich's circle; its members were afterwards called Slavophils. The Slavophils approached the vital questions which occupied us from the opposite side, and were far more absorbed in practical work and real conflict than Stankevich's circle.

It was natural that Stankevich's society should split up between them and us. The Aksakovs and Samarin joined the Slavophils, that is, Khomyakov and the Kireyevskys. Belinsky and Bakunin went over to us. Stankevich's closest friend, one most kindred to his spirit, Granovsky, was one of us from the day he came back from Germany.

If Stankevich had lived, his circle would nonetheless have broken up. He would himself have gone over to Khomyakov or to us.

By 1842 the sifting in accordance with natural affinity had long been over, and our camp stood in battle array face to face with the Slavophils. Of that conflict we will speak elsewhere.

In conclusion I will add a few words concerning those elements of which Stankevich's circle was composed; that will throw some light on the strange underground currents which were silently undermining the strong crust of the Russo-German régime.

Stankevich was the son of a wealthy Voronezh landowner, and was at first brought up in all the ease and freedom of a landowner's life in the country;

[6] T. N. Granovsky (1813–55), professor of European history at Moscow University, and a liberal; his lectures were enormously popular; A. V. Koltsov (1809–42), a poet, of whom below; V. P. Botkin, a well-known critic and friend of Belinsky; M. N. Katkov (1818–87), once a liberal, later Russia's most influential conservative journalist.

then he was sent to the Ostrogozhsk school (and that was something quite original). For fine natures a wealthy and even aristocratic education is very good. Comfort gives unbound freedom and scope for growth and development of every sort, it saves the young mind from premature anxiety and apprehension of the future, and provides complete freedom to pursue the subjects to which it is drawn.

Stankevich's development was broad and harmonious; his artistic, musical, and at the same time reflective and contemplative nature showed itself from the very beginning of his university career. It was to his artistic temperament that Stankevich owed his special faculty, not only of deep and warm understanding, but also of reconciling, or as the Germans say, "transcending" contradictions. The craving for harmony, proportion, and enjoyment makes Germans indulgent as to the means; to avoid seeing the well they cover it over with canvas. The canvas will not withstand any pressure, but the yawning gulf does not trouble the eye. In this way the Germans reached pantheistic quietism and there they rested tranquilly. But such a gifted Russian as Stankevich could not have remained "tranquil" for long.

This is evident from the first question which involuntarily troubled Stankevich immediately after he left the university.

His university studies were finished, he was left to himself, he was no longer led by others; *he did not know what he was to do.* There was nothing to go on with, there was no one and nothing around that could appeal to a live mind. A youth, taking stock of his surroundings and having had time to look about him after school, found himself in the Russia of those days as a lonely traveller might awakening in the steppe; you may go where you will—there are tracks to follow, there are bones of those who

had perished, there are wild beasts and the emptiness on all sides with its dull menace of danger—it is easy to perish and impossible to struggle. The only thing one can do honestly and enjoy doing is study.

And so Stankevich persevered in the pursuit of learning. He imagined that it was his vocation to be an historian, and he took to Herodotus; as was to be expected, nothing came of that.

He would have liked to be in Petersburg in which there was so much of *new* activity and to which he was attracted by the theatre and its nearness to Europe; he would have liked also to be an honorary superintendent of the school at Ostrogozhsk. He resolved to be of use in that "modest office"—but that proved to be even less of a success than his study of Herodotus. He was in reality drawn to Moscow, to Germany, to his own university circle, to his own interests. He could not exist without kindred spirits around him (another proof that there were at hand no interests congenial to him). The craving for sympathy was so strong in Stankevich that he sometimes invented intellectual sympathy and talents and saw and admired in people qualities which they completely lacked.

But—and in this lay his personal power—he did not often need to have recourse to such fictions—at every step he did meet people worthy of admiration, he *knew how* to meet them, and every one to whom he opened his heart remained his passionate friend for life; to everyone Stankevich's influence meant either an immense benefit or an alleviation of his burden.

In Voronezh, Stankevich occasionally went to a local library for books. There he met a poor young man of humble station, modest and melancholy. It turned out that he was the son of a cattle dealer who had business dealings with

Stankevich's father over sales. Stankevich befriended the young man; the cattle dealer's son was a great reader and fond of talking of books. Stankevich got to know him well. Shyly and timidly the young man confessed that he had himself tried his hand at writing verses and, blushing, ventured to show them. Stankevich was amazed at the immense talent, neither conscious nor confident of itself. After that he did not let him go until all Russia was enthusiastically reading Koltsov's songs. It is quite likely that the poor cattle dealer, oppressed by his relations, unwarmed by sympathy or recognition, might have wasted his songs on the empty steppe beyond the Volga over which he drove his herds, and Russia would never have heard those marvellous, deeply national songs, if Stankevich had not crossed his path.

When Bakunin finished his studies at the school of artillery, he received a commission as an officer in the Guards. It is said that his father was angry with him and himself asked that he should be transferred into the regular army. Stranded in some Godforsaken village of White Russia with his battery, he grew morose and unsociable, neglected his duties, and would lie for days together wrapped in a sheepskin. The commander of his battery was sorry for him; he had, however, no alternative but to remind him that he must either perform his duties or go on the retired list. Bakunin had no suspicion that he had a right to take the latter course and at once asked to be relieved of his commission. On receiving his discharge he came to Moscow, and from that date (about 1836) life began in earnest for him. He had studied nothing before, had read nothing, and his knowledge of German was very poor indeed. With a gift for dialectics, for constant, persistent thinking, he had strayed without

map or compass in a world of fantastic conceptions and auto-didactic efforts. Stankevich perceived his talents and set him down to study philosophy. Bakunin learnt German reading Kant and Fichte and then set to work on Hegel, whose method and logic he mastered to perfection, and preached it afterwards to us and to Belinsky, to his female friends and to Proudhon.

However Belinsky drew as much from the same source; Stankevich's views on art, on poetry and its relation to life, grew in Belinsky's articles into that powerful modern criticism, into that new outlook upon the world and upon life which impressed all thinking Russia and made all the pedants and doctrinaires draw back from Belinsky with horror. It was Stankevich who had to curb Belinsky, for the passionate, merciless, fiercely intolerant talent that carried Belinsky beyond all bounds wounded the aesthetically harmonious temperament of Stankevich.

And at the same time it was Stankevich who encouraged the gentle, loving, dreamy Granovsky, who was then plunged in melancholy. Stankevich was a support and an elder brother to him. His letters to Granovsky are full of charm and beauty—and Granovsky, too, loved him dearly!

"I have not yet recovered from the first shock," wrote Granovsky soon after Stankevich's death, "real grief has not touched me yet; I think of it with fear. Now I am still unable to believe that my loss is possible—only at times I feel a stab at my heart. He has taken with him something essential to my life. To no one in the world was I so much indebted. His influence over us was always unbounded and beneficial."

And how many could say or, perhaps, have said it!

In Stankevich's circle only he and

Botkin were well-to-do and completely independent financially. The others made up a very mixed proletariat. Bakunin's relations gave him nothing; Belinsky, the son of a petty official of Chembary, expelled from Moscow University for "lack of ability," lived on the scanty pay he got for his articles. Krasov, on taking his degree, found a situation with a landowner in some province, but life with this patriarchal slaveowner so terrified him that he came back on foot to Moscow with *a wallet on his back,* in the winter, together with some peasants in charge of a train of wagons. Probably a father or mother of each one of them when giving them their blessing had said—and who dare reproach them for it—"Mind you work hard at your studies; and when you've finished them you'll have to strike out on your own, there is nobody to leave you anything, we've nothing to give you either; you'll have to take care of yourself and then of us too." Now, Stankevich had probably been told that he could take a prominent position in society, that he was called by wealth and birth to play a great part— just as in Botkin's household everyone, from his old father down to the clerks, urged upon him by word and example the necessity of making money and piling it up more and more.

What inspiration touched these men? What was it that recreated them? They had no thought, no care for their social position, or for their personal gain or for their security; their whole life, all their efforts were devoted to the public weal regardless of all personal interests; some forgot their wealth, others their poverty, and went forth, without looking back, to the solution of theoretical questions. The interests of truth, the interests of learning, the interests of art, *humanitas,* absorbed everything else.

And the renunciation of this world was not confined to the time at the university and two or three years of youth. The best men of Stankevich's circle are dead; the others have remained what they were to this day. Belinsky, worn out by work and suffering, fell a fighter and a beggar. Granovsky, delivering his message of learning and humanity, died as he mounted his platform. Botkin did not, in fact, become a merchant; indeed, none of them *distinguished* themselves in the government service.

It was just the same in the two other circles, the Slavophils and ours. Where, in what corner of the Western world today, do you find such groups of devotees of thought, such zealots of learning, such fanatics of conviction—whose hair turns grey but whose enthusiasm is forever young?

Where? Point them out. I boldly challenge you—I only except for the moment one country, Italy—and demarcate the field for the contest, i.e., I stipulate that my opponent should not escape from the domain of statistics into that of history.

We know how great were the interest in theory and the passion for truth and religion in the days of such martyrs for science and reason as Bruno, Galileo, and the rest; we know, too, what the France of the Encyclopaedists was in the second half of the eighteenth century; but later? Later *sta, viator!*

In the Europe of today there is no youth and there are no young men. The most brilliant representative of the France of the last years of the Restoration and of the July dynasty, Victor Hugo, has taken exception to my saying this. Properly speaking he refers to the young France of the twenties, and I am ready to admit that I have been too sweeping[7]—but beyond that I will not yield one iota to him. I have their own admissions. Take *Confession d'un enfant du siècle,* and the poems of Alfred de Musset, recall the France depicted in George Sand's letters, in the contemporary drama and novels, and in the cases in the law-courts.

But what does all that prove? A great deal; and in the first place that the Chinese shoes of German make in which Russia has hobbled for a hundred and fifty years, though they have caused many painful corns, have evidently not crippled her bones, since whenever she has had a chance of stretching her limbs, the result has been the exuberance of fresh young energies. That does not guarantee the future, but it does make it extremely *possible.*

[7] Victor Hugo, after reading *Thoughts on the Past* in the French translation, wrote me a letter in defence of the younger generation of France at the period of the Restoration. —A.H.

28

WHAT IS OBLOMOVISM?

By Nikolai Dobrolyubov

The essay which appears below in abbreviated form was first published in the radical journal *Sovremennik* ("The Contemporary") in 1859, during the great public debate preceding the emancipation of the serfs. Its author (1836–61) was then twenty-three years old but was already considered a leading literary critic. In 1856 he had become a follower of the materialist philosopher Nikolai Chernyshevski and in 1857 took over the literary column of *Sovremennik*. His chief contribution to literary criticism was his formulation of the theory of social types as represented in Russian literature. As a follower of Belinsky, he believed that literature must serve society as a positive guide, praising the good and condemning evil.

His essay on Oblomovism became the most celebrated of his writings. Immediately upon its appearance, it was used by the radical camp in its fight with the moderates and the liberals. One of the latter, Alexander Herzen, answered Dobrolyubov with an article entitled "Very dangerous." The term "oblomovshchina" has been incorporated into the Russian language. Lenin used it on many occasions and not long before his death seemed to find the disease still prevalent in Russia. "The old Oblomov," he wrote, "has remained, and for a long while yet he will have to be washed, cleaned, shaken and thrashed if something is to come of him."

For a biography of the creator of Oblomov, the writer Ivan Goncharov, see Janko Lavrin's *Goncharov*. F. Seeley's "The Heyday of the 'Superfluous Man' in Russia," *Slavonic and East European Review*, XXXI, 92–112, is a study of the Oblomov phenomenon. See also Franklin Reeve, "Oblomovism Revisited," *American Slavic and East European Review*, XV, 112–18, and Leon Stilman, "Oblomovka Revisited," *American Slavic and East European Review*, VII, 45–77. For another analysis of Goncharov, see Helen Rapp, "The Art of Ivan Goncharov," *Slavonic and East European Review*, XXXVI, 370–95. The novel itself is available in a paperback edition. There is a chapter on Oblomov in Renato Poggioli's *The Phoenix and the Spider*. There are chapters on Dobrolyubov in Rufus Mathewson's *The Positive Hero in Russian Literature;* Franco Venturi's *Roots of Revolution* (paperback); Eugene Lampert's *Sons against Fathers;* and George Lukacs', *Studies in European Realism*. See also Robert Jackson's "Dostoevsky's Critique of the Aesthetics of Dobrolyubov," *Slavic Review*, June, 1964. Nikolai Chernyshevsky's novel *What Is To Be Done* (paperback), published in 1862, seemed to be an answer to all Dobrolyubov's prayers.

From N. Dobrolyubov, *Selected Philosophical Essays* (Moscow, 1956), pp. 182–94, 204–17.

Where is the one who in the native language of the Russian soul could pronounce for us the mighty word "forward"? Century after century passes, and a half a million stay-at-homes, lubbers and blockheads are immersed in deep slumber, but rarely is a man born in Rūs who is able to pronounce this mighty word . . . Gogol.[1]

. . . Oblomov is not altogether a new personage in our literature, but never has he been presented to us so simply and naturally as he is in Goncharov's novel. Not to go too far back into the past, we shall say that we find the generic features of the Oblomov type already in Onegin;[2] and then we find them repeated several times in the best of our literary productions. The point is that this is our native, national type, which not one of our serious artists could brush aside. But in the course of time, as social consciousness developed, this type changed its shape, established a different relationship with life and acquired a new significance. To note these new phases of its existence, to determine the substance of its new significance, has always been an enormous task, and the talent who succeeded in doing it always did a great deal for the advancement of our literature. This is what Goncharov has done with his *Oblomov*. We shall examine the main features of the Oblomov type, and then we shall try to draw a slight parallel between it and several types of the same kind which have appeared in our literature at different times.

What are the main features of the Oblomov character? Utter inertness resulting from apathy towards everything that goes on in the world. The cause of

this apathy lies partly in Oblomov's external position and partly in the manner of his mental and moral development. The external position is that he is a gentleman: "he has a Zakhar, and another three hundred Zakhars," as the author puts it.[3] Ilya Ilyich (Oblomov) explains the advantages of his position to Zakhar in the following way:

Do I fuss and worry? Do I work? Don't I have enough to eat? Do I look thin and haggard? Am I in want of anything? Have I not people to fetch and carry for me, to do the things I want done? Thank God, I have never in my life had to draw a pair of stockings on. Do you think I would go to any trouble? Why should I? . . . But I need not tell you all this. Haven't you served me since childhood? You know all about it. You have seen how tenderly I was brought up. You know that I have never suffered cold or hunger, that I have never known want, that I don't have to earn my bread and, in general, have never done any work.

Oblomov is speaking the absolute truth. The entire history of his upbringing confirms what he says. He became accustomed to lolling about at a very early age because he had people to fetch and carry for him, to do things for him. Under these circumstances he lived the idle life of a sybarite even when he did not want to. And tell me, pray, what can you expect of a man who grew up under the following circumstances:

Zakhar—as his [Oblomov's] nurse did in the old days—draws on his stockings and puts on his shoes while Ilyusha, already a boy of fourteen, does nothing but lie on his back and put up one foot and then the other; and if it seems to him that Zakhar has done something not in the right way, he kicks him in the nose. If the disgruntled Zakhar takes it into his head to complain, he gets his ears boxed by the adults. After

[1] The epigraph, slightly misquoted, is from volume two of Gogol's *Dead Souls*.

[2] Onegin: hero of Pushkin's novel in verse, *Eugene Onegin*.

[3] Zakhar: Oblomov's personal servant, a serf. The "three hundred Zakhars" are the serfs owned by Oblomov as part of his estate.

that Zakhar combs Ilya Ilyich's hair, helps him on with his coat, carefully putting his arms into the sleeves so as not to incommode him too much, and reminds him that he must do so and so and so and so: on waking up in the morning—to wash himself, etc.

If Ilya Ilyich wants anything he has only to make a sign—and at once three or four servants rush to carry out his wishes; if he drops anything, if he reaches for something he needs and cannot get at it, if something has to be brought in, or it is necessary to run on some errand—he sometimes, like the active boy he is, is just eager to run and do it himself, but suddenly his mother and his father and his three aunts shout in a quintet:

—"Where are you going? What for? What are Vaska and Vanka and Zakharka here for? Hey! Vaska, Vanka, Zakharka! What are you all dawdling there for? I'll let you have it! . . ."

And so Ilya Ilyich is simply not allowed to do anything for himself. Later on he found that this was much more convenient and he learned to shout himself: "Hey, Vaska, Vanka, bring me this, bring me that! I don't want this, I want that! Go and bring it! . . ."

An important factor here is the mental development of the Oblomovs, which, of course, is also moulded by their external position. From their earliest years they see life turned inside out, as it were, and until the end of their days they are unable to understand what their relation to the world and to people should reasonably be. Later on much is explained to them and they begin to understand something; but the views that were inculcated in them in their childhood remain somewhere in a corner and constantly peep out from there, hindering all new conceptions and preventing them from sinking deep into their hearts. . . . As a result, chaos reigns in their heads: sometimes a man makes up his mind to do something, but he does not know how to begin, where to turn.

. . . This is not surprising: a normal man always wants to do only what he can do; that is why he immediately does all that he wants to do. . . . But Oblomov . . . is not accustomed to do anything; consequently, he cannot really determine what he can do and what he cannot do —and consequently, he cannot seriously, *actively,* want anything. . . . His wishes always assume the form: "how good it would be if this were done," but how this can be done he does not know. That is why he is so fond of dreaming and dreads the moment when his dreams may come in contact with reality. When they do, he tries to shift the burden to another's shoulders; if there are no other shoulders, why then, *perhaps* it will get done *somehow.* . . .

Ilya Ilyich was born a small country squire with an estate that provided him with an income that did not exceed ten thousand rubles in assignats;[4] consequently, he could mould the destiny of the world only in his dreams. But in his dreams he was fond of giving himself up to bellicose and heroic ambitions.

Sometimes he liked to picture himself an invincible general, compared with whom not only Napoleon but even Veruslan Lazarevich was a nonentity; he would picture a war and its cause: for example, Africans would come pouring into Europe, or he would organize new crusades and would fight, decide the fate of nations, sack towns, show mercy, execute, perform acts of kindness and generosity.

Sometimes he would picture himself as a great thinker or artist who is followed by admiring crowds. . . . Clearly, Oblomov is not a dull, apathetic type, destitute of ambition and feeling; he too seeks something in life, thinks about something. But the disgusting habit of

---

4 Assignats: paper currency of considerably less value than the silver ruble. They were withdrawn from circulation in 1843.

getting his wishes satisfied not by his own efforts but by the efforts of others developed in him an apathetic inertness and plunged him into the wretched state of moral slavery. This slavery is so closely interwoven with Oblomov's aristocratic habits that they mutually permeate and determine each other, so that it becomes totally impossible to draw any line of demarcation between them. This moral slavery of Oblomov's is, perhaps, the most interesting side of his personality, and of his whole life. . . . But how could a man enjoying the independent position of Ilya Ilyich sink into slavery? If anybody can enjoy freedom, surely he can! He is not in the civil service, he does not go into society, and he has an assured income. . . . He himself boasts that he does not have to bow and scrape and humiliate himself, that he is not like "others" who work tirelessly, fuss and run about, and if they do not work they do not eat. . . . He inspires the good widow Pshenitsyna with reverent love for himself precisely because he is a *gentleman,* because he shines and glitters, because he walks and talks so freely and independently, because "he is not constantly copying papers, does not tremble with fear that he might be late at the office, because he does not look at everybody as if asking to be saddled and ridden on, but looks at everybody and everything boldly and freely, as if demanding obedience." And yet, the whole life of this gentleman is wrecked because he always remains the slave of another's will and never rises to the level of displaying the least bit of independence. He is the slave of every woman, of every newcomer; the slave of every rascal who wishes to get him under his thumb. He is the slave of his serf Zakhar, and it is hard to say which of them submits more to the power of the other. At all events, if Zakhar does not wish to do a thing Ilya Ilyich cannot make him do it; and if Zakhar wants to do anything he will do it, even if his master is opposed to it—and his master submits. . . . This is quite natural: Zakhar, after all, can at least do something; Oblomov cannot do anything at all. It is needless to speak of Tarantyev and Ivan Matveyich, who do everything they like with Oblomov in spite of the fact that they are far inferior to him both in intellectual development and in moral qualities. . . . Why is this? Again the answer is, because Oblomov, being a gentleman, does not wish to work, nor could he even if he wanted to; and he cannot understand his own relation to everything around him. He is not averse to activity as long as it is in the form of a vision and is far removed from reality: thus, he draws up a plan for the improvement of his estate and zealously applies himself to this task—only "details, estimates and figures" frighten him, and he constantly brushes them aside, for how can he bother with them! . . . He is a gentleman, as he himself explains to Ivan Matveyich:

Who am I? What am I? you will ask. . . . Go and ask Zakhar, he will tell you. "A gentleman" he will say! Yes, I am a gentleman, and I can't do anything! You do it, if you known how, and help if you can, and for your trouble take what you like— that's what knowledge is for!

Do you think that in this way he is only shirking work, trying to cover up his own indolence with the plea of ignorance? No, he really does not know how to do anything and cannot do anything; he is really unable to undertake any useful task. As regards his estate (for the reorganization of which he had already drawn up a plan), he confesses his ignorance to Ivan Matveyich in the following way:

I don't know what barshchina[5] is. I know nothing about husbandry. I don't know the difference between a poor muzhik and a rich one. I don't know what a quarter of rye, or oats is, what its price is, in which months different crops are sown and reaped, or how and when they are sold. I don't know whether I am poor or rich, whether I will have enough to eat next year, or whether I shall be a beggar—I don't know anything! . . . Therefore, speak and advise me as if I were a child. . . .

Having reached this point in explaining Oblomov's character we deem it appropriate to turn to the literary parallel we drew above. The foregoing reflections have brought us to the conclusion that Oblomov is not a being whom nature has completely deprived of the ability to move by his own volition. His indolence and apathy are the result of upbringing and environment. The main thing here is not Oblomov, but Oblomovshchina. Perhaps Oblomov would even have started work had he found an occupation to his liking; but for that he would have had to develop under somewhat different conditions. In his present position he cannot find an occupation to his liking because he sees no meaning in life in general and cannot rationally define his own relations to others. This is where he provides us with the occasion for comparing him with previous types, which the best of our writers have depicted. It was observed long ago that all the heroes in the finest Russian stories and novels suffer from their failure to see any purpose in life and their inability to find a decent occupation for themselves. As a consequence, they find all occupations tedious and repugnant, and in this they reveal an astonishing re-

semblance to Oblomov. Indeed, open, for example, *Onegin, A Hero of Our Times, Who Is To Blame? Rudin, Unwanted,* or *Hamlet from Shchigry County*[6]—in every one of these you will find features almost identical with Oblomov's.

Onegin, like Oblomov, gives up society because he was

Weary of inconstancy
And of friends and friendship too.

And so he took to writing:

Abandoning wild gaiety
Onegin stayed at home,
He picked his pen up with a yawn
And wished to write, but diligence
To him was loathsome; nothing
From his pen would come.

Rudin too launched out in this field and was fond of reading to the chosen "the first pages of the essays and works he intended to write." Tentetnikov[7] also spent many years writing "a colossal work that was to deal with the whole of Russia from all points of view," but in this case too, "this undertaking was confined mainly to thinking: his pen was bitten to shreds, drawings appeared on the paper, and then everything was thrust aside." Ilya Ilyich was not behind his brothers in this respect; he too wrote and translated—he even translated Say. "Where is your work, your translations?" Stolz asked him later. "I don't know, Zakhar put them away somewhere. They are lying in the corner, I suppose," Oblomov answers. It appears, therefore, that Ilya Ilyich may have done even more than the others who had set down to their tasks as determinedly as he had. . . . Nearly all the brothers in the Oblomov family set to

5 Barshchina: obligation of the serfs to work on the landowners' land and perform various services. During the first half of the nineteenth century the customary obligation was three days a week, though this was often exceeded. Equivalent to the French *corvée* before 1789.

6 *A Hero of Our Times:* a novel by Lermontov. *Who Is To Blame?* a novel by Herzen; the other works are by Turgenev.

7 A character of Gogol's *Dead Souls*.

work in this field in spite of the difference in their respective positions and mental development. Pechorin alone looked down superciliously upon "the storymongers and writers of bourgeois dramas"; but even he wrote his memoirs. As for Beltov,[8] he must certainly have written something; besides, he was an artist, he visited the Hermitage and sat behind an easel planning to paint a large picture depicting the meeting between Biren who was returning from Siberia and Münnich who was going to Siberia. . . . What came out of this the reader knows. . . . The same Oblomovshchina reigned in the whole family. . . .

"But this is not yet life, it is only the preparatory school for life," mused Andrei Ivanovich Tentetnikov as he, together with Oblomov and the whole of that company, plodded through a host of useless subjects, unable to apply even an iota of them to actual life. "Real life is in the service." And so, all our heroes, except Onegin and Pechorin, go into the service; and for all of them this service is a useless and senseless burden, and all end up by resigning, early and with dignity. Beltov was fourteen years and six months short of qualifying for a clasp because, after working with intense zeal for a time, he soon cooled towards office work and became irritable and careless. . . . Tentetnikov had some high words with his chief, and, moreover, he wanted to be useful to the state by personally taking over the management of his estate. Rudin quarrelled with the headmaster of the high school at which he served as a teacher. Oblomov disliked the fact that all the members of the staff spoke to the chief "not in their natural but in some other kind of voices, squeaky and disgusting." He rebelled at the idea of having to explain to his chief in this voice why "he had sent a certain document to Arkhangelsk instead of Astrakhan" and so he re-

signed. . . . Everywhere we see the same Oblomovshchina. . . .

The Oblomovs resemble each other very closely in domestic life too:

Sound sleep, a stroll, an entertaining book,
A forest glade and a babbling brook,
A dark-eyed beauty,
Young and fresh to kiss sometimes,
The bridle of a restive steed,
Dinner to suit his fastidious needs,
A bottle of light wine,
Solitude, tranquillity,
Holy is the life Onegin leads. . . .

Word for word, except for the steed, this is the kind of life that Ilya Ilyich regards as the ideal of domestic bliss. Oblomov does not even forget the kissing of a dark-eyed beauty.

"One of the peasant women," muses Ilya Ilyich, "with a tanned neck, her sleeves rolled up above her elbows, her sly eyes shyly drooping, just a little, only for appearance sake resisting the squire's embraces, but actually enjoying them . . . only—the wife mustn't see, God forbid!" (Oblomov imagines that he is already married). . . .

The types which great talent has created are long lived; even today there are people who seem to be copies of Onegin, Pechorin, Rudin and the others, and not in the way in which they might have developed under other circumstances, but exactly in the way they were depicted by Pushkin, Lermontov and Turgenev. It is only in the public mind that they become more and more transformed into an Oblomov. It cannot be said that this transformation has already taken place. No, even today thousands of people spend their time talking, and thousands of others are willing to take this talk for deeds. But the fact that this transformation has begun is proved by the Oblomov type which Goncharov has created.

[8] Pechorin: the principal character of *A Hero of Our Times*; Beltov: the hero of *Who Is To Blame?*

His appearance would have been impossible had society, at least some section of it, realized what nonentities all those quasi-talented natures are, which it had formerly admired. In the past they decked themselves in cloaks and wigs of different fashions and were attractive because of their diverse talents; but today Oblomov appears before us in his true colours, taciturn, reclining on a soft couch instead of standing on a beautiful pedestal, wearing a wide dressing-gown instead of an austere cloak. The questions: *What is he doing? What is the meaning and purpose of his life?* have been put plainly and bluntly without being obscured by any secondary questions. This is because the time for social activity has arrived, or will soon arrive.... And that is why we said in the beginning of this essay that we regard Goncharov's novel as a *sign of the times.*

Indeed, look at the change that has taken place in public opinion concerning the educated and smooth-tongued drones who were formerly regarded as genuine leaders of society.

Before us stands a young man, very handsome, adroit and educated. He moves in high society and is successful there; he goes to theatres, balls and masquerades; he dresses and dines magnificently; he reads books and writes well.... His heart is stirred only by the daily events in high society; but he also has ideas about higher problems. He is fond of talking about passions,

> About age-old prejudices
> And the fatal secrets of the grave...

He has some rules of honour: he can

> A lighter quitrent substitute
> For the ancient yoke of barshchina,

sometimes he can refrain from taking advantage of an unsophisticated young woman whom he does not love, and he does not overrate his successes in society. He stands sufficiently high above the society in which he moves to be conscious of its vapidity; he can even abandon this society and retire to his seat in the country, but he finds it dull there too, and does not know what to turn his hand to.... Out of idleness he quarrels with his friend and thoughtlessly kills him in a duel.... Several years later he returns to society and falls in love with the woman whose love he had formerly spurned because it would have meant surrendering his freedom to roam about the world.... In this man you recognize Onegin. But look more closely ... it is Oblomov.

Before us stands another man with a more ardent soul, with wider ambitions. This one seems to have been endowed by nature with all that which were matters of concern for Onegin. He does not have to worry about his toilet and his clothes, he is a society man without that. He does not have to grope for words or sparkle with tinsel wit, his tongue is naturally as sharp as a razor. He really despises men, for he is aware of their weaknesses. He can really capture the heart of a woman, not for a fleeting moment, but for long, perhaps forever. He can sweep away or crush every obstacle that rises in his path. In only one matter is he unfortunate: he does not know which path to take. His heart is empty and cold to everything. He has tried everything; he was sated with all the pleasures that money could buy when still a youth. He is weary of the love of society beauties because it has brought no solace to his heart. Learning has also wearied him because he has seen that it brings neither fame nor happiness; the ignorant are the happiest, and fame is a matter of luck. The dangers of the battlefield too soon bored him because he saw no sense in them, and quickly became accustomed to them. And lastly, he even grows tired of the pure and simple-hearted love of an untamed girl of whom he is really fond because even in her he finds no satisfaction for his impulses. But what are these impulses? Whither do they lead? Why does he not yield to them with every fibre of his being? Because he himself does not understand them and does not take the trouble to think about what he should do with his spiritual strength. And so he spends his life jeering at fools, disturbing the hearts of unsophisticated young ladies, interfering in the love affairs of other people, picking quarrels, displaying valour over trifles and fighting duels over nothing at all. . . . You remember that this is the story of Pechorin, that he himself has explained his own character to Maxim Maximich to some extent, almost in the same words. . . . Please look closer: here too you will see Oblomov. . . .

But here is another man who is more conscious of the path he is treading. He not only knows that he is endowed with great strength, he knows also that he has a great goal before him. . . . It seems that he even suspects what kind of goal it is and where it is situated. He is honourable, honest (although he often fails to pay his debts), ardently discusses not trifling matters, but lofty subjects, and asserts that he is ready to sacrifice himself for the good of mankind. In his mind all problems have been solved, and everything is linked up in a living harmonious chain. He enraptures unsophisticated youths with his overpowering eloquence, and hearing him speak they too feel that they are destined to perform something great. . . . But how does he spend his life? In beginning everything and finishing nothing, attending to everything at once, passionately devoting himself to everything, but unable to devote himself to anything. . . . He falls in love with a girl who at last tells him that she is willing to give herself to him although her mother has forbidden her to do so—and he answers: "Good God! Your Mama disapproves! What an unexpected blow! God, how soon! . . . There is nothing to be done, we must be resigned. . . ." And this is an exact picture of his whole life. . . . You have already guessed that this is Rudin. . . . No, even he is now Oblomov. If you examine this character closely and bring it face to face with the requirements of present-day life you will be convinced that this is so.

The feature common to all these men is that nothing in life is a vital necessity for them, a shrine in their hearts, a religion, organically merged with their whole being, so that to deprive them of it would mean depriving them of their lives. Everything about them is superficial, nothing is rooted in their natures. They, perhaps, do something when external necessity compels them to, just as Oblomov went visiting the places that Stolz dragged him to, he bought music and books for Olga and read what she compelled him to read; but their hearts do not lie in the things they do merely by force of circumstances. If each of them were offered gratis all the external advantages that they obtain by their work they would gladly give up working. By virtue of Oblomovshchina, an Oblomov government official would not go to his office every day if he could receive his salary and regular promotion without having to do so. A soldier would vow not to touch a weapon if he were offered the same terms and, in addition, were allowed to keep his splendid uniform, which can be very useful on certain occasions. The professor would stop delivering lectures, the student would give up his studies, the author would give up writing, the actor would never appear on the stage again and the artist would break his chisel and palette, to put it in high-flown style, if he found a way of obtaining gratis all that he now obtains by working. They only talk about lofty strivings, consciousness of moral duty and common interests; when put to the test, it all turns out to be words, mere words. Their most sincere and heartfelt striving is the striving for repose, for the dressing-gown, and their very activities are nothing more than an *honourable dressing-gown* (to use an expression that is not our own) with which they cover up their vapidity and apathy. Even the best educated people, people with lively natures and warm hearts, are prone in their practical lives to depart from their ideas and plans, very quickly resign themselves to the realities of life, which, however, they never cease to revile as vulgar and disgusting. This shows that all the things they talk and dream about are really alien to them, superficial; in the depth of their hearts they cherish only one dream, one ideal—undisturbed repose, quietism, Oblomovshchina. Many even reach such a stage that they cannot conceive of man working willingly, with enthusiasm. Read the argument in *Ekonomicheskii Ukazatel'* to the effect that everybody would die of starvation resulting from idleness if by the equal distribution of wealth people were robbed of the incentive to accumulate capital. . . .[9]

> Now the riddle has been answered,
> A word for it has now been found.

That word is—*Oblomovshchina.*

Now, when I hear a country squire talking about the rights of man and urging the necessity of developing personality, I know from the first words he utters that he is an Oblomov.

When I hear a government official complaining that the system of administration is too complicated and cumbersome, I know that he is an Oblomov.

When I hear an army officer complaining that parades are exhausting, and boldly arguing that marching at a *slow pace* is useless, etc., I have not the slightest doubt that he is an Oblomov.

When, in the magazines, I read liberal denunciations of abuses and expressions of joy over the fact that at last something has been done that we have been waiting and hoping for for so long, I think to myself that all this has been written from Oblomovka.

When I am in the company of educated people who ardently sympathize with the needs of mankind and who for many years have been relating with undiminished heat the same (and sometimes new) anecdotes about bribery, acts of tyranny and lawlessness of every kind, I, in spite of myself, feel that I have been transported to old Oblomovka. . . .

Who, then, will in the end shift them from the spot to which they are rooted by the mighty word "forward!" which Gogol dreamed of, and for which Rūs has been longing and waiting for so long? So far we find no answer to this question either in society or in literature. Goncharov, who understood and was able to reveal our Oblomovshchina to us, could not, however, avoid paying tribute to the common error which is prevalent in our society to this day: he set out to bury Oblomovshchina and deliver a panegyric over its grave. "Farewell, old Oblomovka, you have outlived your time," he says through the mouth of Stolz, but what he says is not true. All Russia which has read, or will read, *Oblomov* will disagree with him. No, Oblomovka is our own motherland, her owners are our teachers, her three hundred Zakhars are always at our service. There is large portion of Oblomov

---

9 *Ekonomicheskii Ukazatel'* (Economic Guide) : a St. Petersburg economic journal of laissez faire leanings.

within every one of us, and it is too early to write our obituary. . . .

Paying tribute to his times, Mr. Goncharov provided an antidote to Oblomov in the shape of Stolz; but as regards that individual, we must repeat the opinion that we have always expressed, namely, that literature must not run too far ahead of life. Stolzes, men of an integral and active character that makes every idea a striving and translates it into deeds the moment it arises, do not yet exist in our society (we have in mind the educated section of society, which is capable of loftier strivings; among the masses, where ideas and strivings are confined to a few and very practical objects, we constantly come across such people). The author himself admits this when he says about our society:

There! Eyes have opened after slumber, brisk, wide footsteps, animated voices are heard. . . . How many Stolzes with Russian names must appear!

Many must appear, there can be no doubt about that; but for the time being there is no soil for them. And that is why all we can gather from Goncharov's novel is that Stolz is a man of action, always busy with something, running about, acquiring things, saying that to live means to work, and so forth. But what he does and how he manages to do something worthwhile where others can do nothing, remains a mystery to us. He settled the affairs of the Oblomov estate for Ilya Ilyich in a trice—but how? That we do not know. He got rid of Ilya Ilyich's false promissory note in a trice —but how? That we know. He went to see the chief of Ivan Matveyich, to whom Oblomov had given the promissory note, had a friendly talk with him, and after this Ivan Matveyich was called to the chief's office, and not only was he ordered to return the note, but was also

asked to resign. It served him right, of course: but judging by this case, Stolz had not yet reached the stage of the ideal Russian public leader. Nor could he have done so; it is too early. For the time being, even if you are as wise as Solomon, all you can do in the way of public activity is, perhaps, to be a *philanthropic tavern licensee* like Murazov, who performs good deeds out of his fortune of ten million, or a noble landlord like Kostanzhoglo[10]—but further than that you cannot go. . . . And we cannot understand how in his activities Stolz could rid himself of all the strivings and requirements that overcame even Oblomov, how he could be satisfied with his position, rest content with his solitary, individual, exclusive happiness. . . . It must not be forgotten that under his feet there was a bog, that the old Oblomovka was near by, that he would have had to clear the forest to reach the highroad and thus escape from Oblomovshchina. Whether Stolz did anything in this direction, what he did, and how he did it—we do not know. But until we know we cannot be satisfied with his personality. . . . All we can say is that he is not the man who "will be able to pronounce in a language intelligible to the Russian soul that mighty word: 'forward!'"

Perhaps Olga Ilyinskaya is more capable of doing this than Stolz, for she stands nearer to our new life. We have said nothing about the women that Goncharov created, nothing about Olga, or about Agafya Matveyevna Pshenitsyna (or even about Anissya or Akulina, women also with peculiar characters), because we realized that we were totally unable to say anything coherently about them. To attempt to analyze the

[10] Murazov and Kostanzhoglo: characters in *Dead Souls.*

feminine types created by Goncharov would be to lay claim to expert knowledge of the feminine heart. Lacking this quality, we can only admire Goncharov's women. The ladies say that Goncharov's psychological analysis is amazing for its truth and subtlety, and in this matter the ladies must be believed. . . . We would not dare to add anything to their comment because we are afraid of setting foot in a land that is completely strange to us. But we take the liberty, in concluding this essay, to say a few words about Olga, and about her attitude towards Oblomovshchina.

In intellectual development, Olga is the highest ideal that a Russian artist can find in our present Russian life. That is why the extraordinary clarity and simplicity of her logic and the amazing harmony of heart and mind astonish us so much that we are ready to doubt even her imaginary existence and say: "There are no such young women." But following her through the whole novel we find that she is always true to herself and to her development, that she is not merely the creation of the author, but a living person, only one that we have not yet met. She more than Stolz gives us a glimpse of the new Russian life; from her we may expect to hear the word that will consume Oblomovshchina with fire and reduce it to ashes. . . . She begins by falling in love with Oblomov, by believing in him and in the possibility of his moral transformation. . . . She toils long and stubbornly, with loving devotion and tender solicitude, in an effort to fan the spark of life in this man and to stimulate him to activity. She refuses to believe that he is so incapable of doing good; cherishing her hopes in him, her future creation, she does everything for him. She even ignores conventional propriety, goes to see him alone without telling anybody, and, unlike him, is not afraid of losing her reputation. But with astonishing tact she at once discerns every false streak in his character, and she explains to him why it is false and not true in an extremely simple way. He, for example, writes her the letter we referred to above and later assures her that he had written it solely out of concern for her, completely forgetting himself, sacrificing himself, and so forth.

No, she answers, that is not true. If you had thought only of my happiness and had believed that for it it was necessary that we should part, you would simply have gone away without sending any letters.

He says that he fears that she will be unhappy when she learns that she had been mistaken in him, ceases to love him, and loves another. In answer to this she asks him:

Where do you see my unhappiness? I love you now and I feel good; later I will love another, hence, I will feel good with him. You need not worry about me.

This simplicity and clarity of thought are elements of the new life, not the one under the conditions of which present-day society grew up. . . . And then— how obedient Olga's will is to her heart! She continues her relations with Oblomov and persists in her love for him, in spite of unpleasantness, jeers, etc., from outside, until she is convinced of his utter worthlessness. Then she bluntly tells him that she had been mistaken in him and cannot combine her fate with his. She continues to praise and pet him while she rejects him, and even later, but by her action she annihilates him as no other Oblomov was ever annihilated by a woman. Tatyana says to Onegin at the end of the romance:

I love you (why conceal it?),
But to another my troth is plighted,
To him forever I'll be true.

And so, only formal moral duty saves

her from this empty-headed fop; if she were free she would have flung her arms around his neck. Natalya leaves Rudin only because he himself was obdurate from the very outset, and on seeing him off she realizes that he does not love her and she grieves sorely over this. There is no need to speak of Pechorin, who managed only to earn the *hatred* of Princess Mary. No, Olga did not behave to Oblomov in that way. She said to him simply and gently:

I learned only recently that I loved in you what I wanted you to have, what Stolz pointed out to me, and what he and I conjured up. I loved the future Oblomov! You are unassuming and honest, Ilya; you are tender . . . like a dove; you hide your head under your wing—and you want nothing more; you want to coo in the loft all your life. . . . But I am not like that: that is not enough for me; I want something more, but what—I don't know!

And so she leaves Oblomov and strives towards her *something*, although she does not quite know what it is. At last she finds it in Stolz, she joins him and is happy; but even here she does not halt, does not come to a dead stop. Certain vague problems and doubts disturb her, there are things she is trying to fathom. The author did not fully reveal her emotions to us and we may err in our assumptions concerning their nature. But it seems to us that her heart and mind were disturbed by the spirit of the new life, to which she was immeasurably nearer than Stolz. We think so because we find several hints of this in the following dialogue:

"What shall I do? Yield and pine?" she asked.

"No," he answered. "Arm yourself with firmness and serenity. We two are not Titans," he continued, embracing her. "We shall not follow the Manfreds and Fausts and challenge disturbing problems to mortal combat, nor shall we accept their challenge. We shall bow our heads and wait humbly until the hard times pass, and life, happiness, will smile again. . . ."

"But suppose they never leave us: suppose grief disturbs us more and more?" she asked.

"Well, we'll accept it as a new element of life. . . . But no, that cannot be, it cannot happen to us! It is not your grief alone, it is the common ailment of mankind. You have suffered only one drop. . . . All this is frightful when a man loses his grip on life, when he has no support. But in our case. . . ."

He did not specify the *our case*, but it is evident that it is *he* who does not wish to "challenge disturbing problems to mortal combat," that it is *he* who wants to "humbly bow his head. . . ." She is ready for this fight, she longs for it and is always afraid that her tranquil happiness with Stolz may grow into something that resembles the Oblomov apathy. Clearly, she does not wish to bow her head and wait humbly until the hard times pass, in the hope that life will smile again later. She left Oblomov when she ceased to believe in him; she will leave Stolz if she ceases to believe in him. And this will happen if she continues to be tormented by problems and doubts, and if he continues to advise her to accept them as a new element of life and bow her head. She is thoroughly familiar with Oblomovshchina, she will be able to discern it in all its different shapes, and under all masks, and will always be able to find strength enough to pronounce ruthless judgement on it.

. . .

29

GOING TO THE PEOPLE

By Katerina Breshkovskaia

Breshko-Breshkovskaia (1844–1934) is known as "the Grandmother of the Russian Revolution." Her participation in the revolutionary movement began in 1873 and continued until 1917. She helped her father, a landowner, liberate the peasants from serfdom in 1861. With her husband she opened the first zemstvo schools and libraries in the district. But the authorities closed the schools and forbade the family to work among the peasants. Father and husband submitted to the government, but Breshkovskaia went into revolutionary work, renouncing the comforts and privileges of her social position. For the next forty years life was a succession of imprisonments, escapes, and new arrests. When the American journalist George Kennan visited Siberia in 1888 (collecting material for his *Siberia and the Exile System*) Breshkovskaia said to him: "We shall die in exile, and our children and perhaps our children's children, but in the end something will come of it." As a leader of the Socialist Revolutionaries Breshkovskaia opposed the Bolsheviks and emigrated to Czechoslovakia, where she died. She was well known in America where she often raised funds for revolutionary work. Our excerpts are taken from her memoirs written in 1917.

The "going to the people" is analyzed in A. Pedler, "The Russian Narodniki in 1874–5," *Slavonic and East European Review*, VI, 130–41. A larger analysis of the populist movement is James Billington, *Mikhailovsky and Russian Populism*. For more of Breshkovskaia, see W. Walsh (ed.), "Some Breshkovskaia Letters," *American Slavic and East European Review*, IV, 128–40. See also her reminiscences and letters published as *The Little Grandmother of the Russian Revolution*. We have the memoirs of two participants of the movement in the seventies: Prince Peter Kropotkin's *Memoirs of a Revolutionary* (paperback), and Sergei Stepniak, *Underground Russia*. J. M. Meijer in his *Knowledge and Revolution* discusses the background of the populist movement of 1874. See also Donald Treadgold, "The Populists Refurbished," *Russian Review*, X, 185–96, and George Fedotov, "The Religious Sources of Russian Populism," in the same journal, I, 27–39. See also Richard Pipes, "Narodnichestvo: A Semantic Enquiry," *Slavic Review*, September 1964. There is a chapter on the Narodniks in Franco Venturi's *Roots of Revolution* (paperback). See also Arthur Mendel's *Dilemmas of Progress in Tsarist Russia: Legal Marxism and Legal Populism*. Vera Figner's *Memoirs of a Revolutionist* is an account by a participant in the movement. On Breshkovskaia see also Alexander Kerensky, "Catherine Breshkovsky," *Slavonic and East European Review*, Vol. XIII.

Reprinted from Lincoln Hutchinson (ed.), *Hidden Springs of the Russian Revolution: Personal Memoirs of Katerina Breshkovskaia* (Palo Alto, Calif.: Stanford University Press, 1931), pp. 31–39, 55–67, 123–36. Used with the permission of the publishers, Stanford University Press. Copyright 1931 by the Board of Trustees of the Leland Stanford Junior University, renewed 1959 by James S. Hutchinson.

WANDERINGS IN THE UKRAINE, 1874

About that time I too was ready to start. It was not fitting that I go alone, so I chose two young helpers. The first was Maria Kolenkina, who was to go with me as my niece. In preparing herself for the journey she had learned to dye hand-woven materials. She made peasant dresses and passports for us both. My second companion was Jacob Stephanovich, my "nephew" and a shoemaker. Neither my Mashenka ("niece") nor myself could be taken for Little Russians,[1] and since we intended to visit the governments[2] of Kiev and Kherson we preferred the passports and appearance of Great Russian women. The passports were of the government of Orel. We spoke the language of that region, and we planned to explain our manners and education by the fact that we had belonged to the *dvorovye*[3] and had lived with our masters and had learned much from them.

In Kiev we procured detailed military maps of Kiev, Kherson, and Podolia, the governments which we intended to visit, planning to begin our work in the big villages around the sugar factories. On these maps we drew blue-pencil lines south and a little to the west from Belozerie and Smela.

Having disposed of our former belongings, Mashenka and I rose with the sun one day early in June, donned our peasant dresses, adjusted our sacks containing the dyeing outfit, some linen, and other materials, strapped them on our backs, and went to the steamer which ran down the Dnieper to Cherkass. Stephanovich met us at Cherkass.

From there we had a walk of some twenty versts to Belozerie. As we left the steamer I noticed that Mashenka, because of her heavy burden, was walking on the sand with great difficulty. I stopped her and offered to rest. She looked at me in wonder and said, "We *must* hurry. We are expected." All her life that "must" remained the keynote of her actions. It was safe to start the most dangerous and difficult work with her, because for her there was no other law than that of perfect fulfillment of a duty undertaken.

On our way to Belozerie, Stephanovich, of course, made fun of our feminine weakness; nevertheless he transferred part of our things to his own sack. We rested in the shade several times. Before sunset we reached a small hostel in Belozerie and stopped to inquire about a hut to rest. There was no one to be seen, either in the street or in the hostel. The entire population was out in the fields. We met only an old soldier who talked nothing but nonsense. In return for a glass of *horilka*[4] he took us to the other end of the village, showed us an empty hut, and introduced us to its owner.

The next day we opened our dyeing workshop and became acquainted with some girls and young women. The older women were also curious about us and invited me, as the elder, to their houses. Mashenka easily made friends with the village girls, while I made further and further inquiries in my attempt to approach the householders. Stephanovich meantime made boots, but remained with us in Belozerie for only a few days.

The attitude of the village in general was listless. The sands surrounding it scarcely returned the seeds planted, and straw alone remained. The people tried to rent land from the neighboring land-

---

[1] Little Russia: the old name for the Ukraine, in contrast to Great Russia.

[2] Government: a province is meant.

[3] *Dvorovye*: house-serfs who performed personal services for the landowners before the emancipation of 1861.

[4] *Horilka*: Ukrainian name for vodka.

lord, but the factories of Bobrinski[5] had swallowed up the best soil for beet-root plantations, and they had therefore to look for meadows and fields scores of versts away and had to live near them in harvest time. They were despondent, and saw no solution to their problem.

Soon we moved to Smela. This enormous country town, which already contained one sugar refinery and six factories, was spread over a wide area. The house of the landlord, with its garden, park, and lake, surrounded by a sea of trees, seemed to draw away from the noisy, dirty streets, which teemed with factory people. The large market place swarmed with traders. The police and fire stations were at the market place. At the end of the place was a pond, its muddy water surrounded by very steep banks. Earthen huts were dug out of these banks, and the shores of the lake were thus lined with habitations resembling dens for animals. In them the workers who came from other places lived—former *dvorovye*, who had no land, who had come from northern governments. They lived in these huts with their large families; here they were born and here they died.

In Smela we soon found a corner to live in. No one in the town occupied a whole house. Small rooms were rented, usually without tables or seats. The father of the owner of our hut, an old fighter for the welfare of this community, offered us his own room, a dark den, and himself moved into the passage, where he slept on planks. This old man helped me a good deal in understanding the life of the factory population. They had been brought to Smela, when serfdom still existed, from one of the central governments, to work in the factories, having abandoned their land and their houses. With their liberation

as serfs they had got new small patches of land, but only large enough to build their houses on, and were still obliged to work in the factories, receiving a ration of bread as wages. I do not remember further details, but I know that the factory population lived in constant fear of losing their work at the whim of managers and directors. Those with large families had an especially hard time. Our old man was always weak from hunger. His son had his own family to care for; his daughter-in-law was unkind; and the old man, who had been twice flogged and sent to Siberia for defending the common interests, was at the end of his days almost a beggar. An old pink shirt, a jacket, and an old peasant coat were his only clothes. He also had a wooden basin and several wooden spoons, which he kindly put at our disposal.

We used to rise early in the morning, and I would go with Mashenka to the market. Long rows of peasant women sat on the earth beside jugs of milk, sacks of onions, various vegetables, and pieces of salt lard. As we did our modest shopping we observed the customs of our *poissardes*.[6] Never since then have we heard such conversation and such expressions; when the Little Russian woman is excited, she is irrepressible.

At noon we four sat with the old man around the wooden basin and swallowed our soup with great appetites. I talked a great deal with the old man, questioning him concerning the life of the workers and listening to his tales of the past. It was a cruel story. The peasants, transferred from their homes against their wills and placed by their landlords in a position of hopeless slavery, had "revolted" several times, demanding that they be sent back, and refusing to work in the factory. They were punished for

---

[5] Count Bobrinski was the most important Russian sugar manufacturer.

[6] *Poissarde*: idiomatic French for "fishwoman."

this. Every fifth or tenth man was flogged. Detachments of soldiers were left in the place. Like grasshoppers these soldiers devoured everything, leaving not a crust of bread for the inhabitants. The fate of the serf leaders was most terrible. These were the men who had spoken the loudest and had been the most obstinate in defending the rights of the villagers.

To my request that he help me in my revolutionary propaganda in Smela the old man answered: "I have no strength left. I have been cruelly punished. One soldier stood on one arm, another on the other, and two on my legs. I was beaten, beaten until the earth was soaked with blood. That is how I was flogged. And that did not happen merely once or twice. I was exiled to Siberia, came back, and began all over again; but I can't do it any more."

I asked him if there were any younger, bolder peasants who took the interests of the factory people to heart, who spoke with authority at meetings, and who were especially persecuted by the factory authorities. He named two peasants. One of them, a middle-aged workman, with his wife and children lived next door to us. The other, a little older, lived at the other end of the village. He also had a family. I visited the first one and asked if he would not like to read some clever and truthful books. He looked at me questioningly, as if wondering how a simple peasant woman such as I could read at all.

"Well," he answered, "bring them around."

We had brought with us several copies of appeals to the people in the form of proclamations, leaflets, tales, legends, and a fairy tale about the "Four Brethren." I chose one of them and went the next Sunday to see my neighbor. While I was reading, the man listened attentively. His wife watched us wondering-

ly. Several times she came nearer to listen, and then returned to her work. When I finished my reading, he said:

"If such leaflets could be distributed to all the people and explained, something would come of it. But how could we begin all alone? We have tried many times, but as we received no support from other places our attempts were useless. The people must be united and be of the same mind, otherwise nothing can succeed. You ought to go around to the villages and talk to the people."

"If you have reliable comrades whom you can trust," I said, "call them together, and I will read this to them."

We agreed to meet on the next Sunday. I was the first to arrive. The only ones in the hut were the master of the house and his children. I pointed at the children and said: "Should they remain here?"

He looked at me wonderingly. "But they are my children," he replied.

I remembered that when my parents had discussed political matters they had always sent the children out of the room.

Some twenty people filled the hut. They listened attentively. When I had finished, one of the workers asked,

"Where did she learn to read so well?"

"You see, she belongs to the *dvorovye*," explained my host. "She has lived long with the masters; they have taught her."

Then they discussed the subject and agreed to come again the next Sunday. They made no protest against my proposal to prepare the soil for a general revolt; but it was evident that the recent punishments had made a terrible impression on them. They said as one man: "If everyone agreed to rise at the same time, if you went around and talked to all the people, then it could be done. We tried several times to rise. We demanded our rights to the land. It was useless. Soldiers were sent down and the people were punished and ruined. . . ."

It seemed useless to remain longer in Smela, though we had grown to love a people who overlooked all the eccentricities of the "women from Orel." Mashenka and I had already invented an excuse for leaving and were only awaiting the return of Stephanovich in order to start. One day a young man in town clothes suddenly appeared at our room. He had come from Kiev with the password and a message warning us that our address and itinerary were known to the gendarmes and that they were already following us up. In one of his journeys to Kiev, Stephanovich had left our exact address at Luri's office. The office had been searched and all the papers taken, and Luri had been arrested, though he soon escaped and fled abroad. Our comrades in Kiev, therefore, sent us this urgent warning and a little money, and informed us that Stephanovich would join us at Cherkass.

We quickly packed our sacks and explained to our hosts that we had been offered advantageous work elsewhere. With our sacks on our backs we went to the market place, where one could always find a man who would take passengers to Cherkass. We found one who was returning with no passengers. He willingly took us with him. I was glad to ride thus alone with Mashenka. The fare was one ruble each. We trotted steadily on, met no one, and reached Cherkass toward evening. We stopped in a suburb opposite the landing-place and waited for Stephanovich. He arrived the next day and told us that he had traveled on the steamer with gendarmes, who were now galloping to Smela in a troika. After discussing our plans, we decided that it was too dangerous for the three of us to travel about together and that one of us should wait in some quiet place. Mashenka went to the home

of some near relations of mine and remained there several months. . . .

ARREST, 1874

We directed our steps toward Podolia, but I remember only a little of the details of the journey. In one of the villages I gave away my last illegal leaflet and then decided to write an appeal to the peasants myself. Stephanovich made three copies of it. I did this because when I spoke to the peasants they always said, "If you would write down these words and spread them everywhere, they would be of real use, because the people would know then that they were not invented."

In those terribly ignorant times when the only written papers in the villages were the orders issued by the authorities, their faith in a written word was great, all the more so since there was no one in the villages who could write even moderately well. . . .

In the middle of September we reached Tulchin, the small place where the Decembrists had arranged the conference of their South Russian organization. But we had no thought for them; the past had no place in our minds. What we hoped for was to meet here several of those bold rebels who had frightened the whole government of Podolia by their raids in different parts of the district. It had been impossible so far to catch these raiders and many interesting legends were in circulation about them among the people. We failed to get track of them, however, and decided to pass some time in or near Tulchin in order to study the matter more closely.

Tulchin was a big village on the land of a rich Polish landlord. His ancient castle stood at the end of the village, surrounded by a neglected park. At some distance from the park lay the hamlet, Varvaska, where we decided to stay. It was inhabited exclusively by peasants. Tulchin was full of small shop-keepers engrossed wholly in their money affairs. Their entire attention was taken up by the life of the market, which handled products from the neighboring villages in enormous quantities. I decided to take advantage of the market days. Varvaska was so close that it would be quite easy to get there.

We entered a house and asked for a room. After examining our passports,[7] the master decided to take us in. The place was less primitive than those in which we had stayed before. The town was full of Jews, Poles, and other nationalities. Artisans, wanderers, and contrabandists were continually coming and going. In addition, the population lived in constant expectation of raids by the followers of the famous Karmeluk.

Karmeluk was a legendary hero-robber, who became invisible in broad daylight, robbed the rich, and rewarded the poor. It was he whom "not one prison could hold" because of his strength and agility. Stephanovich went into raptures while listening to tales of this hero and of the trust which the poor people placed in him. He pictured to himself the fights of the Zaporogs[8] and passionately dreamed of reviving the bold struggle of the Ukrainians with all that interfered with their peaceful life, still so full of beauty and of poetry. . . .

The master of our house declared that the room he intended to assign to us was not ready, since heavy rains had damaged one wall, and it had to be repaired. Meanwhile we could live in the hut. The hut was divided in two by a partition.

[7] In both pre-revolutionary and present-day Russia all citizens had to, and still must have an internal passport in which police permission to reside in any locality is entered.

[8] One of the groups of Cossacks established on the lower Dnieper beyond the rapids during the seventeenth century. They were feared for their plundering expeditions. Their stronghold was destroyed by Catherine the Great.

We were allowed to sleep on benches in the front part. The host and hostess lived in the other one. They had no children.

My "nephew," the bootmaker, and his "aunt," the dyer, earned no money by their crafts, partly because they were not skilled and partly because all their time was taken up with other matters. The finances of our organization were very meager. Those of us who went among the people had only a little money, though happily one could live on bread with apples and lard.

We were running short of money; so Jacob decided that it was time for him to return to his beloved Kiev. He was anxious to know what had been going on there in our absence. I had only two rubles and a few kopeks to last until he came back. The master knew that my nephew had gone on business and would be back in a few days.

I lay down to sleep on the best bench in the "red corner." My sack served as a pillow. I covered myself with my thin coat and slept soundly. Stephanovich had not taken his tools. They lay in my sack under the bench, together with the military maps, the written proclamations, and a change of linen. True peasants, householders, in contrast with the naïveté with which they regard other people's letters, never allow themselves to inspect the belongings of their visitors. Letters, they consider the property of all the neighbors and even of all the village. To touch or look at another's belongings without his permission is considered very rude; but when one of us sat down to write a letter the host and his guests crowded around, watched attentively, and exchanged remarks:

"What small characters! One can scarcely see them."

"Our scribe at the police station writes as quickly."

"Good, brother, good."

"To whom do you write? Can you both write?"

"Well, read aloud what you have written?"

I read aloud, but not what I had written. It would have been unwise to refuse, but my proclamations were too threatening in tone to be read among a people whom I knew so little.

After Stephanovich's departure, I continued my visits to the market place. On one fine Sunday as I was returning home (I think it was the twenty-seventh of September) with a piece of lard and a few apples, I was stopped. My coat and my kerchief, tied "Russian fashion" under my chin, had distinguished me from the Little Russian crowd. As I walked along the dam which connected Varvaska with Tulchin I heard a carriage. A pair of horses trotted past me; a coachman sat on the box, and the district commissar of police was in the carriage.

"Stop," exclaimed the commissar. "You, there, take your seat on the box." I went on. "Do you hear, you, woman from Orel? Sit down here. You are staying with ———. We are going there. Come along."

I felt that I was lost but had a faint hope that my passport would save me. The master of the house was alone when we arrived and was surprised when the commissar entered.

"Where are this woman's things?" he asked at once.

"She has no things," said the master. "Here is her passport."

He took my passport out of his trunk, thinking that it would protect him. The commissar scrutinized it and saw at once that it was false. Some formality had been omitted.

"Show me her things, I say."

"She has no things," answered the master and looked questioningly at me and at the commissar. Evidently he thought that the police were seeking a large quantity of stolen things but were not looking for my miserable sack.

"It can't be. Give me her things at once."

"She has nothing except this one sack."

"Give me the sack. . . ."

The commissar next had the maps and written sheets in his hands. He cast a swift glance over the first and then took up the paper. He began to read aloud; his face became flushed with exultant joy. I watched, wonderingly. My emphatic and even cruel words he read distinctly, stressing them in triumphant tones. He was intoxicated by his luck and did not notice what was going on around him. Scores of peasants of all ages had in the meantime gathered in the hut. They filled the yard and listened eagerly at the open windows. The commissar's clerk was there. When he had finished reading, the commissar ordered him to call the priest. He wanted to boast of his luck in having caught a political criminal.

The peasants stood around bareheaded. They had taken off their caps at the reading of the "edict." By that time the yard and hut were crammed with people. While we waited for the priest, the commissar came up and began to joke with me. I brusquely pushed him aside, sat down on my host's trunk, and began to eat bread and lard. Soon the young priest came in, looking shyly about.

"Listen, reverend father, listen. Read that aloud," he said to his clerk.

Again the proclamation was read distinctly, solemnly, in a loud voice. The peasants made the sign of the cross and the hut grew ever more crowded. "He is doing my work for me," I thought. At the same time my heart was whispering, "You are caught, my dear, and it serves you right. You should have been more cautious."

The reading was finished. The crowd did not move. The priest in his confusion did not know what to say. The magistrate was sent for. The inspector was aflame. He questioned my host.

"With whom did she come?"

"With a nephew. He has gone to Kiev and will be back in a few days."

"Has anyone been to see her? What did she talk of with you?"

"No one has been here, and she has not told us anything. She has paid the money in advance."

So, from the point of view of my host, I was a most respectable person. I was anxious about Stephanovich and could think of nothing but of how to warn him of my misfortune. It was impossible to speak to anyone privately.

The magistrate soon appeared. He was older and was stern and silent all the time. The inspector had his clerk read the proclamation aloud a third time, to the great satisfaction of the audience, who with heads bared made the sign of the cross. I was also pleased. We had not worked in vain. The proclamation was being read to a large audience very distinctly so that everyone could understand it.

Evening was drawing near but the sun had not yet set. I, thinking only of Jacob, was astonished when the chief commissar of the district was announced. It developed that he had been informed of the event by a messenger and had come from the district town of Bratzlav, thirty versts away. This stout gentleman entered the hut demanding, "Where is she?" I was still sitting on the trunk eating apples. The chief commissar, the *ispravnik*, was about to ask me a question, when the *stanovoi*[9] quickly interrupted, "She does not answer or tell anything about herself." He assumed a pose and began to read the

9 *Ispravnik:* chief of police; *stanovoi:* a bailiff.

proclamation again. The scene was so vivid and picturesque that I can still see and hear the details of what went on. The *stanovoi* had scarcely read the first page when the *ispravnik* exclaimed in an angry voice,

"Enough! Take her to prison under strong guard. Search her first."

Several women were summoned, and in the closet which I had planned to occupy they, who were full of sympathy and curiosity, timidly searched my shabby, almost beggarly clothes, examined my two rubles pityingly and put them carefully back into my pocket.

An escort was waiting for me in the yard—twelve peasants armed with clubs. They put me in a cart and took me to Tulchin. While wandering about the market I had often wondered about a curiously shaped building. A high wall of planks, pointed at the top, hid this building from sight, only its red-tiled roof showing. In my innocence I used to wonder what strange sort of man would build himself such a horrid habitation.

On arriving in Tulchin my cart drove up to this strange building. The wide gates were opened. As we rolled into a bare, dreary yard, a large, thin pig walked slowly about us, grunting plaintively. It had been arrested for trespassing, and since its owner had not appeared it had been starving for a whole week in the prison yard.

The enormous, barn-like building was divided into four big wards. Scores of prisoners could be placed in each of them. At that time they were empty. I was taken into one of them. I had my sack with me, but they had taken out my papers, maps, and tools. The wooden bedsteads were wide and clean. I lay down and went to sleep.

When I woke up the next morning a group of sentinels was at my window. This interested me. I was curious to know what the peasants were thinking about, what they had heard and seen. The windows could be opened. It would be very easy to talk with the guards and to hand whatever I wanted to out to them. I especially hoped to find among them a man who would help me warn Stephanovich of my arrest. We began discussing the reasons for my arrest. When I asked what the *stanovoi* had read aloud, one of the guards stepped forward and repeated the proclamation word for word. This led to further talk and the boldest propaganda on my part. "Quite so," one of them said, "but we cannot do such things by ourselves. If you distributed such leaflets all over the country, it would be another thing. We have tried to enforce those demands. The result was that many were flogged and sent to prison."

It was evident that these people still remembered the early sixties, when liberation without land had caused revolts, and the subsequent penalties had made them hesitate to take separate, non-concerted action. Everywhere I had heard the same argument. . . .

Next day I was taken into a big barn which was filled with officials in uniform. The prosecutor, who had been informed of the event by the police of Bratzlav, had come down from Kamenetz-Podolsk with his staff. The local authorities were there also, and some local officials, who probably had no concern in the affair. There was also a photographer with his apparatus.

They began questioning me, but I refused to answer. They did not insist. I sat on a chair in the middle of the room. The rest stood some distance away. The photographer asked to take my picture. When he was ready, I shut my eyes and made a face. They did not force me to have the picture taken. Obviously my case was one of the first in the experience of the local bureaucracy. It was mainly a matter of curiosity to them.

Besides, the liberal traditions of the sixties were still alive. They were not so harsh in the treatment of "political prisoners" as they later became.

The officials soon left, after having obtained no information. They were replaced by twelve simple women who had sworn to search me conscientiously from head to foot. They approached me diffidently. They were tremendously impressed with the solemnity of the occasion and with the rumors of the events accompanying my arrest. I, myself, had to tell them what to do. The ceremony ended quickly and happily for both sides.

In the course of my long life, I was to undergo this same procedure several times, and I always, during the first months of my imprisonment, refused to be photographed. This gave my friends time to hear of my arrest and to think things out before there was an opportunity for searches and inquiries. If a gendarme appears and suddenly produces a photograph of a close friend, confusion results, and the necessary precautions cannot be taken. . . .

THE FORTRESS, 1876–77

It was September again. The police stations and the Third Department[10] were full of people who had been arrested for spreading propaganda among the factory workers. The big "Trial of the 50" was being prepared and our own inquisition was still being carried on. New participants had been found and additional witnesses were being sought. The prosecutors shrugged their shoulders at our insistent questions. The young heroines were tired, but not one had lost courage. None but the two or three who had been only casually involved in the affair had petitioned for mercy and expressed repentance. It was a hard period

---

10 Third Department: the secret police.

for these casual cases, for they were completely alone. They avoided us in order not to incriminate themselves, and they had no friends outside.

It was decided to transfer some of the prisoners to the fortress[11] in order to make room for the "50." We heard of this from the warders and therefore were not surprised when the noise of rolling carriages sounded in the yard below our windows. About fifty men were taken away before our turn came. I suppose they took first those whose safety they wanted to insure, next those who refused to give evidence, and finally those who had already given evidence.

I was glad that I was to be able to see the conditions in the fortress. When I arrived, many of my comrades of both sexes were already in the Troubetzkoi bastion.[12] All seventy cells in both stories were occupied.

The crowded conditions and the arrangement of the large but dirty and gloomy cells contributed much to the setting up of a widespread system of communication. The beds, tables, and stools were of wood and movable. One could push the table up to the window, put the stool on it, and in this way tap on the iron bar with a pencil, a book, or a bit of broken glass. Those with loud voices could even talk to one another. The warders and guards were horrified at first. There had never been such a scandal in the fortress. After the Decembrists had been incarcerated there, the walls had been covered with felt and painted paper. The guards watched us through the cell "eyes" and ran from cell to cell, opening doors, begging and threatening. When this had no effect,

[11] The Peter and Paul Fortress in St. Petersburg is meant. It was the chief political prison of the old régime, and is now a museum.

[12] So called after the Decembrist Prince Trubetskoi, who had been imprisoned there.

they appealed to the warder. With him they rushed into our cells and took out all objects that could be used for tapping. The furniture was put back into its place, and we were threatened with confinement in the penance cell or worse— "into such a place that you won't live even a month." As soon as they left, the tables were again pushed to the window, and we began to tap again, using any small objects that we had been able to hide. I had kept a toy rod with a magnetized end, such as is used by children when they play with tin fish and swans. I had found it in a thick book which had been given to the fortress library, and had hidden it behind the felt on the wall.

The authorities were unable to stop the tapping, for our party were united and brave. Also I think that after the first day we were not watched very carefully, for we had all either been interrogated already or were hopelessly silent.

In this way we passed a whole year. We were transferred from cell to cell, in order to separate friends, but this merely led to the formation of new friendships and to the invention of new ways of communication. The young Shamarin taught his neighbors to speak through a crude megaphone of folded paper. By using this method, conversations out of the window were audible only to the sentries outside; they reported to the gendarmes, but nothing could be done about it.

During the day we held conversations through the windows. In the evenings we played chess. Both amateurs and experts tapped on the floor with their heels so that they could be heard at a distance of several cells and in this way indicated to their opponents the moves of the imaginary pieces.

Serge Filippovich Kovalik, who was a keen chess-player, enlivened the whole bastion. He was a very clever man and solved easily and quickly the most difficult problems in the game. He was well-read and a student of many sciences, although he was completely indifferent to his reputation as a scientist. In his talks with his comrades he was full of fun and harmless irony. He always spoke of himself humorously and was gay and kindly in his attitude toward others. His comrades loved him as a brother. His capacity to bear easily and cheerfully the discomforts of an outlaw's life strengthened the characters of the rest of us. Many years later when his comrades spoke of him they would relate endless incidents and jokes about him. Hard labor, long exile on the shores of the Arctic Ocean, wore out this grand being before his time. He is three years younger than I am, but he is often ill and already old, he who might have lived to be a hundred in full enjoyment of his strength had he not been a son of cruel Russia.

My cell was in the upper story of the Trubetzkoi bastion, probably on the Neva side, for I often heard water lapping against the wall. I could also hear the musical clock. I often fed the doves, which, when the window was opened, fluttered together in great numbers in the space between the double casements. At that time rations of white and black bread were given to us. I could not eat all of it; so I made small pellets of the soft part and threw them to the doves. I took a particular dislike to one of the birds. He was the smallest one, was very ugly, and had a monstrous beak. He cleared his way rudely, hissing like a serpent, and darted to and fro so threateningly that he scattered the rest of the doves, although there were fifteen of them and they were all twice as large as he. Such impudence on one side and cowardice on the other made me indignant. His presence always spoiled the feeding. When I tried to drive him away, he merely hissed and flew at my head.

Sometimes the birds flew into the cell. The sentries reported this to the gendarmes, who chased them out and grumbled at the waste of bread; but I went on feeding them.

The sentries also reported that there was something wrong with number ———. They had seen me skipping up and down the cell in a sort of ballet dance and mistook this for a sign of madness. The guards peeked through the "eye," but told the sentries that there was no harm—that number ——— always danced. Lack of exercise had always been bad for my health. In the "Preliminary," where the cells were only four or five feet wide, I jumped and stamped on the same spot. While there, I learned the Russian national dance. The warders there were also frightened at first, but soon ceased to worry about it.

It was this dancing that caused my neighbor to the left, Sophia Alexandrovna Leschern von Gertzfeldt, to recognize me, and she tapped a greeting. From that moment dates a friendship unswerving as Sophia Alexandrovna herself. Her earnestness and unflinching devotion to the revolutionary cause cemented our friendship forever. She was a moral tower of strength, and it is a cause for deep regret that there are so few mementoes of her and so few contemporaries who could tell the truth about her.

Sophia was still in her prime. She was very kind to me. We were both cheerful and did not notice privations, especially since we were better fed in the fortress than we had been elsewhere. There were plenty of books, in various languages, which were constantly added to by the Red Cross. One old magazine contained a communication in cipher to the effect that Nechaev was interned in the Alexeevski ravelin,[13] that attempts were be-

13 Alexeevskii ravelin was so named after Tsarevich Alexis, imprisoned there by his father,

ing made to poison him, and that he had refused all food. Evidently the books were transmitted from ravelin to ravelin and the gendarmes had not noticed the cipher. . . .

PREPARATION FOR THE TRIAL, 1876–77

Our leaders, Kovalik, Voinaralski, Rogachev, Myschkin, had long discussions about our coming appearance before the judges and the answer we should make to the indictment. The indictment was so petty that it inspired only disgust. Even an attempt to refute it would be humiliating. We did not intend to argue with Zelihovski, but we wished to formulate a condemnation of a governmental policy which had forced the thinking portion of the population to take up arms against it.

The question was discussed in every corner of the prison. Voinaralski drew up a summary of the speech he proposed to make, in which he pictured the political and economic phases of Russian life. His outline was logical, terse, reserved. The facts spoke for themselves. Of the origin and history of our movement he said nothing himself, but incorporated a statement written by Kovalik. Kovalik declared that he himself would refuse to speak in court, for he was convinced that our protest should stick to the form already planned, that is, of refusing to recognize the court in any way. He was sure that we should be given no opportunity to tell the truth, because we would be silenced after the first word. Myschkin, on the contrary, declared that although he would refuse to be tried he would certainly make a speech, and begged us to agree with him. He said that his heart was so full

of indignation that he could not force himself to be silent. We decided to let him have his say, provided he prefaced his speech with the introduction written by Kovalik.

To my mind, Myschkin's speech was a historical event. For the first time a living word of truth was heard in Russia, spoken fearlessly and forcefully by a helpless prisoner face to face with an autocratic government. Those who heard it were enraptured. The lawyers, who were men of advanced views, unanimously declared that they had never heard anything more admirable.

While in the fortress, all of us, except Andreeva, the casual prisoner who had taken no part in our affairs either in or out of prison, agreed to refuse to participate in the proceedings on the ground that the accused would not be allowed to explain their case freely and that anyhow the trial would be conducted behind closed doors and the speeches would not be published. We tried to communicate our decision to our comrades in the House for Preliminary Detention, who were anxious to know our attitude toward the trial, and to our great joy we soon learned through secret channels that most of our comrades in the "Preliminary" agreed with us.

At the end of the winter we were told that we would be summoned, in groups, to the office of the fortress in order to read the hundreds of thousands of briefs which had been accumulated. Evidence and minutes, in big blue carton portfolios, were so numerous that they had to be brought to the fortress in carts like cordwood. The documents were so divided that each region was treated separately and only those of us, such as Voinaralski and Kovalik, who had had time to work in several places were involved in several groups. The number of these groups, which in reality formed one huge, All-Russian organization, so

---

Peter the Great. Sergei Nechaev was a famous Russian revolutionary who died in the fortress in 1883.

magnified the importance of the case as to frighten the higher authorities, rouse hopes of promotion among the numerous large and small bureaucrats, and prompt to political action and Socialistic propaganda thousands of young people who until that time had sought an outlet for their energy almost exclusively in attempts at educational work.

Our visits to the office offered a chance to see each other and to exchange notes. We began to "read" industriously in groups of five and six. I personally found no pleasure in this, because I found so much evidence of the moral instability of some of our comrades who had been completely worn out by suffering. It was painful and sad. I was also repelled by the presence of the authorities, who watched the readers carefully. The more indifferent among us enjoyed the readings. They contrived to talk to each other by innocent gestures, and exchanged notes while pretending to be engrossed in the study of their cases. As a matter of fact everyone really read but little, and that very carelessly, for they had already become familiar with a good deal of the evidence through the questionings at the preliminary inquiries. Besides, they attached no importance to a trial the outcome of which was predetermined. The reading was considered mainly as a diversion in the dreary drama of prison life.

We were offered a choice of counsel for the trial. At first we decided not to have any, but we soon got hints from friends on the outside that we ought not to refuse, that the solicitors themselves wanted to make out a case against the authorities and would be able to do this only if they were defending us. These same friends advised us as to our choice. The kindness of the lawyers in offering their services was also a factor in our decision.

Each of the attorneys had one or two clients who maintained their innocence and wished to make a real defense, and appearing for them would open the opportunity to participate actively in all the proceedings and make it possible to be of service to other clients who, though they did not wish to defend themselves, might be helped in various ways.

I was advised to engage a young and very promising solicitor, N. Karabchevski. He attended the trial, during the whole five or six months that it lasted, for the sole purpose of helping me communicate with my comrades. He fought for justice for us and displayed much patience in the fulfillment of his duty. With much finesse and delicacy he conducted the case of Vera Pavlovna Rogacheva, who regretted that she had agreed to take no part in the protest.

I am convinced that the group of solicitors who took part in the "Trial of the 193" represented the quintessence of noble and human understanding of jurisprudence and that they defended our cause because they realized all the cruelty and dishonesty with which we had been treated. They had seen with their own eyes how many noble young people had either perished or been crippled for life through the pitiless ambition of officials seeking personal rewards. To their honor these solicitors spared no words in describing the actions of the "justice."

We made much use of bribery. Gendarme officers, in return for fees, would allow interviews; and oh, those interviews! What sorrows, joys, tears, and hopes they caused. The whole prison was deeply interested in each of them, for without them we were completely cut off from the world. Even if only two or three out of seventy were allowed these opportunities, all the others could get from them items of interest concerning revolutionary and public life.

I must say something about our "free"

wives. They had the welfare of the whole prison at heart. They got information from their husbands as to the special needs of each of us and with the help of the Red Cross bought supplies for us. Fictive fiancées, sisters, and cousins of all degrees were invented. In order to obtain permission to send us things they had to go through many formalities, but they never gave up and in the end got what they wanted.

In the big reception rooms in the prison large numbers of visitors would sit, awaiting their turn. There you could see weeping mothers and red-eyed, pale young wives. Fathers and brothers came rarely. Still more rare were husbands. This was chiefly due to the fact that wives and husbands were nearly always imprisoned together. The majority of the prisoners were unmarried, however, and that is why fiancés and bridegrooms had to be invented.

During the four years that we of the "193" were imprisoned the Red Cross did some admirable work. It was under the direction of the Kornilov sisters, Liubov Ivanovna Serdukova and Alexandra Ivanovna (after she had been liberated under bond). They were helped by Sophia Perovskaia,[14] who had also been released under bond, and, later on, by Vera Nicolaevna Figner[15] and other wonderful girls. They undertook to visit all of the prisons and to collect money, clothes, and books for their helpless friends. Peasant women too came from faraway places to help us, one of these being Myschkin's mother. I cannot say enough in praise of her efficient help and the fearlessness of her relations with the authorities. The Red Cross organization was perfect. Records of needs were kept; and the free comrades contributed either money or work. Groups of young girls, for instance, made clothes for prisoners and for Siberian exiles. . . .

[14] As an accomplice in the assassination of Alexander II Perovskaia was, with four others, executed in 1881.

[15] Figner was arrested in 1883, and spent twenty-two years in Schlüsselburg Fortress. She was released during the revolution of 1905.

30

FROM A VILLAGE DIARY

By Gleb Uspenskii

The works of Gleb Uspenskii, whether journalism or fiction, have not been translated into English. Yet his writing is a powerful document of Russian social history of his time. "The work of our Narodnik writers," noted George Plekhanov, the father of Russian Marxism, "must be studied as attentively as one studies statistical works on the Russian national economy." The piece from which we print only excerpts below first appeared in the Populist monthly *Notes of the Fatherland* in 1877–79, and was reprinted several times in the following decade. The author had worked in the province of Samara as a clerk in a village savings association, while his wife taught in the local school. His perceptive observations based on long-time residence in the countryside tended to destroy all the chief tenets of Russian Populism. In regard to the province of Samara, which is described below, it should be noted that statistics collected there in 1877 indicated that nine desiatins of land were needed to live reasonably well in the area. In fact local holdings ranged from 1.3 to 6.8 desiatins on the average. As a result arrears in payments for the land were high, and constantly growing.

Many Russian writers of this period wrote about the peasantry and its mentality. Leo Tolstoy contributed *The Power of Darkness* (1866). Ivan Turgenev followed with *Virgin Soil* (1877). Anton Chekhov wrote *The Peasants* (1897) and *In the Ravine* (1900). Ivan Bunin wrote *The Village* (1910) and *Dry Valley* (1911). For an account of the village by a Russian contemporary see Sergei Stepniak-Kravchinskii, *The Russian Peasantry*. A Western observer who first visited the villages in the 1870's is Sir Donald Mackenzie Wallace, author of *Russia* (paperback). Vladimir Lenin paid particular attention to the class structure of the village in *The Development of Capitalism in Russia*, first published in 1900. Two secondary accounts are Sir John Maynard's *Russia in Flux* (paperback), and the classic *Rural Russia under the Old Regime* by Geroid Robinson. The only other piece of Uspenskii available in English is an unidentified fragment in Moissaye Olgin's *The Soul of the Russian Revolution*, pp. 227–47.

From G. Uspenskii, *Pol'noe Sobranie Sochinenii*, V (Moscow, 1940), 125–31, 133–38, 145–47, 231–33, 239–42. Translated by Sylvia Fain. The editor is indebted to Professor Richard Wortman for suggesting the passages for translation.

While strolling about the country place where I spent the summer of 1878 I could see an old peasant walking toward me. He was carrying a little girl, about one-and-a-half years old. Another about twelve, was walking beside him. They were walking slowly, as beggars do who are always watching for someone who might give them alms, fixing their attention on every window, every door, looking over fences and into half-open doorways. They resembled beggars, too, in their outward appearance. Even for country folk they were poorly dressed. The man's trousers were ragged and torn, exposing his bare body beneath, and he was barefoot. The little girl was so thin and jaundiced that she seemed ill. Her blond hair was disheveled and hung in uneven dirty strands, with little cakes of dirt visible between them. The other girl's appearance also bespoke poverty and ineradicable untidiness. . . .

When this little group came up I expected the man to beg; but he said nothing, only stopped and bowed.

"Are you begging?" I asked uncertainly.

"What!" said the peasant, looking at me with obvious astonishment. "I am the local watchman— Merciful heaven!—"

"Oh, well then, excuse me for—"

"The watchman, the watchman, dear sir— God forbid I should be reduced to— These are my grandchildren come to visit, and we're just out for a walk— No! God preserve us from such a thing—"

I again begged his pardon, and said:

"The little girls are so thin, that's why—"

"That they are, my friend, and how else when there's no food for them?"

"How is it they have no food?"

"There isn't any, that's all. We had a cow, but the Lord took her from us— she died— So, no milk."

"Then what do you feed this little one?" I asked.

"What do we feed her? Same things we eat—kvas,[1] bread—"

"To such a little child?!"

"And just what would you do?—God willing, this fall the heifer will be grown, and we'll sell her. And for the summer I have to be watchman for the master— Adding in what I make from that, God willing we'll buy a cow before winter. But in the meantime, we have to endure— can't be helped!—"

"You stand watch at night?"

"Just so, only at night. But if I had a horse, my days would not be wasted—"

I should mention here that in the village where I was living there is a lot of construction work, and the peasants could earn good pay doing day labor in their free time.

"If you have a horse," continued the peasant, "they'll pay seventy kopecks a day; so I would really be all set at the end of the summer. That is something to grieve a body, my friend, for I haven't a horse, nor any way to get one— I haven't a wife any longer, she's been dead two years now. Their father," he said, pointing to the girls, "my daughter's husband, they took him into the army, so there I was, alone to feed them, and no way to manage— Ah, but if I only had some old horse—there were some for fifteen rubles at the fair— Then, no matter what, I'd be able to be on my feet again come winter."

"Well, there's a cooperative, a bank here— Why don't you get your fifteen rubles from the bank?"

"That bank gives nothing to us, mister—"

"What do you mean? Why not?"

"Because they don't, that's all. Besides, dear sir, you have to have someone sign for you, and where would I find anyone willing to do that? Now somebody with

---

[1] A fermented drink, made from bread.

means, he can have all he wants from that bank. But somebody like me, who has nothing—who would back me up? If something were to happen, nobody would be willing to back me up."

The district where the unfortunate watchman lives is unquestionably the richest area that I myself have ever seen. The whole region is wealthy, and bountifully supplied with natural riches. It lies along the Volga, in the steppe of Samara province. This is the breadbasket of Russia, where five puds² of grain sown commonly returns a hundred—often even more. Besides the wonderful land, what lush meadows there are, what abundant feed for cattle, not to mention the beauty of the place! The wide Volga is a plentiful source of food. There are not many places like this, where fish can be had so cheaply. But besides the Volga, the many smaller rivers which flow through the region provide so much edible life that, as they say, "You'll never catch it all, you'll never eat it all." And how many different kinds of birds and wildfowl fly and sing in the meadow marshes and over the lakes of this steppe region, and hide in the fragrant high grasses. "Paradise!" So one might say, looking upon all this natural beauty, all this natural wealth. . . .

This village I am talking about is provided with just as many of these natural blessings as other parts of the region. It is situated along a stream; and another, an even wider, deeper, and richer stream, flows not more than a third of a mile away. The lands and meadows which the peasants farm are wonderfully fertile and rich. Besides that, as a supplement to this natural wealth, monetary resources are available in the village as well—a savings and loan association, in which every one of the seventy village households is a member. Finally, so that the reader may be completely convinced

of the prosperity of this village, I must say that although there is still no school here, and no doctor, still, since the Emancipation of February 19, 1861, there is not, has not been, and most probably will not be, a single kopeck of arrears in this village. I can back up this argument on behalf of the area's prosperity with the official survey. But my personal observations lead me to the conclusion that such faithfulness and regularity in meeting their obligations, which is generally such a difficult burden for the peasant, has been accomplished here without any special labor. For the quitrent income from the mill, the river, the tavern, etc., is enough to cover all taxes and dues. For instance, the tavern keeper alone pays 600 silver rubles yearly to the commune for his license to trade.

What else, then, is lacking, so that a man living here will have enough food, clothing, and shoes, and would be if not rich, then at least not a beggar?— And yet just imagine—among such blessings not a day passes that you do not run into some happening or scene or conversation that instantly shatters all your fantasies, spoils all your deductions and views about the people's life: in a word, leaves you completely unable to comprehend how the things you see could occur in the given conditions.

Here, alongside the home of a peasant who has 20,000 rubles in savings, lives an old woman and her granddaughters, with nothing to fall back on, and no fuel to cook her dinner, unless she can pick up some splinters of firewood somewhere —not to mention winter, when she will freeze from the cold.

"But aren't there communal forests?" you, the dilettante of rural customs, exclaim with astonishment.

"Oh yes, but they won't let us gather firewood there."

² A pud equals 36 pounds.

"Why not?"

"Well, some are allowed to, but not everyone." Or:

"Alms, sir, for the sake of heaven!"

"You,—do you live here?"

"Yes, I live here."

"Well then, how has it happened you have come to such a condition?"

"How did it happen? I'll tell you— We used to live well, mister. But one day my husband was working in the manor house, and fell from the roof— They said we should take him to the city, but I had no way to get him there— Now I am alone with the children— The commune took our land."

"How could the commune take your land? Why?"

"And just who was going to pay the poll tax for it? They first relieved us of the poll tax, but when they saw we weren't able to work the land, they took it too."

"What about hiring someone to help?"

"Where would we get the money?"

"What do you mean, where? You have your own money, money you and your husband have saved—you have cash, in the communal funds!— I know there are several hundred rubles there. You can hire someone, and buy food for yourselves too. Why do you go around begging? Ask for money from the communal funds—part of it is your own money!"

"Oh, is that so? And *they* will give it to *us*, I suppose— Alms, for the sake of heaven, God will bless your mercy—"

Finally, consider the watchman I described above: here is a member of the commune who cannot obtain a loan of 15–20 rubles, although available resources include not only communal funds, but also a village bank run by the village assembly and supplied with credits of 15,000 rubles by the State Bank. This member of the commune sees no chance of recovering by doing the type of work he and all his countrymen do, yet it is clear to all that he could easily work off a 20 ruble debt. . . .

In such a prosperous region, where the land is held communally, in a place with a savings association and a bank, in a place where there are no arrears in land payments, can it be that a working man cannot support his family, and has nothing to eat!? . . . Certainly this seems like the result of some sorcery! Admittedly, if in this village of seventy households you were to meet only that watchman, or the old woman I described earlier, you would be puzzled, and hard put to explain their situation. But what would you say should you come across such incomprehensible phenomena at each step, phenomena which convinced you that such personal disasters are taken lightly in this wealthy village where it would seem everything favors prosperity. . . .

The first thing one notices from observing the contemporary rural order is the almost complete absence of moral bonds among members of the village commune. During serfdom, the village people were united by the awareness of common misfortunes, for all were bound to obey every whim of the landlord. The master had a right to interfere with a family's affairs, and arbitrarily direct a man's private life: he could determine his profession, make him a scientist, a musician, a cook, or a tailor; he could arrange marriages regardless of a man's own wishes, and so forth. The continual possibility of such arbitrariness bound the commune through the same belittling of human dignity. . . . Nowadays no one interferes with the family life except the government, which conscripts soldiers. Nowadays everyone answers for himself, and runs his own affairs as he knows best. But the bond of the "moral yoke," that unity fostered by common resentments, has not been replaced by any positive appreciation of the necessity for general prosperity, and for a better life for all. In place of the old arbitrary rule has come neither knowledge, nor development, nor even a kind word between neighbors. Nothing has destroyed the old habit of trembling before authority, seeing oneself as a perpetual laborer, or the habit of making daily bread the goal of one's entire existence on earth. These habits hold the peasant in their power to this day.

Arbitrary authority is much less of a factor in the peasant family life now than during the days of serfdom. And yet little value is placed on another's existence, and no sympathy or concern for another's private interests. A sick child may cry all night and all day, or all week, while the parents worry and grieve for him—but the family knows nothing of medicine, and no one comes with help or skill, exactly as it was when they were all serfs. A doctor who earns 1,200 rubles yearly serving a population of 300,000, says:

"But I can't be everywhere at once!" The doctor's assistant can't be everywhere at once, either. . . . And meanwhile, a child is dying—and his death impresses those who loved him with the weight of their cares and their ignorance. . . .

There is a school, but the teacher only cares about earning his bread, has little knowledge himself, and is poverty-stricken. In the summer, he likes to keep to himself, or visit with his neighbor the priest. And when he is teaching, how can he cope with all his sixty students? Even teaching them the alphabet is a major task. As he himself told me, he shouted himself hoarse doing it. How could he have any time for cultivating social consciousness? What is needed is simply socially conscious and concerned vil-

lagers, and lots of them—but there are none.

There is no enlightenment which could come into the peasant family from the outside and give these people a better and a wider perspective on the world about them, which would let them breathe freely, and show them that man is destined for more than shedding sweat and blood. Without all this, each peasant household remains burdened with cares, which would disappear if only they were the subject of the *common village concern*. Each such household then is like an isolated island, where a stubborn struggle with life goes on from day to day, with a patience and frantic labor which is scarcely comprehensible to its inhabitants. The weight of those cares is so great that it seems impossible to exist in the face of them. It is this burden of cares which forces the peasant family to struggle so, and thus produces a deep fatalism in their way of thinking:

"It is God's will that thousands and millions of people struggle just as we do." This is how each peasant household explains its lot to itself, as the family rises at cock's crow to begin another day's work. . . .

There are a great many examples which may be given to demonstrate the complete isolation of the peasant family, and the alienation of the members of the commune from one another. For instance, merchants will use their influence with the rural authorities to persuade the commune to lease its fishing rights or vodka-selling rights to them. The more persuasive they are—that is, the more vodka they give to the elders and officers —the less they will have to pay to lease the commune's commercial rights. Ordinarily meetings called to deal with this kind of communal business include all the members of the commune; but this is because the merchants will provide a glass or two of vodka for everybody. The motivation for deciding to lease the village's commercial rights, then, generally has nothing to do with concern for the common interest. This is confirmed by the absolute unconcern which all the members show in the money which is thus earned. The members of the commune know that no one will get his share of the 600 rubles which is paid to the commune by the tavern. They leave this money, as it almost always happens, to the plunder of the people who have access to the village funds. . . .

If only there were some mutual concern for one another's welfare among the villagers, the money taken in from the tavern could be used for a thousand useful things—if only those matters were considered worthy of common attention. Why could not that peasant who broke his leg be taken to a hospital at the commune's expense? Then he would soon be able to start working again—and his family would be saved from ruin. A doctor's assistant could be sent for; or that talented self-taught lad could be sent to a high school, later to return to be the communal clerk, perhaps. These things are not done, because in all these ventures there is no real monetary gain for any member of the commune, and monetary gains are the only kind they think about —they know nothing about any kind of profit other than personal.

Because of this complete absence of "social consciousness" in today's rural thinking the communal use of the land generally does not spare the villagers from death by starvation. Amazing cases of this type happen very simply. Here is a peasant family, for instance, which pays a poll tax for two, and farms a double allotment of land. A household like this will have one working man, though perhaps five or six mouths to feed. Now if this man has

fallen from the roof and broken his leg, he stays at home unable to work. The money in the communal cash fund, to which he has contributed, and which would pay for a doctor and hospital care, has been squandered—perhaps by the village clerk or one of the elders. But the disabled man would anyway not expect to be helped through communal money. So he stays home, work stops on the family's land, and the family grows poor. They cannot pay the double poll tax, so they ask the commune to reduce their tax by half. The commune takes away half the tax obligation, but *also takes the land* which goes with it. Deprived of land and income, the family grows still poorer. Thus it may well be that the following year the second allotment will also have to be taken away from them, leaving the family completely without land, forced to wander about the world like beggars. Yet the man is a member of a commune well provided with lands, forests, and sums of money. Who will rescue him in such a plight? His family might help, his relations and friends might save him— blood ties and personal relationships to private persons can help—but there is no *communal* concern for him as an individual. The workings of the communal system can destroy him, but cannot help him stand on his feet. They give the land which was taken away from him to another, someone who has not been afflicted by misfortunes which have forced him to lose heart. But he has been ruined, must wander from place to place, hire himself out as a laborer to his neighbor, who too is a fully privileged member of the commune. Where is the much-praised "harmony" of the communal system??

I submit, in conclusion, still another incident which I investigated, to prove that contemporary rural institutions are not at all durable or harmonious. Adjoining this village's land is a large estate with 600 desiatins[3] of land, including 100 desiatins of forest (which in this area is quite valuable). The owner of this estate does not manage his own lands, but only visits the estate in the summer. Under the former owner, this land was readily leased by the local people and neighboring peasants. But the new owner proposed to sell it in one piece to the commune as a whole. To facilitate this purchase and let all the villagers participate in it, he proposed that the peasants pay him for this land —not with money—but with the very forest they would be buying as part of the estate! Under the terms he proposed, the peasants acting as a group would cut down four desiatins of this forest each year, and deliver the wood to the landlord, who would pay them at the going rates for the wood and the carting. The whole operation was to be completed in twenty-five years. Thus, at the end of the last year, although the old forest would have been cut down, the peasants would have a new one—the twenty-five year growth. At the same time, they would have had the use of the other five-sixths of the estate since the day the agreement was signed. The whole affair was to be arranged through the commune, and guaranteed by the whole village. But it is already two years since the offer was made, and nothing is to be seen of this guarantee. The peasants continue to rent land for cash, either from neighboring landlords or from peasants who have fallen into difficulties and lost their allotments. They will pay each other 3–5 rubles per desiatina. At the same time the estate owner is overwhelmed by requests from some peasants who want to buy portions of the estate. One peasant even wanted to buy the entire estate, on the suggested terms, but the landlord does not want to sell the land in any other way but to the whole commune. But the *whole commune* does not agree, the members cannot get together, and so they remain passive while this good, cheap, needed land lies unused. What is the reason for such an incomprehensible phenomenon?

From my conversations with the peasants upon this subject I could be sure of only one thing: the mutual dissensions among members of this commune had reached an almost dangerous level. Should the whole commune buy the estate (several peasants explained to me), it would be necessary to choose one man who would deal with the landlord, make accounts of the required woodcutting operations each year, and keep track of working days for each villager. This would have to be a man the whole commune could trust. But there is no such man among the seventy households! Now the villagers choose elders and the tax collector, but these are official persons who deal with the government, and anyway the law says they must choose such officers. But to choose *their own man*, who would watch over the common interest as well as his own, seems impossible to these people. Each thinks that a man can look only to his own private interests, and that anyone in a position of special privilege must finally end up better off than all the others. Whomever I named, the village people said he could not be trusted.

"It doesn't matter what a man says, just see what he does if you give him a chance—" This is how the village people characterize each other.

This lack of trust in an as yet unselected manager, lack of faith in the possibility that any person would not take advantage of others if he could,

[3] A desiatina equals 2.7 acres.

is just as prevalent among the wealthy peasants as among the poor ones. These two rather distinguishable rural groups are equally reluctant to conclude a deal which would be profitable to everyone. For the poor not to allow the strong to become still stronger is a real pleasure. And their confidence that if all participated equally in a purchase the strong would get more than the poor, that the poor would turn out to be only laborers for the richer, is so strong, and based on what seem to them such irrefutable facts, that the landlord's plan seems completely impracticable. . . .

It seems to me that one, small, generally unnoticed factor provides the clue to understanding the essence of the rural way of life. To this day you very frequently hear the word *barshchina*— the collective term for labor dues—in rural conversations. But since serfdom and labor dues are a past affair, you attach little significance to it. Yet it appears that although this word really belongs to the past, the remnants of this past are far from effaced today. And so, as you observe rural life you become convinced that in the contemporary village there is not a phenomenon, there is not a character trait, not even one habit, which the labor dues system alone will not explain.

Now what actually was this *barshchina*, the labor dues system? In general outline, this was work performed by the whole village for one manor house—this labor was an obligation the peasants had been burdened with from time immemorial, something they never questioned. The lord, to whom the village belonged, could change either for the better or for the worse. But for the village all these changes meant nothing: they had to work all the same, whether for conservatives or liberals or even radicals, whoever came to live in the

manor house. A landlord demanded only one thing from the village—*work*; work which took up the greater part of the day, of the year, of one's lifetime, work for someone else. This fundamental principle of *barshchina* was strengthened in the people's mind by all possible means, and finally produced a completely defined ideal for the creature known as the *muzhik* (the peasant). The ideal required, first, unquestioning fulfilment of another's commands; second, that this fulfilment be deeply rooted in a conviction that a peasant's own life is a matter of little concern.

In this way, serfdom has left us a legacy of peasants who are, first, tireless workers who struggle and labor at their work, who sweat and toil from day to day; second, men who pay their dues in full—and for whom these dues and obligations are the first care before which all private cares must fade; third, men who do not argue, whatever happens—they only ask "What must I do?" "How much is my tax?" Tax assessments are almost the only subject discussed in the village assembly. Personal or private village matters never come up —such things have never been learned. Fourth, to work, and to struggle, is the goal of life, the thread joining days and years into a whole human life. Our peasant is at peace after tiring and exhausting himself at his work, because he has done exactly as demanded of him. He forces his son to marry "a good worker" disregarding all other considerations.

It is in the name of this ideal that the peasant continues to live as he did in the days of serfdom. Where the system of obligatory labor was dominant, the peasant has remained almost a serf. Just as in the past, he goes out to the fields before sunrise, he struggles to pay his dues, keeps silent with unthinking indifference, fulfills everything that the elders order him to do. In such villages the peasants have a completely worked-out view of themselves and of their place in God's world. Thanks to it, they know what it is they do, and why they must struggle. Here is why it seems that the peasants of a poor village, overloaded with work and taxes, without any supplementary income, with less land and poorer land than their neighbors, still live better, keep up their payments better, are wiser and healthier than those in a village where the *barshchina* ideal was for some reason weaker.

But are there really, in this prosperous village, so few personal needs that no one voices them? How many children in the village grow up illiterate, not knowing how to count or read or write? How many do not know what the moon or the sun are, or where money comes from—in short, who know exactly nothing? How many poor people are there in the village, how many beggars, how many cripples, orphans, and homeless? How many have met accidental misfortunes and been left to the arbitrary whims of fate? Some thought ought to be given to these problems—some thought which is not taken up with other worries. But no one concerns themselves with these things, because no one knows that such things deserve concern or worry. The commune's affairs consist exclusively of land or tax distribution, and vodka drinking. If there is no distribution, the men get together and drink vodka—nothing else ever happens. . . .

The peasant today still does not try to live for his own private interests, and is barely aware of them in his own daily life. How else would you explain, for instance, a scene like the following. A mill. There are several carts of grain awaiting their turn. Peasants of various ages are sitting on the ground or on the carts, waiting. On the hill nearby is the new house of the man who leases the mill, a merchant. He is sitting at an open window, drinking hot tea, cup after cup, and constantly wiping his fat neck and red face with a towel.

"Look!" says one of the waiting men. "See the red-faced devil drinking tea!"

"Brother, is he drinking tea!"

"I've been counting and counting the cups, but I gave up. The housekeeper just keeps bringing him more and more."

"You'd think he would burst!"

"Are you kidding? He can take it all right."

"Sure, all he has to do is drink tea."

"That's all!—and there's nothing to it, you just sit and drink, that's all there is to it."

"That's how he does his business, too."

"You and I, my friend, break our backs to earn a kopeck. But there he is, doing nothing, not dirtying his pretty white hands, and raking in money while he drinks his tea— See there, how he fills his trousers!"

Many of the peasants lying about sigh in agreement.

"What cunning! He has set up a granary there, that's all, nothing more. But every year he pockets about 2,000 rubles from it— Ah, but you and I groan over every penny."

More comments on this theme could be heard all around. But let us go up to the speaker and ask:

"Whose mill is that?"

"Ours!"

"Is this the communal mill?"

"Yes. That fellow over there (pointing to the hill)—the one drinking tea—we lease the mill to him."

And then a story followed, as if to prove the dishonesty of the miller who was drinking tea. You may judge for yourself as to that. Ever since anyone could remember, the peasant told me, a small shed had stood near the mill, which was rented from the peasants by grain merchants. These merchants bought up grain in small batches from all over the village. "That one there, drinking tea," that "scoundrel," had leased the mill and the old granary from the village, but then had built a large sturdy barn in place of the old rickety granary. Ever since, each winter he has earned no less than 2,000 rubles from this granary, literally without lifting a finger.

The tone with which this "cunning" is described is somewhat obsequious, and resentment is clearly audible in it. And actually it is offensive to see how this merchant sits and drinks tea, all the while getting rich. But no one so much as suggests that a member of the commune might have built the granary, that someone could have been appointed to watch over the mill and report its accounts to the commune. There are no customs or procedures for such common enterprises. This, too, is a result of the old labor dues system. Under that system, the peasant concerned himself only with his own little plot, only occasionally showing off at the tavern. Someone else took care of the real income and expenses. For the *muzhik* it was all right if he was given the glass of vodka prescribed by the customary ritual; but the commune's income—this was not the peasant's affair. It was as if heaven had reserved this activity for outsiders.

Here is another brief illustration of the extent to which the peasant has divorced himself from really vital communal affairs. Public and appanage lands which are rented out everywhere at very low prices and in large quantities fall into the hands of these peasants only through a middleman. That is, these lands are first leased by a merchant, who rents the whole portion. Afterward the peasants lease land in small bits from him for three times the original rental price. Announcements of sales and rentals of field and forest lands are constantly circulated among village clerks and village elders. But I saw no case where the commune itself resolved to lease land. The peasants know about available land, but they wait to see who will take the land.

"Who leased that meadow?"

"Some city fellow."

"Where is his agent?"

"Right over there."

And the peasants will go to the land agent, who leased the land yesterday for one ruble a desiatina, and lease it from him today for three, four or six rubles. The merchant takes in the money, and sits in the hot afternoon drinking tea. The people look at him from afar (never up close), and grumble with anger:

"Look at the scoundrel! See how he steams his tummy while he rakes in the cash—"

31

KILLING AN EMPEROR

By David Footman

The assassination of Alexander II on March 1, 1881, was the most daring act of the Russian revolutionary movement in the nineteenth century. It astounded the country and brought the Party of the People's Will into unprecedented prominence. It should be noted that the party resorted to violence for its own reasons and condemned political assassination as such. Upon the assassination of President Garfield the executive committee of the party protested, "in the name of all Russian revolutionaries, against such violent acts as the assault of Guiteau. In a country where the liberty of the individual makes an honest struggle of opinions possible, and where the free will of the people determines not only the law but even the personality of the rulers, political assassination, as a weapon, is only an expression of the same spirit of despotism the destruction of which in Russia we consider to be our task. Despotism of an individual is equally as despicable as despotism of a party; violence can be justified only when it is directed against violence."

The excerpts which follow give the text of sections of the trial account and of the manifestos issued by the revolutionaries to explain their action. The texts are taken from the biography of the revolutionary Zhelyabov; the author is a fellow of St. Anthony's College, Oxford.

For a general account of the revolutionary movement, see Avrahm Yarmolinsky, *Road to Revolution* (paperback). W. E. Mosse, *Alexander II* (paperback), is a biography of the assassinated emperor. Samuel Kucherov, *Courts, Lawyers and Trials under the Last Three Tsars*, analyzes the Russian legal system and political trials. Vera Figner, *Memoirs of a Revolutionary*, is an autobiography of a member of the People's Will, while *Underground Russia* by Sergei Kravchinskii (Stepniak) is an account by a former revolutionary. Lev Tikhomirov, mentioned below as the author of the letter to Alexander III, wrote *Russia, Economic, Political, and Social*. The last chapters of Franco Venturi's *Roots of Revolution* (paperback) are devoted to the People's Will. *Katkov*, by Martin Katz, is a biography of the most influential journalist of the time and his reactions to the assassination.

THE MANIFESTO

On March 2, a manifesto was issued to the Workers of Russia. It had been composed beforehand, presumably by Zhelyabov and Grinevitski:

"Workers of Russia!

"Today, March 1, Alexander the Ty-

rant has been killed by us, Socialists. He was killed because he did not care

From David Footman, *Red Prelude* (New Haven, Conn.: Yale University Press, 1945), pp. 202–3, 218–35. Footnotes by the editor. Used by permission of the publisher and Christy & Moore, Ltd.

for his people. He burdened them with taxes. He deprived the peasant of his land; he handed over the workers to plunderers and exploiters. He did not give the people freedom. He did not heed the people's tears. He cared only for the rich. He himself lived in luxury. The police maltreated the people and he rewarded them instead of punishing them. He hanged or exiled any who stood out on behalf of the people or on behalf of justice. That is why he was killed. A Tsar should be a good shepherd, ready to devote his life to his sheep. Alexander II was a ravening wolf and a terrible death overtook him. . . ."

On the evening of March 1 Tikhomirov started to work on the open letter to Alexander III, perhaps the most famous of all the People's Will manifestoes. This was not finally issued until the 12th. The draft had to be considered and approved by the Executive Committee, and Tikhomirov also desired to discuss it with some of his liberal publicist friends.

This open letter is long, too long perhaps to be really effective propaganda. The following are among its salient passages:

"Your Majesty:

"While fully comprehending your deep sorrow, the Executive Committee would not be justified in postponing this explanation through reasons of natural delicacy. There is something higher than the most legitimate of personal feelings. It is the duty to our country, to which all individual sentiments must be sacrificed. . . .

"The tragedy of the Ekaterinski Canal was neither fortuitous nor unexpected. The events of the last ten years made it inevitable. And that must clearly be understood by him whom fate was now placed at the head of the administrative machine. . . .

"The Administration may well be able to arrest and hang a number of individuals, and to suppress a number of revolutionary groups. But the issue remains unchanged. It is the circumstances of the age that create revolutionaries, the whole nation's discontent, the urge of all Russia towards a new social order. . . .

"There are but two ways—Revolution, inevitable, unavertible by any executions, or the voluntary transfer of supreme power to the hands of the People. . . .

"We turn to you, disregarding that suspicion which the misdeeds of the Administration have aroused . . . we turn to you as a citizen and a man of honour. We trust that no personal bitterness will cause you to forget your duty or to cease to wish to know the truth. We too have cause for bitterness. You have lost a father. We have lost fathers, brothers, wives, children, and our dearest friends. We are prepared to suppress our personal feelings if the good of Russia demands it; and we expect the same of you. . . .

"We do not impose conditions, as these have been imposed by history. We merely state them. They are:

"(1) A general amnesty for all political crimes, as those have not been crimes, but rather the fulfilment of social duty.

"(2) The summoning of representatives of the whole nation to consider the existing social and economic order and its modification in accordance with the nation's desire. . . .

"And so, Your Majesty, decide. There are two ways before you. On you depends the choice. We can only beg of fate that your judgment and your conscience lead you to choose the only path consistent with the good of Russia, with your honour, and with your duty towards your country."

THE TRIAL OF THE SIX

Some days before the trial took place Pobyedonostsev,[1] whose influence was considerable now that his former pupil had ascended the throne, warned the young Emperor that public opinion was "disquietened by rumours of the possibility of the lives of the tsaricides being spared." Alexander III said: "Do not be alarmed. No one would dare approach me with such a proposal. I can promise you that all six will be hanged."

Shortly after this, on March 25, Zhelyabov addressed a memorandum to the authorities:

"As our activities have been directed solely against the Administration, the Court of the Senate, being composed of members of the Administration, is an interested party and therefore not competent to judge the issue. . . . The sole tribunal competent to adjudicate is the nation, acting by means of a national plebiscite or referendum, or else through a freely elected Constituent Assembly. . . . Failing that, the social conscience might be able to make itself felt in a trial by jury. I accordingly request and require a trial by jury. I have no doubt that this would lead to our acquittal as it led to the acquittal of Zasulich."

This was a warning to the authorities, if such were needed, of the attitude that Zhelyabov was likely to adopt at the trial. They had experience of the tendency of political prisoners to launch out on indictments of the Administration. The necessary precautions had already been taken. Arrangements had been made for the censorship of accounts of the proceedings in the Russian press, and to ensure that only carefully selected individuals, officials for the most part, should be admitted to the court. None the less there was still a certain danger of leakage. Accordingly Fuchs, who had

been appointed president of the court, was approached in turn by Loris-Melikov,[2] by Nabokov (the Minister of Justice) and by Pobyedonostsev, who informed him that His Imperial Majesty would prefer to see the proceedings made as short as possible; it would be undesirable for the accused to be allowed to make long speeches, or for Zhelyabov to be given the opportunity to expound his political views.

II

The proceedings opened at 11 A.M. on March 26. The court consisted of ten persons, including Fuchs, the president, and representatives of the Estates of the Empire. The merchant class was represented by the Mayor of Moscow and the peasants by one Helker, a rural district headman. The prisoners sat in a row: Rysakov, Mihailov, Helfmann, Kibalchich, Perovskaya and Zhelyabov, in that order. The arrangement was intentional. The more malleable prisoners came first, and Zhelyabov last, so that he would not be able to give a lead to the others. All were represented by counsel except Zhelyabov. Apart from Rysakov the prisoners were calm and in good spirits. From time to time Zhelyabov whispered to Perovskaya until he was stopped by an officer of the court.

Each of the accused was called upon to give his name, age, and religion. When it came to Zhelyabov's turn he objected to the form in which the charge had been communicated to him and required an answer to his memorandum demanding a trial by jury. His objections were overruled and the formalities proceeded.

"Name?"

"Andrei Ivanovich Zhelyabov."

"Age?"

"Thirty."

---

[1] For Pobyedonostsev, see the reading (No. 33) later in this volume.

[2] Count Mikhail Loris-Melikov (1825–88) became minister of the interior in 1880.

"Religion?"

"I was baptised into the Orthodox Church but am no longer a member. At the same time I admit the teaching of Christ to be the basis of my moral convictions. I believe in truth and justice. I consider religion without deeds to be of no value. I hold it to be the duty of a sincere Christian to fight on behalf of the weak and oppressed; and, if need be, to suffer for them. That is my faith."

"Address and occupation?"

"My last place of residence was in the Ismailovski Polk. I have lived at various addresses as ordered by the Executive Committee. My sole occupation has, for several years, been the liberation of my fellow-countrymen."

The clerk of the court read the charge against the prisoners: "That they did enter into a secret society calling itself the Russian Social Revolutionary party and having as its aim to overthrow by force the form of government and the social structure at present existing in this Empire; and that they did undertake a series of attempts against the Sacred Person of His Late Imperial Majesty. . . ." The twenty-four counts of the charge covered the attack on the Ekaterinski Quay, the mine in the Malaya Sadovaya, and (this last concerned Zhelyabov alone) the attempt on the railway at Alexandrovsk.

The prisoners were told to plead.

Zhelyabov, when it came to his turn, said:

"I admit I am a member of the People's Will, in accordance with my convictions. I have acted as agent of the Executive Committee. At one time I devoted several years to peaceful propaganda. I was forced to abandon that form of activity. By the time I came to settle in Petersburg I had become convinced that the main enemy of the Russian social movement was the Russian bureaucracy."

The President: "I will not permit expressions of that nature."

Zhelyabov: "I do not plead guilty of belonging to a secret society composed of the six persons here and a few others. Some of them have taken a leading part in revolutionary activities, but they do not form a secret society in the terms of the charge. In any case Mihailov had nothing whatever to do with the matter at issue."

Muraviev, the acting public prosecutor, informed the court that he proposed to read the depositions of Colonel Dvorzhitski and of two other witnesses who had been wounded by the explosion and were unable to attend in person; also that he proposed to read the depositions of Goldenberg. Counsel for the accused raised no objection. Zhelyabov announced that he wished to call Kolotkevich and Kurshunikov (Barannikov). To this the prosecution objected in view of a rule that the evidence of other political prisoners was not to be accepted in political trials as their "natural inclination would be to distort rather than to clarify the issue." Zhelyabov replied that in that case he objected to the depositions of Goldenberg. There ensued a legal argument: finally Zhelyabov's objection was overruled on the grounds that, as Goldenberg was dead, the rule did not apply to his case. Zhelyabov then demanded proof of the death of Goldenberg, and the court pronounced that sufficient evidence of his death had been produced at the Trial of the Sixteen.

This concluded the preliminaries and the trial began. . . .

III

The hearing of the witnesses occupied two whole days and, to ensure that the trial should be concluded on the third, proceedings were resumed at ten in the morning. Muraviev started his speech for the prosecution:

"Gentlemen, called as I am to undertake the prosecution in this most appalling of crimes ever committed upon Russian soil, I feel overwhelmed by the immensity of my task. Before the fresh-filled grave of our adored Monarch, amid the universal tears of a great Empire mourning the so unexpected and so terrible end of its Father and Reformer, I fear lest my weak powers. . . ."

It must be remembered, in justice to Muraviev, that this somewhat florid style was the fashion of his day. It must be remembered, too, that it was not his main task to establish the facts. The facts were largely admitted. . . . The counsel had been appointed by the court. They realised the nature of the trial and the effect on their subsequent careers if they showed a tendency to make trouble. It was natural for them to emphasize their reluctance at being put in a position where they were forced to speak on behalf of the accused and they confined themselves to appeals for such mercy as the court might feel inclined to show. A striking exception was Gerard, who defended Kibalchich.

Gerard stood up to the prosecution. "I well appreciate," he said, "the emotion which animated the prosecutor . . . but your duty, gentlemen of the court, is to keep your judgment free from emotion." Gerard's main concern was to explain the circumstances in which Kibalchich had become a revolutionary. He told the court of Kibalchich's arrest on account of the *Tale of Four Brothers;* of his three years in prison awaiting trial; of his frustrated attempt to resume his normal studies. He exposed the whole story of the Trial of the 193 and of the police measures that had preceded and accompanied that trial. Again and again the president called him to order. "The actions of our administrative authorities," the president declared, "are not a subject for consideration by this court."

IV

Zhelyabov had refused the services of counsel and was therefore entitled to make a speech in his own defence. This, in spite of the precautions taken to avoid publicity, was a matter of some concern to the authorities. The bureaucracy continued to be intensely suspicious of any court of law. After the first day of the trial Count Baranov, the prefect of Petersburg, had complained to the Minister of Justice of the "weakness" of Fuchs in the face of the accused. According to a report which there seems no reason to doubt, on the morning of the 28th the president received a personal message, purporting to come from the Emperor, which pointed out the "extreme undesirability" of allowing Zhelyabov to speak at all. Fuchs was thus in a difficult position. But he was a man of integrity, and, in any case, to refuse Zhelyabov his legal right might well entail consequences quite other than those intended. Zhelyabov was allowed to make his speech, but only within limits that were strictly defined.

The following is the account that appeared in the *Times:*

The speeches of Zhelyabov, Mihailov, and Kibalchich were all more or less explanatory of the unhappy conditions of society and government in Russia. Although the Procuror in his case for the Crown went fully into the whole question of Socialism and Nihilism at home and abroad, and particularly dwelt upon the aims of the Russian Revolutionary Party, in order to explain the heinous character of the prisoners' views and aims, yet the prisoners referred to, as well as their advocates, were frequently requested to confine themselves to the circumstances of the crime of the first of March, and not to go into the general questions upon which the prosecution dilated at such length. The speech of Zhelyabov was the most remarkable of all. With an air of assurance, changing to one of defiance when interrupted by the Court or the disapproving murmurs of the audience, Zhelyabov tried to lay bare the state of things and the social conditions which had made him and his fellow-conspirators what they are now. When the incidents just referred to occurred, and he glared round the Court like a wild beast at bay, there stood the wiry type of the fierce and unyielding demagogue.

The *Times* correspondent goes on to describe how Zhelyabov exposed the distress of the peasantry and the misdeeds of officials "who did everything for themselves and nothing for the people." There is nothing of this in the official stenographic account of the proceedings which has come down to us. It has been suggested that the court records were subjected to a secret censorship. Be that as it may, we must turn to the official account for all we can know of the one occasion accorded to Zhelyabov to attempt a public declaration of his faith.

Zhelyabov: "Gentlemen of the court, a sincere worker in any cause will hold his cause dearer than his life. Today our cause has been more grossly misrepresented than our own personal actions; and so it is our duty to explain our party's aims and methods. I maintain that the picture drawn by the prosecutor was false, and this I intend to prove by the documents and evidence on which he based his speech. The Programme of the Workers' Section served as basis for allegations that we do not recognise ordered government. Relying on the text of this programme I maintain that we are adherents of ordered government, not anarchists. It is an old story that we are anarchists. We affirm that as long as there are common interests it will be necessary to maintain a government. I would like to explain our principles—."

President: "No. The law allows you only to dispute those statements of fact on the part of the prosecution which you consider untrue."

Zhelyabov: "Then I will keep to the points of the indictment. We are not anarchists. We stand for Federal Government. We advocate a Constituent Assembly. How can we then be regarded as anarchists? Further, we criticise the existing economic system, and we maintain—"

President: "You are now using your right of defence in order to advance theories. Economic and social theories are not matters for consideration by this court."

Zhelyabov: "The prosecutor remarked that the event of March 1 was not a mere fact but was history. I agree; and accordingly this event must be considered in the light of the factors concerned."

President: "The crime of March 1 is a historical fact. But our business now is to consider your personal participation, and you are entitled to speak on that only."

Zhelyabov: "The prosecutor lays the responsibility for March 1 on the whole party, not merely on the accused here in court. It is therefore only logical to refer to the aims and methods as laid down in the party's publications."

President: "You have merely the right to deal with your personal participation. This court does not regard you as authorised to speak on behalf of the party, and, for the purposes of this court, the party has nothing to do with the question of your guilt. The prosecutor referred to your party, and in view of this you have the right to deal with any views attributed by the prosecutor to the party which you yourself do not hold. But I warn you that this is no place for the airing of political theories; further that I will not allow anything to be said derogatory to the law, to the authorities or to religion. That is my duty as president and I intend to fulfil it."

Zhelyabov: "My original plan for my defence was very different. I had intended to say only a few words. But, as the prosecutor has devoted five hours to misrepresenting facts which I had considered to be clear, I submit that a defence within the limits you now set me is inconsistent with the freedom you allowed to the prosecution."

President: "My attitude is dictated by the nature of the crime with which you are charged. Within these limits and so far, but only so far, as you can do so without offence to the law and to the existing social order you may use that freedom."

Zhelyabov: "I shall confine myself to the evidence called by the prosecutor. He has produced various documents, a brochure by Morozov and a lithographed manuscript found in my possession. He considers that these are evidence. On what grounds? Because they were in my possession. Now they are in his. Have I the right to say they represent his convictions because he has them? How can he maintain that they represent mine? As to Morozov's pamphlet, I have not read it, but I know of its contents. As a party we disapprove of its line of argument, and we have asked our émigré friends abroad, so long as they are abroad, not to express views on the tasks of the party in Russia. Now, apparently, we are to be held responsible for the views of Morozov because at one time in the past certain members of the party, like Goldenberg, took the attitude that our whole task was to clear our way by a series of political murders. At present terrorism is only one among a whole row of other means designed to secure the amelioration of our national life. I—as the prosecutor said of him-

self—have also the right to call myself a Russian."

(*A murmur among the public: Zhelyabov turned and glowered at them and then continued.*)

"So much for the aims of the party. Now for its methods. I wish to make a short historical sketch, as the prosecutor did. Every social phenomenon must be regarded in the light of its past. To understand our present methods of struggle you must understand our history. For we have a history, short in years but rich in experience. Gentlemen of the court, if you were to look into the records of political trials, that open book of the past, you would find that the Russian Peoples' party did not always use bombs, and that we, as a party, have had our youth, a youth of radiant dreams. If this is now all past and gone it is through no fault of ours."

President: "You are exceeding the limits which I laid down. Restrict yourself to your own personal activities."

Zhelyabov: "I am coming to that. We looked for means of helping the people, and the means we chose was to take up positions as common working men and women with a view to the peaceful propagation of socialist ideas. This surely was harmless. What happened? Those concerned were imprisoned or sent into exile. An entirely peaceful movement, opposed to violence, opposed to revolution, was crushed. I took part in this movement, and this the prosecutor lays to my charge. I have to explain its character, as an integral part of my defence."

President: "But you were acquitted."

Zhelyabov: "None the less the prosecutor lays it to my charge."

President: "Confine yourself to facts directly connected with the matter in hand."

Zhelyabov: "I wish to point out that in 1873, '74, and '75, I was not a revolutionary as the prosecutor alleges. My aim was to work for the good of the people by the spread of socialist ideas. I did not approve of violence, I was not concerned with political matters—my companions even less so. In 1874, as far as we had political ideas, we were anarchists. To this extent I agree with the prosecutor. Indeed, there is much truth in what he says. But fragments of truth, taken from different periods and put together again in a purely arbitrary manner, are apt to form, to use his own expression, 'a bloody fog.' "

President: "Is this with reference to yourself?"

Zhelyabov: "It is. I say that all I wished to do was to work in a peaceful manner among the people. I was put in prison. There I became a revolutionary. I now pass to the second stage of the socialist movement. This stage—no, possibly I should cease trying to defend my principles and instead merely request that the prosecutor's speech be printed word for word as he said it, and published for the world to judge.[3] Well, perhaps after all I will make the attempt. This temporary movement to the people showed our ideas to be impracticable and doctrinaire. But we found that there was much in Russian popular tradition that we could build on. Because of this and because the authorities made it impossible for us to spread our ideas by peaceful means we socialists became Narodniks. We decided to work on the needs and desires of which the people were already conscious. That is the distinguishing mark of Narodnichestvo. From dreamers we became workers. We took to deeds, not words. Action meant some use of force. But force was not used to any great extent. So things went

on up to 1878. In that year, as far as I know, there first appeared the idea of more radical action, of cutting the Gordian knot. The movement that culminated in the event of March 1 began to take shape in the winter of '77–'78. The year 1878 was a transitional year, as can be seen from the pamphlet 'A Death for a Death.' The party had not yet grasped the significance of the political front, although circumstances were forcing it into open war against the political system."

President: "Now you are talking of the party again—"

Zhelyabov: "I was one of its members."

President: "Speak only of yourself."

Zhelyabov: "Circumstances were forcing me, among others, to declare war against the existing political structure. All the same I spent the summer of 1878 in a village, propagandising peacefully. In the winter 1878–79 there seemed to be no solution. I spent the spring of 1879 in the South. For me it was a time of anxiety and distress. I knew that my comrades were feeling the same perplexities, especially in the North, and that in the North there had come a split in the Zemlya i Volya society. Some of its members held the same views as myself and a few of my friends in the South. We eventually joined forces at Lipetsk. There we drew up a new programme and policy. But the Lipetsk conference did not cover so narrow a field as the prosecution makes out. The basic principles of the new policy were as follows: the political structure—"

President: "I will not allow you to continue, as you refuse to obey my directions. You are now indulging in a historical dissertation."

Zhelyabov: "I am accused of taking part in the Lipetsk conference."

President: "No. You are accused of taking part in the attempt at Alexan-

---

[3] The proceedings of the case were not published until 1906, when the Russian censorship was considerably relaxed.

drovsk, which was a consequence of the Lipetsk conference."

Zhelyabov: "If I am merely accused of participation in the Alexandrovsk attempt and the event of March 1, then all I have to say is 'Yes,' as the facts have been proved. But a bald affirmation is not a defence."

President: "We are considering the question of your motive."

Zhelyabov: "In that case I submit that an explanation of the development of my ideas—"

President: "I will admit an explanation of your personal convictions as far as they concern the events under consideration. But I will not admit an account of the views of the party."

Zhelyabov: "I do not understand the distinction."

President: "I am asking you to confine your remarks to your own physical and moral participation in these events."

Zhelyabov: "I answered this question at the beginning of the proceedings. If I may add nothing further, then I must merely draw the court's attention to my previous statements."

President: "If you have nothing to add—"

Zhelyabov: "I have given the bare outlines, the skeleton. I wish now to give the soul."

President: "Your own soul, not that of the party."

Zhelyabov: "Yes, mine. I took part in the Lipetsk conference. This conference led to a series of events as the result of which I am here in the dock. I must therefore explain the decisions taken at Lipetsk. According to the prosecutor the task we then set ourselves was to attempt to kill. This is untrue. The task we set ourselves was not so narrow. Our basic principle—my basic principle if you will—was that the Social Revolutionary party should bring about a revolution. To this end we were to organise

revolutionary forces on the widest possible scale. Up till then I had not seen the necessity of organisation. Like other simple socialists I had felt that certain matters, the supply of prohibited literature for instance, should be organised. Otherwise I had relied on individual initiative. But once we had set ourselves the task of carrying out an armed revolution it was obviously necessary to establish a strong, centralised machine, and we—myself included—devoted vastly more time and effort to this work than to preparing assassinations. After Lipetsk I became a member of the body at the head of which stands the Executive Committee, and I devoted all my powers to the creation of a strong centralised organization, consisting of a number of semi-autonomous groups working on a common plan and inspired by a common idea. My personal task, the object of my life, had been to work for the common good. I tried first to do this by peaceful means. Later on I was forced to turn to violence. I would willingly abandon violence if there were the possibility of serving my ideals by peaceful means—of peacefully expounding my views and organising those of my way of thinking. I repeat again as my last word, to avoid any misunderstanding, a peaceful solution is possible. I myself would at once abandon terrorist activity if the conditions—"

President: "You have nothing more to say in your defence?"

Zhelyabov: "In my defence, nothing. But I wish to correct an earlier statement. In the interests of justice I drew the attention of the court to the part played by Timothy Mihailov, that is, to the fact that Mihailov was in no way involved either in the bomb attack or in the Malaya Sadovaya mine. I now understand that my attempt to prevent a miscarriage of justice has wounded the feelings of Timothy Mihailov. I accordingly wish to declare that should this matter be raised again I would not repeat my statement. I hasten to add that we, the accused and the prosecutor, conform to very different moral standards."

V

After the conclusion of the speeches for the defence, and before pronouncement of verdict and sentence, the accused had the right to give their "final word." They were called upon one by one. Rysakov said:

"I do not belong to the terrorist section as the prosecutor said. I deny having worked for it. This is true, because I do not approve of terrorism as a method of struggle. I only heard of it here in this court. . . . I do not approve of open warfare with the authorities. I am convinced that no good would come of violent action. . . . And I am not the only one to oppose terror. Goldenberg did the same."

Timothy Mihailov said:

"I have not the education to explain myself. . . . I belong to the Social Revolutionary party, but a party for protecting the workers, not for starting revolutions, at least as far as I could understand. . . . It is difficult to make my meaning clear because I am uneducated."

Helfmann confined herself to correcting police statements of her previous history. "I wish to point out" she said, "that when I came back to Petersburg [as an 'illegal' in 1879] it was not in order to escape the police but because I had devoted myself to the service of that cause which I had been and have been serving."

Kibalchich recapitulated the prosecutor's theories regarding social unrest in Russia. He then said:

"There now comes the question of how to prevent the repetition of regrettable events such as that with which we are here concerned. He [the prosecutor] appears to believe that the one sure method is to make no move towards conciliation and to rely entirely upon the gallows and the firing squad. I regret that I cannot agree with the prosecutor that the methods he suggests will lead to the result desired."

Kibalchich went on to a matter with which he had been deeply occupied during the ten days of his detention.

"There is one thing more. I have drafted a project for a flying machine. I am of the opinion that my invention is practicable. My draft contains full details, and the necessary designs and calculations are attached. It now appears unlikely that I shall have the opportunity of discussing my invention with qualified experts, and as the possibility exists of my plans being exploited by unauthorised persons, I wish now publicly to declare that my project and sketch are to pass into the sole possession of my counsel, M. Gerard."

Perovskaya said:

"The prosecutor has made a number of charges against us. With regard to his statements of fact I have dealt with these in my preliminary examination. But I and my friends are also accused of immorality, brutality and contempt for public opinion. I wish to say that anyone who knows our lives and the circumstances in which we have had to work will not accuse us either of immorality or of brutality."

Zhelyabov said:

"Only this. During the preliminary examination I said little, knowing that any statement of mine would merely be used by the prosecution for their own ends. Now I regret having said what I have said here in court. That is all." . . .

32

A SLAVOPHILE STATEMENT

By Ivan Aksakov

With his brother Konstantin, and with Iurii Samarin, Ivan Aksakov (1823–86) led the second Slavophile generation. The first period of Slavophilism, inaugurated by Aleksei Khomiakov (mentioned below) and Ivan Kireevskii, came to a close with the Crimean War (1854–56). The second period may be said to have ended with Ivan Aksakov's death. He had been a civil servant in various parts of Russia during the 1840's. After fighting in the Crimean War as a volunteer, he played a leading part in the Moscow Slavic Committee (1858–78). The Committee was disbanded by the government, and Aksakov was exiled from Moscow for a speech criticizing Russian foreign policy. He continued to edit various Slavophile journals until his death. The speech reprinted below was made shortly after Alexander II's assassination. It provides an illustration of the Slavophile doctrine of "democratic autocracy."

Additional speeches by Ivan Aksakov are reprinted in Olga Novikova, *Russia and England*, pp. 24–35, 53–60, 98–106. Some of the works of the Slavophiles Alexei Khomiakov and Ivan Kireevsky are translated in Volume I of the anthology *Russian Philosophy* edited by James Edie *et al.* Biographies are *Ivan Aksakov* by Stephen Lukashevich, and *Konstantin Aksakov* by Edward Chmielewski. See also Peter Struve, "Ivan Aksakov," *Slavonic and East European Review*, Vol. II. Nicholas Riasanovsky has written *Russia and the West in the Teaching of the Slavophiles*. See also Edward Thaden, *Conservative Nationalism in 19th Century Russia*, and a chapter on the Slavophiles in John Maynard's *Russia in Flux* (paperback). There is an essay on "Personality and Society in the Ideology of the Slavophiles" by Andrzej Walicki in *California Slavic Studies*, Vol. II. The Slavophiles are discussed in three chapters of Richard Hare's *Pioneers of Russian Social Thought* (paperback). Peter Christoff has written *Khomiakov*, a biography of the first Slavophile leader. Janko Lavrin has articles on "Kireevsky and the Problem of Russian Culture," in the *Russian Review*, April, 1961, and "Khomiakov and the Slavs," *ibid.*, January, 1964.

ADDRESS TO THE ST. PETERSBURG BENEVOLENT SLAVIC COMMITTEE

Gentlemen,—I came from Moscow to take part in your assembly, and to join my Moscow voice to yours. I should greatly like to convey to you what is said and thought at Moscow, but it is beyond expression by spoken word.

From Olga Novikova, *Skobelev and the Slavonic Cause* (London: Longmans, Green & Co., 1883), pp. 354–62.

378

How, indeed, are we to define the impressions which fill our souls at this moment? It is sorrow, it is grief, it is shame and horror—a kind of solemn foreboding horror. Divine judgment is now risen up against us. It is God Himself, living in history, who is sending us His terrible revelations. We are now standing before Him, and called upon to answer. What is the answer we are giving? Is there any answer we could give? Let everyone appeal to his conscience. Is he not partly to be blamed for the infamy which has deserved the punishment of God and stained our country in the eyes of the whole world? Let us not deceive ourselves. We are on the edge of ruin. One step more in the fatal direction we followed with such criminal light-headedness, and we attain to blood and chaos! This is no exaggeration, no mere words. Do not flatter yourselves with dreams. If our country is mute, it is because she is wondering and amazed. Do you realise the meaning of the silent wondering of many millions of people? Their breast is swelling like an ocean, full of heavy thoughts. No external calamity could be compared to the moral burden caused by the villainy of March 1.

The Emperor is murdered; the same Emperor who was the greatest benefactor to his country, who emancipated, bestowing upon them human and civil rights, tens of millions of Russian peasants. He is murdered; not from personal vengeance, not for booty, but precisely because he is the Emperor, the crowned head, the representative, the first man of his country, that vital, single man, who personified the very essence, the whole image, the whole strength and power, of Russia. From time immemorial that power constituted the strength of the country. The attempt directed against the person of the Tzar is always directed against the whole people; but in this case the whole historical principle of the national life has been attacked, the autocratic power bestowed upon the Emperor by the country itself. Who are those who dared to bring that awful shame upon the people, and, as if by mockery, in the name of the people? Who are they? Is it merely a handful of criminals, blood-thirsty blockheads, enslaved by the demon of destruction? Where did they come from? Let us address that question sternly to ourselves. Is it not the product of our moral treason, of which is guilty almost all the so-called liberal press? Can it be anything else but the logical, extreme expression of that Westernism which, since the time of Peter the Great, demoralised both our government and our society, and has already marred all the spiritual manifestations of our national life? Not content to profit by all the riches of European thought and knowledge, we borrowed her spirit, developed by a foreign history and foreign religion. We began idolising Europe, worshipping her gods and her idols! Who is to be blamed? Some forty years ago has not Khomiakov warned us, threatening us with Divine punishment for 'deserting all that is sacred to our hearts'? But really, what are these 'Anarchists,' 'Social Democrats,' and Revolutionists, as they call themselves? Have they the smallest particle of Russian spirit in all their aspirations and aims? Is there the slightest shade in their teachings of a protest against the real shortcomings of which Russia is suffering? Just the opposite; what they despise most is precisely the Russian people. In their servile imitation of foreign teaching and foreign idols, they only borrow what can easily be explained, if not excused, in Western Europe by historical and social conditions. There results of that kind are the natural protest caused by unequal partition of land, the unjust reign of the *bourgeoisie* over the fourth class—deprived of all civil organisation and political rights—a protest, therefore, against the present constitutional forms.

But that injustice is exactly what we do not possess. Thank God, and thanks to that very martyr-Emperor so brutally murdered, our 'fourth class,' or our peasantry, forming almost eighty per cent of the whole realm, now possess land, organisation, and the most complete self-government. To this very day, that fourth class is the keeper of our historical instinct, of our religion, and of the whole element of our political organism. They, and not the so-called 'Intelligentsia,' are the real supporters of our country. The memory of our 'Zemskie assemblies,' summoned by the will of the autocratic power, is not lost in our history, and no efforts of our *bureaucracy*, and the pseudo-liberal worshippers of the Western political organisation, will be strong enough to stop in the future the renovation of that precious homogeneous union between the sovereign and the land (*zemstvo*).

And is it not monstrous that now, when violent protests are heard everywhere in the West against constitutionalism and parliamentarism, that in Russia the so-called 'Intelligentsia' should be craving for the constitutional rags that Europe will have the charity to throw to her valets!

Who accepts the causes has also to accept their logical consequences. Who accepts the Western Constitution has also to bear the last expression of Western political life, viz., social revolution with all its manifestations.

But can such be the result of the historical thousand years' harvest of the Russian people? Its patience conquered all, every kind of misfortune, and remained, in spite of all, faithful to its civil and moral principles. Worse than all the external calamities was the moral treason of its leading class, powerful through knowledge and development. The reforms of Peter the Great weakened our memory and disabled us from understanding our own history—so very different from that of the West. Conquest is not at the bottom of our historical life, as is the case in all the Western countries. Our history begins with quite a voluntary and rational appeal to power. The same appeal was repeated much later, in 1612, and gave the foundation to the present reigning dynasty, empowered with autocracy, and nothing and nobody could induce the country to alter that shape of government. Such was the will, such was the inspiration of the national spirit.

Our history does not possess, therefore, that fundamental fact, which characterises the political life of the Western powers of Europe, the antagonism between the people and a power imposed by conquest. That antagonism, however, is the very foundation of Western constitutionalism. It is a mere agreement; a compromise between two camps hostile to each other, mistrusting each other; a kind of treaty, surrounded with all sorts of conditions. To evade those conditions *without contradicting the letter of the agreement,* constitutes the great talent of the rulers as well as of those who are ruled. Struggle for power—that is the real sense of the political life of European countries. The foundation of their administration is a kind of mechanical apparatus; the centre of power and mind, of an *unlimited power,* belongs to the majority of voices based upon the numbers of the representatives. Thus some ten voices—often bribed and bought—automatically decide the destinies of the people, forming the actual majority, in comparison of which the parliamentary majority is a few grains of sand compared to the sandy wilderness of Sahara. But that autocrat, composed of several numerical units, bears no moral responsibility before its conscience and the country, responsibility which falls heavily on the one personal representative of the supreme power. More than that, the so-called lowest class, forming the great bulk of the country, is not even represented in the Chambers. It is simply excluded, it is despised by the Western 'Intelligentsia.'

During the First Republic the French Representative Assembly declared—quite legally as far as the form was concerned, and in the name of the people—that the worship addressed to God was null, and replaced by adoration of the 'Goddess of Reason'; and all that in the face of tens of millions of true believers, but of men deprived of any legal voice, and thus unable to protest at all. The same thing happened in France the other day. It is ordered now to put in all the primary schools, instead of the word God, the word *Nature*. Is this not a study illustrative of popular Western representation? What is the use of political rights which allow, in the name of liberty and law, such a revolting infraction of freedom and truth?

Such are the kinds of freedom promised to Russia by worshippers of European liberal institutions. But the instincts and the notions of freedom in the Russian people are higher and broader than in any part of the world, because they are free from the conventional and formal element, and are based on *moral truth*. They are easily traced in our self-government, the broadest of Europe, and in the largest application of the *elective element*. There was no antagonism between our Emperor and the people, as our superior power has been voluntarily recognised by the whole country.

The Russian people has not entrusted full power to a heartless, soulless, mechanical apparatus, but to the 'holiest of beings'—to a man with a human soul, with a Russian heart, and a Christian conscience. The people know, and know well, the drawbacks of every human institution, but feel at the same time the power to overcome and improve them. And our former Tzars have not deceived their hopes and confidence; they held majestically and rigorously their imperial title, and asked for advice the whole Russian land in the shape of our *Zemskié Sobory,* and the land never failed to bring in response the love and the truthful thoughts of the whole nation. There was no mentioning any political rights, or supporting any kind of political doctrine. It was the regular, the natural manifestation of national life itself. Neither the people nor the autocratic Tzar ever thought themselves otherwise than in a constant moral and intellectual alliance of unity. The superior power, far from finding itself attacked, was supported by millions of loving hearts and intellects. And therefore, after the destructive calamities which took place before the year 1612, after that epoch, it gradually became, to the amazement of the whole world, one of the most powerful countries. The Emperor Peter the Great's reforms have changed all that. I admit that change had its cause, its *raison d'être;* but now it exists no more; any obstinacy shown in that direction by the government or the 'Intelligentsia' would be fatal, and has already been the cause of our present state. But, if our administration has forsaken for a time its national traditions, the nation itself remains faithful.

There is, however, another side of the question, of which I beg permission to say a few words. All that Nihilism, Socialism, that last word of Western European life, has a moral underlining. The idea of a State could nowhere be developed with such fullness and consistency as in the heathen world, where it constituted the highest idea of truth. Christianity showing man the highest vocation outside and above the State, designated the principle of Divine truth as the moral source of every strength and power. But, as soon as the Christian world forgets the notion of God, the modern foundation of the State is shaken, as Christianity is the only great principle subduing, moderating in due limits, the development of mere State principle. Society, which repudiates Christianity, but at the same time is unable to give up the exigencies inspired by Christian truths, individual freedom, and other Christian ideals—such a society is doomed to search only in the State for the realisation of all these ideals, though they are perfectly unattainable in that region. In rejecting the spiritual weapon, that highest moral motive for good, based upon faith in supernatural truth, there remains only material force, however legal it may be.

But a Christian cannot simply cease to be a Christian; he will continually struggle with his former God, in his own soul and in the outside world. And the more he struggles the more discontented he becomes. Therefore the final fate of every Christian society which excluded Christ from itself is rebellion and revolution. But rebellion creates nothing, and from rebellion to rebellion you come to anarchy, to a complete self-negation. The beginning of all this is to be traced already in Western Europe. In denying the existence of God and his soul, man deifies the body, and is subdued by animal instincts. Such is the political and spiritual path recommended to Russia.

After she has been covered with the so-called Liberal constitutional organisation by our social revolutionists, and that part of our 'Intelligentsia' who stupidly imagine that you may stop halfway, they try to displace from her historical and Christian ground that Russia, which to this moment we call 'Holy Russia,' and simple people generally designated themselves as 'Christians' and 'Orthodox world.'

No, that shall never happen! Our people is hostile to Liberalism preached along with the negation of Christian faith and Christian morality, and which expresses the greatest contempt for the political and spiritual belief of the Russian land.

The time is come for us to bethink ourselves. The time is come to fix our mobile heart, our mobile thoughts, on the rock of Divine and national truth. I am happy to have been able to express aloud, in the name of the Slavic society, the civil and moral aims and ideals of the Russian people. But that is not sufficient. It is necessary—it is absolutely necessary—for us to implore our Emperor to allow us, the whole country, the whole nation, to surround his throne and to express fearlessly, openly to the whole world, our horror and indignation to all who dare to make any attempt against what is most sacred to our national feeling, the historical principle of the autocracy, which constitutes the very foundation of our political life. Yes; let us implore that the old union between the Emperor and the country shall be revived, based upon reciprocal, sincere confidence, love, and union of souls.

33

THE SLAV ROLE IN
WORLD CIVILIZATION

By Nikolai Danilevsky

Danilevsky (1822–85) is known principally for his *Russia and Europe*, published in 1869. The work was called "the most complete catechism of Slavophilism," and its author recognized as the spokesman for the Panslavs. The book went through many Russian editions and appeared in German in 1920 but has never been translated into English. During the reign of Alexander III it was recommended by the Ministry of Education as a textbook for history teachers. Danilevsky was also a noted scientist, specializing in fisheries, and published a two-volume work on Darwinism in 1885–89. The excerpt below is taken from the last chapter of *Russia and Europe*.

The first biography of the man is Robert MacMaster's *Danilevsky: A Totalitarian Philosopher*. There is an essay on him by Hans Kohn in Ernest Simmons (ed.), *Continuity and Change in Russian and Soviet Thought*. There is a chapter on Danilevsky in Pitirim Sorokin's *Social Philosophies of an Age of Crisis* (reprinted in paperback as *Modern Historical and Social Philosophies*). Rostislav Fadeev's *Opinion on the Eastern Question* is a statement by a Russian Panslav. There are three monographs on Panslavism: *Panslavism* by Hans Kohn (paperback); *The Emergence of Russian Panslavism*, by Michael Petrovich; and *Seventy Years of Panslavism in Russia, 1800–1870*, by F. Fadner. See also Edward Thaden's *Conservative Nationalism in 19th Century Russia*, and a chapter on Panslavism in *European Ideologies*, edited by Felix Gross. On Russian activities in the Balkans see the classic *Russia and the Balkans* by B. H. Sumner, and David MacKenzie's *The Serbs and Russian Panslavism, 1875–8*.

And now let us turn to the Slav world, and chiefly to Russia, its only independent representative, in order to examine the results and the promises of this world, a world still only at the beginning of its cultural-historical life. We must examine it from the viewpoint of the above four foci of reference: religion, culture, politics, and socio-economic structure, in order to elucidate what we rightfully expect as well as hope from the Slav cultural-historical type.

Religion constituted the most essential element of ancient Russian life, and at the present time, the overwhelming spiritual interest of the ordinary Russian is also involved in it; in truth, one cannot but wonder at the ignorance and the impertinence of these people who could insist (to gratify their fantasies)

From Hans Kohn (ed.), *The Mind of Modern Russia* (New Brunswick, N.J.: Rutgers University Press, 1955), pp. 200–211. Copyright 1955 by The Trustees of Rutgers College in New Jersey.

on the religious indifference of the Russian people.

From an objective, factual viewpoint, the Russian and the majority of Slav peoples became, with the Greeks, the chief guardians of the living tradition of religious truth, Orthodoxy, and in this way they continued the high calling, which was the destiny of Israel and Byzantium: to be the chosen people. . . .

We have already pointed to the special character of the acceptance of Christianity by Russia, not through subjection to a culturally higher Christian nation, nor through political supremacy over a nation, nor by way of an active religious propaganda—but out of an inner discontent, a dissatisfaction with paganism, and out of the unfettered search for truth. . . . The religious aspect of the cultural activity belongs to the Slav cultural type and to Russia in particular; it is its inalienable achievement, founded on the psychology of its people and on its guardianship of religious truth.

If we turn to the political aspect and to the extent to which the Slav peoples have manifested their ability to set up their body politic, we find the situation at first sight discouraging, because all the Slav peoples, with the exception of Russia, either did not succeed in establishing independent states, or were incapable of preserving their independence. The Slavophobes conclude from this that the Slav peoples are politically incapable. Such a conclusion cannot stand up if we face the facts as they are. These facts tell us that the vast majority of the Slav tribes (at least two-thirds of them, if not more) have built a huge, continuous state, which has already had an existence of a thousand years and is all the time growing in strength and power in spite of the storms which it has had to weather during its long historical life. This one fact of the first magnitude

demonstrates the political sense of the Slavs or at least of a significant majority of them.

If the German Empire [of the Middle Ages], after a relatively short period of glory and power, turned into a political *monstrum,* are we then entitled to conclude that the German race is incapable of political life? Of course not, because the German race also has created the powerful British Empire, and therefore we must ascribe the political situation of Germany exclusively to unfavorable domestic and foreign circumstances, and not to a deep-rooted incapacity. This is confirmed by Prussia's actions, which reveal political sense of a fairly long standing (at least since the Great Elector) and led to Bismarck's success.

In judging the political incapacity of the Slavs one also hears of the alleged lack of unity of the Russian state, because there are in it, maybe, about a hundred peoples of different nationalities. But it is forgotten that all this diversity disappears before the preponderance of the Russian race—qualitatively and quantitatively. Even if all the Western and Southwestern Slav peoples were really incapable of political life, nonetheless one must recognize the high political sense of the Slav race as a whole, in view of the Russian state alone.

The example of the Ukraine, which for a long time was torn from the rest of Russia but voluntarily united with her after gaining her independence, furnishes the proof that there is more than one Slav people gifted with deep political insight; therefore, we may hope that when the opportunity arises, other Slavs will display the same insight, voluntarily recognizing the hegemony of Russia after having gained their independence, and realizing that the circumstances in which the Ukraine found itself at the time of Bogdan Khmelnitsky and in which the Western Slavs find themselves now are essentially similar. Popular enthusiasm, favorable circumstances, and the genius of a leader placed at the head of a popular movement can achieve independence for them. But preservation of their independence and of the Slav character of life and culture will be impossible without a close mutual union with Russia.

Whatever the future may bring we are entitled, on the evidence of the past alone, to consider the Slavs among the most gifted families of the human race in political ability. Here we may turn our attention to the special character of this political ability and show how it manifested itself during the growth of the Russian state. The Russians do not send out colonists to create new political societies, as the Greeks did in antiquity or the English in modern times. Russia does not have colonial possessions, like Rome or like England. The Russian state from early Muscovite times on has been Russia herself, gradually, irresistibly spreading on all sides, settling neighboring nonsettled territories, and assimilating into herself and into her national boundaries foreign populations. This basic character of Russian expansion was misunderstood because of the distortion of the original Russian point of view through Europeanization, the origin of every evil in Russia. . . .

But the expansion of the state, its attainment of stability, strength, and power, constitutes only one aspect of political activity. It has still another one, consisting of the establishment of equal relationships between the citizens themselves and between them and the state, i.e., in the establishment of civil and political freedom. A people not endowed with this freedom cannot be said to possess a healthy political sense. Is the Russian people capable of freedom?

Naturally our "well-wishers" give a negative answer: some regard slavery as a natural element of the Russians, and others are afraid, or pretend to be afraid, that freedom in Russian hands must lead to all sorts of excesses and abuses. But on the basis of Russian history and with knowledge of the views and traits of the Russian people, one can only form an opinion diametrically opposed to this view—namely, that there hardly ever has existed or exists a people so capable of enduring such a large share of freedom as the Russians and so little inclined to abuse it, due to their ability and habit to obey, their respect and trust in the authorities, their lack of love for power, and their loathing of interference in matters where they do not consider themselves competent. If we look into the causes of all political troubles, we shall find their root not in the striving after freedom, but in the love for power and the vain cravings of human beings to interfere in affairs that are beyond their comprehension. . . .

This nature of the Russian people is the true reason why Russia is the only state which never had (and in all probability never will have) a political revolution, i.e., a revolution having as its aim the limitation of the power of the ruler . . . All the troubles in Russian history were popular rebellions without politi cal character, in the strict meaning of the word; their causes were doubt in the legitimacy of the ruling person, dissatis faction with the serfdom that was oppressing the people to an ever greater extent than had been foreseen by the laws, and finally high-handedness and violence, which necessarily develop in Russia's borderlands, in the unceasing struggle of the Cossacks with the Tartars and other nomads. . . .

With legality in the succession of the throne secured, with civil order introduced among the Cossacks, and finally with the liberation of the peasants, all the reasons which in former times had agitated the people disappeared; and even an ordinary rebellion, going beyond the limits of a regrettable misunderstanding, has become impossible in Russia so long as the moral character of the Russian people does not change. . . .

To what degree moderation, an easygoing nature, and common sense characterize both the Russian people and Russian society has been clearly demonstrated by the events of the last years. As far as the historical memory of mankind can go back, one can scarcely find faster, more sudden changes, within the general social conditions of popular life than those that took place before our eyes. . . . The change from oppressive servitude to full freedom was sudden. . . . Even when the new authority of the communal organization was not yet established, and the people existed in critical moments without any direct close authority, public order was nowhere disturbed, and no incitements could swerve the population from giving full confidence to the government either then or later. . . . It thus became clear to all, even to those who were ill-disposed to the reform and almost expected it to result in the fall of the hated colossus, that here (as always) Russia could lean on her broad, unshakable foundations. . . .

And so, what do we see? The abuses and the oppression from which Russia suffered before the reforms of the present reign were not smaller, but in many respects they were even more severe than the ones from which France suffered until the Revolution; the transformation was more radical than the one carried out by the French National Assembly. Yet, whereas the broken dam in France released a general flood of harmful antisocial instincts and passions, in Russia it could not disturb the peace, respect, and trust towards the authorities, but even emphasized them and strengthened all the foundations of the state. Are we not then entitled to assert that the Russian people and Russian society, in all social classes, are capable of accepting and enduring any amount of freedom, and that to advise its restriction can only be done by a distorted belief in self-created dangers or (what is even worse) under the influence of certain secret motives, unfair and hostile to Russian aspirations? Thus we may conclude that the Russian people, by their attitude towards the power of the state, by their ability to sacrifice to it their own personal interests, and by their attitude towards the use of political and civil freedom, are gifted with wonderful political sense.

In the socio-economic sphere, Russia is the only large state which has solid ground under its feet, in which there are no landless masses, and in which, consequently, the social edifice does not rest on the misery of the majority of the citizens and on the insecurity of their situation. In Russia only there cannot and does not exist any contradiction between political and economic ideals. This contradiction threatens disaster to European life, a life which has embarked on its historical voyage in the dangerous seas between the Charybdis of Caesarism or military despotism and the Scylla of social revolution. The factors that give such superiority to the Russian social structure over the European, and give it an unshakable stability, are the peasant's land and its common ownership. On this health of Russia's socio-economic structure we found our hope for the great socio-economic significance of the Slav cultural-historical type. This type has been able for the first time to create a just and normal system of human activity, which embraces not only human relations in the moral and political sphere, but also man's mastery of nature, which is a means of satisfying human needs and requirements. Thus it establishes not only formal equality in the relations between citizens, but a real and concrete equality.

However, as regards the prominent place of the Slav cultural-historical type in the field of culture proper, one must admit that so far the Russian and other Slav achievements in the sciences and in the arts are insignificant in comparison with the accomplishments of the two great cultural types, the Greek and the European. . . . Let us concentrate all our attention upon Russia, the only independent Slav state. The establishment of a state, we said, is the first historical activity of a people emerging through circumstances from a purely ethnographic existence, and such a people must progress to a certain point before it can become culturally productive. The difficulty of the political task which was the lot of the Russian people was such that it is no wonder that it took one thousand years and demanded all the national energy; yet the incomparably easier task of the Western peoples took the same length of time to be fulfilled. I have already mentioned the special obstacles that geography presented to the establishment and the consolidation of the Russian state. The large forests and steppes gave to a sparse population, still living at the ethnographic stage of its development, the possibility of escape from the burdens imposed by the state, the choice of refusing them without active opposition. When such a fate befalls a population already accustomed, from an earlier time, to living in a state and already possessed of some measure of education (as happened in the United States of America), and when security from outside attacks is assured without the necessity of a strong union or political centralization, then national activity

is directed in a struggle against nature, in the acquisition of wealth, whose value the population has already learned to understand. This is what gave American culture a primarily technical and industrial character. In Russia, on the contrary, where foreign enemies threatened on all sides, at first primarily from the East and later from the West, a lack of the governmental centralization needed to repel the enemies would inevitably have entailed the irrevocable loss of national independence.

Thus arose the need for the utmost concentration of governmental power, i.e., for an autocratic and monolithic government which would with unlimited strength drive and direct individual activity towards general goals. The conditions of American life, on the other hand, led to technical activity, under the weakest possible federative-democratic direction. In both cases, scientific and artistic activities receded into the background; their time had not yet come. The intense governmental activity of the Muscovite State was still further intensified by the Petrine reforms, the essential character of which was purely political and governmental, and not at all cultural. In principle everything was sacrificed to the state. . . . From the time of Peter, according to an expression adopted quite aptly in our country, all the people were harnessed into state service. The nobility were harnessed directly and the other classes indirectly; the merchant class by the fiscal character given to industry; the peasantry by its attachment either to the state or to the nobility. The necessity for such an enslavement of all the national forces for political goals could be explained by the fact that the European states, with which Russia had, *volens nolens*, to come into close political contact, had in the course of their existence become thickly populated, had achieved a harmonious order, and had accumulated a large scientific and industrial capital. Armies, which in the Middle Ages had not numbered more than a few tens of thousands, began from the time of Louis XIV on to number hundreds of thousands of soldiers, equipped with expensive armaments, the manufacture of which required a significant technological development in the country. This applied to an even greater degree to the navy. . . .

Scientific and artistic activity can thrive only under conditions of leisure, of an overflow of forces that remain free from daily toil. Could much leisure be left over among Russians and Slavs? . . . All these considerations fully answer, it seems to me, the question why until now Russia and the other Slav countries could not occupy a respected position in purely cultural activities. . . . But indications of these aptitudes, of these spiritual forces, which are necessary for brilliant achievements in the fields of science and art are now indisputably present among the Slav peoples in spite of all the unfavorable conditions of their life; and, consequently, we are justified in expecting that with a change in these conditions, these peoples will bring forth remarkable creations. . . .

The Slav cultural type has already produced enough examples of artistic and, to a lesser degree, scientific achievements to allow us to conclude that it has attained a significant degree of development in these fields. The relative youth of the race and the concentration of all its forces upon other, more urgent types of activity have not, until now, given the Slavs the opportunity of acquiring cultural significance, in the exact meaning of the phrase. This should not embarrass us; rather, it points to the right path in our development. As long as there is no strong foundation, we cannot and we must not think of the erection of a du-

rable edifice; we can only set up temporary buildings, which cannot be expected to display the talents of the builder in every respect. The political independence of the race is the indispensable foundation of culture, and consequently all the Slav forces must be directed towards this goal. Independence is indispensable in two respects: without the consciousness of Slav racial unity, as distinct from other races, an independent culture is impossible; and without fruitful interaction between the Slav peoples, liberated from foreign powers and from their national divisions, diversity and richness of culture are impossible. A well-known example of the beneficial influence of unity is the relationship and interaction between the spiritual developments of Great Russia and the Ukraine.

The requisite preliminary achievement of political independence has still another importance in the cultural as well as in all other spheres: the struggle against the Germano-Roman world (without which Slav independence is impossible) will help to eradicate the cancer of imitativeness and the servile attitude towards the West, which through unfavorable conditions has eaten its way into the Slav body and soul. Only now has the historical moment for this cultural development arrived: only with the emancipation of the peasantry can the period of Russian cultural life begin, and her purely state period of life (which consisted in leading the people from tribal will to civil liberty) end. But first, as a *sine qua non* condition of success, strong and powerful Russia has to face the difficult task of liberating her racial brothers; for this struggle, she must steel them and herself in the spirit of independence and Pan-Slav consciousness.

Thus, on the basis of our analysis of the preceding cultural-historical types and of the peculiarities of the Slav world, we can maintain the fundamental hope that the Slav cultural-historical type will, for the first time in history, accomplish a synthesis of all aspects of cultural activity—aspects which were elaborated by its precursors on the historical scene, either in isolation or in incomplete union. We may hope that the Slav type will be the first to embody all four basic cultural activities, the religious, the political, the esthetic-scientific, and the socio-economic. . . .

Two sources on the banks of the ancient Nile begin the main flow of universal history. One, heavenly and divine, has reached Kiev and Moscow with unsullied purity by way of Palestine and Tsargrad [Constantinople]; the other, earthly and human, divided itself into two main streams, that of esthetic-scientific culture and that of politics, which flowed through Athens, Alexandria, and Rome into Europe, drying up temporarily, then enriching themselves with new and ever more abundant waters. On Russian soil a new fountainhead, a fourth river, originates, providing the popular masses with a just socio-economic structure. These four streams will unite on the wide plains of Slavdom into a mighty sea.

34

THE FALSEHOOD OF DEMOCRACY

By Konstantin Pobedonostsev

Pobedonostsev (1827–1907) began his long career as a civil servant in the 1840's. In 1859 he became professor of civil law at Moscow University and wrote a three-volume text on the subject which was used until the end of the century. He was a member of the government committee which drafted the judicial reforms of 1864. In the following year he became tutor of the Imperial children, the future Alexander III and Nicholas II. From 1872 he was a member of the State Council and from 1880 to 1905 occupied the important post of Procurator of the Holy Synod. In that office his name became synonymous with ultra-conservative policies. He is said to have served as a a model for Dostoevski's Grand Inquisitor. The volume from which we have chosen selections was translated into English, German, French, and Italian.

There is yet no biography of the man, but several articles can be used. See "Pobedonostsev and Alexander III," *Slavonic and East European Review*, VII, 30–54. Warren Walsh has written on "Pobedonostsev and Pan-Slavism," *Russian Review*, VIII, 316–21. P. Schilovsky's "Reminiscences of Pobedonostsev," *Slavonic and East European Review*, XXX, 364–75, discusses some of the relevant memoirs. Arthur Adams has written "Pobedonostsev and the Rule of Firmness," *Slavonic and East European Review*, XXXII, 132–39, and "Pobedonostsev's Thought Control," *Russian Review*, XI, 241–46. Robert Byrnes analyzes "Pobedonostsev as a Historian," in Stuart Hughes (ed.), *Teachers of History*, pp. 105–21, and "The Pobedonostsev Family," *Indiana Slavic Studies*, II, 63–78; see also his "Pobedonostsev on the Instruments of Russian Government," in *Continuity and Change in Russian and Soviet Thought*, edited by Ernest Simmons. Also of interest is the translation of Pobedonostsev, "Russia and Popular Education: A Reply to Prince Kropotkin," *North American Review*, CLXXIII (1901), 349–54. See also Robert Byrnes, "Dostoevski and Pobedonostsev," *Essays in Russian and Soviet History*, edited by John S. Curtiss. M. Wren writes on "Pobedonostsev and Russian Influence in the Balkans," *Journal of Modern History*, XIX, 130–41. For an essay on Pobedonostsev see Richard Hare, *Portraits of Russian Personalities between Reform and Revolution*. See also Edward Thaden, *Conservative Nationalism in 19th Century Russia*. The *Reflections of a Russian Statesman* are now available in paperback.

THE NEW DEMOCRACY

What is this freedom by which so many minds are agitated, which inspires so many insensate actions, so many wild From K. Pobedonostsev, *Reflections of a Russian Statesman* (London: Grant Richards, 1898), pp. 26–44, 62–69, 75–79.

390

speeches, which leads the people so often to misfortune? In the democratic sense of the word, freedom is the right of political power, or, to express it otherwise, the right to participate in the government of the State. This universal aspiration for a share in government has no constant limitations, and seeks no definite issue, but incessantly extends. . . . For ever extending its base, the new Democracy now aspires to universal suffrage—a fatal error, and one of the most remarkable in the history of mankind. By this means, the political power so passionately demanded by Democracy would be shattered into a number of infinitesimal bits, of which each citizen acquires a single one. What will he do with it, then? How will he employ it? In the result it has undoubtedly been shown that in the attainment of this aim Democracy violates its sacred formula of "Freedom indissolubly joined with Equality." It is shown that this apparently equal distribution of "freedom" among all involves the total destruction of equality. Each vote, representing an inconsiderable fragment of power, by itself signifies nothing; an aggregation of votes alone has a relative value. The result may be likened to the general meetings of shareholders in public companies. By themselves individuals are ineffective, but he who controls a number of these fragmentary forces is master of all power and directs all decisions and dispositions. We may well ask in what consists the superiority of Democracy. Everywhere the strongest man becomes master of the State; sometimes a fortunate and resolute general, sometimes a monarch or administrator with knowledge, dexterity, a clear plan of action, and a determined will. In a Democracy, the real rulers are the dexterous manipulators of votes, with their placemen, the mechanics who so skilfully operate the hidden springs which

move the puppets in the area of democratic elections. Men of this kind are ever ready with loud speeches lauding equality; in reality, they rule the people as any despot or military dictator might rule it. The extension of the right to participate in elections is regarded as progress and as the conquest of freedom by democratic theorists, who hold that the more numerous the participants in political rights, the greater is the probability that all will employ this right in the interests of the public welfare, and for the increase of the freedom of the people. Experience proves a very different thing. The history of mankind bears witness that the most necessary and fruitful reforms—the most durable measures—emanated from the supreme will of statesmen, or from a minority enlightened by lofty ideas and deep knowledge, and that, on the contrary, the extension of the representative principle is accompanied by an abasement of political ideas and the vulgarization of opinions in the mass of the electors. It shows also that this extension—in great States—was inspired by secret aims to the centralisation of power, or led directly to dictatorship. In France, universal suffrage was suppressed with the end of the Terror, and was re-established twice merely to affirm the autocracy of the two Napoleons. In Germany, the establishment of universal suffrage served merely to strengthen the high authority of a famous statesman who had acquired popularity by the success of his policy. What its ultimate consequences will be, Heaven only knows!

The manipulation of votes in the game of Democracy is of the commonest occurrence in most European states, and its falsehood, it would seem, has been exposed to all; yet few dare openly to rebel against it. The unhappy people must bear the burden, while the Press, herald of a suppositious public opinion, stifles the cry of the people with its shibboleth, "Great is Diana of the Ephesians." But to an impartial mind, all this is nothing better than a struggle of parties, and a shuffling with numbers and names. The voters, by themselves inconsiderable unities, acquire a value in the hands of dexterous agents. This value is realised by many means—mainly, by bribery in innumerable forms, from gifts of money and trifling articles, to the distribution of places in the services, the financial departments, and the administration. Little by little a class of electors has been formed which lives by the sale of votes to one or another of the political organisations. So far has this gone in France, for instance, that serious, intelligent, and industrious citizens in immense numbers abstain from voting, through the difficulty of contending with the cliques of political agents. With bribery go violence and threats, and reigns of terror are organised at elections, by the help of which the respective cliques advance their candidates; hence the stormy scenes at electoral demonstrations, in which arms have been used, and the field of battle strewn with the bodies of the killed and wounded.

Organisation and bribery—these are the two mighty instruments which are employed with such success for the manipulation of the mass of electors. Such methods are in no way new. Thucydides depicts in vivid colours their employment in the ancient republics of Greece. The history of the Roman Republic presents monstrous examples of corruption as the chief instrument of factions at elections. But in our times a new means has been found of working the masses for political aims, and joining them in adventitious alliances by provoking a factitious community of views. This is the art of rapid and dexterous generalisation of ideas, the composition of phrase and formulas, dissem-inated with the confidence of burning conviction as the last word of science, as dogmas of politicology, as infallible appreciations of events, of men, and of institutions. At one time it was believed that the faculty of analysing facts and deducing general principles was the privilege of a few enlightened minds and deep thinkers; now it is considered a universal attainment, and, under the name of convictions, the generalities of political science have become a sort of current money, coined by newspapers and rhetoricians.

The faculty of seizing and assimilating on faith these abstract ideas has spread among the mass, and become infectious, more especially to men insufficiently or superficially educated, who constitute the great majority everywhere. This tendency of the people is exploited with success by politicians who seek power; the art of creating generalities serves for them as a most convenient instrument. All deduction proceeds by the path of abstraction; from a number of facts the immaterial are eliminated, the essential elements collated, classified, and general formulas deduced. It is plain that the justice and value of these formulas depend upon how many of the premisses are essential, and how many of those eliminated are irrelevant. The speed and ease with which abstract conclusions are arrived at are explained by the unceremonious methods observed in this process of selection of relevant facts and in their treatment. Hence the great success of orators, and the extraordinary effect of the abstractions which they cast to the people. The crowd is easily attracted by commonplaces and generalities invested in sonorous phrases; it cares nothing for proof which is inaccessible to it; thus is formed unanimity of thought, a unanimity fictitious and visionary, but in its consequences actual enough. This is called the "voice of the people," with the pendant, the "voice of God." It is a deplorable error. The ease with which men are drawn by commonplaces leads everywhere to extreme demoralisation of public thought, and to the weakening of the political sense of the people. Of this, France to-day presents a striking example, and England also has not escaped the infection.

THE GREAT FALSEHOOD
OF OUR TIME

. . . Among the falsest of political principles is the principle of the sovereignty of the people, the principle that all power issues from the people, and is based upon the national will—a principle which has unhappily become more firmly established since the time of the French Revolution. Thence proceeds the theory of Parliamentarism, which, up to the present day, has deluded much of the so-called "intelligence," and unhappily infatuated certain foolish Russians. It continues to maintain its hold on many minds with the obstinacy of a narrow fanaticism, although every day its falsehood is exposed more clearly to the world.

In what does the theory of Parliamentarism consist? It is supposed that the people in its assemblies makes its own law, and elects responsible officers to execute its will. Such is the ideal conception. Its immediate realisation is impossible. The historical development of society necessitates that local communities increase in numbers and complexity; that separate races be assimilated, or, retaining their polities and languages, unite under a single flag, that territory extend indefinitely; under such conditions direct government by the people is impracticable. The people must, therefore, delegate its right of power to its representatives, and invest them with administrative autonomy. These repre-

sentatives in turn cannot govern immediately, but are compelled to elect a still smaller number of trustworthy persons—ministers—to whom they entrust the preparation and execution of the laws, the apportionment and collection of taxes, the appointment of subordinate officials, and the disposition of the militant forces.

In the abstract this mechanism is quite symmetrical: for its proper operation many conditions are essential. The working of the political machine is based on impersonal forces constantly acting and completely balanced. It may act successfully only when the delegates of the people abdicate their personalities; when on the benches of Parliament sit mechanical fulfillers of the people's behests; when the ministers of State remain impersonal, absolute executors of the will of the majority; when the elected representatives of the people are capable of understanding precisely, and executing conscientiously, the programme of activity, mathematically expressed, which has been delivered to them. Given such conditions the machine would work exactly, and would accomplish its purpose. The law would actually embody the will of the people; administrative measures would actually emanate from Parliament; the pillars of the State would rest actually on the elective assemblies, and each citizen would directly and consciously participate in the management of public affairs.

Such is the theory. Let us look at the practice. Even in the classic countries of Parliamentarism it would satisfy not one of the conditions enumerated. The elections in no way express the will of the electors. The popular representatives are in no way restricted by the opinions of their constituents, but are guided by their own views and considerations, modified by the tactics of their opponents. In reality, ministers are autocratic, and they rule, rather than are ruled by, Parliament. They attain power, and lose power, not by virtue of the will of the people, but through immense personal influence, or the influence of a strong party which places them in power, or drives them from it. They dispose of the force and resources of the nation at will, they grant immunities and favours, they maintain a multitude of idlers at the expense of the people, and they fear no censure while they enjoy the support in Parliament of a majority which they maintain by the distribution of bounties from the rich tables which the State has put at their disposal. In reality, the ministers are as irresponsible as the representatives of the people. Mistakes, abuse of power, and arbitrary acts are of daily occurrence, yet how often do we hear of the grave responsibility of a minister? It may be once in fifty years a minister is tried for his crimes, with a result contemptible when compared with the celebrity gained by the solemn procedure.

Were we to attempt a true definition of Parliament, we should say that Parliament is an institution serving for the satisfaction of the personal ambition, vanity, and self-interest of its members. The institution of Parliament is indeed one of the greatest illustrations of human delusion. Enduring in the course of centuries the tyranny of autocratic and oligarchical governments, and ignoring that the evils of autocracy are the evils of society itself, men of intellect and knowledge have laid the responsibility for their misfortunes on their rulers and on their systems of government, and imagined that by substituting for these systems government by the will of the people, or representative government, society would be delivered from all the evils and violence which it endured. What is the result? The result is that, *mutato nomine,* all has remained essen-

tially as before, and men, retaining the weaknesses and failings of their nature, have transfused in the new institutions their former impulses and tendencies. As before, they are ruled by personal will, and in the interests of privileged persons, but this personal will is no longer embodied in the person of the sovereign, but in the person of the leader of a party; and privilege no longer belongs to an aristocracy of birth, but to a majority ruling in Parliament and controlling the State. . . .

Thus the representative principle works in practice. The ambitious man comes before his fellow-citizens, and strives by every means to convince them that he is more than any other worthy of their confidence. What motives impel him to this quest? It is hard to believe that he is impelled by disinterested zeal for the public good.

In our time, nothing is so rare as men imbued with a feeling of solidarity with the people, ready for labour and self-sacrifice for the public good; this is the ideal nature, but such natures are little inclined to come into contact with the baseness of the world. He who, in the consciousness of duty, is capable of disinterested service of the community does not descend to the soliciting of votes, or the crying of his own praise at election meetings in loud and vulgar phrases. Such men manifest their strength in their own work, in a small circle of congenial friends, and scorn to seek popularity in the noisy marketplace. If they approach the crowd, it is not to flatter it, or to pander to its basest instincts and tendencies, but to condemn its follies and expose its depravity. To men of duty and honour the procedure of elections is repellent; the only men who regard it without abhorrence are selfish, egoistic natures, which wish thereby to attain their personal ends. To acquire popularity such men have little scruple in assuming the mask of ardour for the public good. They cannot and must not be modest, for with modesty they would not be noticed or spoken of. By their positions, and by the parts they have chosen, they are forced to be hypocrites and liars; they must cultivate, fraternise with, and be amiable to their opponents to gain their suffrages; they must lavish promises, knowing that they cannot fulfil them; and they must pander to the basest tendencies and prejudices of the masses to acquire majorities for themselves. What honourable nature would accept such a role? Describe it in a novel, the reader would be repelled, but in elections the same reader gives his vote to the living *artiste* in the same role. . . .

On the day of polling few give their votes intelligently: these are the individual, influential electors whom it has been worth while to convince in private. The mass of the electors, after the practice of the herd, votes for one of the candidates nominated by the committees. Not one exactly knows the man, or considers his character, his capacity, his convictions; all vote merely because they have heard his name so often. It would be vain to struggle against this herd. If a level-headed elector wishes to act intelligently in such a grave affair, and not to give way to the violence of the committee, he would have to abstain altogether, or to give his vote for his candidate according to his conviction. However he might act, he could not prevent the election of the candidate favoured by the mass of frivolous, indifferent, and prejudiced electors.

In theory, the elected candidate must be the favourite of the majority; in fact, he is the favourite of a minority, sometimes very small, but representing an organised force, while the majority, like sand, has no coherence, and is therefore incapable of resisting the clique and the faction. In theory, the election favours the intelligent and capable; in reality, it favours the pushing and impudent. It might be thought that education, experience, conscientiousness in work, and wisdom in affairs, would be essential requirements in the candidate; in reality, whether these qualities exist or not, they are in no way needed in the struggle of the election, where the essential qualities are audacity, a combination of impudence and oratory, and even some vulgarity, which invariably acts on the masses; modesty, in union with delicacy of feeling and thought, is worth nothing.

Thus comes forth the representative of the people, thus he acquires his power. How does he employ it, how will he turn it to advantage? If energetic by nature he will attempt to form a party; if he is of an ordinary nature, then he joins himself to one party or another. The leader of a party above all things requires a resolute will. This is an organic quality, like physical strength, and does not by any means inevitably accompany moral excellence. With limited intellect, with infinite egoism and even wickedness, with base and dishonest tendencies, a man with a strong will may become a leader in Parliament, and may control the decisions of a party which contains men far surpassing him in moral and intellectual worth. Such may be the character of a ruling force in Parliament. To this should be joined another decisive force—eloquence. This also is a natural faculty, involving neither moral character, nor high intellectual culture. A man may be a deep thinker, a poet, a skilful general, a subtle jurist, an experienced legislator, and at the same time may not enjoy the gift of fluent speech, while, on the contrary, one with ordinary intellectual capacity and knowledge may possess a special gift of eloquence. The union of this gift with a plenitude of intellectual power is a rare and exceptional phenomenon in Parliamentary life. The most brilliant improvisations, which have given glory to orators, and determined grave decisions, when read are as colourless and contemptible as descriptions of scenes enacted in former times by celebrated actors and singers. Experience shows that in great assemblies the decision does not belong to reason, but to daring and brilliancy; that the arguments most effective on the mass are not the most symmetrical—the most truly taken from the nature of things, but those expressed in sounding words and phrases, artfully selected, constantly reiterated, and calculated on the instinct of baseness always dominant in the people. The masses are easily drawn by outbursts of empty declamation, and under such influences often form sudden decisions, which they regret on cold-blooded consideration of the affair. . . .

What is a Parliamentary party? In theory, it is an alliance of men with common convictions, joining forces for the realisation of their views in legislation and administration. But this description applies only to small parties; the large party, which alone is an effective force in Parliament, is formed under the influence only of personal ambition, and centres itself around one commanding personality. By nature, men are divided into two classes—those who tolerate no power above them, and therefore of necessity strive to rule others; and those who by their nature dread the responsibility inseparable from independent action, and who shrink from any resolute exercise of will. These were born for submission, and together constitute a herd, which follows the men of will and resolution, who form the minority. Thus the most talented persons submit willingly, and gladly entrust to stronger hands the control of affairs and the mor-

al responsibility for their direction. Instinctively they seek a leader, and become his obedient instruments, inspired by the conviction that he will lead them to victory—and, often, to spoil. Thus all the important actions of Parliament are controlled by the leaders of the party, who inspire all decisions, who lead in combat, and profit by victory. The public sessions are no more than a spectacle for the mass. Speeches are delivered to sustain the fiction of Parliamentarism, but seldom a speech by itself affects the decision of Parliament in a grave affair. Speech-making serves for the glory of orators, for the increase of their popularity, and the making of their careers; only on rare occasions does it affect the distribution of votes. Majorities and minorities are usually decided before the session begins. . . .

Such is the Parliamentary institution, exalted as the summit and crown of the edifice of State. It is sad to think that even in Russia there are men who aspire to the establishment of this falsehood among us; that our professors glorify to their young pupils representative government as the ideal of political science; that our newspapers pursue it in their articles and feuilletons, under the name of justice and order, without troubling to examine without prejudice the working of the parliamentary machine. Yet even where centuries have sanctified its existence, faith already decays; the Liberal intelligence exalts it, but the people groans under its despotism and recognises its falsehood. We may not see, but our children and grandchildren assuredly will see, the overthrow of this idol, which contemporary thought in its vanity continues still to worship.

THE PRESS

From the day that man first fell falsehood has ruled the world—ruled it in human speech, in the practical business of life, in all its relations and institutions. But never did the Father of Lies spin such webs of falsehood of every kind, as in this restless age when we hear so many falsehoods uttered everywhere on Truth. With the growing complexity of social problems increases the number of relations and institutions pervaded with falsehood through and through. At every step appears some splendid edifice bearing the legend, "Here is Truth." Do you enter—you tread on falsehoods at every step. Would you expose the falsehoods which have angered you, the world will turn on you with anger greater still, and bid you trust and preach that this is truth, and truth unassailable.

Thus we are bidden to believe that the judgments of newspapers and periodicals, the judgments of the so-called Press, are the expression of public opinion. This, too, is a falsehood. The Press is one of the falsest institutions of our time. . . .

In our age the judgment of others has assumed an organised form, and calls itself Public Opinion. Its organ and representative is the Press. In truth, the importance of the Press is immense, and may be regarded as the most characteristic fact of our time—more characteristic even than our remarkable discoveries and inventions in the realm of technical science. No government, no law, no custom can withstand its destructive activity when, from day to day, through the course of years, the Press repeats and disseminates among the people its condemnations of institutions or of men.

What is the secret of this strength? Certainly not the novelties and sensations with which the newspaper is filled, but its declared policy—the political and philosophical ideas propagated in its articles, and selection and classification of its news and rumours, and the peculiar illumination which it casts up-

on them. The newspaper has usurped the position of judicial observer of the events of the day; it judges not only the actions and words of men, but affects a knowledge of their unexpressed opinions, their intentions, and their enterprises; it praises and condemns at discretion; it incites some, threatens others; drags to the pillory one, and others exalts as idols to be adored and examples worthy of the emulation of all. In the name of Public Opinion it bestows rewards on some, and punishes others with the severity of excommunication. The question naturally occurs: Who are these representatives of this terrible power, Public Opinion? Whence is derived their right and authority to rule in the name of the community, to demolish existing institutions, and to proclaim new ideals of ethics and legislation?

But no one attempts to answer this question; all talk loudly of the liberty of the Press as the first and essential element of social well-being. Even in Russia, so libelled by the lying Press of Europe, such words are heard. Our so-called Slavophiles, with amazing inconsistency, share the same delusion, although their avowed object is to reform and renovate the institutions of their country upon a historic basis. Having joined the chorus of Liberals, in alliance with the propagandists of revolution, they proclaim exactly in the manner of the West: "Public Opinion—that is, the collective thought, guided by the natural love of right in all—is the final judge in all matters of public interest; therefore no restriction upon freedom of speech can be allowed, for such restriction can only express the tyranny of the minority over the will of the mass."

Such is a current proposition of the newest Liberalism. It is accepted by many in good faith, and there are few who, having troubled to analyse it, have discerned how it is based upon falsehood and self-deception.

It conflicts with the first principles of logic, for it is based on the fallacious premiss that the opinions of the public and of the Press are identical.

To test the validity of this claim, it is only needful to consider the origin of newspapers, and the characters of their makers.

Any vagabond babbler or unacknowledged genius, any enterprising tradesman with his own money or with the money of others, may found a newspaper, even a great newspaper. He may attract a host of writers and feuilletonists, ready to deliver judgment on any subject at a moment's notice; he may hire illiterate reporters to keep him supplied with rumours and scandals. His staff is then complete. From that day he sits in judgment on all the world, on ministers and administrators, on literature and art, on finance and industry. It is true that the new journal becomes a power only when it is sold in the market—that is, when it circulates among the public. For this talent is needed, and the matter published must be attractive and congenial for the readers. Here, we might think, was some guarantee of the moral value of the undertaking—men of talent will not serve a feeble or contemptible editor or publisher; the public will not support a newspaper which is not a faithful echo of public opinion. This guarantee is fictitious. Experience proves that money will attract talent under any conditions, and that talent is ready to write as its paymaster requires. Experience proves that the most contemptible persons—retired moneylenders, Jewish factors, newsvendors, and bankrupt gamblers—may found newspapers, secure the services of talented writers, and place their editions on the market as organs of public opin-

ion. The healthy taste of the public is not to be relied upon. The great mass of readers, idlers for the most part, is ruled less by a few healthy instincts than by a base and despicable hankering for idle amusement; and the support of the people may be secured by any editor who provides for the satisfaction of these hankerings, for the love of scandal, and for intellectual pruriency of the basest kind. Of this we meet with evidence daily; even in our own capital no search is necessary to find it; it is enough to note the supply and demand at the newsvendors' shops, and at the railway stations. All of us have observed the triviality of conversation in society; in provincial towns, in the government capitals, the recreations of the people are well known—gambling, scandal, and anecdotes are the chief. Even conversation on the so-called social and political questions takes in a great measure the form of censure and aphorisms, plentifully supplemented with scandal and anecdote. This is a rich and fruitful soil for the tradesmen of literature, and there, as poisonous fungi, spring up organs of calumny, ephemeral and permanent, impudently extolling themselves as organs of public opinion. The great part which in the idle life of government towns is played by anonymous letters and lampoons, which, unhappily, are so common among us, is played in the newspaper by "correspondence," sent from various quarters or composed in the editorial offices, by the reports and rumours invented by ignorant reporters, and by the atrocious practice of blackmailing, often the strongest weapon of the newspaper press. Such a paper may flourish, attain consideration as an organ of public opinion, and be immensely remunerative to its owners, while no paper conducted upon firm moral principles, or founded to meet the healthier instincts of the people could compete with it for a moment.

This phenomenon is worthy of close inspection, for we find in it the most incongruous product of modern culture, the more incongruous where the principles of the new Liberalism have taken root, where the sanction of election, the authority of the popular will, is needed for every institution, where the ruling power is vested in the hands of individuals, and derived from the suffrages of the majority in the representative assemblies. For the journalist with a power comprehending all things, requires no sanction. He derives his authority from no election, he receives support from no one. His newspaper becomes an authority in the State, and for this authority no endorsement is required. The man in the street may establish such an organ, and exercise the concomitant authority with an irresponsibility enjoyed by no other power in the world. That this is in no way exaggeration there are innumerable proofs. How often have superficial and unscrupulous journalists paved the way for revolution, fomented irritation into enmity, and brought about desolating wars! For conduct such as this a monarch would lose his throne, a minister would be disgraced, impeached, and punished; but the journalist stands dry above the waters he has disturbed, from the ruin he has caused he rises triumphant, and briskly continues his destructive work.

This is by no means the worst. When a judge has power to dishonour us, to deprive us of our property and of our freedom, he receives his power from the hands of the State only after such prolonged labour and experience as qualify him for his calling. His power is restricted by rigorous laws, his judgments are subject to revision by higher powers, and his sentence may be altered or commuted. The journalist has the fullest power to defame and dishonour me, to injure my material interests, even to restrict my liberty by attacks which force me to leave my place of abode. These judicial powers he has usurped; no higher authority has conferred them upon him; he has never proven by examination his fitness to exercise them; he has in no way shown his trustworthiness or his impartiality; his court is ruled by no formal procedure; and from his judgment there lies no appeal. Its defenders assure us that the Press itself heals the wounds it has inflicted; but any thinking mind can see that these are mere idle words. The attacks of the Press on individuals may cause irreparable injury. Retractions and explanations can in no way give them full satisfaction. Not half of those who read the denunciatory article will read the apology or the explanation, and in the minds of the mass of frivolous readers insulting or calumnious suggestions leave behind an ineffaceable stain. Criminal prosecution for defamation is but the feeblest defence, and civil action seldom succeeds in exposing the offender, while it subjects the offended to fresh attack. The journalist, moreover, has a thousand means of wounding and terrifying individuals without furnishing them with sufficient grounds for legal prosecution.

It is hard to imagine a despotism more irresponsible and violent than the despotism of printed words. Is it not strange and irrational, then, that those who struggle most for the preservation of this despotism are the impassioned champions of freedom, the ferocious enemies of legal restrictions and of all interference by the established authority. We cannot help remembering those wise men who went mad because they knew of their wisdom.

PUBLIC INSTRUCTION

. . . Take, for instance, the phrases, repeated unto weariness among us, and everywhere: Free Education, Obligatory Attendance, the Restriction of Child-Labour During the Years of Obligatory Attendance. There can be no question that learning is light, and that ignorance is darkness, but in the application of this rule we must take care to be ruled by common-sense, and so to abstain from violating that freedom, of which we hear so much, and which our legislators so ruthlessly restrict. Inspired by an idle saying that the schoolmaster won the battle of Sadowa, we multiply our model schools and schoolmasters, ignoring the requirements both of children and of parents, of climate, and of nature itself. We refuse to recognise, what experience has shown, that the school is a deceptive formality where its roots have taken no hold among the people, where it fails to meet the people's necessities, and to accord with the economy of its life. That school alone is suited to the people which pleases them, and the enlightening influence of which they see and feel; but all schools are repugnant to them to which they are driven by force, under threats of punishment, or which are organised, in ignorance of the people's tastes and necessities, on the fantasies of doctrinaires. In such schools the work becomes mechanical; the school resembles an office with all the formality and weariness which office life involves. The legislator is satisfied when he has founded and organised in certain localities a certain number of similar institutions adorned with the inscription —School. For these establishments money must be raised; attendance is secured under penalty; a great staff of inspectors is organised whose duty it is to see that parents and poor and working men send their children to school at the established age. Already all Governments have transgressed the line at which pub-

lic instruction begins to show its reverse side. Everywhere official education flourishes at the expense of that real education in the sphere of domestic, professional, and social life which is a vital element of success.

But infinite evil has been wrought by the prevalent confusion of knowledge and power. Seduced by the fantasy of universal enlightenment, we misname education a certain sum of knowledge acquired by completing the courses of schools, skilfully elaborated in the studies of pedagogues. Having organised our school thus, we isolate it from life, and secure by force the attendance of children whom we subject to a process of intellectual training in accordance with our programme. But we ignore or forget that the mass of the children whom we educate must earn their daily bread, a labour for which the abstract notions on which our programmes are constructed will be vain; while in the interests of some imaginary knowledge we withhold that training in productive labour which alone will bear fruit. Such are the results of our complex educational system, and such are the causes of the aversion with which the masses regard our schools, for which they can find no use.

The vulgar conception of education is true enough, but unhappily it is disregarded in the organisation of the modern school. In the popular mind the function of a school is to teach the elements of reading, writing, and arithmetic, and, in union with these, the duty of knowing, loving, and fearing God, of loving our native land, and of honouring our parents. These are the elements of knowledge and the sentiments which together form the basis of conscience in man, and give to him the moral strength needed for the preservation of his equilibrium in life, for the maintenance of struggle with the evil impulses of his nature and with the evil sentiments and temptations of the mind. It is an unhappy day when education tears the child from the surroundings in which he first acquired the elements of his future calling, those exercises of his early years through which he acquires, almost unconsciously, the taste and capacity for work. The boy who wishes to become a bachelor or a master of arts must begin his studies at a certain age, and in due time pass through a given course of knowledge; but the vast majority of children must learn to live by the work of their hands. For such work physical training is needed from the earliest age. To close the door to such preparation, that time may be saved for the teaching of schools, is to place a burden upon the lives of the masses who have to struggle for their daily bread, and to shackle in the family the natural development of those economic forces which together constitute the capital of the commonwealth. The sailor qualifies for his calling by spending his boyhood on the sea; the miner prepares for his work by early years spent in the sub-terranean passages of mines. To the agriculturist it is even more essential that he shall become accustomed for his future work, that he may learn to love it in childhood, in the presence of nature, beside his herds and his plough, in the midst of his fields and his meadows.

Yet we waste our time discussing courses for elementary schools and obligatory programmes which are to be the bases of a finished education. One would include an encyclopaedic instruction under the barbarous term *Rodino-vyedenie* (knowledge of the fatherland); another insists on the necessity for the agriculturist to know physics, chemistry, agricultural economy, and medicine; while a third demands a course of political economy and jurisprudence. But few reflect that by tearing the child from the domestic hearth for such a lofty destiny, they deprive his parents of a productive force which is essential to the maintenance of the home, while by raising before his eyes the mirage of illusory learning they corrupt his mind, and subject it to the temptations of vanity and conceit.

35

RUSSIAN LIBERALS

By Paul Milyukov

In 1903 the Chicago industrialist Charles R. Crane brought Paul Milyukov to the University of Chicago for a summer course of lectures entitled "Russian Civilization." Milyukov's lectures were published during his second visit to this country. Below is reproduced part of the conclusion to his volume. A prominent student of Kluchevsky, Milyukov (1859–1943) began as a historian and wrote the most popular historical work of pre-revolutionary Russia, *Outlines of Russian Culture*, part of which has been published in English (in three paperback volumes). In the 1890's he was deprived of his teaching post at Moscow University for political reasons. He soon became the leader of Russian liberalism. In the years 1905–17 he headed the Constitutional Democratic party (Kadets) and became the Duma's leading deputy. He was foreign minister of the first Provisional Government and opposed the Bolshevik rise to power. In 1918 he left Russia for France where he continued to write and publish a newspaper until his death.

For a biography of Milyukov see *A Russian European*, by Thomas Riha. See also the the same author's "Miliukov and the Progressive Bloc in 1915," *Journal of Modern History*, Vol. XXXII, and "Riech': Portrait of a Russian Newspaper," *Slavic Review*, December, 1963, as well as "1917: A Year of Illusions," *Soviet Studies*, July, 1967. For other articles about Miliukov see the following: Alexis Goldenweiser, "Paul Miliukov: Historian and Statesman," *Russian Review*, Vol. XVI; Boris Elkin, "Paul Miliukov," *Slavonic and East European Review*, Vol. XXIII; Robert Tuck, "Paul Miliukov and Negotiations for a Duma Ministry, 1906," *American Slavic and East European Review*, Vol. X; and Clarence Smith, "Miliukov and the Russian National Question," *Harvard Slavic Studies*, Vol. IV. See also the chapter on Miliukov in Donald Treadgold, *Lenin and His Rivals*, as well as Michael Karpovich, "Two Types of Russian Liberalism: Miliukov and Maklakov," in *Continuity and Change in Russian and Soviet Thought*, edited by Ernest Simmons. *Russia Today and Tomorrow* is another English volume by Miliukov himself.

For a history of Russian liberalism until 1905 see George Fischer, *Russian Liberalism*. Fedor Rodichev, a prominent Russian liberal, has written "The Liberal Movement in Russia," *Slavonic and East European Review*, Vols. II and VII. In the latter volume there is also his essay on "The Veteran of Russian Liberalism, Ivan Petrunkevich." Bernard Pares has contributed "Two Great Russian Liberals, Peter Struve and Sergius Bulgakov," *ibid.*, Vol. XXIII. There is a study of "The Russian Liberals and the 1906 Anglo-French Loan to Russia," *ibid.*, Vol. XXXIX. Ariadna Tyrkova has written "The Cadet Party," *Russian Review*, Vol. XII, and "Russian Liberalism," Vol. X of the same journal. See also V. King, "The Liberal

Movement in Russia, 1904–5," *Slavonic and East European Review*, Vol. XIV; E. Tartak, "The Liberal Tradition in Russia," in *European Ideologies*, edited by Felix Gross; Donald Treadgold, "The Constitutional Democrats and the Russian Liberal Tradition," *American Slavic and East European Review*, Vol. X; and Marc Raeff, "Reflections on Russian Liberalism," *Russian Review*, July 1959. For an analysis of the Russian political spectrum before 1917 see Sergei Utechin, *Russian Political Thought* (paperback).

. . . If, now, we ask once more whether the Russian political tradition is firm and solid, we may answer that a real tradition here, just as in the sphere of religion, was broken by Peter the Great, and that since Peter's time no new tradition has sprung up, while the ancient one, having been entirely forgotten, cannot possibly be renewed. It is clear, therefore, that the existing political form, however firm and solid it may prove to be, owes its solidity not so much to any tradition as to the force of inertia, and to such multiform and numerous measures as the autocracy has been obliged to take in self-defense. And this very system of self-defense, whether from material violence or from public opinion, serves to prove how small are the resources of an ideal nature which may be relied upon by the autocracy. This observation we found to have been made already by Speransky, about a century ago.

While these lectures were proceeding at the University of Chicago, many of my hearers may have listened to the eloquent words of Professor Iyenaga on the subject of the civilization of his native country, Japan. For myself, as a Russian, his course of lectures was particularly instructive. When Mr. Iyenaga spoke of the old spirit of the Japanese warrior class—their gentry, the *booshi* —a spirit which he said was still living in the present generation; when he exalted the spirit of self-sacrifice with which the Japanese noblemen parted with half of their feudal income in order to maintain the national unity; when he

explained to us how the historical and religious claims of the central power at last overcame the opposing forces of the feudal elements; when he told us about the opposition of the popular religion to religious innovations, how the old popular belief kept on co-existing with the established church, and how the educated classes have recently grown irreligious—it seemed to me as if I were listening to the well-known melodies of a musical composition which in its *ensemble* was entirely strange. I think I have the key to the explanation of this similarity in parts and dissimilarity of the whole. The processes of "restoration" and "renaissance" which Professor Iyenaga described appear to have been the same as they were in Russia during the process of her political unification and Europeanization. But the tempo of these processes was quite different. Things that with us took centuries to pass away, in Japan appear to have been crowded in the short space of some decades. Now, one of the consequences of this rapidity of process is that the ancient tradition of Japan, as it were, had no time to die out, and has kept enough of its vitality to be able to enter into some degree of combination with the elements of the new life and culture.

A like combination was dreamed of by Russian Slavophils, but Russian history has provided us with ample evidence that no possibility of such com-

From P. Milyukov, *Russia and Its Crisis* (Chicago: University of Chicago Press, 1905), pp. 552–64. The book is now available in paperback.

bination between new and old exists any longer in Russia. The old tradition was too long a time in dying out, and elements of the new culture struck root too deeply. No living elements of the old historical tradition are now in existence. That is why some facts of Japanese life, as they were related by my brilliant colleague, may awaken in a Russian some reminiscences of a past never to be recalled, and may remind him of some aspirations long buried under new currents of life and thought.

But there is one discordant note in this comparison. Recent as is the new culture of Japan, and comparatively old as is our own new culture; heterogeneous as may be the mixture of the elements of old tradition and of new culture in Japan, and homogeneous as are the elements of progress with us, yet Professor Iyenaga appears to have had nothing to tell of any serious social or political struggle in his country, and it is chiefly with the elements of such struggle that I had to deal.

One explanation of the difference may be that society in Japan is not so much democratized as in Russia. It may be that it is not so much demanded by public opinion in Japan as in Russia. But another explanation is that much more is given. Japan enjoys the elementary condition of progress—a free political life—which we are yet striving to attain. The statesmen that reformed Japan seem to have acted upon the same wise counsel as was given to Alexander I by the greatest of Russian statesmen, Speransky, to the effect that patriotic battles should be permitted, not in the streets, not in the lecture-rooms of universities, not in annual sessions of Zemstvos, but within the walls of a national diet. The point of this advice was to keep in advance of public opinion. I do not know what Russian life would be like now, if, nearly a century ago, Emperor Alexan-

der had yielded to the patriotic pressure of Speransky and had inaugurated an era of political freedom. It is quite possible that the political opposition would have taken a much more peaceful form; that the old spirit of the warrior class, so prominent at the time of Catherine II and Alexander I, would have been preserved in a larger degree than it is now; that moderate elements would have played a much more conspicuous part in political life and in public opinion; that the struggle between the government and public opinion would not have taken the form of a continuous war between two different races, each possessing its own "patriotism" and its own "loyalty." All this might have been, and something of it may still come, if political conditions are made more normal; but with the system of self-defense of the autocracy, the actual events of our political life took an entirely different direction.

From what has just been said it may be inferred that the Russian government had the possibility of a choice, and that it freely chose the line it now follows. To be sure, this free choice would have been impossible had there been any social forces to compel the government to take another course. Thus the uncertainty of political issues is chiefly due to the absence of such social forces as would be able to determine these issues, in the same way as they have been determined wherever those social forces were present. Not satisfied, however, with this *a priori* inference, we reviewed the chief data of the social history of Russia, and found that the inference was true. The social orders in Russian history have always been subservient to the aims of the state. They have had no privileges, except such as resulted from their state duties and such as were given them by the state. This was the position of the social orders at the time when the Muscovite state was in process of formation, and particularly during the sixteenth and seventeenth centuries. The ties between these classes and the government were somewhat relaxed when the most impending national military aims of the Muscovite state were attained: and an attempt was even made by the government of Catherine II to transform the social orders of Russia into a kind of privileged orders like those of mediaeval Europe. But this attempt to form a substitute for the missing social tradition came too late, and therefore proved a failure. For here, as well as in the realms of religion and of political institutions, the past had left no legacy of tradition to the present. And this conclusion, we saw, proved equally true, whether we studied the history of the nobility, of the gentry, or of the bourgeoisie.

The tradition of the Russian nobility was purposely and systematically discarded by the government itself. We have seen how the ancient aristocracy of lineage was crushed by Ivan IV in the sixteenth century, and how the second aristocracy, that of state service, was democratized by the measures of Peter the Great. We know that the third aristocracy, that of the courtiers of the eighteenth century, was too dependent upon the government to form any real social force. Then we saw that the Russian gentry, though having moments of great brilliancy in its history, had little or no chance of ever becoming independent. This was, to be sure, the class most needed by the government to serve as military power and political support. In return for this service, the members of the gentry were actually granted whatever they wanted: lands and peasants, places in the state service, appointments by the Tsar. The whole peasant class was sacrificed to the pressing needs of the state. There was a time, in the

middle and the second half of the eighteenth century, when it seemed as if the gentry would become interested in affirming their social position through the use of political privileges. But just then the government, having no more need of the gentry for military purposes, was ready to listen to the cry for freedom rising loud and louder from the oppressed peasantry. So, instead of political representation, the gentry were granted predominance in local government. This, however, they did not appreciate as a class privilege; they looked upon their local duties and rights merely as stepping-stones to the state service. Thus the chance for getting political privileges was lost, and when, some three-quarters of a century later, the gentry were dispossessed of their slaves, they claimed in vain the right of voice in a reform which was to deprive them of a third of their income.

Little has been said about the Russian bourgeoisie, for the reason that until very recent times there was no bourgeoisie in Russia worthy of the name. The dependence of the Russian trading and commercial class on the government was still greater than that of the gentry; and this could but be expected, since the cherishing and fostering of Russian industries are entirely due to state measures.

Thus we were obliged to conclude that there was on the stage no social force which could influence political life and take part in the development of political ideas. Nevertheless there *were* in Russia a political life and a political development. Who, then, were the representatives, and what rôle did they play in the history of Russian civilization?

We have seen that in the beginning these were men of the gentry, the first to become educated. The state itself was obliged to give them education, for the purpose of its own Europeanization.

Their class feeling was weak, but this very weakness made them more sensitive to the ideal side of education. Thus, men of the gentry who, so long as they represented their class, were politically insignificant, became stronger and stronger after they began to represent general public opinion. With their political idealism they were undermining chiefly their class privileges, and the government was not entirely averse to this kind of public opinion. But then, after having attained the first great aim of their program—the liberation of the peasants—they looked to the second—political freedom. And here their successes were for a long time checked by the self-defense of autocracy. What, now, are their means of attaining their second aim? Is it as yet the ideal force of public opinion alone, or are there other and stronger means at their disposal?

We must observe, first, that already, in attaining their primary aim, they used forces other than those of mere opinion. We had occasion to mention that the emancipation of the peasants was in a large degree the result of a social danger steadily increasing in proportion as serfdom was becoming unbearable. Not less important was it that the economic growth of the country was checked or impeded by the preservation of slavery; and thus economic reasons, together with social and philanthropic ones, tended in the direction of emancipation.

All these and other reasons may likewise have played a part in the second phase of the political struggle. What must be mentioned first is the enormous growth of the politically conscious social elements that make public opinion in Russia. The gentry still play a part among these elements, but are by far not the only social medium of public opinion, as they were before the emancipa-tion of the peasants. Members of the ancient gentry are now found in all branches of public life: in the press, in public instruction, in the liberal professions, not to speak of the state service, and particularly the local self-government. But it would be impossible to say what is now the class opinion of the gentry. The fact is that the gentry are no longer a class; they are too much intermingled with other social elements in every position they occupy, including that of landed proprietors. By this ubiquity the gentry have added to the facilities for the general spread of public opinion; but as a class they influence public opinion in an even smaller measure than in former times. The "men of mixed ranks," the *raznochintsy*, have enormously increased in all vocations; and the democratic spirit brought by them, and fostered by the liberal and radical press, is a distinctive feature of the educated class in present-day Russia.

Of course, this educated class is not politically homogeneous, and the political opinions cherished by its various representatives are widely different. We have distinguished the two chief currents, which we called the liberal and the socialistic.[1] Now, the predominant feature of political life in Russia, owing to its abnormal conditions, is that political opinion, instead of differentiating and splitting into small groups and factions, tends rather toward united and common action against the general enemy, which is represented by these abnormal conditions. This process of unification of public opinion is twofold. First, only such shades of political opinion as are more or less radical are represented. There being no "spoils,"

[1] There is no real conservative opinion in Russia; there is only an official opinion, that of the government, which does not count here.

political opinion, having had no chance to back the private interests of any particular group or person, is disinterested, abstractly humanitarian, largely democratic, and thus naturally radical. That is why the scale on which a reconciliation and unification of public opinion are striven for is not so large as to preclude the possibility of such unification. In the second place, the scope of divergence among different shades of opposition is steadily diminishing just in the measure that political struggle is going on. In studying the history of the liberal and socialistic currents, we have found that the chasm existing between them at their inception was perpetually narrowing, so as to make possible at last almost an alliance, or at least concerted action for an aim which was admitted to be general. We have seen that the liberal current was gradually radicalized and democratized, and that it one by one eliminated from its program such elements as might have only a class interest. At the same time, as we have noted, the utopian element was slowly but steadily vanishing from the socialistic programs; and thus the way has been paved for the transformation of a revolutionary into a political party, and of its methods of struggle from oriental to European.

Political reform—this is now the general cry of all shades of political opinion in Russia. But is this only an opinion? Are there no interests, no organizations, ready to fight for political freedom? Are there no impelling forces to extort it from a reluctant government?

We have found the answer in the study of the present situation. Yes, the impelling forces are there, and they are twofold: the material crisis and the political disaffection. The picture here drawn, at any period before January, 1905, might have been considered an exaggeration; but now nobody can think it an overstatement. Russia is passing through a crisis; she is sick; and her sickness is so grave as to demand immediate and radical cure. Palliatives can be of no use; rather, they but increase the gravity of the situation. To pretend that all is right in Russia, except for a few "ill-intentioned" persons who are making all the fuss, is no longer ridiculous, it is criminal. Upon quite peaceful and law-abiding citizens, who never shared in any political struggle and never had any definite political opinions, the feeling begins to dawn that the system of self-defense practiced by the government precludes general progress and the development of private initiative, just as, forty years ago, progress was precluded by the further existence of serfdom. Indeed, the development of private initiative is held by the government itself to be the chief need of the present time, and the chief remedy for the present industrial, commercial, and agricultural crisis which has become endemic in Russia. It would be presumption on the part of a historian to predict what, under these conditions, will be the probable result of the secular conflict between Russian opposition and alleged tradition, between public opinion and government. We must leave to history its whims, says Herzen. And we must acknowledge that there is a large scope for the whims of history in the situation as we have described it. Increased and united as they are, the forces of opposition are still not strong enough to replace the government by a violent overthrow. But they are strong enough to make the use of violence continuous, and by increasing this to preclude any further peaceful work of civilization. No form of government can survive, we may say with Speransky, which possesses no moral force and is obliged to carry all its orders into execution by mere material force. And if the only question that remains is, How long will the material force of the bayonets side with the government? then the position is desperate. Where thirty-five thousand policemen are sent to the villages, while no student of statistics is permitted to enter them, the condition of affairs must be recognized as utterly indefensible. And a good political strategist, if he will not surrender, ought to take thought not as to further defenses, but as to a more tenable position.

It may, of course, have been inferred, from what has been said in the preceding, what this tenable position is, in the view of Russian public opinion. Russia wants a political representation, and guaranties of what are called the fundamental rights of individuality; i.e., freedom of belief and of speech, the right of association and of public meetings, liberty of the press, a strict regime of law, and the free course of justice, which implies the repeal of arbitrary edicts and regulations, the abolition of extraordinary tribunals, and last, but not least, a habeas-corpus act, i.e., security from arbitrary arrest and domiciliary search. There is no general opinion as to the kind of representative institutions wanted, but a medium current may easily be found. Public opinion will not now be satisfied with a consultative chamber, and will not join the extremists who want a federative republic and a referendum; i.e., immediate legislation by the people. The great majority will be glad to have what was once claimed

by the liberals of Tver, i.e., a constitution similar to that which was sanctioned in Bulgaria by the Russian Tsar twenty-five years ago. One must know that the Bulgarian constitution is consistently democratic, and that it includes both of the features claimed by the democratic liberals of Russia; i.e., universal suffrage and one chamber. The habitual argument of the conservatives, that Russia is not ready for a constitution, is cut short by this example of Bulgaria. The broad democratic basis of the constitution of that country did not correspond to the degree of political development of the Bulgarian people; but it proved highly valuable as a means of promoting their political education, and precludes for a long time any discussion about further changes in the form of government, which cannot fail to establish a good and durable political tradition, and to concentrate all struggle within the legal frame of guaranteed institutions.

Whether this example of political wisdom, which takes care, not only of the present, but also of the future, will be followed by Russian statesmen is an open question. But for a historian there is no question as to whether there will or will not be any political reform at all. History may have its whims, but it also has its laws; and if the law of Russian history is progress, as we have tried to demonstrate, political reform may not be avoided. To deny it is to despair of the future of Russia.

36

INDUSTRIAL WORKERS IN THE 1880's

From the Reports of Factory Inspectors

The early stages of industrialization everywhere were marked by hardships for the workers, and Russia was to be no exception to this. The conditions under which the Russian worker performed his duties were often appalling. Although Russia had a fair amount of legislation designed to protect the worker, particularly female and child labor, enforcement was another matter. Rapid industrialization and the welfare of the workers often turned out to be conflicting commitments. The factory inspectorate, established by the Ministry of Finance in the early 1880's, was designed to keep the government informed of violations of its protective legislation. But reporting violations only seldom resulted in the prosecution of guilty factory owners. Under existing political conditions the workers could not organize, and strikes were illegal. The situation improved decisively only after the 1905 revolution had demonstrated the potential strength of the growing industrial labor force.

There is a section on Russian labor in Volume III of *Readings in Russian History*, edited by Warren Walsh. Sergei Turin has written *From Peter the Great to Lenin: A History of the Russian Labor Movement*. There is much useful information in Manya Gordon's *Workers before and after Lenin*. There are two articles on the factory inspectorate: "The Formative Years of the Russian Factory Inspectorate, 1882–5" by Frederick Giffin in the *Slavic Review*, December, 1966, and "Factory Inspection under the Witte System," by Theodore Von Laue in the *American Slavic and East European Review*, October, 1960. Von Laue has three articles on Russian Labor: "The Russian Peasant in the Factory," *Journal of Economic History*, Vol. XXI (1961); "Russian Labor between Fields and Factory, 1892–1903," *California Slavic Studies*, Vol. III (1964); and "Tsarist Labor Policy, 1895–1903," *Journal of Modern History*, Vol. XXXIV (1962). See also two articles by Gustav Rimlinger: "Autocracy and the Factory Order in Early Russian Industrialization," *Journal of Economic History*, March, 1960, and "The Management of Labor Protest in Tsarist Russia, 1870–1905," *International Review of Social History*, Vol. V (1962). See also Jacob Walkin, "The Attitude of the Tsarist Government toward the Labor Problem," *American Slavic and East European Review*, Vol. XIII, and Reginald Zelnik, "An Early Case of Labor Protest in St. Petersburg: The Alexandrovsk Machine Works in 1860," *Slavic Review*, September, 1965.

From S. Dmitriev (ed.), *Khrestomatiia po Istorii SSSR*, III (Moscow, 1952), 504–15. Translated by Syliva Fain. The excerpts from inspectors' reports have been rearranged in topical fashion.

... Sanitary conditions in the workers' settlement of Yuzovka[1] are highly conducive to the contraction and spread of disease. The market place and streets are full of filth. The air is rotten with the stench from factory smoke, coal and lime dust, and the filth in gutters and organic wastes on streets and squares. The interiors of most workers' living quarters are just as unhygienic. ... Petty clerks and some skilled workers live in "shacks." These are long buildings divided into several large and small sections. Inside, they are extremely dirty and crowded with tenants. The majority of workers live in so-called "cabins" built in the outskirts of the settlement, along the river Kalmius. These cabins are simply low, ugly mud huts. The roofs are made of earth and rubbish. Some of them are so close to the ground that at first sight they are nearly unnoticeable. The walls are covered with wood planks or overlaid with stones which easily let in the dampness. The floors are made of earth. These huts are entered by going deep down into the ground along earthen stairs. The interiors are dark and close, and the air is damp, still, and foul-smelling. The "cabins" are untidy, and far more unsightly than the "shacks." The furnishings are completely unhygienic, although frequently the workers live here with their families and infant children. ...

The coal miners are housed in mud huts much like those in Yuzovka. The hut walls are sloppily boarded up or covered with stone, and sometimes whitewashed. There are dirt floors, and no

[1] Yuzovka was founded in 1869 as a result of the construction of a metallurgical plant by the Welshman John Hughes—hence the name. Located in the Donets Basin, it had a population of 49,000 in 1914. In 1924 it was renamed Stalino and by 1959 had a population of 701,000. Since 1964 it has been called Donetsk.

proper ceiling—only the bare rafters and the roof. Inside there is generally an oven, a table, and a bench. Beds are rare. ... The roof and walls let in dampness, so that even in summer the atmosphere is musty and putrid. Only a dim half-light comes in through the tiny windows, and even in daytime the darkness is barely dissipated by the dim flickering light of smoky oil lamps. Even in their leisure hours the miners cannot get enough light and fresh clean air, while they work all day or all night in the close and heavy atmosphere of the underground tunnels. Because of such living conditions, the miners are emaciated, weakened figures with sickly pale faces, and poor eyesight. ...

The buildings used for workers' quarters at Moscow factories are either the open, barrack type, or are partitioned into small individual compartments. ... Bachelors are always housed in barracks, but some married workers may live there too, if space is limited. Most of the married workers have their own rooms. However, this division is not strictly observed in a considerable number of factories. Married men are indeed separated from single men and women sometimes, but the rule is rather an undifferentiated mixture of sexes and ages, so that all sleep in one and the same barracks, or are thrown together indiscriminately into the compartments. ... In either type of housing, the furnishings are always very plain: generally there are rows upon rows of largely bare plank beds—occasionally iron ones. ... The workers are required to furnish their own bedding, so most of them sleep in their own sheepskin coats or in tunics. ... In factory No. 45, the workers live in a basement, where the air is extremely musty and damp. Instead of beds, loose boards are laid across wooden sawhorses. Two or three men sleep on such a "bed.". . . . Factory No. 109 is still worse: the workers are given straw mattresses, but ten kopecks a month is deducted from their pay as rental. A worker who lives there one year pays the employer far more than the cost of the mattress. Yet after he leaves, the mattress remains the employer's property, and is rented out to another worker. . . .

In the majority of factories there are no special quarters for the workers. This applies to workers in paper, wool, and silk finishing. Skilled hand craftsmen like brocade weavers can earn good wages, and yet most of them sleep on or under their looms, for lack of anything else. Only in a few weaving factories are there special sleeping quarters, and these are provided not for the weavers, but for other workers—the winders and dyers, etc. Likewise, the velveteen cutters almost always sleep on the tables where they work. This habit is particularly unhealthy, since the work areas are always musty and the air is saturated with dye fumes—sometimes poisonous ones. Carpenters also generally sleep on their workbenches. In bastmatting factories, workers of both sexes and all ages sleep together on pieces and mats of bast which are often damp. Only the sick workers in these bast factories are allowed to sleep on the single stove. In silk factory No. 61, the young female workers sleep side by side on the floor of their workroom. . . . Conditions are similar in dye works No. 82: workers sleep all over the plant, even in the washing room and the bleach room, in the midst of harmful fumes. . . . There are no special sleeping quarters, either, in tarpaulin factory No. 83. The female canvas makers sleep together with their children on the benches where they sew, in rooms filled with the sharp odor of fresh tarpaulins. . . .

Working conditions in factories and mines also promote disease and illness. . . . The Semyonov and Alexandrov mines I visited are themselves structurally defective. There are frequent caveins, which make the inadequate ventilation even worse. The air becomes so thick in the underground passages that the lamps go out—or as the miners say, "the sun stops shining." Can you imagine how hard it is to breathe this air! . . . After a mine shaft has been dug out and reinforced, the horizontal passageways are built. These are wide tunnels about seven feet high. The lateral tunnels, or "stoves," branch off from the main tunnels. The width of the "stoves" varies from three and a half to four and a half feet. Thus the miners must always be stooped over. These "stoves" are much more cramped than the main tunnels, since the miners must lie on their sides, and prop themselves on their elbows to face the coal-rock wall. They chip off pieces of coal with a chisel-like instrument called a "hack." . . .

Many of the workers in the steel mills are always literally "working with fire." For when steel is smelted, the metal is heated white-hot for stamping and rolling rails. The air where these processes take place becomes intolerably hot. While inspecting one of these mills I saw steel rails being made. The workers use hooks to haul a thick piece of steel four or five feet long which has been heated until it seems to breathe flame, and turn it onto the rollers. Once the piece of steel has passed through the rollers and the new rail, like a fiery snake, is seized again by the workers' hooks, the metal has cooled off considerably. But even at this point it radiates heat, throwing off thousands of fiery metal sparks at the slightest impact. At this moment, it would be almost impossible to stand within a yard of the rail for the heat—yet the workers stand almost next to the red-hot metal, and endure this heat day and night, year after year. Such working conditions weaken the men and make them susceptible to frequent illness. It is enough for an exhausted worker to go from this extreme heat, even for a short time, into the cold winter weather and the open air in order to catch a cold. The intensity of flaming light in which these men work also is undoubtedly harmful to the eyes.

. . . Work at the mill never stops, day or night. There are two twelve hour shifts a day, which begin at 6:00 A.M. and 6:00 P.M. The men have a half-hour for breakfast (8:30–9:00) and one hour for dinner (1:00–2:00).

. . . Sanitary conditions in factories everywhere are as a rule completely unsatisfactory. . . . Here are some examples from my notes: In candy factory No. 11, "the shop buildings are extremely dark and dirty. Most of the chocolate department is in the basement, which is poorly lit and damp. The workers continually track in mud from the courtyard which is saturated with excrements and slops." In cloth factory No. 48 which was typical of such establishments, "the air in the dye-house was so saturated with steam when I inspected it that it was impossible to see anything. I groped my way about the dyeing room as if blindfolded —evidently, there was no ventilation at all. The machines were very crowded together, and belts crisscrossed in all directions. Moving around the machines is extremely hazardous, and accidents could easily happen to the soberest and most careful workers."

In chemical factory No. 144 "musty gases in rooms where tinned salt is prepared are so strong that someone unaccustomed to them could remain there only a few minutes. In the department where mercury is prepared, the only precautions against the deadly fumes are the cloths which the workers tie over their mouths. Not only are there no more reliable safety measures than this, but the family of one of the workers actually lives in an adjoining room.". . .

In plant No. 115 "in some departments, especially in the spinning room and the old weaving building, the machines are very crowded together. The lack of ventilation causes terribly thick cotton dust to accumulate in the combing and scutching rooms. Devices to evacuate the dust are inadequate. Much of the machinery, particularly in the scutching room, is uncovered and dangerous. There is no ventilation in the singe and burn room, and the smoke there is so thick and heavy that I was unable to remain there more than two or three minutes. . . ."

The worst violations of hygienic regulations were those I saw in most of the flax-spinning mills where linen is produced. . . . Although in western Europe all the dust-producing carding and combing machines have long been covered and well ventilated, I saw only one Russian linen mill where such a machine was securely covered. Elsewhere, the spools of these machines were completely open to the air, and the scutching apparatus is inadequately ventilated. . . .

Because of this lack of ventilation and protective covering, I invariably saw such dust in carding shops of the spinning mills I visited that I would become completely covered with it, like flour, in just a few minutes. This dust was especially heavy in those spinning mills where the poorer grades of flax are processed. There the dust literally drifts in thick clouds, so that it becomes difficult not only to breathe, but also to see anything in the grayish fog. However undemanding our workers generally are, as I saw for myself, even they consider it necessary to take precautions against this awful dust. These workers have improvised a "respirator": they take a long bundle of flax, put it over their mouths, and tie the ends around in back of the head, and thus try to save their lungs.

To cut down on the putrid fumes which are produced in the wetting vats, the flaxen yarns can be wetted quickly with lukewarm running water, then rinsed again with clean water. But I saw such measures taken only in the factory mentioned above (that of I. I. Syenko), where they effectively reduced the vat fumes to a barely perceptible odor. In all the other linen mills these departments were extremely dirty, the floors were sticky and the rooms filled with heavy putrid fumes. In several factories, as, for example the Kyekin mill, these vat rooms smell just like refuse pits. . . .

The very worst, most unhealthy conditions I saw were in tobacco factories. . . . The shops where tobacco is chopped and dried are so filled with caustic dust and nicotine fumes that each time I entered one of these rooms I had spasms in my throat and my eyes watered. If I stayed there very long I even became dizzy, though I am a smoker myself. Yet even women sometimes work in this atmosphere, as I myself can testify. Children work in these tobacco factories as wrappers, baggers (making the little paper tobacco bags), and packers. There were even children under twelve working there. . . .

According to my observations of 181 industrial establishments, only 71 pay their workers regularly. But even this figure, I suppose, is much higher than it should be, since factory owners and directors quite naturally would say yes when I asked if wages were paid regularly, and I myself did not always have an

oportunity to check up on the truth of their statements. Terms varied, but monthly wages are the most prevalent, even in the government service. But this leaves more than one hundred factories, that is, a significant majority, in which wages are not fixed, and depend completely on the will and the financial position of the owner or manager. The number of "accountings" per year is relatively fixed, but that is all. When an accounting is made, the mutual liabilities of employer and employee are summed up, but there is not necessarily any concurrent payment of wages.

In the steel mill at Yuzovka, wages for one month are given out about the middle of the next. In this way the factory office always has two weeks' wages on hand for each employee. The workers are given their money in a special tin box, which also contains an account of the wages, fines, and other deductions. Should a man's monthly wages just cover his fines he will be so notified by a slip in his box. . . .

Steel orders have been slow recently, so that there is frequently not enough work. This has meant lower wages or none at all from time to time, and has put most workers, especially those with families, in a quite unfavorable and sometimes very serious financial position. When work is steady, the workers can buy food and necessary supplies. But when work is slow, they must buy everything on credit, counting on their future earnings—and the merchants will charge them at least 30 per cent extra for this privilege. . . .

In Moscow and its environs, company stores are the rare exception, and the workers buy groceries and supplies from independent merchants. But since, in most cases, the workers are unable to obtain any large amounts of credit on their own, the factory sends them to certain shops which have agreed to extend credit on the factory's guarantee. I learned that many factory owners get rebates from the shopkeepers, generally at a rate of five to ten kopecks on the ruble. Outside Moscow and its nearest suburbs, even in populated localities where there are already local shops, factories generally have their own private stores. In the city of Kolomna, for example, almost all the factories either have their own store, or require their workers to buy as they may direct and thus earn a tidy profit. In the matting factories, for instance, the workers are obliged to obtain all their provisions exclusively through the factory. There is no factory store, but it is rumored that the factory earns a 10 to 15 per cent commission from the Kolomna merchants from whom the workers buy. In places far from populated areas company stores are unquestionably necessary; nevertheless some factory owners line their own pockets by charging high prices for everything. In so doing, they still further reduce the workers' wages, which are relatively small to begin with. . . .

. . . Fines are as varied as the factories themselves. The factory administration is free to determine the grounds for fines and the amounts payable. There are only a few factories (like that of the Malyutin brothers, No. 49) where fines are small and are rarely levied. In the majority of factories, fines are all too common; they may be very heavy, and are imposed for the most varied causes. For instance, during the working year 1881-82, in factory No. 115, 5,702 rubles were collected for infringements of various factory rules alone (excluding damage or losses inflicted upon the owner for which the workers paid). In many industrial establishments the grounds for fines and the sizes of fines

are not fixed in advance. The factory rules may contain only one phrase like the following: "Those found violating company rules will be fined *at the discretion of the manager.*"

The degree of arbitrariness in the determination of fines, and thus also in the determination of the worker's wages, was unbelievably extreme in some factories. In Podolsk, for instance, in factories No. 131 and No. 135, there is a ten-ruble forfeit for leaving the factory before the expiration of one's contract. But as applied, this covers much more than voluntary breach of contract on the worker's part. This fine is exacted from every worker who for any reason has to leave the factory. Cases are known of persons who have had to pay this fine three times. Moreover, fines are levied for so many causes that falling under a severe fine is a constant possibility for each worker. For instance, workers who for any reason came into the office in a group, instead of singly, would be fined one ruble. After a second offense, the transgressors would be dismissed—leaving behind, of course, the ten-ruble fine for breach of contract.

In factory No. 135 the workers are still treated as serfs. Wages are paid out only twice a year, even then not in full but only enough to pay the workers' taxes (other necessities are supplied by the factory store). Furthermore this money is not given to the workers directly, but is sent by mail to their village elders and village clerks. Thus the workers are without money the year around. Besides, they are also paying severe fines to the factory, and these sums will be subtracted from their wages at the final year-end accounting.

Extreme regulations and regimentation is very common in our factories— regulations entangle the workers at every step and burden them with more or less severe fines which are subtracted from their often already inadequate wages. Some factory administrators have become real virtuosos at thinking up new grounds for fines. A brief description of a few of the fines in factory No. 172 is an excellent example of this variety: on October 24, 1877, an announcement was posted of new fines to be set at the discretion of the office for fourteen different cases of failure to maintain silence and cleanliness. On December 4, 1881, an announcement prescribed fines for four additional reasons. On September 4, 1882, there was a similar notification of fines for four more offenses. There were also dozens of minor fines prescribed for certain individual offenses: for example, on August 4, 1883, a huge fine of five rubles was set for singing in the factory courtyard after 9:30, or at any time in any unauthorized place. On June 3, 1881, a fine was to be levied from workers who took tea and sugar, bread, or any kind of foodstuffs into the weaving building, "in order to avoid breeding any insects or vermin." On March 4, 1881, an escalating fine was announced for any worker who washed out his laundry in the sleeping quarters, or at the well in the courtyard. On May 14, 1880, a fine was set for anyone who wrote with pencil, chalk, or anything else on the walls in the dyeing or weaving buildings. On December 8, 1881, an announcement stated: "Any workers'

child who starts a fight or hits someone with his fists will be fined three rubles for the first offense." On December 29, 1879, any weavers or dyers who entered the metal shop or carpentry shop for any reason would be fined. On May 30, 1880, the factory office announced that singing on workdays was forbidden to all hand weavers, cutters, and laborers in the factory under threat of fine. On November 29, 1877, unmarried men were strictly forbidden to visit the family or women's quarters. . . .

All the money collected for fines and miscellaneous deductions is at the disposal of the factory owner, and in some places this is a very sizable sum—as much as several thousand rubles a year. This could be a substantial source of supplementary income for an unscrupulous manager. In the majority of factories, the owner never reveals what is done with this money. Only in a few factories is an account of these monies given, yet this is still no guarantee that the money has really been used for the designated ends. . . .[2]

[2] The table below will give the reader some idea of monthly wages in various industries for 1884–85 (in rubles):

	Men	Women	Children
Paper mills	16.00	9.50	7.00
Cotton mills	15.50	9.00	6.25
Silk factories	20.00	13.00	3.50
Dye shops	13.75	6.75	7.25
Glass shops	29.00	10.50	5.50
Tobacco plants	16.60	11.50	10.00
Machine building	29.00	. . .	8.00

37

AN ECONOMIC POLICY
FOR THE EMPIRE

By Sergei Witte

Count Witte (1849–1915) was a talented statesman and Russia's greatest finance minister. Born into a German Baltic family, he began his career in the railroad business. In 1892 he became minister of finance, a post he held for the next eleven years. "The Witte Era" was one of economic expansion and rapid industrialization. After Russia's defeat by Japan in 1904–05, Witte was named chief Russian delegate to the peace conference, obtained advantageous terms for Russia, and returned home in triumph. He became premier on the eve of the issuance of the October Manifesto. However, the Emperor resented the concessions he had been forced to make and dismissed Witte in April, 1906, after the Premier had successfully negotiated a huge loan from France. Witte belonged to no party, though he was by nature a conservative, and had no sympathy with the revolution.

Below we reproduce a sample of Witte's thinking on Russia's economic future. "No other document of this period available to us," says Professor Theodore Von Laue, who discovered, translated, and published the memorandum, "contains such a precise formulation of the government's economic policy and its official motives." It is not a polished piece of writing but a hastily composed fighting credo provoked by the Emperor's temporary opposition to the further importation into Russia of foreign capital. The memorandum was intended to influence only the top bureaucrats, not the public, who in fact never heard of it.

For a more extensive presentation of Witte's views, see his autobiography, *The Memoirs of Count Witte*. Theodore Von Laue has written *Sergei Witte and the Industrialization of Russia*. James Mavor, *An Economic History of Russia*, Vol. II, is a study of the entire nineteenth century. For a Marxist interpretation, see Peter Liashchenko, *History of the National Economy of the USSR*. See also Raymond Goldsmith, "The Economic Growth of Russia, 1860–1913," *Economic Development and Cultural Change*, IX (1961), 441–75, and Alexander Gerschenkron, *Economic Backwardness in Historical Perspective*, in which the author's essays on Russia are reprinted. See also "Russian Industrialists Look to the Future," by Ruth Roosa, in *Essays in Russian and Soviet History*, edited by John S. Curtiss. There is a chapter on Russia in Herbert Feis's *Europe, the World's Banker, 1870–1914* (paperback). Vladimir Lenin wrote *The Development of Capitalism in Russia* in 1900. For a general assessment see Herbert Ellison, "Economic Modernization in Imperial

From T. H. Von Laue, "Sergei Witte on the Industrialization of Imperial Russia," *Journal of Modern History*, XXVI, 61–74.

Russia," *Journal of Economic History,* December, 1965, and the *Cambridge Economic History of Europe,* Vol. VI, Part II. See also Alexander Gerschenkron, "The Rate of Industrial Growth of Russian since 1885," *Journal of Economic History,* 1947, Supplement VII. On foreign capital see Olga Crisp, "French Investment in Russian Joint Stock Companies, 1894–1914," *Business History,* June, 1960. There is a chapter on Witte as a finance minister in Vladimir Gurko's *Features and Figures of the Past.* See also J. Westwood, "John Hughes and Russian Metallurgy," *Economic History Review,* April, 1965.

REPORT OF THE MINISTER OF FINANCE TO HIS MAJESTY ON THE NECESSITY OF FORMULATING AND THEREAFTER STEADFASTLY ADHERING TO A DEFINITE PROGRAM OF A COMMERCIAL AND INDUSTRIAL POLICY OF THE EMPIRE. EXTREMELY SECRET

The measures taken by the government for the promotion of national trade and industry have at present a far deeper and broader significance than they had at any time before. Indeed, the entire economic structure of the empire has been transformed in the course of the second half of the current century, so that now the market and its price structure represent the collective interest of all private enterprises which constitute our national economy. Buying and selling and wage labor penetrate now into much deeper layers of our national existence than was the case at the time of serf economy, when the landlord in his village constituted a self-sufficient economic little world, leading an independent life, almost without relation to the market. The division of labor; the specialization of skills; the increased exchange of goods among a population increasingly divided among towns, villages, factories, and mines; the greater complexity of the demands of the population—all these processes rapidly developed in our fatherland under the influence of the emancipation of the serfs, the construction of a railroad network,

the development of credit, and the extraordinary growth of foreign trade. Now all organs and branches of our national economy are drawn into a common economic life, and all its individual units have become far more sensitive and responsive to the economic activities of the government. Because of the extremely interlaced network of contemporary economic relationships, any change in the conditions of one or the other industry, of one or the other branch of trade, credit, or communications, touches and influences, often in hidden ways, the fate of a considerable majority of our enterprises.

As a result of such fundamental transformation of the economic interests of the country, every major measure of the government more or less affects the life of the entire economic organism. The solicitude shown to various branches of industry, a new railroad, the discovery of a new field for Russian enterprise, these and other measures, even if partial and of local application only, touch the entire ever more complicated network and upset the established equilibrium. . . .

In view of these facts, the minister of finance concludes that the country, which in one way or the other is nurtured by the commercial and industrial policy of the government, requires above all that this policy be carried out according to a definite plan, with strict system and continuity. Isolated and unco-ordinated acts of encouragement can never offset the pernicious and painful shocks which the economic organism suffers from a change of the guiding policy. Even the most beneficial measures of the government in the realm of economic policy during the first years of their operation often seem to impose a hardship on the population. It is a difficult matter; years, even decades, must pass before the sacrifices can bear fruit. Wise statesmanship requires, then, that these difficult years be suffered patiently, as the experience of other peoples shows that the sacrifices demanded by the coherent and steadfast adherence to a firm and just economic system are always rewarded a hundred fold. Any change of basic policy before the fruits of sacrifice have had time to mature leads to the complete loss of all capital invested in the previous system, or it leads to new sacrifices in the pursuit of a new system. A government with an unsteady commercial and industrial policy is like a businessman who constantly reorganizes his production without producing anything. No matter how great the technical perfection of such a business, it always ends in ruin.

When I became minister of finance, I acted on the conviction that the government, no matter which commercial and industrial system it follows, is guided by the property interests of the entire people and that in order to compensate them for their losses one has merely to wait for the positive results of the government's economic system. This lasts years and sometimes decades. In taking over the ministry of finance in 1892, I felt obliged to make clear to myself the foundations of the commercial and industrial policy of my predecessors and to bend all efforts toward continuing and finishing what they had begun or had taken over from their predecessors. The necessity of such succession and continuity seemed to me so paramount

that I relinquished my own personal views. I realized, of course, that there were very weighty arguments against the protectionist system and against high tariffs. But I supposed that even the proponents of free trade must be aware that it would be extremely harmful from the government view point to repudiate the protective system before those industries had been securely established for whose creation whole generations had paid by a high tariff. I assumed that an absolutely perfect tariff system did not exist and that each system had positive and negative features. And I furthermore concluded that in making a choice one should throw one's weight in favor of the system already existing, for which the people bore such heavy sacrifices and to which the country's economy is already adapted. Besides, it was clear to me that any commercial and industrial policy touching very directly the property interests of the population would always have its defenders and opponents. I considered it my duty to listen attentively to the latter, and I recognized the necessity of alleviating the measures which inevitably brought temporary damage to some. Nevertheless, I did not waver in my fundamental aim to complete in detail what was so boldly begun in the reign of Alexander III and of Your Imperial Highness. . . .

These conclusions find special confirmation in the facts of our industrial development. The absence of a strictly enforced plan and sudden changes from protectionism to almost unlimited free trade did not permit our industry to develop calmly. What was created yesterday was destroyed today; and only by the will of Emperor Alexander III was a customs tariff established which gave positive protection to our industries. His wise command was realized in the tariff of 1891, which was worked out while I was still one of the directors of the departments in the ministry of finance. It has been the starting point of our industrial system.

Now, as the attacks on the existing commercial and industrial policy continue and even increase in bitterness, I consider it my duty to review once more its chief foundations and to submit them to Your Imperial Highness. In order to be the true executor of Your Imperial Majesty's will, I must have instruction not for individual measures but for a comprehensive commercial and industrial policy. The country needs, above all, a firm and strict economic system.

In Russia at the present moment the protectionist system is in force. Its principal foundations were laid down in the tariff of 1891.

What are the tasks of the protectionist system?

Russia remains even at the present essentially an agricultural country. It pays for all its obligations to foreigners by exporting raw materials, chiefly of an agricultural nature, principally grain. It meets its demand for finished goods by imports from abroad. The economic relations of Russia with western Europe are fully comparable to the relations of colonial countries with their metropolises. The latter consider their colonies as advantageous markets in which they can freely sell the products of their labor and of their industry and from which they can draw with a powerful hand the raw materials necessary for them. This is the basis of the economic power of the governments of western Europe, and chiefly for that end do they guard their existing colonies or acquire new ones. Russia was, and to a considerable extent still is, such a hospitable colony for all industrially developed states, generously providing them with the cheap products of her soil and buying dearly the products of their labor. But there is a radical difference between

Russia and a colony: Russia is an independent and strong power. She has the right and the strength not to want to be the eternal handmaiden of states which are more developed economically. She should know the price of her raw materials and of the natural riches hidden in the womb of her abundant territories, and she is conscious of the great, not yet fully displayed, capacity for work among her people. She is proud of her great might, by which she jealously guards not only the political but also the economic independence of her empire. She wants to be a metropolis herself. On the basis of the people's labor, liberated from the bonds of serfdom, there began to grow our own national economy, which bids fair to become a reliable counterweight to the domination of foreign industry.

The creation of our own national industry—that is the profound task, both economic and political, from which our protectionist system arises. The advantages derived from the successful completion of this system are so numerous that I select here only the principal ones.

National labor, which at present is intensively employed only for a short agricultural season, will find full application and consequently become more productive. That, in turn, will increase the wages of the entire working population; and that again will cause an improvement of the physical and spiritual energy of the people. The welfare of Your Empire is based on national labor. The increase of its productivity and the discovery of new fields for Russian enterprise will always serve as the most reliable way for making the entire nation more prosperous.

The demand not only for raw materials but also for other articles will be met to a considerable extent by the work of the people themselves. And consequently the payment to foreigners, which at present consumes a considerable part of our national revenue, will be reduced. The import of foreign goods will then be determined not by the weakness of our industry but by the natural division of labor between nations, by which an industrially developed nation buys abroad only what it cannot advantageously produce at home; purchase abroad then enriches rather than exhausts it. Thanks to that, the accumulation of new capital from national savings is considerably facilitated, and that, in turn, promotes a further growth of productivity.

Within the country, exchange between the products of the soil and of labor will expand and give greater purchasing power to the grain market, which then can afford to pay higher prices for agricultural goods, thanks to which export prices also will rise. As a result, the income derived from land will also increase. And that, in turn, will make it possible for land cultivators, small and large, to improve their agricultural techniques and to raise the productivity of the land. The improvement of agricultural techniques will inevitably reduce the extreme fluctuation of harvests, which at present imposes such a heavy strain upon our national prosperity.

The gradual growth of industry in the country, always accompanied by falling prices for manufactured goods, will make it possible for our export trade to deal not only in raw materials, as at present, but also in industrial goods. Our present losses in the European trade can then be converted into profits in the Asiatic trade. . . .

A new industry cannot arise on short order. Protective duties must, therefore, be continued for decades in order to lead to positive results. Meanwhile, in the course of the long preparatory period, the population will need the products of industry. And as domestic production cannot yet satisfy the domestic demand, the consumers are forced to buy foreign goods at increased prices because of the customs duties; and they have to pay almost as much for the goods of domestic origin. So, for instance, an Englishman pays for a pood of pig iron 26 kopecks, an American 32 kopecks, but a Russian up to 90 kopecks.

Of all charges against the economic policy of Russia, the minister of finance is most keenly aware of the following: that because of the tariff a Russian subject pays for many items considerably more than the subjects of other countries; that the costs of production rise in proportion as they are determined by the value of capital goods; that the cost of living also grows for both rich and poor; and that the paying powers of the population are strained to the utmost, so that in many cases consumption is directly curtailed. The minister of finance recognizes that the customs duties fall as a particularly heavy burden upon the impoverished landowners and peasants, particularly in a year of crop failure. These imposts are a heavy sacrifice made by the entire population, and not from surplus but out of current necessities. Naturally, the question is asked: Are there no ways to avoid or to reduce those sacrifices which have such an enervating effect on our economy?

It must be stated first of all that the system, because it is coherently carried out, is already beginning to show results. Industry numbers now more than 30,000 factories and mills, with an annual production surpassing 2,000,000,-000 rubles. That by itself is a big figure. A widespread and tight net of economic interests is linked to the welfare of that industry. To upset it by a shift to free trade would undermine one of the most reliable foundations of our national well-being; such a shock would adversely affect its general level. In several branches, our industry grew very rapidly. Thus the smelting of pig iron, not exceeding 10,000,000 pood at the beginning of the century, rose to 36,000,000 pood in the last decade and to 114,000,000 pood in 1897, i.e., it trebled in ten years. And if it did not meet the demand, it was only because the demand itself rose from 102,000,000 pood in 1893 to 166,000,000 pood at present. In 1893, 131,000,000 pood were smelted. Still more characteristic was the development of the cotton industry, which produces goods of wide popular consumption. That industry formerly used foreign raw materials exclusively; at the present, thanks to the protective tariff, it obtains up to 30 per cent of the required cotton inside the empire. Its annual productivity grew from 259,000,000 rubles in 1885 to 531,000,000 rubles in 1896, i.e., more than double. The import of yarn from abroad fell from 296,000 pood to 127,000 pood. Now the value of imported cotton fabrics does not exceed 5,000,000 rubles, and that is accompanied by a noticeable increase of exports from Russia to Persia, Bokhara, Middle Asia, China, etc. That export, which amounted to 3,500,000 rubles in the past decade, now attains 12,000,000 rubles.

In this way the sacrifices of the population are not borne in vain. Industry has grown very considerably as compared with the condition in which the tariff of 1891 found it. Russian enterprise has found itself new outlets; internal trade has developed. But much remains still to be done before we can say that the building is finished. Domestic production grows, but the consumption of the population grows still more rapidly. It can be satisfied only with the very considerable help of the import of foreign goods, which, therefore, is growing despite the development of domestic production. Thus for the years 1886–90

an average of 410,000,000 rubles worth of foreign goods was imported; from 1891 to 1895, 585,000,000 rubles; and in 1897, 560,000,000 rubles worth. We pay the foreigners for their goods almost as much as the government takes annually from the people in the form of indirect taxes. And if we talk about the heavy burden which the government budget imposes upon a considerable part of the population of the empire— that additional tribute paid to foreigners represents an almost unbearable burden, particularly for the agricultural population. One cannot, therefore, ignore the fact that even goods which we are beginning to produce at home are still imported from abroad. Thus, although the metallurgical industries grew considerably after the tariff of 1891, their extent is still insufficient. In 1897 we imported metals (crude or in finished goods) for 152,000,000 rubles. The natural conditions of our economy are such that all this could be extracted and processed inside the country. The same is true of other industrial commodities, woolens, cotton textiles, hides, pottery, furniture, etc., of which we import from abroad 62,000,000 rubles worth, only because our domestic industry cannot catch up quickly with our growing domestic demand. Among raw materials and semi-finished goods, of which we import 250,000,000 rubles worth, one can find many like wool, cotton, fat, hides, anthracite, etc., which could be produced in greater quantity at home. The extensive import of so many commodities which could be, or which are already, produced in the country serves as a true indication that our domestic production, despite its great successes in recent years, is not yet large enough to satisfy the needs of the population. Under these conditions our industries are not only unable to free the population from the heavy duties imposed by the tariff, but they also charge, at the same time, highly monopolistic prices for their own goods. It is one of the most irrefutable economic laws that only such industries work cheaply as produce their goods in such large quantities that the supply of goods either equals the demand or even exceeds it and finds its outlet in foreign markets. If the conditions of production are what we see in Russia, i.e., if only part of the goods is produced at home and the remainder abroad, then the consumer, i.e., the entire population, is compelled to pay dearly for both foreign and domestic products.

It is obvious that our domestic industry, no matter how extensively it has developed, is quantitatively still small. It has not yet reached such proportions as to give birth to the creative forces of knowledge, the mobility of capital, and the spirit of enterprise. It has not yet attained the pitch of healthy competition which would enable it to produce cheaply and repay the population for its sacrifices by the cheapness and abundance of its products. It is not yet an equal partner of agriculture in providing goods for export and bearing the tax burden. But that partnership must be accomplished, and in the shortest time possible. Economic conditions in the past years have become very complex, and the protective tariff has borne down extremely heavily upon the population. It has been too difficult for the population to provide for both itself and an almost monopolistic industry. The task of our present commercial and industrial policy thus is still a very difficult one. It is necessary not only to create industries but to force them to work cheaply; it is necessary to develop in our growing industrial community an energetic and active life—in a word, to raise our industries qualitatively and quantitatively to such a high level that they cease to be a drain and become a source of prosperity in our national economy.

What do we need to accomplish that? We need capital, knowledge, and the spirit of enterprise. Only these three factors can speed up the creation of a fully independent national industry. But, unfortunately, not all these forces can be artificially implanted. They are mutually interconnected; their own proper development depends upon the very growth of industry.

The accumulation of capital is possible only to the extent that the productivity of an enterprise yields an unused surplus. In Russia, where the great majority of the population is still engaged in agriculture, that surplus of income over expenditure is insufficient for the accumulation of new capital. Actually, the savings of which account is kept—those which go into banks and savings institutions—amount to about 200,000,-000 rubles a year. And a considerable part of them (about 130,000,000 rubles) is spent for the purchase of mortgages from land banks, i.e., they are consumed by the needs of rural and urban economy. The creation of larger funds—say, for the construction of railways—always requires the help of the government in our country. Only the industrial regions of Your Empire show a real ability to create new capital for economic application. This capital appears also as the chief promoter of our industrial progress. But, as the influence of these industrial regions in our vast national economy is relatively small, these savings seem insufficient for the quick creation of an independent national industry.

We have thus neither capital, nor knowledge, nor the spirit of enterprise. The extension of popular education through general, technical, and commercial schools can have, of course, a beneficial influence; and Your Majesty's government is working on that. But no matter how significant the promotion of enlightenment, that road is too slow; by itself, it cannot realize our goal. The natural school of industry is first of all a lively industry. Institutions of learning serve only as one aid toward that end. The first investment of savings awakens in man the restlessness of enterprise, and with the first investment in industry the powerful stimulus of personal interest calls forth such curiosity and love of learning as to make an illiterate peasant into a railway builder, a bold and progressive organizer of industry, and a versatile financier.

Industry gives birth to capital; capital gives rise to enterprise and love of learning; and knowledge, enterprise, and capital combined create new industries. Such is the eternal cycle of economic life, and by the succession of such turns our national economy moves ahead in the process of its natural growth. In Russia this growth is yet too slow, because there is yet too little industry, capital, and spirit of enterprise. But we cannot be content with the continuation of such slow growth. No matter how great the results attained by the present protectionist system, to accomplish what is still ahead and what the entire country so impatiently waits for is by all accounts the most difficult matter. We have to develop mass-production industries, widely dispersed and variegated, in which not customs duties but the more powerful and beneficial laws of competition play the dominant role. We must give the country such industrial perfection as has been reached by the United States of America, which firmly bases its prosperity on two pillars—agriculture and industry. . . .

We cannot wait for the natural accumulation of capital in a country in which the majority of the population is experiencing hard times and which surrenders a considerable part of its surplus to the government in the form of taxes. And we cannot continue to make the population pay dearly for what it buys—that is too much of a burden for the population and for agriculture, its primary occupation. Neither can we repudiate the protectionist system and grant free or at least easier access to foreign goods; we cannot thus give up the industries which the people created with such heavy sacrifices—for that would mean to deprive the country, already so destitute of capital, of the industries which it has protected by the sweat of its brow. . . .

The influx of foreign capital is, in the considered opinion of the minister of finance, the sole means by which our industry can speedily furnish our country with abundant and cheap goods. Each new wave of capital, swept in from abroad, knocks down the immoderately high level of profits to which our monopolistic entrepreneurs are accustomed and forces them to seek compensation in technical improvements, which in turn, will lead to price reductions. Replenishing the poor store of popular savings by foreign capital makes it possible for all capital in the country to flow more freely over a broader field and to work up not only the fat but also the leaner sources of profit. . . .

But in recent times objections have been raised against the influx of foreign capital. It is said that this influx is detrimental to basic national interests, that it tries to siphon off all profits from our growing Russian industries, that it will lead to the sale of our rich productive forces to foreigners. It is no secret, of course, to the minister of finance that the influx of foreign capital is disadvantageous primarily to entrepreneurs, who are harmed by any kind of competition. Not only our own, but also foreign, capitalists who have already obtained an advantageous place in Russian industry join in these heart-rending complaints and thus try to guard their monopolistic profits. But, as frequently happens in the public discussion of economic problems, the interested voices are hiding behind impartial but little-informed representatives of public interests; and what is undesirable for private groups is, by a misunderstanding, eagerly interpreted as harmful to our economy as a whole.

The extent of the influx of foreign capital into Russia is usually much exaggerated. The foreign corporations formed in 1896 numbered twenty-two, with a basic capital of 80,000,000 rubles. In 1897 their number was fifteen, with 55,000,000 rubles capital. Even if one adds foreign capital invested in Russian corporations (12,000,000 rubles in 1896 and 22,000,000 in 1897) one finds that, all together, foreign capital does not amount to more than one-third of the capital of all joint-stock companies formed annually. One should also remember that the corporation is still something very strange and unpopular with Russian entrepreneurs. The organization which they prefer is the personal enterprise or at least the family partnership. A considerable part of Russian capital is invested in such enterprises; the number of these formed every year equals that of the joint-stock companies. It would seem, then, that of the total amount of capital invested every year in the further development of our industries, foreign capital scarcely constitutes more than one-fifth or one-sixth.

Ninety-two million rubles in 1896; 77,000,000 rubles in 1897; 376,000,000 rubles all together since 1887—do these statistics prove that there is a danger for our vast Russian economy? Can our productive forces be sold at such a figure? That much foreign capital is no more than a leaven, which derives its significance not from its size but from the energy which it sets free in our sluggish industrial community. Foreign capital, five times smaller than Russian, is nonetheless more visible; it arouses attention because it carries with it better knowledge, more experience, and more initiative. But it deposits these cultural forces in Russia, and with that we really cannot find fault.

There are complaints that our protectionist system obstructs the import trade, that we do not bring in many foreign goods but instead open our doors wide to foreign capital. As a matter of fact, we imported foreign capital to the amount of 92,000,000 rubles in 1896 and 77,000,000 rubles in 1897, but foreign goods to the amount of 585,000,000 rubles and 560,000,000 rubles, respectively, i.e., six or seven times more than capital. But, on the other hand, if we look more deeply into the character of foreign capital, we find that in the last analysis it flows to us not in the form of money—our currency is furnished with a sufficient quantity of tokens—but, by a complex exchange process, in the form of useful goods. The import of foreign capital constitutes a part of the import of foreign goods, but with the difference that it is not spent for immediate consumption by the population but saved for productive purposes, for constructive investment in industry.

If we compare our import from abroad for the past years (1896 and 1897) with the average for the years 1888–90, we see that the import of pig iron, iron ore, steel, machines, apparatus, iron and steel products, iron ships —in a word, of capital goods which have long been protected and are necessary not for the consumer but for the producer—amounted to 98,000,000 rubles in 1896 (when 92,000,000 rubles of foreign capital was imported). In 1897 it amounted to 82,000,000 rubles (when 77,000,000 rubles of foreign capital was imported). In the woolen and silk industries the import of thread fell off and was replaced by the import of raw wool and silk, as the processing of these raw materials for the domestic consumer was done more and more by our own industries. In the cotton industry the import of finished goods, thread, and even raw cotton declined. It is obvious that the very character of our import changes; consumers' goods are replaced by producers' goods. And it seems hardly understandable to the minister of finance when it is said in the same breath that it is advantageous for the country to buy abroad, say, cotton fabrics year after year and yet that it is harmful for the same country to buy abroad the machines which could produce such fabrics inside the country. Why does everybody wholeheartedly approve if a country does not consume all its income but spends part of it for further production, and why should they at the same time consider it a danger if it practices equal thrift with its foreign purchases?

Apparently such falsehoods grow from dissatisfaction with the fact that the revenue from these new enterprises will go to the foreign capitalists and that the owners of the imported machinery which is set to work in the country will also be foreigners. But then the factories which produce abroad for the Russian consumer also belong to foreigners and are also founded by foreign capital; their revenue does not go to Russia, either. But there is a basic difference: the machinery imported into Russia and set to work here, even though it belongs to a foreigner, operates in a Russian setting. And it will not work by itself. It demands raw materials, fuel, lighting, and their auxiliary materials, and it demands human labor. All that, its owner must buy in Russia. Taking all this into account, it seems that the greater part of a ruble spent for any product of

foreign enterprise at work on Russian territory goes for the payment of various ingredients of production bought inside the country; and only the remaining part goes to the foreign capitalist as reward for his capital, knowledge, enterprise, and risk. How much of the price of a given commodity goes to the worker and how much to the entrepreneur may be seen, for instance, from analyses published by the American department of labor about the relationship between wages, entrepreneurial profit, and the price of goods. In the cotton industry 30 per cent goes to the workers, but only $6\frac{1}{2}$ per cent to the entrepreneur; in the glass industry 38 per cent goes to the workers, but only 9 per cent to the entrepreneur; in metallurgy and machine-building, 35 per cent to the worker and 10 per cent to the entrepreneur; in railway companies, 34 per cent to the workers and less than 3 per cent to the entrepreneurs. In this manner, out of one ruble paid for the finished commodity produced with the help of foreign capital, approximately 25–40 kopecks accrue to the Russian worker. Another considerable part is spent for raw materials and other auxiliary items, and only 3–10 kopecks is left as the entrepreneur's profit. But in paying for an imported commodity, the entire ruble leaves the country; and neither the producers of raw materials and fuel nor the worker receives a single kopeck. . . .

One has to consider also the fact that it is generally held advantageous to sell finished goods and dangerous to sell productive forces. The buyer obviously must be guided by the contrary principle. If in our present situation we cannot satisfy all our demands from our own resources and have to resort to purchasing abroad, it will be more advantageous for us to buy not finished goods but capital, which is one of the most necessary productive forces, particularly in industry. This consideration apparently is lost sight of by those who look so apprehensively at the prospect of paying dividends to foreigners.

What is that percentage, that outflow abroad of a part of our national income, which is so threatening to our future? Foreign capital comes to us from countries in which the capitalists are not spoiled by the fat profits to which our Russian capitalists are accustomed. It gravitates to us because in these countries capitalists are used to small profits. It works its way into our industry only because it is satisfied wherever it goes with smaller profits than its Russian predecessors. A new hundred million, flowing into the country from abroad during a given year, lowers by the laws of competition the rate of interest of all capital previously invested in Russian industry, which amounts to billions. If the country pays for these new hundred million rubles ten million in dividends, it gains still a considerably larger sum from the lower interest rates for the capital already invested in its economy. As the billions of national capital become cheaper, the prices of all industrial products will also fall considerably. We have at our disposal cheap labor, tremendous natural riches, and only the high price of capital now stands in the way of getting cheap goods. So why not let foreign capital help us to obtain still more cheaply that productive force of which alone we are destitute? Then we will be able to raise our industry to such a level that it can provide us with cheap goods in sufficient quantity not only for domestic consumption but also for export. Even at present we are getting closer to that goal. By bringing the transformation which is occurring under our eyes to its natural conclusion, we will eventually be able to pay the interest charges for capital received from Europe out of the profits of our Asiatic trade.

The entire country could be brought to that level if, with the help of new capital, the products of our industries could be made more cheaply and their productive forces could work more intensively for both domestic consumption and export. As history shows, these are the conditions under which a people rapidly becomes able to save and begins to accumulate its own capital. Only the first steps on that road are difficult. One has to take them, however, even with the help of foreign capital. Any further accumulation proceeds naturally by the laws of geometric progression. According to the experience of other industrially developed nations, millions give rise to billions. The fact that quantitatively the amount of foreign capital is small serves as the best indication that our economic policy does not aim at founding our further industrial growth primarily on foreign capital. We admit only a little of it, no bigger than a seed, which, embedded in our own thrift, should in the very near future produce national capital. In a way, obeying the laws of economic circulation, foreign capital against its will raises its own competitors. Tempted into Russia by higher dividends, it brings with it industrial energy, knowledge, a willingness to take risks, and in the end it will lower its dividends and amass so much native capital as to reduce imperceptibly its own influence. The presence of foreign capital will thus stand out only at the beginning of the process of industrialization.

It must also be stated that the influx of foreign capital does not proceed so easily and freely as is necessary to assure its continuation until the demands of the country no longer require the help of foreign savings. On the contrary, there are in our country such obstacles to its influx as exist in no other civilized country. We do not have the corporation laws which are in effect in the majority of civilized countries. Under such laws, everyone who wishes can form a joint-stock company by fulfilling certain conditions stipulated by law. In Russia a foreign company can be opened only by a special decree of the Committee of Ministers, which requires the confirmation of Your Imperial Highness. Russian joint-stock companies in which foreigners are shareholders are permitted to have only a minority of foreigners on their board of directors. In ten provinces of tsardom Poland, in eleven provinces of the western regions of Russia, in Turkestan, the Steppe regions, and the Amur district, neither foreign companies nor Russian companies with foreign participation are permitted to acquire property or exploit natural resources. A new company is admitted into Russia only with the permission of the local administration, and the acquisition of the right to exploit natural resources for a stated period is decided entirely on an individual basis and then only after preliminary investigation by the local administration into the actual needs of such enterprise. All foreign companies are subject to Russian laws and regulations as well as to ordinances and rules *which may be subsequently issued*. In permitting the activities of foreign companies in Russia, the government retains *the right to revoke at any time that permission and to demand the liquidation of any company.* Obviously, every detail of the influx of foreign capital into Russia is kept under strictest control by the central and local government. Whether this influx will be increased, decreased, or stopped altogether depends on their estimate and their interpretation of public welfare. Under these circumstances, one should rather speak of an excess of government control of foreign capital, which takes

its chances in going to Russia, and of unnecessary limitations imposed upon its freedom of investment. . . .

Considering the fact that the influx of foreign capital is the chief means for Russia in her present economic condition to speed up the accumulation of native capital, one should rather wish that our legislation concerning foreigners might be simplified. Historical experience shows that those human energies which accompany foreign capital are a useful creative ferment in the màss of the population of the most powerful nation and that they become gradually assimilated: mere economic ties change into organic ones. The imported cultural forces thus become an inseparable part of the country itself. Only a disintegrating nation has to fear foreign enslavement. Russia, however, is not China!

I have now analyzed the chief bases of the economic system which has been followed in Russia since the reign of Alexander III. . . .

To obtain cheaper goods, of which the population stands in such urgent need, by a substantial tariff reduction would be too expensive. It would forever deprive the country of the positive results of the protective system, for which a whole generation has made sacrifices; it would upset the industries which we have created with so much effort just when they were ready to repay the nation for its sacrifices.

It would be very dangerous to rely on the competition of foreign goods for the lowering of our prices. But we can attain the same results with the help of the competition of foreign capital, which, by coming into Russia, will help Russian enterprise to promote native industry and speed up the accumulation of native capital. Any obstructions to the influx of foreign capital will only delay the establishment of a mature and all-powerful industry. The country cannot

afford to defer that goal for long. The
burden of expensive manufactured
goods so oppresses the population that,
unless we resort to the help of foreign
capital for the quick development of our
industry, it would be better to give up
the tariff of 1891 altogether. Without the
help of foreign capital, which can create
an industry in a country surrounded by
high tariff barriers, a tariff is merely
preventive and not creative; such a tariff
can destroy a country. The tariff of
1891 was a beneficial measure only because of the subsequent trade treaties
and of the influx of foreign capital. One
cannot give up these logical corollaries
and not run the risk of rendering the
original measure harmful to national
welfare.

As our industries grow with the help
of foreign capital, it will be possible
gradually and in strict accordance with
the course of our industrial development
to lower our tariffs. Such reduction,
however, ought to be timed to the renewal of our trade treaties, because,
without a cautious reduction adjusted
to the conditions of our industry, we
will not be able to defend the interests
of our foreign trade. The coming renewal of our trade treaties on favorable
terms will be a difficult matter economically as well as politically. In dealing
with countries which buy our agricultural exports, we should insist on their
lowering their tariffs for our goods. But
this time the conflict with the interests
of native agriculture in these countries
with whom we must deal may be even
more bitter than at the time of the mem-
orable tariff war with Germany. It will
be possible to obtain from them better
conditions for our exports only if we,
on our part, are in a position to offer
them lowered tariffs for their industries.
A trade agreement is nothing but a
mutual exchange of such tariff reductions. If we voluntarily reduce our tariff

before 1904 without receiving compensation from foreign governments, then
we cannot induce them to reciprocate at
the time of the conclusion of a new
treaty. They not only will not agree to
making concessions to our exports but
under pressure from their native agrar-
ians might even raise their barriers.
That is the reason why our protective
tariff should stand unchanged until
1904.

If we carry our commercial and industrial system, begun in the reign of
Alexander III, consistently to the end,
then Russia will at last come of age
economically. Then her prosperity, her
trade and finance, will be based on two
reliable pillars, agriculture and industry; and the relations between them,
profitable to both, will be the chief motive power in our economy. Russia will
move closer to that goal with the help of
foreign capital, which, anyway, is required to make the protective tariff of
1891 effective.

Your Imperial Highness may see from
the foregoing that the economic policy
which the Russian government has followed for the last eight years is a carefully planned system, in which all parts
are inseparably interconnected. Other
persons, perhaps, can devise a better
system to establish the needed equilibrium more successfully in a different
way. Upon assuming the direction of
the ministry of finance, I found a protective system almost in full operation.
This system seemed to me then, and still
seems to me now, completely justified. I
bent all my efforts to speed its beneficial
results and to alleviate, principally with
the help of foreign capital, the hardships
of the transition period. It is possible
that we could have pursued a different
policy. But in following the directives of
Your Imperial Highness in such an inti-
mately interdependent matter as our na-

tional economy, I believed it my duty as minister of finance to ask Your Majesty to consider this point: even if it were possible to follow a different economic policy, it would, no matter how beneficial its ultimate results, produce in the immediate future a sharp break. Such an unnecessary shock would aggravate the hardships now existing. Only by a system strictly sustained, and not by isolated measures, can a healthy development be guaranteed to our national economy.

Pledging all my efforts to fulfil still better the will of my sovereign, I make bold to ask that it may please Your Imperial Highness to lend your firm support to the foundations of our economic system as I have analyzed them. They form, in essence, the following program:

1. To keep the tariff of 1891 unchanged until the renewal of our trade treaties.

2. To work in the meantime by all means for reducing the prices of industrial goods, not by increasing the import of goods from abroad but by the development of our domestic production, which makes mandatory the influx of foreign capital.

3. To postpone a lowering of our tariff until the time of the renewal of our trade treaties, so that, in turn, we can insist upon favorable terms for our agricultural exports.

4. Not to impose in the meantime new restraints on the influx of foreign capital, either through new laws or new interpretations of existing laws or, *especially, through administrative decrees.*

5. To maintain unchanged our present policy toward foreign capital until 1904, so that with its help our domestic industries can develop in the meantime to a position of such strength that in the renewal of trade treaties we may be able to make genuine reductions on several of our tariff rates.

6. To review in 1904, at the time of the renewal of the trade treaties, the problem of foreign capital and to decide then whether new safeguards should be added to existing legislation.

In submitting this program to favorable consideration by Your Imperial Highness, I respectfully ask that it may please you, my sovereign, to make certain that it may not be endangered henceforth by waverings and changes, because our industries, and our national economy in general, require a firm and consistent system carried to its conclusion.

If this program does not find the support of Your Imperial Highness, then, pray, tell me which economic policy I am to pursue.

STATE SECRETARY S. IU. WITTE
III/22/1899

38

THE NATIONAL PROBLEM IN RUSSIA

By Richard Pipes

Most students of Russia would agree that the nationalities question was one of the basic causes of the Russian Revolution. Yet one finds practically nothing on the subject in most treatments of Russian history. In view of the fact that almost 60 per cent of the Russian Empire's population were non-Russian, such neglect of a vital problem is inexcusable. The fact remains that very little has been written on the subject in English. Below we reproduce the bulk of the introductory chapter of a study of the problem in the first years of the Soviet era. Richard Pipes is professor of Russian history at Harvard University.

D. S. Mirsky's *Russia* is the only general history of the period up to the revolution which gives extensive analyses of the development of Russia's national minorities. For the Ukraine, see Mikhail Hrushevsky's *A History of the Ukraine* and the symposium entitled "The Role of the Ukraine in Modern History," *Slavic Review,* June, 1963, pp. 199–262. Central Asia is covered in Richard Pierce, *Russian Central Asia, 1867–1917,* and Serge Zenkovsky, *Pan-Turkism and Islam in Russia.* For the Caucasus, see W. E. D. Allen, *A History of the Georgian People.* One of several studies of the Jewish problem is Louis Greenberg, *The Jews in Russia* (2 vols.). See also Nicholas Vakar, *Belorussia: The Making of a Nation.* For Poland, see the *Cambridge History of Poland* in two volumes. The fate of Russia's nationalities during 1917 is discussed in E. H. Carr's *Bolshevik Revolution,* Vol. I. For a legal analysis, see Leonid Strakhovsky, "Constitutional Aspects of the Imperial Russian Government's Policy toward National Minorities," *Journal of Modern History,* XIII, 467–92.

. . . The first systematic census, undertaken in 1897, revealed that the majority (55.7 per cent) of the population of the Empire, exclusive of the Grand Duchy of Finland, consisted of non-Russians. The total population of the Empire was 122,-566,500. The principal groups were di-

Reprinted by permission of the publishers from Richard Pipes, *The Formation of the Soviet Union: Communism and Nationalism, 1917–1923* (Cambridge, Mass.: Harvard University Press, 1955), pp. 2–21. Footnotes have been omitted. Copyright 1954, by The President and Fellows of Harvard College.

vided, by native language, as follows (the figures are in per cent):

Slavs:

Great Russians	44.32
Ukrainians	17.81
Poles	6.31
Belorussians	4.68
Turkic peoples	10.82
Jews	4.03
Finnish peoples	2.78
Lithuanians and Latvians	2.46
Germans	1.42
Caucasian Mountain peoples (*gortsy*)	1.34
Georgians	1.07
Armenians	0.93
Iranian peoples	0.62
Mongolians	0.38
Others	1.03

One of the anomalies of pre-1917 Russia was the fact that although, to quote one observer, "the Russian Empire, Great Russian in its origin, ceased being such in its ethnic composition," the state, with some exceptions, continued to be treated constitutionally and administratively as a nationally homogeneous unit. The principle of autocracy, preserved in all its essentials until the Revolution of 1905, did not permit—at least in theory—the recognition of separate historic or national territories within the state in which the monarch's authority would be less absolute or rest on a legally different basis from that which he exercised at home. In practice, however, this principle was not always consistently applied. At various times in history Russian tsars did grant considerable autonomy to newly conquered territories, partly in recognition of their special status, partly in anticipation of political reforms in Russia, and in some cases they even entered into contractual relations wtih subject peoples, thus limiting their own power.

Poland from 1815 to 1831 and Finland from 1809 to 1899 were in theory as well as in practice constitutional monarchies. Other regions, such as the Ukraine from 1654 to 1764, Livonia and Estonia from 1710 to 1783 and from 1795 to the 1880's, enjoyed extensive self-rule. But those exceptions were incompatible with the maintenance of the principle of autocracy in Russia itself. Sooner or later, for one reason or another, the privileges granted to conquered peoples were retracted, contracts were unilaterally abrogated, and the subjects, together with their territories, were incorporated into the regular administration of the Empire.

At the close of the nineteenth century, Finland alone still retained a broad measure of self-rule. Indeed, in some respects, it possessed greater democratic rights than Russia proper; Finland under the tsars presented the paradox of a subject nation possessing more political freedom than the people who ruled over it. It was a separate principality, which the Russian monarch governed in his capacity as Grand Duke (*Velikii Kniaz'*). The tsar was the chief executive; he controlled the Grand Duchy's foreign affairs; he decided on questions of war and peace; he approved laws and the appointments of judges. The tsar also named the resident Governor General of the Grand Duchy, who headed the Finnish and Russian armies and the police on its territory, and who was responsible for the appointments of the local governors. A State Secretary served as the intermediary between the Russian monarch and the Finnish organs of self-rule. The Finns had complete control over the legislative institutions of the state. They possessed a bicameral legislative body, composed of a Senate and a Seim (Diet). The Senate considered legislative projects and performed the function of the supreme court of the state. The Seim was the highest legislative organ in the country. Called every five years on the basis of nationwide elections, it initiated and voted on legislation pertaining to its domain. No law could become effective without its approval. Finnish citizens in addition enjoyed other privileges. Every Finnish subject, while in Russia proper, could claim all the rights of Russian citizens, although Russian citizens in Finland were considered foreigners. In every respect, therefore, Finland had a uniquely privileged position in the Russian Empire, which resembled more closely the dominion relationship in existence in the British Empire than the customary colonial relationship prevalent in other parts of Russia. The Finns had originally acquired these privileges from the Swedes, who had ruled their country before the Russian conquest. The tsars preserved them because Finland was acquired by Alexander I, a monarch of relatively liberal views, who, for a time, had thought of introducing a constitutional regime into Russia proper.

Prior to 1917, the Russian Empire also possessed two protectorates, the Central Asian principalities of Bukhara and Khiva. In 1868 and 1873 respectively, these states recognized the sovereignty of the Russian tsar and ceded to him the right to represent them in relations with other powers. They also granted Russians exclusive commercial privileges and were compelled to abolish slavery in their domains. Otherwise, they enjoyed self-rule.

The remaining borderlands of the Empire were administered, in the last decades of the *ancien régime*, in a manner which did not differ essentially—though it differed in some particulars—from that in effect in the territories of Russia proper. Whatever special powers the Imperial Government deemed necessary to grant to the authorities administering these territories were derived not so much from a recognition of the multinational character of the state or from a desire to adapt political institutions to the needs of the inhabitants, as from the impracti-

cability of extending the administrative system of the Great Russian provinces in its entirety to the borderland. . . .

Russian law also made special provisions for certain groups of non-Russian subjects. Russia, prior to 1917, retained the system of legally recognized classes and class privileges, long since defunct in Western Europe. Within this system there was a social category of so-called inorodtsy, a term which has no exact equivalent in English and can best be rendered by the French *peuples allogènes*. The inorodtsy comprised the Jews and most of the nomadic peoples of the Empire, who were subject to special laws rather than to the general laws promulgated in the territories which they inhabited. For the nomadic inorodtsy, this meant in effect that they possessed the right to self-rule, with their native courts and tribal organization. Their relations with the Russian authorities were limited to the payment of a fixed tribute or tax, usually to an agent of the Ministry of Interior or of State Properties. By settling on land and abandoning nomadic habits, an inorodets changed from his status to that of a regular Russian citizen, with all the duties and privileges of the class which he had joined; as long as he retained his inorodets status, he gave nothing to the government and received nothing in return. Russian treatment of the nomads was, on the whole, characterized by tolerance and respect for native traditions. Much of the credit for this must be given to the great liberal statesman M. M. Speranskii, who, at the beginning of the nineteenth century, had laid down the basic principles for their administration.

For the other subgroup of inorodtsy, the Jews, membership in this class entailed stringent restrictions (most of them stemming from eighteenth-century legislation). These forbade them to move out of a strictly defined area in the southwestern and northwestern parts of the Empire, the so-called Pale of Settlement, to purchase landed property, or to settle outside the towns. Such disabilities brought severe social and economic suffering, for the Jews were crowded into towns where they had no adequate basis for livelihood and had to rely heavily on primitive handicraftsmanship and petty trade to survive. By creating abnormal economic conditions in the Jewish communities and preventing them from taking their place in the life of society, the restrictive legislation contributed to the large number of Jews found in radical movements at the beginning of the twentieth century. The Jew could alter his status only by adopting Christianity.[1]

At no point in its history did tsarist Russia formulate a consistent policy toward the minorities. In the early period of the Empire, approximately from the middle of the sixteenth until the middle of the eighteenth century, the attitude of the government toward its non-Russian subjects was influenced strongly by religion. Where discrimination existed, the principal reason was the desire of the regime to convert Moslems, Jews, and other non-Christians to the Orthodox faith. Toward the end of the eighteenth century, with the secularization of the Russian monarchy, this religious element lost its force, and political considerations loomed ever larger. Thereafter, the treatment of the minorities, as of the Great Russians themselves, was largely determined by the desire on the part of the monarchs to maintain and enforce the principle of autocracy; minority groups which challenged this effort in the name of national rights were treated as harshly as were Russian groups which challenged it in the name of democracy or freedom in general.

[1] Exceptions were made only in the case of certain categories of Jews who were either rich merchants or had a higher education.

The period from the accession of Alexander III (1881) to the outbreak of the 1905 Revolution was that in which persecution of the minorities culminated. The Russian government perhaps for the first time in its entire history adopted a systematic policy of Russification and minority repression, largely in an endeavor to utilize Great Russian national sentiments as a weapon against growing social unrest in the country. During this period, Finnish privileges were violated through a suspension of the legislative powers of the Seim (1899), the introduction of the compulsory study of Russian in Finnish secondary schools, the subordination of the Finnish Ministry of Post and Telegraphs to the corresponding Russian institution, and other restrictive measures. Polish cultural activity was severely limited; the Jewish population was subjected to pogroms inspired or tolerated by the government, and to further economic restrictions (for instance, the revocation of the right to distill alcohol); the Ukrainian cultural movement was virtually brought to a standstill as a result of the prohibitions imposed on printing in the Ukrainian language (initiated in the 1870's); the properties of the Armenian church were confiscated by the Viceroy of the Caucasus (1903). It was, however, not accidental that this era of Russification coincided with the period of greatest governmental reaction, during which the Great Russian population itself lost many of the rights which it had acquired in the Great Reforms of Alexander II (1856–81).

The outbreak of the Revolution of 1905 and the subsequent establishment of a constitutional monarchy brought to a halt the period of national persecution but it did not repair all the damage done in the previous quarter-century. The Dumas, especially the First, in which the minorities were well represented, gave only slight attention to the national question, though they provided an open rostrum of discussions on that topic. In 1907, the government regained supremacy over the liberal elements; it changed the electoral laws in favor of the Russian upper classes, among whom supporters of the autocracy were strong, depriving the remainder of the population of a proportionate voice in the legislative institutions of the state. The borderlands, where liberal and socialist parties enjoyed a particularly strong following, were hardest hit by the change, and some (Turkestan, for instance) lost entirely the right to representation.

NATIONAL MOVEMENTS IN RUSSIA

The paradox—and tragedy—of Russian history in the last century of the *ancien régime* was the fact that while the government clung to the anachronistic notion of absolutism, the country itself was undergoing an extremely rapid economic, social, and intellectual evolution, which required new, more flexible forms of administration. The nineteenth century was a period when capitalism and the industrial revolution penetrated Russia, stimulating the development of some social classes which had previously been weak (a middle class, an industrial proletariat, and a prosperous, land-owning peasantry), and undermining others (e.g., the landed aristocracy). Western ideas, such as liberalism, socialism, nationalism, utilitarianism, now found a wide audience in Russia. The Russian monarchy, which until the nineteenth century had been the principal exponent of Western ideas in Russia, now lagged behind. The second half of the reign of Alexander I (1815–25) marked the beginning of that rift between the monarchy and the articulate elements in Russian society which, widening continuously, led to conspiratorial movements, terrorist activity, and revolution, and finally, in 1917, to the demise of monarchy itself.

The national movement among the minorities of the Russian state, which also began in the nineteenth century, represented one of the many forms which this intellectual and social ferment assumed. Because the traditions and socio-economic interests of the various groups of subjects, including the minorities, were highly diversified, their cultural and political development tended to take on a local, and in some cases, a national coloring. Romantic philosophy, which first affected Russia in the 1820's, stimulated among the minority intellectuals an interest in their own languages and past traditions, and led directly to the evolution of cultural nationalism, the first manifestation of the national movement in the Russian borderlands.

Next, in the 1860's and 1870's, the spread of Russian Populism, with its emphasis on the customs and institutions of the peasantry, provided the minority intellectuals with a social ideology and induced them to establish contact with the broad masses of their own, predominantly rural, population. Finally, the development of modern political parties in Russia, which took place about 1900, led to the formation of national parties among the minorities, which in almost all instances adopted either liberal or socialist programs and affiliated themselves closely with their Russian counterparts. Until the breakdown of the tsarist regime, such Russian and minority parties fought side by side for parliamentary rights, local self-rule, and social and economic reforms; but while the Russian parties stressed the general needs of the whole country, the minority parties concentrated on local, regional requirements. The fact that the minorities in Russia developed a national consciousness before their fellow-nationals across the border (the Ukrainians in Austrian Galicia, Armenians in the Ottoman Empire, Azerbaijanis in Persia, and so on) was a result of the more rapid intellectual and economic growth of the Russian Empire.

The refusal of the tsarist regime to recognize the strivings of the minorities was part of the larger phenomenon of its failure to respond to the growing clamor on the part of all its citizens for fundamental reforms, and had equally dire results.

THE UKRAINIANS AND BELORUSSIANS

The Ukrainians and Belorussians (22.3 and 5.8 million respectively in 1897) descended from the Eastern Slav tribes which had been separated from the main body of Russians as a result of the Mongolian invasions and Polish-Lithuanian conquest of the thirteenth and fourteenth centuries. For over five centuries, these two parts of Eastern Slavdom developed under different cultural influences. By the end of the eighteenth century, when Moscow had conquered the areas inhabited by the other Eastern Slavic groups, the dissimilarities caused by centuries of separate growth were too considerable to permit a simple fusion into one nation. Through contact with their western neighbors, those peoples had acquired distinct cultural traditions with their own dialects and folklores. Moreover, the steppes of the Black Sea region had for several centuries following the Mongolian invasion remained a no man's land, where runaway serfs, criminal elements, or simply adventurers from Poland, Muscovy, or the domains of the Ottoman Empire had found a haven. In the course of the sixteenth and seventeenth centuries, those groups to which the Turkic name "Cossack" (freebooter) was applied had formed an anarchistic society, with a center along the lower course of the Dnieper, which lived in complete freedom, hunting, fishing, or pillaging. In the course of time, these Cossacks—with their ideal of unlimited external and internal freedom—developed a new socio-economic type of great importance for the future Ukrainian national consciousness.

Tied by the bonds of religion and the memory of common origin, but separated by cultural and socio-economic differences, the Ukrainians and Belorussians did not coalesce completely with their Great Russian rulers. The rapid economic development of the rich Ukrainian agriculture following the liberation of the serfs, especially in the last two decades of the *ancien régime*, when the Ukrainian provinces became one of the world's leading grain-exporting regions, created an additional basis for Ukrainian nationalism. There now emerged a prosperous class of independent farmers, without parallel in Russia proper. On the whole, the Ukrainian peasantry knew neither the communal type of land ownership nor the service relationship between peasant and landlord (*barshchina*). Its soil was individually owned, and paid for by money, not by personal labor.

During the eighteenth and part of the nineteenth century, it was still an open question whether the cultural and economic peculiarities of the Ukrainian people would lead to the the formation of a separate nation. The absence of a Ukrainian intelligentsia and centripetal economic forces militated against; the Cossack tradition and the interests of the Ukrainian peasants for. Throughout its existence, the Ukrainian movement had to develop in an atmosphere of skepticism in which not only the validity of its demands but the very existence of the nationality it claimed to represent was seriously questioned by persons unconnected with the movement. This accounts, at least in part, for the great vehemence with which Ukrainian nationalists tended to assert their claims.

The cultural phase of the Ukrainian movement began in the 1820's, under the stimulus of the ideas of Western romanticism transmitted through Russia. Scholars began it by undertaking ethnographic studies of the villages of southwestern Russia, where they uncovered a rich and old folklore tradition and the ethos of a peasant culture, the existence of which had been scarcely suspected. On this basis, there arose in Russia and in the Ukrainian provinces a sizable provincial literature which reached a high point with the publication in 1840 of the *Kobzar,* a collection of original poems in Ukrainian by Taras Shevchenko, then a student at the Saint Petersburg Academy of Arts. This began the transformation of a peasant dialect into a literary, and, subsequently, a national language: In 1846, a number of writers and students at Kiev founded the Cyril and Methodius Society—a secret organization permeated with the spirit of utopian socialism, German idealism, and the notions of international brotherhood and social equalitarianism. Present also was a strong element of cultural Pan-slavism. This society, like others of similar type in Russia proper, was suppressed in 1847.

In the second half of the century, the Ukrainian movement patterned itself after Populism, prevalent in Russia at the time. It devoted itself to the social problems of the peasantry, and displayed strong sympathy for peasant customs and manners. The cultural movement received a temporary setback in the 1870's when the Russian government, suspecting a liaison between the "Ukrainophiles" (as the Ukrainian Populists were called) and Polish nationalists, issued edicts which for all practical purposes forbade printing in the Ukrainian language. For the next thirty years, its center shifted to Galicia, where it en-joyed greater freedom owing to Vienna's interest in utilizing Ukrainian (Ruthenian) patriotism as a counterbalance to Polish nationalism in this province.

Until the end of the nineteenth century, the Ukrainians had no political parties of their own. In the Ukraine, as in Galicia, there were numerous provincial organizations of a cultural character, the so-called *Hromady* (Communities), devoted to the study of Ukrainian life, but they took no part in political activity. It was only in 1900 that a society of young Ukrainians founded the first political organization, the Revolutionary Ukrainian Party (or RUP for short). This party, established in Kharkov, represented a merger of various groups dissatisfied with the purely cultural activity of the older generation, and determined to give the Ukrainian movement a political expression. The RUP utilized the local Hromady to spread its influence to the provincial towns and villages. Its headquarters were located in Kiev, but the nerve center was abroad, in Lemberg (Lwów, Lviv), where the RUP printed propaganda to be smuggled into Russia, and engaged in other illegal activities. The RUP united several divergent tendencies: separatist, anarchistic, Marxist, Populist, and others. At first the extreme nationalist, irredentist element won the upper hand; the first program of the RUP (1900) demanded unconditional independence for a "greater Ukraine" extending between the Don and the San rivers. But before long, the more moderate elements prevailed and the RUP withdrew the demand for Ukrainian independence from its program, replacing it with a demand for autonomy within the Russian Empire. The RUP played a part in stimulating agrarian disorders in the Ukraine in 1902–3, and in spreading ideas of Ukrainian nationalism among the masses. It also served as a training ground for many of the future political leaders of the Ukrainian cause.

A few years after its formation, the RUP began to fall apart, as the various groups which it had united stepped out to form independent parties. The first to depart were the separatists (*samostiiniki*) who, dissatisfied with the gravitation of the party toward Russian socialist organizations, founded the National Ukrainian Party (NUP) in 1902. Next went the extreme left radicals, who, in 1905, joined the Russian Social Democratic Labor Party. The remainder of the RUP adopted the Social Democratic program and renamed itself the Ukrainian Social Democratic Labor Party (USDRP). Its program included the demand for Ukrainian autonomy and the establishment of a regional Seim (Diet) in Kiev. In 1905, the liberal elements of the Ukrainian society who had not been associated with the RUP formed a separate Ukrainian Democratic Radical Party (UDRP). Thus within a few years, a large number of Ukrainian parties appeared on the scene—an early manifestation of the extreme factionalism which was to become a characteristic trait of Ukrainian political life. The USDRP and UDRP were the most influential, though none of them seems to have had a numerous following or a very efficient apparatus. The USDRP co-operated closely with the Russian Marxists, whereas the UDRP supported the Russian Kadets.

The Belorussian movement developed more slowly than the Ukrainian. Its cultural phase did not get well under way until the beginning of the twentieth century, with the publication of the *Nasha niva* (Our Land), the first newspaper in the Belorussian language. The first Belorussian national party was the Belorussian Revolutionary Hromada, founded in 1902 in St. Petersburg by a group of students associated with the Polish Socialist Party (PPS), and later renamed the Belorussian Socialist Hromada. The Hromada took over the program of the PPS, adding to it a statement on the national question, which demanded the introduction of federal relations in Russia, with territorial autonomy for the provinces adjoining Vilna and national-cultural autonomy for all the minorities of the region. The Belorussian movement, operating in one of Western Russia's poorest areas, and having to compete with Polish, Jewish, Russian, and Lithuanian parties, remained ineffective and exercised no influence on political developments in prerevolutionary Russia.

THE TURKIC PEOPLES

By 1900 Russia had within its borders nearly fourteen million Turks—several million more than the Ottoman Empire itself. The remaining Moslems were either of Iranian stock, or else belonged to North Caucasian groups whose racial origin is uncertain.

Culturally and economically, the most advanced Turks in Russia were the Volga Tatars (over two million in 1897) who inhabited the regions adjacent to Kazan. Descendants of the Kazan Khanate which had been conquered by Ivan IV, the Volga Tatars had early abandoned the nomadic habits of their ancestors and had settled in the cities and on the soil. Taking advantage of the geographic location of their territory, they developed considerable commercial activity, serving as middlemen between Russia and the East. This economic position they retained after the Russian conquest. A statistical survey undertaken at the beginning of the nineteenth century revealed that the Tatars owned one-third of the industrial establishments in the Kazan province, and controlled most of the trade with the Orient. The Volga Tatars were the first of the Turks in Russia, or for that matter, anywhere in the world, to develop a middle class. This enabled them to assume leadership of the Turkic movement in Russia.

The Crimean Tatars and the Azerbaijani Turks were next in order of cultural advancement. Both these groups had come relatively late under Russian dominion, the former in 1783, the latter in the first decade of the nineteenth century. The Crimean Tatars were the remnants of the Crimean Khanate which, at one time, had dominated the Black Sea steppes and from the middle of the fifteenth century to the Russian conquest had been under the protection of the Ottoman Sultan. At the time of the Russian occupation, they had numbered, according to contemporary estimates, one half million, but several waves of mass migration to Turkish Anatolia had reduced that number by 1862 to one hundred thousand. In 1897 there were in the Crimea 196,854 Tatars. The Crimean Tatars owed their cultural advance partly to contact with other nations, made possible by their geographic location, and partly to the wealth acquired from subtropical horticulture.

The Azerbaijanis (1,475,553 in 1897) lived along the Kura River valley of Transcaucasia. They formed a smaller part of that branch of the Turks, the majority of whom then, as now, inhabited northwestern Persia. The Azerbaijanis were an agricultural people, consisting of a peasantry and landowning aristocracy. With the development of the Baku oil industries on their territory, the Azerbaijanis also acquired the beginning of an urban middle class.

The Central Asian Uzbeks (about two million in 1897, not counting those inhabiting Khiva and Bukhara) also were largely settled, and had developed an urban trading and artisan class. At the time of the Russian conquest they were politically and economically the rulers of Turkestan.

The remaining Turkic groups in Russia consisted largely of seminomads: Bashkirs of the southwest Ural region (1,493,000 in 1897); the Kazakhs and Kirghiz (4,285,800), and the Turkmens of Central Asia (281,357 in 1897); and the numerous small tribes of Siberia. The majority of those groups combined cattle-breeding and the tending of sheep with agriculture.

Nearly all the Turkic peoples spoke similar dialects of the same language and had a common racial descent. An observer might have expected, therefore, that "Turkism" or "Pan-Turkism" would provide the basis for a national movement of the Turkic groups in Russia. This, however, did not prove to be the case. The concept of a single Turkic people emerged only at the end of the nineteenth century and, before the Revolution of 1917, had not had an opportunity to affect even the Turkic intelligentsia, let alone the broader masses of the population.

The Turks in Russia, insofar as they felt a sense of unity, were much more conscious of their common Moslem faith than of their common ethnic origin. Since Islam, like most Oriental religions, is not only a set of beliefs but also a way of life, it affects family relations, law, commerce, education, and virtually every other aspect of human existence. This religious bond provided the main basis of the Turkic movement; it was, prior to 1917, always more important than the ethnic element. But it also presented great difficulties to the slowly developing national movement among the Russian Turks which from the first took on an openly westernizing character, and as such was anticlerical. Its leaders found themselves thus in the position of having to uproot the very ideas which provided the *raison d'être* of their movement.

The national awakening of Russian Turks had its beginning in the Crimea.

Its leader was Ismail-bey Gasprinskii (Gaspraly or Gaspirali) who, in 1883–84, established in his native city of Bakhchisarai a Turkish-language newspaper, the *Terdzhiman* (*Tercüman*, meaning Interpreter) which before long became the prototype for all Moslem periodical publications in Russia and served as an organ of Moslems throughout the entire country. Gasprinskii also founded a new school system, based on the principles of modern education, to replace the *medresse,* which taught Arabic and restricted instruction to subjects bearing on religion. On the basis of the experience which these efforts provided, there grew up in Russia within one generation a considerable network of periodical publications and "new-method," or so-called *dzhaddidist* (*jadidist*) schools. By 1913 Russia had sixteen Turkic periodical publications, of which five were daily newspapers. All except three of those were written in the dialect of the Volga Tatars which was quickly gaining acceptance as the literary language of all Russian Turks. In the same year, there were published in Russia 608 books in Turkic languages in a total edition of 2,812,130 copies, of which 178 titles and 1,282,240 copies were devoted to religious subjects, while the remainder were secular. The reformed school system, which the tsarist government allowed to develop freely, spread to the Volga region and from there to Turkestan. On the eve of the First World War, Russian Turks had access to a considerable number of elementary and several secondary schools of the secular, Western kind which taught youth in their native languages free from government interference or supervision. From educational institutions of this kind, supported largely by wealthy Kazan or Baku merchants, emerged the intelligentsia which, during the Russian Revolution and the first

decade of Soviet rule, was to play a crucial role in the history of the Moslem borderlands.

Beginning with the Russian Revolution of 1905, the political movement among Russian Turks took two parallel courses. There was an All-Russian Moslem movement, and there were local movements of the various national groups. Occasionally the two forms actively supplemented one another, occasionally they conflicted, but they never merged completely. In 1905 and 1906, the leading representatives of the Moslem intelligentsia met in three congresses, the first and third at Nizhnii Novgorod (now Gorkii), the second at Moscow. At those meetings, the principle of unity of all Russian Moslems was asserted through the establishment of a Moslem Union (*Ittifāq-ul-Muslimīn* or *Ittifāk*) and agreements for the caucusing of the Moslem deputies in the Russian Dumas. The Third Congress (August 1906) adopted resolutions urging the introduction of regional autonomy into Russia, without specifying whether or not it was to rest on the national principle.

In the First and Second Dumas, in which they had thirty and thirty-nine deputies respectively, the Moslems formed a separate Moslem Faction in which the Volga Tatar Saadri Maksudov (Maksudi) later came to play a dominant role. The majority of them supported the Russian liberals or Kadets, though small socialist groups were also present within the Faction. The change of electoral laws, effected in 1907 to favor the election of Russian deputies, reduced the number and importance of Moslems in the last two Dumas.

Simultaneously with the All-Russian Moslem movement—which was dominated by liberal elements—there developed regional Turkic parties, generally of a more radical character. The

Volga Tatars again led the way. In 1906 two Volga Tatar writers, Fuad Tuktarov and Gaijaz (Ayaz) Iskhakov (Iskhaky), founded a local counterpart of the Russian Socialist Revolutionary Party, which, grouped around the newspaper *Tang* (Dawn), advocated the immediate transfer of all land to the people and, wherever possible, of factories to the workers. The relations of their party, the *Tangchelar* (*Tançelar*), with the pro-Kadet Ittifak were cool and occasionally hostile.

In Azerbaijan a group of young Turkic intellectuals, many of whom had been closely associated with the local Bolshevik organization during the 1905 Revolution, formed in Baku in 1911–12 the Moslem Democratic Party *Mussavat* (*Musavat*). Its original leader was a young journalist, Mehmed Emin Resul-zade. The first program of this Party had a pronounced Pan-Islamic character, expressing the desire for the reëstablishment of Moslem unity throughout the world and the revival of the ancient glories of Islam. It advanced no specific demands for the Azerbaijani people. Indeed, the very concept of a distinct Azerbaijani nation did not come into being until 1917, when local nationalists applied to their people the geographic name of the Persian province inhabited by Turks.

These two parties, established among the leading Turkic peoples in Russia, had no counterparts among the smaller Turkic groups which were to acquire national organizations only during the Revolution of 1917.

THE PEOPLES OF THE CAUCASUS

The term Caucasus (*Kavkaz*) is applied to the territory adjoining the northern and southern slopes of the Caucasian Mountains which stretch between the Caspian and Black seas, a thousand-mile-long chain with elevations surpassing those of the European Alps. Under tsarist administration this area was divided into six provinces or *gubernie* (Baku, Tiflis, Erivan, Elisavetpol, Kutais, and Chernomore), five regions or *oblasti* (Batum, Daghestan, Kars, Kuban, and Terek), and one separate district or *okrug* (Zakataly). Topographically, the Caucasus can be divided into two main parts, separated from each other by the Caucasian range. The Northern Caucasus (*Severnyi Kavkaz*) includes the steppes stretching from the mountains toward the Volga and Don rivers and the northern slopes of the mountains themselves. South of the range is Transcaucasia (*Zakavkaz'e*), an area covered by mountains of medium height and traversed by three river valleys: the Rion, Kura, and Araks (Aras). The total territory of the Caucasus is 158,000 square miles.

The Caucasian population is extraordinarily heterogeneous. It may safely be said that no other territory of equal size anywhere in the world displays a comparable diversity of languages and races. The mountains of the Caucasus, situated near the main routes of Asiatic migrations into Europe and to the Near Eastern centers of civilization, have offered a natural haven for peoples seeking escape from wars and invasions, and in the course of the past three thousand years nearly every one of the peoples inhabiting or passing through the region has left its mark on the Caucasus' ethnic composition. In 1916 the Caucasus had 12,266,000 inhabitants, divided into the following principal groups:

Russians, Ukrainians, Belorussians	4,023,000
Azerbaijanis and other Moslems	2,455,000
Armenians	1,860,000
Georgians	1,791,000

Caucasian Mountain
peoples 1,519,000
Other European peoples . 140,000
Other indigenous peoples . 478,000

The greatest ethnic heterogeneity is to be found in the Northern Caucasus, and especially in its eastern sections, Daghestan and Terek. The term "Caucasian Mountain peoples" (*Kavkazskie gortsy*, or simply *gortsy*) has no ethnic significance; it is merely a general term used to describe the numerous small groups inhabiting the valleys and slopes of the Caucasian range. There one can find living side by side the descendants of the Jews carried into captivity by the Babylonians, of the Avars, who had ravaged Eastern Europe between the sixth and eighth centuries; and of numerous other small peoples, some of whom number no more than a few hundred. In Transcaucasia, on the other hand, in addition to the Azerbaijani Turks, there are two sizable national groups: the Georgians and the Armenians. Their racial origin is still a matter of dispute, but it is certain that they have inhabited their present territories continuously for over two thousand years. Their history has been closely associated with that of the entire Near East, and, at various times, they have been subjected to the dominant powers in that region, the Persians, Greeks, Romans, Arabs, Byzantines, Mongolians, and Turks.

The central factor in the historical development of the Georgians and the Armenians was their adoption of Christianity in the fourth century. As a result of this, they entered into contact with Byzantium and, through it, with Europe. This bond with the West not only brought these two peoples under different cultural influences from those of their neighbors, but also developed in them a consciousness of distinctness, of separateness from the civilization of the Near East, which remained long after

they had been cut off from the main body of their co-religionists by the spread of Islam. Surrounded on all sides by Moslems, the Christian Georgians and Armenians always felt themselves drawn to Europe and were susceptible to Western ideas. For the same reason, they passed voluntarily under Russian dominion, and once incorporated into Russia, got along well with their Christian rulers. Eastern Georgia became a vassal of Russia at the end of the eighteenth century to escape Persian misrule; it was not allowed to enjoy the privileges of vassalage for long, however, and in 1801 it was incorporated into the Russian Empire by a tsarist edict. Russian Armenia came under Russian rule as one of the prizes of the victorious wars which the tsars waged with Persia at the beginning of the nineteenth century. Russia ruled only a small part of the Armenian population, the majority of which continued to live on territories of the Ottoman Empire.

The Caucasus is a purely geographic, not a historic or cultural concept. There never was, or could have been, a "Caucasian" national movement. The ethnic, religious, and socio-economic divergencies separating the main groups of the population from each other, not only prevented the emergence of a united cultural or political movement, but actually led to internal frictions and at times to armed conflicts. Instead of one, there were separate national movements of the principal ethnic groups.

The Georgians were primarily a rural people, composed of a largely impoverished ancient feudal aristocracy (5.26 per cent of the entire Georgian population in 1897) and a peasantry. The Georgian urban class was small and insignificant. It was the *déclassé* nobility which, from the beginning, assumed the leadership over the cultural and political life of Georgia. The Georgians possessed nearly all the elements that usually go into the formation of national consciousness: a distinct language, with its own alphabet; an ancient and splendid literary heritage; a national territory; and a tradition of statehood and military prowess. In the 1870's, a cultural movement arose among the Georgian aristocracy, which, with its interest in the newly liberated peasant, assumed forms akin to Russian populism.

The political phase of the national movement in Georgia acquired a somewhat unusual character. Whether it was due to the fact that the carriers of the national ideology in Georgia did not belong to the middle class but to an anti-bourgeois nobility, or whether it was caused by the general receptivity to Western ideas characteristic of the Georgians, or by still other causes, the Georgian movement became from its very inception closely identified if not completely fused with Marxian socialism. Marxism was introduced into Georgia in the 1880's and at once encountered an enthusiastic reception. In the First Duma, six of the seven Georgian deputies were Social Democrats; in the Third, two out of three. Georgian socialists did not form separate organizations of their own, but joined the regional branches of the Russian Social Democratic Labor Party, where they soon attained considerable prominence. They had no national demands. Noi Zhordaniia, one of the chief theoreticians of the movement, stated repeatedly that all demands for autonomy were utopian, and that Georgia would obtain sufficient self-rule as a result of the anticipated future democratization of Russia. At the beginning of the twentieth century, a small group of intellectuals, dissatisfied with this attitude, left the Social Democratic Party and founded a separate organization, *Sakartvelo* (Georgia), which in time transformed itself

into the Georgian Party of Socialist-Federalists. Their program, close in social questions to that of the Russian Socialist Revolutionary Party, called for the establishment of a Russian Federal Republic with autonomy for Georgia. Its popular following, however, judging by elections to the Dumas, was small. About 1910 the Georgian Mensheviks somewhat modified their views and adopted formulae calling for extraterritorial cultural autonomy for Georgia.

The absence of territorial demands in the program of the most powerful party of the Georgian movement need not be interpreted as an indication of the lack of Georgian national sentiment. The national ideals of the Georgian intelligentsia were identified, ideologically and psychologically, with the goals of Russian and international socialism. As long as this attitude persisted—that is, as long as Georgian intellectuals believed Marxist socialism capable of dealing with the problems posed by the development of the Georgian nation—there was no necessity to advance territorial demands.

The position of the Armenians was different from that of the Georgians in several important respects: instead of living in a well-defined area of their own, the Armenians were scattered in small groups among hostile Turkic peoples throughout Eastern Anatolia and Transcaucasia, and had a numerous, influential middle class. The paramount issue for the Armenians, ever since the massacres which their population had suffered in the Ottoman Empire in the 1890's, was Turkey and the Turks. Their main concern was how to save the defenseless Armenian population from further massacres engendered by the religious and socio-economic conflicts between the Armenian bourgeoisie or petty bourgeoisie and the Turkic land-owning and peasant classes, as well as by the cynical attitude of the central government of Turkey. In this respect, the problems facing the Armenians were not unlike those confronting the Jews in the western regions of the Empire. Then there was also the question of devising a political solution which would be suited to the ethnic distribution of the Armenian population and provide its urban classes with commercial advantages. The Armenian movement acquired early in its history a conspiratorial, para-military character. It was essentially middle and lower-middle class in content, and much less socialist in spirit than the political movements in Georgia or in most of the remaining Russian borderlands.

The cultural movement in modern Armenia had begun already in the 1840's, at first under the influence of German and French, and then of Russian, ideas, and was actively supported by Armenian merchants residing in the Levant and Western Europe. Its organization centered around the separate Armenian Church establishments and its head, the Catholicos. In the 1890's there were numerous Armenian schools, as well as many societies and cultural centers, supported by the church in Russian Armenia.

The first Armenian political party was the *Hnchak* (Clarion), founded in 1887 in Switzerland. This party was socialist in character. In the 1890's, some of its members separated and founded the *Dashnaktsutiun* (Federation) which during the next quarter of a century came to occupy a dominant role in Armenian political life. The Dashnaks were, in their social program and in their general reliance on terroristic methods of struggle against the Ottoman government, somewhat akin to the Russian Socialist Revolutionaries, though the latter refused to establish direct relations with the Dashnaktsutiun on the grounds that it was allegedly a

petty-bourgeois, nationalistic group which employed socialist slogans only as camouflage. The national program adopted by the Dashnaktsutiun in 1907 made the following demands concerning the Russian Caucasus:

Transcaucasia, as a democratic republic, is to be a component part of the Federal Russian Republic. The former is to be connected with the latter in questions of defense of the state, foreign policy, monetary and tariff systems.

The Transcaucasian Republic is to be independent in all its internal affairs: it is to have its parliament, elected by means of universal, direct, equal, secret, and proportional vote. Every citizen, regardless of sex, is to have the right to vote beginning at the age of twenty.

Transcaucasia is to send its representatives, elected by the same system of universal elections, to the All-Russian Parliament.

The Transcaucasian Republic is to be divided into cantons, which are to have the right to broad local autonomy, and communes with an equal right to self-rule in communal matters.

In determining cantonal borders, it is imperative to take into account the topographical and ethnographical peculiarities of the country in order to form groupings as homogeneous as possible.

The Dashnak program also demanded cultural autonomy, and the right to use local languages in addition to the governmental language of all Russia. Whereas in Russia the Armenian population was too scattered to permit application of national autonomy, the party did request territorial rights for the Armenians in that part of its program which dealt with the Ottoman Empire.

The North Caucasian peoples had no indigenous national parties despite the fact that they were less assimilated and in many respects more dissatisfied with Russian rule than were the peoples of Transcaucasia. The mountains of the Caucasus had been conquered by Russia in some of the bloodiest and longest campaigns of its entire history. No other acquisition had cost Russia as much effort as that impoverished land inhabited by the wild and independent mountaineers. The forceful expulsions carried on by the tsarist regime, the mass migrations of the people of whole regions following the Russian conquest, punitive expeditions, Cossack encroachments on land, the hostility of the men of the mountains for the inhabitant of the plains, of the Moslem for the Christian—all this created a suitable foundation for national animosities. But it was not sufficient to produce an organized national movement. The North Caucasian mountain peoples possessed no ethnic unity and formed no cultural community; they were isolated from each other by mountain ranges. Moreover, some of the groups feuded among themselves, largely as a result of great discrepancies in the distribution of land.

The Caucasus therefore had not one but several national movements developing side by side. Of unity, there was none. The Georgians had their eyes turned to Russia, to Europe, and to socialism; the chief concern of the Armenians was the Turk on both sides of the frontier; the Azerbaijanis participated in the All-Russian Moslem movement; and the inhabitants of the mountains had developed as yet no definite political orientation.

The national movements among the minorities inhabiting the Russian Empire arose under the stimulus of the same forces which had affected Russian society in the nineteenth century: Romantic idealism, with its glorification of the *Volk* and of historic traditions; Populism, with its idealization of the peasantry; the spirit of Western enlightenment; socialism.

Two features of the minority movements stand out. In the first place, before 1917, among the peoples discussed, there had been in evidence no separatist tendencies. The Russian Empire was considered by most of its inhabitants to be a permanent institution which required not destruction but democratization and social reform. In the second place, in most of the borderlands, there was an alliance between nationalism and socialism. This phenomenon was perhaps due to the fact that the majority of the nationality groups did not possess indigenous middle classes, which in Russia proper, as in other European countries, formed the backbone of the liberal forces. On the other hand, the nationalists could not ally themselves with Russian rightist groups because the Russian rightists automatically opposed them.

39

THE SPEECH FROM THE THRONE

By Nicholas II

When the 524 deputies of the First Duma assembled in the Winter Palace on April 26, 1906, to hear the Emperor open Russia's first parliament, they were a sight to behold. Some two hundred of them were peasants, most of whom had never been in the capital before. Only half were Russians, with the rest divided among Ukrainians, Poles, Jews, Tartars, Bashkirs, and other nationalities, many of whom had come in their colorful native dress. As they stood on one side of the immense hall they faced the dignitaries of the court and the government assembled on the other side. It was an unprecedented confrontation. On the government side there glittered gold and diamonds which, as one radical deputy put it, were "the crystallized sweat of the Russian people's labor." The assembly, dubbed "the Duma of National Hopes," expected a great deal, perhaps too much and too quickly, by way of immediate reform and concessions. The Emperor's speech was brief and colorless. The deputies, once they assembled in the Taurida Palace, assigned to them for their meetings, spelled out their desires in great detail. The stage for the drama was set.

The Birth of the Russian Democracy, by A. Sack, has a section on the First Duma with dozens of portraits of the deputies and excerpts from their pronouncements. Vasili Maklakov's *The First State Duma* is, so far, the only work in English devoted to that body. Sidney Harcave's *First Blood* reprints the programs of three of the major parties represented in the Duma—the Constitutional Democrats or Kadets, the Socialist Revolutionaries or the SR's, and the Social Democrats or the SD's. Volumes VIII–XIII of Vladimir Lenin's *Collected Works* are devoted to the period 1905–6. We have the accounts of three perceptive British observers who were in Russia at the time of the Duma's meetings: Sir Bernard Pares wrote *My Russian Memoirs* and *A Wandering Scholar*; Maurice Baring left his account in *A Year in Russia*; and we have *The Dawn in Russia* by H. Nevinson.

SPEECH FROM THE THRONE OF HIS MAJESTY THE EMPEROR . . .

The care for the welfare of the fatherland which is entrusted to me by Almighty Providence has prompted me to summon the elected representatives of the people to assist in our legislative tasks.

I welcome you, those best people whom I commanded my beloved sub-

From *Pravo* (St. Petersburg), 1906, pp. 1764-68. Translated by Sylvia Fain.

jects to choose from among themselves, with an ardent faith in Russia's brilliant future.

Difficult and complicated tasks await you. I believe that you are inspired and united by love for your country. I will protect the new institutions which I have granted my people in the firm conviction that you will devote all your strength to selfless service to the fatherland; to the clarification of the needs of the peasantry which is so close to my heart; and to the promotion of popular enlightenment and the national well-being; remembering that for spiritual greatness and prosperity of the state we need not freedom alone, but order based on law.

My fervent desire to see my people happy, and to pass on to my son a strong, prosperous and enlightened state, would then be fulfilled.

May the Lord bless the labors which I shall undertake in union with the State Council and the State Duma, and may this day henceforth be known as the day of Russia's moral renewal, the day of the renaissance of her best forces. Set about the work with which I have charged you with reverence, and justify the faith which the Tsar and the people have placed in you. May God be with us in our labors!

May the Lord help me and you!

THE REPLY OF THE STATE DUMA

Your Imperial Majesty:

In your speech to the Duma, you were pleased to affirm your intention to protect the new institutions which called upon the people to support a legislature which would act in unity with its monarch. This solemn promise of a monarch to his people is a firm guarantee that our legislative system will grow steadily, developing in accordance with strict constitutional principles. The State Duma, for its part, will strive to improve the principles of popular government, and will submit for Your Majesty's confirmation a bill establishing a popular legislature founded on the principle of universal suffrage, according to the unanimously expressed will of the people.

Your Majesty's call to unity in working for the good of the fatherland finds a lively response in the hearts of all members of the State Duma. We have members from all classes and all peoples of Russia, and we are united by a common fervent desire to renew Russia, and to create a state system founded on firm guarantees for civil liberties and on the peaceful coexistence of all classes and all nationalities.

The State Duma feels obliged to point out, however, that the conditions in which the country is living are such as to frustrate any truly fruitful work directed to the rejuvenation of the country's strengths.

The country has concluded that the arbitrariness of the administrative officials who separate the Tsar from the people is the fundamental shortcoming in the national life. With a united voice the country has loudly declared that the renewal of national life is possible only on the basis of freedom, the right of independent popular action, popular participation in the legislative power, and popular control over the executive power. In Your Majesty's Manifesto of October 17, 1905, Your Imperial Majesty was pleased to proclaim from the height of the Throne a firm resolve to build Russia's future on the basis of these very principles. The entire people met this news with a unanimous cry of joy.

Yet the first days of freedom were clouded by severe trials. The persons responsible are all those who still deny the people access to the Tsar, and who violate all the principles of the Imperial Manifesto of October 17th. They have covered the country with the shame of unjust executions, pogroms, firing squad shootings, and imprisonments.

The consequences of these administrative measures over the past months have so deeply influenced the spirit of the people that civic peace will remain impossible until it becomes clear to the people that no one has the power to commit violence in Your Majesty's name, until all Ministers are responsible to the popular representatives, and until the administrative system at all levels is revised accordingly.

Sire, only a ministry which has been made responsible to the people can appreciate the magnitude of the monarch's responsibilities; only a ministry which enjoys the confidence of the majority of the Duma can foster popular confidence in the Government; and only when there is such confidence can the Duma's work proceed peacefully and properly. But first of all it is imperative to free Russia from the exceptional laws—the state of emergency and martial law—which irresponsible officials have particularly abused.

Together with the establishment of administrative responsibility to the legislature, it is imperative to follow the basic principle of true popular representation, so that the unity of the monarch with the people can be the sole source of legislative power. Thus all barriers between the Supreme Power and the people must be removed. Likewise no limits should be set to the legislative competence of the popular legislature in unity with the monarch. The State Duma feels obliged to declare to Your Imperial Majesty in the name of the people that the entire population can join in the creative task of renewing the national life with true inspiration and

true faith in the development of national prosperity only when nothing will stand between the people and the Throne, no State Council of officials chosen only from the highest classes of the people; when the levying of taxes and duties becomes the responsibility of the popular legislature alone; and when no special laws whatever will set limits to the legislative competence of the popular legislature. The State Duma also considers it incompatible with the national interests that any money bill passed by the Duma be subject to alteration by any bodies or persons not representing the mass of the taxpayers.

Now, as to urgent legislation: The State Duma, fulfilling the duties with which the people have charged it, considers it urgently necessary to agree upon precise laws guaranteeing personal immunity, freedom of conscience, freedom of speech and the press, freedom of union and assembly, and freedom to strike. No reform of social relationships is feasible without precise guarantees and strict enforcement of these rights, which were promised to us in the October 17th Manifesto. The Duma likewise considers it necessary to secure the right for citizens to petition the popular legislature.

The State Duma holds firmly to the conviction that neither freedom nor order founded on right can be strong or lasting without strict observance of the principle of the equality of all citizens before the law (without exception). The State Duma will therefore work out bills for the full equalization of all citizens, and for the abolition of all restrictions and privileges accruing to anyone by reason of class, nationality, religion, or sex. The State Duma will also strive to emancipate the country from the administrative tutelage which obstructs her path, leaving limitations on civic freedoms to the independent judicial power alone. The State Duma considers the use of the death penalty intolerable, even by judicial sentence. Capital punishment ought never to be meted out in any circumstances. The State Duma considers itself entitled to speak for the entire people in expressing the unanimous desire to see the day when capital punishment is abolished forever. In anticipation of such a law, the country awaits a suspension of all death sentences by Your Majesty's decree.

Clarification of the needs of the rural population and the undertaking of legislative measures appropriate to meet them is the most immediate problem facing the State Duma. The working peasantry, the largest part of our population, are impatiently awaiting satisfaction of their acute need for land. The first Russian State Duma will not have fulfilled its duty if it does not work out a law to provide land for the peasants by use of state appanage, cabinet, monastery, and church lands, and by compulsory expropriation of privately owned land.

The State Duma also deems it necessary to work out laws which will secure equal rights for the peasants and do away with the arbitrary and tutelary authority which they have so long endured. The State Duma recognizes as equally urgent the satisfaction of the needs of the working class by legislative measures which will protect the position of the wage laborer. As a first step in this direction, the wage laborers must be guaranteed freedom of organization and independent activity to improve their material and spiritual welfare, regardless of their line of work.

The State Duma likewise considers it its duty to do all it can to raise the level of popular enlightenment; thus we should at once turn our attention to laws concerning universal free education.

The Duma will also give special attention to an equitable distribution of the tax burden, which today weighs disproportionately on the poorest classes of the people, and to the study of the most advisable use of the state revenues.

Fundamental reform of local administration and local self-government is no less essential a legislative task. The entire population should be enlisted for equal participation in local self-government according to principles of universal suffrage. Remembering the burden of service which the people bear in your Majesty's army and navy, the State Duma is concerned with strengthening the principles of equity and justice in the armed forces.

Finally, the State Duma considers it necessary to list among our urgent problems the satisfaction of the long-pressing demands of the various nationalities. Russia is a state populated by many tribes and peoples. A true spiritual union of all these tribes and peoples can be possible only when each is enabled to live its own peculiar and separate way of life. The State Duma will thus also concern itself with ways to satisfy these just demands.

Your Imperial Majesty! There is one question which comes before all our tasks, a question which deeply concerns the entire people and which disturbs us as delegates of the people, preventing us from initiating our legislative activities. The first word which was spoken in this hall, the word which brought shouts of sympathy from the entire Duma, was the word *amnesty*. The country awaits it; an amnesty granted to all those convicted for religious or political reasons, and for all violations of agrarian laws.

These are the demands of the popular conscience, which are impossible to deny and whose fulfilment cannot be delayed. Sire, the Duma awaits from you a full political amnesty, as a first guarantee of the mutual understanding and mutual agreement between the Tsar and the people.

40

THE GOVERNMENT'S DECLARATION
TO THE FIRST DUMA

The Emperor refused to receive the Duma delegation delegated to bring him the chamber's answer to his speech. Instead the aged premier Ivan Goremykin, in a barely audible voice, read to a hushed chamber the government's reply rejecting most of its demands. It came as a shock, and, henceforth, the Duma continued to demand the government's resignation. The cabinet, for its part, was almost unanimous in its desire to dissolve the rebellious Duma. It was only waiting for a convenient pretext, which came in early July. The Emperor and the government had clearly expected very different results. But they were not ready for the beginning of orderly legislative work; Goremykin, by way of first bills, presented budgetary requests for a hothouse and a laundry at a provincial university. It seemed to be a deliberate mockery of the legislature. Actually the blunder merely reflected the bureaucracy's total unfamiliarity with the new ways of governing. As the Minister of Finance remarked, "Thank God, we don't have a parliament."

The rights of the Duma, as granted by the new Fundamental Laws of 1906, are printed in Walter Dodd (ed.), *Modern Constitutions*, Vol. II. Sergei Witte's *Memoirs* give the background of the government's preparations for the First Duma. *The Secret Letters of the Last Tsar*, edited by Edward Bing, contains the Emperor's letters to his mother during the period under review. For an intimate picture of the imperial court see A. Mosolov's *At the Court of the Last Tsar*. We have the memoirs of three important government officials of the period: Vladimir Gurko, deputy Minister of Interior, wrote *Features and Figures of the Past*, with a chapter on Goremykin and the First Duma. Vladimir Kokovtsov, who was then Minister of Finance, wrote *Out of My Past*. Alexander Izvolsky, then Foreign Minister, wrote *Recollections of a Foreign Minister;* he was the Duma's only defender in the cabinet. For a moderate English view of the Duma written at the time see Sir Donald Mackenzie Wallace's *Russia* (paperback).

From Gosudarstvennaia Duma, *Stenografi-cheskii Otchet* (St. Petersburg), 1906, pp. 321–24, 352–53. Translated by Sylvia Fain.

THE GOVERNMENT'S DECLARATION TO THE FIRST DUMA, MAY 13, 1906

The Chairman of the Council of Ministers:

The Council of Ministers has studied carefully the reply made by the State Duma to the welcoming address which His Imperial Majesty was pleased to deliver to us in joint assembly. We have noted that the desires and suggestions expressed in this address concern both legislative and administrative subjects.

The Government believes that all its activity must be based on the observation of strict legality, and we have discussed the views expressed by the State Duma in this light. The Government first of all wishes to express its readiness to co-operate fully in resolving those questions raised which are within the State Duma's sphere of legitimate legislative activity.

Such co-operation should be expected, since the Government is obliged to explain its views on substantive matters to the Duma, and to defend its own proposals. Thus we shall co-operate on the question regarding the alteration of the franchise, although the Government does not consider this matter a subject for immediate discussion. The State Duma is just beginning its legislative work, and has yet to demonstrate clearly the necessity for altering the means by which it has itself been constituted.

The Council of Ministers has paid particular attention to the Duma's discussion of measures for the immediate satisfaction of the urgent needs of the rural population and of the working class; measures proposing equal rights for peasants and persons of other classes; a plan for universal primary education; a search for possible ways of establishing a more proportionate distribution of the tax burden; and a reform of local government and self-government, with due attention for the peculiarities of border districts.

The Council of Ministers is equally concerned with another matter brought up in the Duma's reply—the issuance of new laws to guarantee personal immunities, the freedom of conscience, of speech and the press, assembly and association, in place of the temporary rules now in force. In fact the terms of these rules themselves stipulate that they should be replaced by permanent ones as soon as the new legislative system should be established. However, as for these new laws, the Council of Ministers deems it necessary to specify that the executive must be furnished with real means of enforcement. For even when laws have been passed by the orderly processes of government, violations and abuses of civil freedoms can occur. The Government must be equipped to counter such infringements of the law which threaten our state.

The Council of Ministers feels obliged to declare that the solution of the land problem through the means proposed by the Duma is absolutely impermissible. The Duma's reply suggested the use of the state appanage, cabinet, monastery and church lands, as well as compulsory expropriation of privately owned lands, which would include those lands purchased by some of the peasants themselves. The State cannot recognize the right of private property in land for some, and at the same time deny it to others. Neither can the State take away the right to private ownership of land without at the same time taking away the right of private ownership of all kinds of property. The inalienable and inviolable right of private property is the foundation stone of the popular well-being and social progress of all states at all stages of development. Private property is the fundamental basis of a state's existence: without the right of private property there would be no state. Moreover, the nature of the land problem does not require the use of means such as those proposed by the Duma. Surely there are many types of state action which have yet to be tried, many legal steps which could be taken. Certainly the land question can be successfully resolved without any acts which would erode the very foundations of our state and sap the nation's vitality.

The rest of the Duma's legislative proposals are concerned with establishing ministerial responsibility to the Duma as the popular representative body; the abolition of the State Council; and the elimination of the limits on the Duma's legislative competence which were established by special decree. The Council of Ministers does not consider itself entitled even to discuss these proposals, since they concern a fundamental alteration of our state system. Nor does the State Duma have the right to initiate an examination of such matters.

Finally, the State Duma has expressed concern for strengthening the principles of equity and justice in the army and navy. The Government wishes to state that these principles have long been established in His Imperial Majesty's armed forces. The Emperor is concerning himself at present with improving the material well-being of all ranks of the armed services, as the latest measures on this subject testify. Finding ways and means to implement these measures more broadly will be one of the chief tasks of the Government and the newly established legislature.

Turning to the second desire expressed by the State Duma—the elimination of exceptional laws and arbitrariness on the part of individual official persons— the Council of Ministers notes that these matters are the exclusive concern of the state administration. The powers of the State Duma in this area are limited to the right of interpellation of Ministers and department chiefs, should charges of illegal acts be made against them or against any of their subordinates. Aside from that, the establishment of strict legality based on principles of order and justice is the particular responsibility of the Government, which must see to it that all of its agents and agencies always abide by these principles. As for the exceptional laws for the maintenance of public order during emergencies, which the State Duma has criticized, the Government, too, is aware of their shortcomings. The administration is now in process of formulating better ones to replace them. Satisfactory or not, these laws have indeed had to be used throughout the country because murders, robberies, and shocking acts of violence have become everyday occurrences. The fundamental responsibility of a state is, after all, the defense of the lives and property of its law-abiding citizens. The Council of Ministers is fully aware of its responsibility to the country in this regard. We wish to declare, however, that until the disturbances which have enveloped the country come to an end, and until new laws have been passed to equip the government with effective means for combatting the lawlessness and violence which endanger both public and private safety, the Government will be forced to continue to maintain order by all legal means now at its disposal.

The State Duma's petition for a general political amnesty would include pardon for those sentenced by the courts, as well as release from administrative punishments for persons subjected to them by infringements of the State of Emergency regulations, or of martial law. The pardoning of persons sentenced by the courts, whatever the nature of their crime, is the sole prerogative of the Emperor, who extends his mercy to criminals in keeping with the general welfare. For its part, the Council of Ministers feels that a general amnesty in the present seditious times would not promote the general good, but would only precipitate more murders, robberies, and violence.

As for those persons who have been deprived of their freedom by administrative order, the Council of Ministers has undertaken a very thorough review of these administrative decisions, so that freedom may be restored to all those who will not abuse it in order to threaten the public safety which is at present so menaced by crime.

Aside from considerations on the proposals taken from the Duma's address, the Council of Ministers must also give a general outline of its own proposals in the area of legislation:

The strength of the Russian state is based first of all on the strength of its agricultural population: Russia cannot be prosperous until our peasants have all they need to be successful, for agriculture is the foundation of our national economic life. Thus the peasant question must always be viewed in light of its tremendous significance for the state: the peasant question is the most important facing us today. Accordingly, the Council of Ministers cautions that special care will be demanded in the pursuit of ways and means to solve this problem. Much caution will also be necessary in this matter to avoid any shocks to the unique peasant way of life, which is so deeply rooted in history.

However, in the opinion of the Council of Ministers, the reforms which will be needed follow naturally from the decision to grant peasant participation in legislative activity. The class isolation of the peasants must give way to unity of the peasants with the other classes in a relationship of civic law and order, and justice. Also, all those limitations on private property rights in respect to allotment lands, which were established to insure punctual redemption payments, must be abolished.

The equalization of the peasants with other classes in their civil and political rights must in no way deprive the state of either the right or the obligation to pay special attention to the needs of the peasantry. Measures are required which will aim both at improving agricultural methods on the lands the peasants now farm, and also at increasing the size of present peasant landholdings from free state appanage lands and through purchase of privately owned lands with the co-operation of the Peasant Land Bank.

There is a vast field for productive work ahead of us. Raising agricultural production, which is today at a very low level of development, will increase national productive output and raise the level of the general wealth. There are huge tracts of land suitable for agriculture which today lie empty in the Asiatic provinces of the Empire. Thus a program of resettlement should be one of the primary concerns of the Government.

The Government recognizes the urgency of raising the educational and moral level of the masses, as does the State Duma, and so has been working out proposals for universal primary education which will enlist all the forces at our command. The Council of Ministers is concerned about properly established secondary and higher education as well, and in the near future will submit a project for reform of our secondary schools to the State Duma. This reform would leave room for both public and private initiative in this area, and would include a project for reforms of the autonomous higher educational institutions.

The Council of Ministers is convinced that the moral renewal called for by our Sovereign is unthinkable without the establishment of true principles of legality and order throughout the land. Thus we stress the primary importance of local courts, and desire that they might be established so that justice would be easily accessible to all, and judicial organization simplified and judicial proceedings made quicker and cheaper.

Along with the project for a reform of the local judicial system, the Council of Ministers will submit to the State Duma projects for changes in the existing rules regarding civil and penal responsibility of official persons. Respect for the sanctity and inviolability of law can become rooted in the population only with the conviction that unpunished lawbreaking is impossible for anyone, local person or government representative alike.

While aiming at as fully equitable a distribution of the tax burden as is possible, the Council of Ministers proposes to submit to the Duma proposals concerning an income tax, changes in the provisions of the inheritance taxes and stamp taxes, and a review of several kinds of indirect taxes.

Finally, the Council of Ministers deems it necessary to call attention to projects for a reform of the internal passport regulations, which propose the abolition of internal passports and residence permits.

In conclusion, the Council of Ministers is fully cognizant of the precedent-setting nature of the measures we will take in revising the national laws along the principles expressed in the Imperial Manifesto of October 17, 1905. The Government holds to the conviction that the capability of the state, its external and internal strength, unalterably depends upon an executive power which exercises its authority by fixed rules, but firmly and energetically. The Government intends to conduct itself in this way, steadfast in the consciousness of its responsibility for the maintenance of public order. The Council of Ministers is confident that the State Duma, in the certainty that the peaceful progress in our state depends on an intelligent balance of freedom and order, will join its peaceful, constructive efforts to ours in order to achieve that public peace which Russia so desperately needs.

THE DUMA'S VOTE OF NO CONFIDENCE IN THE GOVERNMENT

The Chairman: Here is the text of the motion as revised according to the views expressed by various deputies:

"WHEREAS, having perceived in the declaration of the Chairman of the Council of Ministers a clear indication that the Government has absolutely no desire to satisfy the popular demands and expectations for land, for civil rights and liberties which were set forth by the State Duma in its reply to the Speech from the Throne, and which must be satisfied before peace is possible in our land and before a popular legislature can begin to work productively;

WHEREAS, finding that the Government has, by its refusal to satisfy the popular demands, revealed a clear disregard for the true interests of the people and a clear unwillingness to avert new shocks and dislocations in our country, which has been ravished by poverty, lawlessness, and a continued subjection to sacrosanct arbitrary power;

EXPRESSING before the nation our complete lack of confidence in a Ministry which is not responsible to the popular legislature; and

RECOGNIZING as the most necessary condition of national peace and productive work in the popular legislature to be the immediate resignation of the present Ministry and its replacement by a Ministry enjoying the confidence of the State Duma;

The State Duma now proceeds to the consideration of its current business." Will those members who accept this resolution please remain seated; those opposed, please rise. The motion is carried by majority vote. (Prolonged applause.)

A Voice: We have to count the votes for and against.

The Chairman: In that case, would those who stood up please rise once more?

Voices: It was a majority against seven dissenting!

Voices: No, it was more than seven!

Kokoshkin (a deputy from Moscow): To avoid misunderstandings in the future there must be an exact count of the votes taken. It will not do to rely on guesswork.

Voices: True, true!

The Chairman: In view of the doubts expressed I will repeat the balloting: those in favor of the motion kindly remain seated, those opposed kindly rise.

Stakhovich (deputy from Orël Province): I understood that there would be a recess, and then a debate on the motion, but I see I was mistaken. I must call attention to the fact that all debate on a motion should be held only after the motion is printed and distributed, so that it could be discussed and debated upon line by line, but no one has requested that this be done. Also please note that initiation of this kind of motion ought to be undertaken by a Member of the Duma, not by the Presidium. The Presidium takes care of procedural forms and clerical work, and beyond that should not take upon itself any legislative initiative. This initiative must come from the Members of the Duma. If there should be no proposals made on the text of a motion, the chairman must put it to the vote as is.

Chairman: No one has opposed this revised motion. Now, if those who stood would please reaffirm their vote by rising once again. . . .

Secretary of the State Duma: Eleven persons are standing. . . .

The Chairman: The motion has passed by a majority, with eleven opposing votes.

41

WE NEED A GREAT RUSSIA

By Peter Stolypin

The agrarian issue wrecked the First Duma; it continued to endanger the fate of the Second Duma as well, although the latter was dissolved on another pretext. There was clearly no basis of agreement between a government determined to protect private landed property and a Duma eager to confiscate it. And yet in retrospect it seems that Stolypin's solution to the land problem was a sensible and promising program which, in the decade in which it was applied, produced some impressive results. The man himself was probably the last Russian statesman of stature produced by the old regime. He stood head and shoulders above his colleagues, and his relations with the Duma indicated that he was interested in collaboration with the legislature provided it was a moderate body. But the chasm between the bureaucracy and the Second Duma, more radical than its predecessor, was too deep to bridge, and Stolypin found a way out of the impasse by violating the new Russian constitution and restricting the electoral law. Henceforth the Duma would be more conservative and would not advocate the socialist schemes abhorrent to the regime.

The solution of the land problem adopted by the Third Duma is described by the Octobrist chairman of its Agrarian Commission, Sergei Shidlovskii, in "The Imperial Duma and Land Settlement," *Russian Review*, November, 1912. The same issue also contains an article by his Kadet rival, Aleksandr Manuilov, "Agrarian Reform in Russia." Another Kadet deputy, Vasilii Maklakov, has written "The Peasant Question and the Russian Revolution," *Slavonic and East European Review*, Vol. II (1923), and "The Agrarian Problem in Russia before the Revolution," *Russian Review*, 1950. Vladimir Lenin's biting comments on Stolypin's program are scattered throughout his *Collected Works*, Vols. XIII–XX, covering the period 1907–14. For articles on the Stolypin land reform see Donald Treadgold, "Was Stolypin in Favor of the Kulaks?" *American Slavic and East European Review*, Vol. XIV; George Yaney, "The Concept of the Stolypin Land Reform," *Slavic Review*, June, 1964; and W. Mosse, "Stolypin's Villages," *Slavonic and East European Review*, June, 1965. For studies of the agrarian problem as a whole see Geroid Robinson, *Rural Russia under the Old Regime*; George Pavlovsky, *Agrarian Russia on the Eve of Revolution*; and Donald Treadgold, *The Great Siberian Migration*. Alfred Levin's *The Second Duma* should also be consulted. See also Bertram Wolfe, "Lenin, Stolypin and the Russian Village," *Russian Review*, Vol. VI, and the memoirs of Stolypin's daughter, Maria Bock, "Stolypin in Saratov," in the same journal, Vol. XII.

From Gosudarstvennaia Duma, *Stenograficheskie Otchety* (St. Petersburg), May 10, 1907, pp. 433–45. Translated by Sylvia Fain.

Members of the State Duma: I have listened to the debates on the land question, studied them from the stenographic record, and have decided that, before the conclusion of this debate, I must make a statement about the questions raised here, and about the Government's own proposals. I do not propose to present the Government's entire agrarian program. One of our subordinate departments intends to do that before the Agrarian Commission. I learned only today that fundamental decisions are being made in this Commission; yet members of the Government are not invited to its sessions, and the materials at the Government's disposal are not being used.

I consider it necessary to confine myself to questions raised and discussed here. I proceed from the view that all persons with an interest in this matter most sincerely desire that it be solved. I think that the peasants most certainly desire a solution to the problem so central to their very existence. And I think the landlords must want their neighbors to be people who are peaceful and happy, and not angry people on the verge of starvation. I think all Russians who long for peace in their land desire a speedy solution to the problem which undoubtedly contributes to the growth of sedition and rebellion. Thus I will ignore all those insults and accusations which have been made here against the Government. Nor will I stop to discuss attacks which resembled hostile pressure on the regime. Nor will I discuss the principle of class revenge—former serfs against nobles—which some here have advanced. Rather, I will try to take a statesman-like point of view; and will try to handle this question completely objectively, and even dispassionately. I shall try to cover all the views which have been expressed here, remembering that opinions which dis-

agree with the Government's views cannot be considered products of seditious thought. Now, judging from the debate which has occurred here, and from the preliminary discussion of the question, there is clearly little chance that these various views will be brought together, or that the Agrarian Commission will be given precisely defined tasks. Thus it seems to me even more imperative that the Government make known its general position.

As to the proposals of the various parties, I will first examine those made by parties on the Left. I will not dispute the statistics they have cited which seem to me highly debatable. I also readily agree with the picture they have drawn of agricultural Russia's impoverishment. Alarmed by this very process, the Government has already begun to take steps to improve the lot of the agricultural class. I must only say that the method those on the Left have suggested, the path they would choose, will overturn all existing civic relationships. It will lead to the subordination of the interests of the whole population to the interests of one class, albeit a large one. It will lead, gentlemen, to a social revolution. It seems to me that these speakers from the Left are well aware of this. One of them invited the regime to take extralegal measures in this situation. He declared that the whole problem of the present moment consists precisely in the destruction of the present state system with its landowning bureaucratic base, and the creation of a modern state based on new cultural principles constructed on the ruins of the old. Why does he propose that reason of state prevail over the legal limits of state authority? Because this will enable the state to return to its proper path of legality? No—rather because he believes the particular extralegal state action he advocates will strike a death blow to the existing state system and the present state structure. In a word, nationalization of the land, with or without compensation, will lead to such a social upheaval, to such a shift of all values, to such an alteration of all social, legal, and civic relations as history has never seen. But, of course, this is no argument against the Leftists' proposal, if such upheavals are considered Russia's means of salvation. Let us assume for the moment that the Government sees the nationalization of land as a good, and that it takes lightly the destruction of the entire class of landowners (an educated class, and a large one, whatever has been said here). Suppose that the Government concurs in this destruction—what will come of this? Would even the basic problem of land allocation be solved? Would this method permit the peasants to farm their own land?

There are statistics which can give us the answer, and this is what they say: even if all the land without any exception, both privately and municipally owned land, were distributed to the peasants who now hold land allotments, then in Vologda province, with the presently available land, there would be 147 desiatins of land per household; there would be 185 in Olonets, and 1,309 in Archangel; while in fourteen provinces there would be less than 15 desiatins per family, and only 9 in Poltava, and 8 in Podolsk province. These disparities are explained by the extremely uneven distribution of public and private ownership of land from one province to another, and by the variations in allotment size. One-fourth of the privately owned land in the Empire is located in the twelve provinces where peasant allotments are above 15 desiatins per household. Only one-seventh of the privately owned land

is located in the ten provinces where peasant allotments are the smallest, or about 7 desiatins for each household. These figures take into account all the land of all landowners, that is, not only the 107,000 nobles, but also the 490,000 peasants who have bought their own land, and the 85,000 burghers (these last two groups together hold nearly 17 million desiatins of land). Thus it follows that an equal division of all the land can scarcely satisfy the peasant's need for land. Instead, we must resort to that very thing which the government is proposing—resettlement. And we must abandon the idea of giving land to all the laboring people without providing any for the rest of the population.

The inadequacy of a general land distribution as a solution to our peasant problem is likewise confirmed by statistics for population growth over the last ten years in the fifty provinces of European Russia. Gentlemen, Russia's population is increasing faster than that of any other country in the world, by a rate of 1.5 per cent per year. This means a natural annual increase of 1,625,000 souls, or 341,000 households, in European Russia alone. Thus, merely keeping up with the population increase would require three and a half million desiatins of additional land a year (allowing 10 desiatins per household). It is clear, gentlemen, that expropriation and redistribution of all privately owned land will not solve our land problem. Such an expropriation would only be a stop-gap measure.

But leaving aside the economic consequences of a land redistribution, what would such a move mean morally? What is the pattern of life in our villages? Everyone must cultivate the same crops in the same way, the commune land must be periodically re-divided, and it is impossible for a farmer with initiative to try out new ideas on the land temporarily in his care. Now, if everyone and everything were made equal, the land would become common, like water and air. But no human hand touches water or air, and no labor improves them. Otherwise there would undoubtedly be a price to pay for the improved water and air, with rights of ownership established for them. I daresay that land which would be distributed to the citizens, and which local Social Democratic officials would expropriate from some to give to others, would soon take on just those properties of water and air. It would be used, but no one would ever improve it, or put his labor into it, since the results of his labor would pass on to another. In general, the incentive to labor, that prudence which makes people work, would be scrapped. Each citizen—and there have always been and always will be some idlers and parasites in any society—will know that he has the right to have land and to till it if he so desires. But once the knowledge of this right begins to bore him, he may leave the land and go a-roaming. Everybody will be equal— but all can be equalized only at a lower level. It is impossible to equalize a lazy man with a conscientious one, or a weak mind with a capable one. Consequently, the cultural level of the country will deteriorate. A good farmer, a resourceful one, will be deprived of the opportunity to apply his knowledge to the land.

We must realize that in such conditions a new revolution would be accomplished: the gifted, strong, and capable man would establish his right to property and to the results of his labors by *force*. Truly, gentlemen, property has always been based on force, backed by a moral right. Remember, the distribution of marshlands under Catherine the Great was justified by the necessity of utilizing huge uncultivated areas. (Voice from the Center: "Oh, really!") Now *that* was reason of state. In this way the right of the capable and gifted created property rights in the West. Is it possible that this experience will be repeated? Will we see the reestablishment of property rights in a Russian countryside ruined by an exaggerated egalitarianism? And this recarved and equalized Russia—would she be richer and more powerful? The power of a country consists of the wealth of its people. The state as a whole would gain nothing from a general land redistribution. Not a single additional piece of bread would be added to the national wealth, while cultural life and activity would have perished. Temporarily, peasant allotments would be enlarged, but as the population grows, land hunger would return. Masses of impoverished peasants would leave the land to join the urban proletariat. But even supposing that this picture is an incorrect and exaggerated one, who would deny that such a shock, such a huge social revolution would not, perhaps, affect Russia's very survival as a nation?

Now gentlemen, these spokesmen for the Left propose to destroy the existing state system. They propose to ruin Russia in order to build a new fatherland on the ruins. I think that in the second millennium of her life Russia will not permit herself to be ruined. I think that she will be renewed, and that she will improve her way of life and advance in the family of nations. But this will not be the result of decomposition, for decomposition means death.

Now we turn, gentlemen, to another project set before us, that of the party of the Popular Freedom [Kadets]. This party offers no sweeping solutions, but confines itself to the problem of increasing the size of peasant landholdings. Their project does not recognize or create any right to land at all, for anyone. I must confess that I do not understand all of their plan, which seems contradictory on many points. The party's spokesman was very critical of the principle of the nationalization of land. I expected that he would, logically, advocate the recognition of the principle of private property. He did so—but only partially. He recognized the right of the peasants to the inviolate use of their land in perpetuity. But, at the same time, he avowed the necessity of denying the large landlords any such rights, in order to give the peasants more land. But once the principle of expropriation has been admitted in one case, what is to prevent expropriation of the peasants' own land, should that ever be considered necessary? Thus, it seems to me that in this respect the project of the Leftist parties is much more honest and straightforward. They recognize the possibility of a revision of working norms, taking away extra land from all householders. The principle proposed by the Kadet party is one of mandatory quantitative expropriations, that is, the principle that land may be taken from those who have much in order to give it to those who have little. In the final analysis this principle leads to nothing other than the nationalization of the land. Under their program, if a landowner has, say, 3,000 desiatins, 2,500 would be taken away. But with a change in farming methods and with the growth of population, he will doubtless run the risk of losing his remaining 500 desiatins. It seems to me, too, that no peasant in need of land would understand why he

should be moved to some place far away, if the neighboring landlord still has land, and a grand house where he lives "in style." Why must he go to Siberia in search of land? Why should he not be assigned land from the neighboring estate? It also seems clear to me that this project would abolish the right of private ownership of land insofar as the right to buy and sell land freely would disappear. No one will apply their labor to land knowing that the fruits of their labor may after several years be expropriated. The Kadet speaker estimated the compensation paid for expropriated land would average 80 rubles per desiatin in European Russia. This could hardly encourage those who have invested heavily in the development of land which originally cost 200–300 rubles per desiatin. The prospect of an expropriation which would entail such losses could hardly encourage them to make any further investments in their property.

But there is one further point which deserves the most serious attention: The Kadet speaker declared that we must let the peasants run their own affairs, in whatever way they choose. The law is not called upon to instruct the peasant or to impose any theories upon him, however basic and correct these theories may be considered by the legislators. Leave each peasant to his own initiative—only then can we really help the population. It is impossible not to welcome such a declaration. The Government itself continually emphasizes one thing in all that it does: we must remove those fetters which have been placed on the peasants and give each one the opportunity to choose for himself that method of using the land which most suits him.

The Kadet project also put forth another interesting principle: the principle of state aid. It is proposed that the Treasury pay half the value of the land which is expropriated for the peasants. I will return to this in a moment, but here I will point out that this seems to me somewhat contradictory to the principle of expropriation which this party advanced. How can they simultaneously accept compulsory expropriation *and* advocate a necessity for the whole state, for all classes of people, to come to the aid of the neediest part of the population? If this last is the goal, then why is it necessary to deal so harshly with 130,000 landlords? For not only would they be treated unfairly, but they would be taken from their accustomed labor, which is after all a useful contribution to society. But, gentlemen, is it impossible to manage without some form of expropriation?

Before submitting to you in general outlines the views of the Government, I will dwell on yet another method for solving the land question which has settled in many heads. I am talking about violence. You all know, gentlemen, how easily our simple peasant listens to all sorts of rumors, how easily he is aroused to extralegal action and to violence, especially in order to satisfy his hunger for land. Our ignorant peasants have already paid for their excesses several times. I must say that at present the danger of new violence and new troubles in the countryside is rising. The Government must take into account two things: on the one hand, it is necessary and evidently widely desired and urged that the Government set to work on new legislation aimed at improving our national life without departing from sound legal principles. The Government must welcome this desire and do everything possible to meet it. But along with this there exists another current of thinking. There are

some who want to stir up discontent in the land, to sow seeds of rebellion and doubt. They wish to destroy confidence in the Government, undermine its authority, and thus to unite all forces hostile to the Government. It was from this very rostrum, gentlemen, that someone shouted: "We have come here not to buy land, but to take it!" (Voices: True! That's right!) From these very halls, gentlemen, letters went out to the provinces, to the country, letters which were printed in the provincial newspapers and aroused much confusion and indignation in the localities. The authors of these letters denied responsibility, but just think, gentlemen, what went on in the minds of those country people who read them. The letters advised the peasants to resort to violence and seize land by force, in view of the Government's alleged crimes, its coercive tactics, and cruel oppression. I shall not trouble you, gentlemen, with a survey of these documents. I will be frank, as a Minister must be when speaking to the Duma, and I will say only that the very existence of such writings suggests that renewed attempts to acquire land by force and violence will be made. I must say that at the present time this danger is still remote. However, it is vitally important to define the limits beyond which open addresses to the people become really dangerous. The Government, of course, cannot allow anyone to overstep this limit, otherwise it would cease to be the Government and would become an accomplice to its own destruction. All that I have said, gentlemen, has been a critique of those various proposals which in the Government's opinion do not supply the answers or solutions which Russia awaits. Violence will not be tolerated. And in the Government's view, nationalization of the land would be a national disaster. The project of the Kadets, that is, semi-expropriation, semi-nationalization, would in the last analysis lead to the same results as the proposals from the Left.

Where is the way out? Where are the answers? Does the Government intend to limit itself to half-measures and mere maintenance of order?

Before speaking of methods we should first clarify our goal. The Government wants above all to promote and enhance peasant land ownership. It wants to see the peasant earning well and eating well, since where there is prosperity there is enlightenment *and also true freedom*. But for this it is necessary to give opportunity to the capable, industrious peasant, who is the salt of the Russian earth. He must be freed from the vise of his present situation. He must be given the chance to consolidate the fruits of his labor and consider them his inalienable property. Let property be general where the commune is operative still; let it be household ownership where the commune no longer exists.; but let it be hereditary, with firm legal guarantees. The Government should then assist such peasant smallholders with advice and credit facilities. Now a stubborn problem immediately presents itself: what of all those peasants who farm their land, but who do not have enough land? All these land-hungry peasants should be given the chance to utilize Russia's existing land reserves—as much land as they need, on favorable terms. We have heard here that we would need 57 million desiatins in order to give enough land to all the peasants. Now I repeat, I am not disputing these figures. It has been pointed out that the Government has at its disposal only 10 million desiatins of land. But,

gentlemen, the Government only recently began to set up a land fund. The Peasant Bank has at its disposal more land than it can handle. Some here have attacked the Peasant Bank, and the attacks were rather serious in nature. Someone said the Bank should be done away with. In the Government's opinion, it is not necessary to do away with anything. Rather, the project we have begun should be improved. In this matter we must return to the idea to which I alluded earlier— the ideal of state assistance. Let us pause to recall, gentlemen, that a state is a single organism. If the parts of the organism are at odds with each other, then the state becomes a "house divided against itself" and must inevitably perish. At the present time our state is ailing, and the peasantry is the sickest part. They must be helped. A simple, completely automatic, completely mechanical method has been proposed to aid them: to seize and divide up all 130,000 existing estates. Is this in the interest of the state as a whole? Does this sound like the story of Trishkin, who cut off the bottom of his coat so he could add length to his sleeves? Gentlemen, it is impossible to strengthen a sick body by feeding it with pieces of its own flesh. The organism must be infused with nutrient fluids before it can overcome a disease. The whole state must be mobilized to fight the illness; all parts of the state must come to the aid of that part which at present seems weakest. The idea that all elements of the state must come to the aid of its weakest part may appear to be the principle of socialism; but if this be socialism it is state socialism, which has often been practiced in western Europe, and has had real and visible results. In our country, this principle would be realized if the Government were to take responsibility for paying a part of the interest which the peasants will have to pay for the land granted to them. The matter would come to the following: the state would buy pieces of land offered for sale, which together with the state lands and independent crown lands would comprise a state land fund. With so much land on the market, land prices would not rise. The peasants who are farming now but who need more land could apply to the land fund. But the peasantry is at present unable to pay the relatively high interest rates set by the Government. Therefore the state should pay that part of the required interest which the administration may determine is beyond the peasant's ability to pay. This difference would be made up from the state budget, and would be included with the estimated annual expenses. Thus, it would come about that the entire state and all classes of the population would be helping the peasants acquire the land they need. All taxpayers, all civil servants, merchants, professional people, the peasants themselves, and the estate owners, would have taken part in this. Everyone would share equally in this task. It would not be made the burden of one small class of 130,000 persons, whose destruction would mean the loss of important sources of culture, whatever may be said to the contrary.

Now the Government has already taken steps in this direction. The interest rates charged by the Peasant Bank have been temporarily reduced. This approach is more flexible, and less sweeping, than the Kadet proposal that the Government pay half the cost of the land which the peasants may purchase. Now if, together with this, a procedure were established for leaving the communes, thus building up the class of hardy individual proprietors, and if

there were a program of planned resettlement, if land loans were easily available, and if expanded agricultural credit facilities were created—if these things were done, hope would be seen, even if the full program of land reforms which the Government has proposed might not be enacted. And, viewing the land problem as a whole, perhaps this notorious question of compulsory expropriation would appear in a clearer light. It is time to put this question in its proper perspective; it is time, gentlemen, not to see it as a magic formula, a panacea for all evils. Expropriation seems a bold move only because it will also create a class of ruined landowners. Compulsory expropriation might really seem necessary in some circumstances. But, gentlemen, only as an exceptional measure, and not a general rule; and only accompanied by clear and precise legal guarantees. Compulsory expropriation could be qualitative instead of quantitative. It should be used chiefly when the peasants can settle locally, and in order to improve their methods of cultivation. It ought to be considered only when necessary to help make a transition to improved means of cultivation—perhaps to facilitate setting up watering places for livestock, digging wells, building roads, or to allow the farmers to consolidate separated bits of land into one or two good-size holdings. But, gentlemen, I am not giving you a full agrarian program, as I said earlier. I am only calling your attention to the outstanding features of the Government's proposals. We have offered to submit a more complete project to the Agrarian Committee, should they elect to hear us.

I have been concerned with the problem of our agrarian landholding system for some ten years. I can assure you that this matter will require prolonged and unpleasant, difficult work. It is impossible to solve this question all at once; it must be solved over a period of time. This has required decades in Western countries. We propose to you a moderate path, but a true one. Those who oppose our state system prefer the path of radicalism, a path of emancipation from Russia's historic past, and from its cultural traditions. They need great upheavals—we need a great Russia! (Applause from the Right.)

42

MEMORANDUM TO NICHOLAS II

By Peter Durnovo

It would be difficult to find a more farsighted prediction of the consequences of World War I for Russia that that contained in the following pages. Their author, Durnovo (1844–1915) was a clever bureaucrat, hated by the revolutionaries and the liberals. First assigned to the Ministry of Justice, he was transferred to the Ministry of the Interior, where he headed the police department (1884–94). From 1900 he was deputy minister of the Interior and minister under Witte (1905–6). With Witte's fall he was appointed to the State Council, Russia's upper chamber, heading its right wing until his death. His memorandum was submitted to the Emperor in February, 1914, but had no effect. Found in the Emperor's papers by the Bolsheviks, it was first published by them in 1922. The Soviet historian Tarle rightly called it "the swan song of the conservative school."

For a general consideration of Russia's foreign relations in the modern period, see the volume edited by Ivo Lederer, *Russian Foreign Policy*. On the Straits problem, see two articles by Robert Kerner, "Russia and the Straits Question, 1915–17," *Slavonic and East European Review*, VII, 589–600, and "Russia, the Straits and Constantinople," *Journal of Modern History*, I, 400–415. For a brief characteristic of Durnovo, see Marc Aldanov, "P. N. Durnovo, Prophet of War and Revolution," *Russian Review*, II, 31–45. Russia's economic relations with other powers is described in M. S. Miller, *The Economic Development of Russia, 1905–1914*. Alexander Iswolsky, Russian foreign minister of the period, has written *Recollections of a Foreign Minister*; so did his successor, Sergei Sazonov, in his *Fateful Years, 1909–1916*. The European diplomatic setting is portrayed in A. J. P. Taylor's *The Struggle for Mastery in Europe, 1848–1918*. The two alliances attacked by Durnovo are analyzed in *The Franco-Russian Alliance*, by Georges Michon, and *The Anglo-Russian Convention*, by Rogers Churchill. See also G. Bolsover, "Aspects of Russian Foreign Policy, 1815–1914," *Essays Presented to Sir Lewis Namier*, edited by Richard Pares and A. J. P. Taylor. A recent paperback is Barbara Jelavich's, *One Hundred Years of Russian Foreign Policy, 1814–1914*. Clarence J. Smith's *The Russian Struggle for Power, 1914–17* is a study of the diplomacy of the First World War. *England, Russia, and the Straits Question*, by Vernon Puryear, is a historical study of the problem of the Straits. Durnovo's fellow bureaucrats described the man in *Features and Figures of the Past*, by Vladimir Gurko, and *Out of My Past*, by Vladimir Kokovtsov. For a study of foreign capital in Russia see Herbert Feis, *Europe, the World's Banker, 1870–1914* (paperback).

A Future Anglo-German War Will Become an Armed Conflict between Two Groups of Powers.—The central factor of the period of world history through

From F. Golder (ed.), *Documents of Russian History, 1914–1917* (New York: The Century Co., 1927), pp. 3–23. Used by permission of Appleton-Century-Crofts.

which we are now passing is the rivalry between England and Germany. This rivalry must inevitably lead to an armed struggle between them, the issue of which will, in all probability, prove fatal to the vanquished side. The interests of these two powers are far too incompatible, and their simultaneous existence as world powers will sooner or later prove impossible. On the one hand, there is an insular State, whose world importance rests upon its domination of the sea, its world trade, and its innumerable colonies. On the other, there is a powerful continental empire, whose limited territory is insufficient for an increased population. It has therefore openly and candidly declared that its future is on the seas. It has, with fabulous speed, developed an enormous world commerce, built for its protection a formidable navy, and, with its famous trademark, "Made in Germany," created a mortal danger to the industrial and economic prosperity of its rival. Naturally, England cannot yield without a fight, and between her and Germany a struggle for life or death is inevitable.

The armed conflict impending as a result of this rivalry cannot be confined to a duel between England and Germany alone. Their resources are far too unequal, and, at the same time, they are not sufficiently vulnerable to each other. Germany could provoke rebellion in India, in South Africa, and, especially, a dangerous rebellion in Ireland, and paralyze English sea trade by means of privateering and, perhaps, submarine warfare, thereby creating for Great Britain difficulties in her food supply; but, in spite of all the daring of the German military leaders, they would scarcely risk a landing in England, unless a fortunate accident helped them to destroy or appreciably to weaken the English navy. As for England, she will find Germany absolutely invulnerable. All that she may achieve is to seize the German colonies, stop German sea trade, and, in the most favorable event, annihilate the German navy, but nothing more. This, however, would not force the enemy to sue for peace. There is no doubt, therefore, that England will attempt the means she has more than once used with success, and will risk armed action only after securing participation in the war, on her own side, of powers stronger in a strategical sense. But since Germany, for her own part, will not be found isolated, the future Anglo-German war will undoubtedly be transformed into an armed conflict between two groups of powers, one with a German, the other with an English orientation.

It Is Hard To Discover Any Real Advantages to Russia in Rapprochement with England.—Until the Russo-Japanese War, Russian policy had neither orientation. From the time of the reign of Emperor Alexander III, Russia had a defensive alliance with France, so firm as to assure common action by both powers in the event of attack upon either, but, at the same time, not so close as to obligate either to support unfailingly, with armed force, all political actions and claims of the ally. At the same time, the Russian Court maintained the traditional friendly relations, based upon ties of blood, with the Court of Berlin. Owing precisely to this conjuncture, peace among the great powers was not disturbed in the course of a great many years, in spite of the presence of abundant combustible material in Europe. France, by her alliance wtih Russia, was guaranteed against attack by Germany; the latter was safe, thanks to the tried pacifism and friendship of Russia, from *revanche* ambitions on the part of France; and Russia was secured, thanks to Germany's need of maintaining amicable relations with her, against excessive intrigues by Austria-Hungary in the Balkan peninsula. Lastly, England, isolated and held in check by her rivalry with Russia in Persia, by her diplomats' traditional fear of our advance on India, and by strained relations with France, especially notable at the time of the well-known Fashoda incident, viewed with alarm the increase of Germany's naval power, without, however, risking an active step.

The Russo-Japanese War radically changed the relations among the great powers and brought England out of her isolation. As we know, all through the Russo-Japanese War, England and America observed benevolent neutrality toward Japan, while we enjoyed a similar benevolent neutrality from France and Germany. Here, it would seem, should have been the inception of the most natural political combination for us. But after the war, our diplomacy faced abruptly about and definitely entered upon the road toward rapprochement with England. France was drawn into the orbit of British policy; there was formed a group of powers of the Triple Entente, with England playing the dominant part; and a clash, sooner or later, with the powers grouping themselves around Germany became inevitable.

Now, what advantages did the renunciation of our traditional policy of distrust of England and the rupture of neighborly, if not friendly, relations with Germany promise us then and at present?

Considering with any degree of care the events which have taken place since the Treaty of Portsmouth, we find it difficult to perceive any practical advantages gained by us in rapprochement with England. The only benefit—improved relations with Japan—is scarcely a result of the Russo-English rap-

prochement. There is no reason why Russia and Japan should not live in peace; there seems to be nothing over which they need quarrel. All Russia's objectives in the Far East, if correctly understood, are entirely compatible with Japan's interests. These objectives, in their essentials, are very modest. The too broad sweep of the imagination of overzealous executive officials, without basis in genuine national interests, on the one hand, and the excessive nervousness and impressionability of Japan, on the other, which erroneously regarded these dreams as a consistently executed policy—these were the things that provoked a clash which a more capable diplomacy would have managed to avoid.

Russia needs neither Korea nor even Port Arthur. An outlet to the open sea is undoubtedly useful, but the sea in itself is, after all, not a market, but merely a road to a more advantageous delivery of goods at the consuming markets. As a matter of fact, we do not possess, and shall not for a long time possess any goods in the Far East that promise any considerable profits in exportation abroad. Nor are there any markets for the export of our products. We cannot expect a great supply of our export commodities to go to industrially and agriculturally developed America, to poor, but likewise industrial, Japan, or even to the maritime sections of China and remoter markets, where our exports would inevitably meet the competition of goods from the industrially stronger rival powers. There remains the interior of China, with which our trade is carried on chiefly overland. Consequently, an open port would aid the import of foreign merchandise more than the export of our own products.

Japan, on her part, no matter what is said, has no desire for our Far Eastern possessions. The Japanese are by nature a southern people, and the harsh environment of our Far Eastern borderland cannot attract them. We know that even within Japan itself northern Yezo is sparsely populated, while apparently Japanese colonization is making little headway even in the southern part of Sakhalin Island, ceded to Japan under the Treaty of Portsmouth. After taking possession of Korea and Formosa, Japan will hardly go farther north, and her ambitions, it may be assumed, will turn rather in the direction of the Philippine Islands, Indo-China, Java, Sumatra, and Borneo. The most she might desire would be the acquisition, for purely commercial reasons, of a few more sections of the Manchurian railway.

In a word, peaceable coexistence, nay, more, a close rapprochement, between Russia and Japan in the Far East is perfectly natural, regardless of any mediation by England. The grounds for agreement are self-evident. Japan is not a rich country, and the simultaneous upkeep of a strong army and a powerful navy is hard for her. Her insular situation drives her to strengthen her naval power, and alliance with Russia would allow her to devote all her attention to her navy, especially vital in view of her imminent rivalry with America, leaving the protection of her interests on the continent to Russia. On our part, we, having the Japanese navy to protect our Pacific coast, could give up once for all the dream, impossible to us, of creating a navy in the Far East.

Thus, so far as our relations with Japan are concerned, the rapprochement with England has yielded us no real advantage. And it has gained us nothing in the sense of strengthening our position in Manchuria, Mongolia, or even the Ulianghai territory, where the uncertainty of our position bears witness that the agreement with England has certainly not freed the hands of our

diplomats. On the contrary, our attempt to establish relations with Tibet met with sharp opposition from England.

In Persia, also, our position has been no better since the conclusion of this agreement. Every one recalls our predominant influence in that country under the Shah Nasr-Eddin (1829–96), that is, exactly at a time when our relations with England were most strained. From the moment of our accord with the latter, we have found ourselves drawn into a number of strange attempts to impose upon the Persian people an entirely needless constitution, with the result that we ourselves contributed to the overthrow, for the benefit of our inveterate enemies, of a monarch who was devoted to Russia. That is, not only have we gained nothing, but we have suffered a loss all along the line, ruining our prestige and wasting many millions of rubles, even the precious blood of Russian soldiers, who were treacherously slain and, to please England, not even avenged.

The worst results, however, of the accord with England—and of the consequent discord with Germany—have been felt in the Near East. As you know, it was Bismarck who coined that winged phrase about the Balkan problem not being worth to Germany the bones of a single Pomeranian grenadier. Later the Balkan complications began to attract much more attention from German diplomacy, which had taken the "Sick Man" under its protection, but even then Germany, for a long time, failed to show any inclination to endanger relations with Russia in the interests of Balkan affairs. The proofs are patent. During the period of the Russo-Japanese War and the ensuing turmoil in our country, it would have been very easy for Austria to realize her cherished ambitions in the Balkan peninsula. But at that time Russia had not yet linked her destinies with England, and Austria-Hungary was forced to lose an opportunity most auspicious for her purposes.

No sooner had we taken the road to closer accord with England, however, than there immediately followed the annexation of Bosnia and Herzegovina, a step which might have been taken so easily and painlessly in 1905 or 1906. Next came the Albanian question and the combination with the Prince of Wied. Russian diplomacy attempted to answer Austrian intrigue by forming a Balkan league, but this combination, as might have been expected, proved to be quite unworkable. Intended to be directed against Austria, it immediately turned on Turkey and fell apart in the process of dividing the spoils taken from the latter. The final result was merely the definite attachment of Turkey to Germany, in whom, not without good reason, she sees her sole protector. In short, the Russo-British rapprochement evidently seems to Turkey as tantamount to England's renouncing her traditional policy of closing the Dardanelles to us, while the creation of the Balkan league, under the auspices of Russia, appeared as a direct threat to the continued existence of Turkey as a European power.

Fundamental Alignments in the Coming War.—Under what conditions will this clash occur and what will be its probable consequences? The fundamental groupings in a future war are self-evident: Russia, France, and England, on the one side, with Germany, Austria, and Turkey, on the other. It is more than likely that other powers, too, will participate in that war, depending upon circumstances as they may exist at the war's outbreak. But, whether the immediate cause for the war is furnished by another clash of conflicting interests in the Balkans, or by a colonial incident, such as that of Algeciras, the funda-

mental alignment will remain unchanged.

Italy, if she has any conception of her real interests, will not join the German side. For political as well as economic reasons, she undoubtedly hopes to expand her present territory. Such an expansion may be achieved only at the expense of Austria, on one hand, and Turkey, on the other. It is, therefore, natural for Italy not to join that party which would safeguard the territorial integrity of the countries at whose expense she hopes to realize her aspirations. Furthermore, it is not out of the question that Italy would join the anti-German coalition, if the scales of war should incline in its favor, in order to secure for herself the most favorable conditions in sharing the subsequent division of spoils.

In this respect, the position of Italy is similar to the probable position of Rumania, which, it may be assumed, will remain neutral until the scales of fortune favor one or another side. Then, animated by normal political self-interest, she will attach herself to the victors, to be rewarded at the expense of either Russia or Austria. Of the other Balkan States, Serbia and Montenegro will unquestionably join the side opposing Austria, while Bulgaria and Albania (if by that time they have not yet formed at least the embryo of a State) will take their stand against the Serbian side. Greece will in all probability remain neutral or make common cause with the side opposing Turkey, but that only after the issue has been more or less determined. The participation of other powers will be incidental, and Sweden ought to be feared, of course, in the ranks of our foes.

Under such circumstances, a struggle with Germany presents to us enormous difficulties, and will require countless sacrifices. War will not find the enemy unprepared, and the degree of his preparedness will probably exceed our most exaggerated calculations. It should not be thought that this readiness is due to Germany's own desire for war. She needs no war, so long as she can attain her object—the end of exclusive domination of the seas. But, once this vital object is opposed by the coalition, Germany will not shrink from war, and, of course, will even try to provoke it, choosing the most auspicious moment. *The Main Burden of the War Will Fall on Russia.*—The main burden of the war will undoubtedly fall on us, since England is hardly capable of taking a considerable part in a continental war, while France, poor in manpower, will probably adhere to strictly defensive tactics, in view of the enormous losses by which war will be attended under present conditions of military technique. The part of a battering-ram, making a breach in the very thick of the German defense, will be ours, with many factors against us to which we shall have to devote great effort and attention.

From the sum of these unfavorable factors we should deduct the Far East. Both America and Japan—the former fundamentally, and the latter by virtue of her present political orientation—are hostile to Germany, and there is no reason to expect them to act on the German side. Furthermore, the war, regardless of its issue, will weaken Russia and divert her attention to the West, a fact which, of course, serves both Japanese and American interests. Thus, our rear will be sufficiently secure in the Far East, and the most that can happen there will be the extortion from us of some concessions of an economic nature in return for benevolent neutrality. Indeed, it is possible that America or Japan may join the anti-German side, but, of course, merely as usurpers of one or the other of the unprotected German colonies.

There can be no doubt, however, as to an outburst of hatred for us in Persia, and a probable unrest among the Moslems of the Caucasus and Turkestan; it is possible that Afghanistan, as a result of that unrest, may act against us; and, finally, we must foresee very unpleasant complications in Poland and Finland. In the latter, a rebellion will undoubtedly break out if Sweden is found in the ranks of our enemies. As for Poland, it is not to be expected that we can hold her against our enemy during the war. And after she is in his power, he will undoubtedly endeavor to provoke an insurrection which, while not in reality very dangerous, must be considered, nevertheless, as one of the factors unfavorable to us, especially since the influence of our allies may induce us to take such measures in our relations with Poland as will prove more dangerous to us than any open revolt.

Are we prepared for so stubborn a war as the future war of the European nations will undoubtedly become? This question we must answer, without evasion, in the negative. That much has been done for our defense since the Japanese war, I am the last person to deny, but even so, it is quite inadequate considering the unprecedented scale on which a future war will inevitably be fought. The fault lies, in a considerable measure, in our young legislative institutions, which have taken a dilettante interest in our defenses, but are far from grasping the seriousness of the political situation arising from the new orientation which, with the sympathy of the public, has been followed in recent years by our Ministry of Foreign Affairs.

The enormous number of still unconsidered legislative bills of the war and navy departments may serve as proof of this: for example, the plan of the organization of our national defense proposed to the Duma as early as the days of Secretary of State Stolypin (1906–11). It cannot be denied that, in the matter of military instruction, according to the reports of specialists, we have achieved substantial improvements, as compared with the time before the Japanese War. According to the same specialists, our field artillery leaves nothing to be desired; the gun is entirely satisfactory, and the equipment convenient and practical. Yet, it must be admitted that there are substantial shortcomings in the organization of our defenses.

In this regard we must note, first of all, the insufficiency of our war supplies, which, certainly, cannot be blamed upon the war department, since the supply schedules are still far from being executed, owing to the low productivity of our factories. This insufficiency of munitions is the more significant since, in the embryonic condition of our industries, we shall, during the war, have no opportunity to make up the revealed shortage by our own efforts, and the closing of the Baltic as well as the Black Sea will prevent the importation from abroad of the defense materials which we lack.

Another circumstance unfavorable to our defense is its far too great dependence, generally speaking, upon foreign industry, a fact which, in connection with the above, will create a series of obstacles difficult to overcome. The quantity of our heavy artillery, the importance of which was demonstrated in the Japanese War, is far too inadequate, and there are few machine guns. The organization of our fortress defenses has scarcely been started, and even the fortress of Reval, which is to defend the road to the capital, is not yet finished.

The network of strategic railways is inadequate. The railways possess a rolling stock sufficient, perhaps, for normal traffic, but not commensurate with the colossal demands which will be made upon them in the event of a European war. Lastly, it should not be forgotten that the impending war will be fought among the most civilized and technically most advanced nations. Every previous war has invariably been followed by something new in the realm of military technique, but the technical backwardness of our industries does not create favorable conditions for our adoption of the new inventions.

The Vital Interests of Germany and Russia Do Not Conflict.—All these factors are hardly given proper thought by our diplomats, whose behavior toward Germany is, in some respects, even aggressive, and may unduly hasten the moment of armed conflict, a moment which, of course, is really inevitable in view of our British orientation.

The question is whether this orientation is correct, and whether even a favorable issue of the war promises us such advantages as could compensate us for all the hardships and sacrifices which must attend a war unparalleled in its probable strain.

The vital interests of Russia and Germany do not conflict. There are fundamental grounds for a peaceable existence of these two States. Germany's future lies on the sea, that is, in a realm where Russia, essentially the most continental of the great powers, has no interests whatever. We have no overseas colonies, and shall probably never have them, and communication between the various parts of our empire is easier overland than by water. No surplus population demanding territorial expansion is visible, but, even from the viewpoint of new conquests, what can we gain from a victory over Germany?

Posen, or East Prussia? But why do we need these regions, densely populated as they are by Poles, when we find it difficult enough to manage our own Russian Poles? Why encourage centripetal tendencies, that have not ceased even to this day in the Vistula territory, by incorporating in the Russian State the restless Posnanian and East Prussian Poles, whose national demands even the German Government, which is more firm than the Russian, cannot stifle?

Exactly the same thing applies to Galicia. It is obviously disadvantageous to us to annex, in the interests of national sentimentalism, a territory that has lost every vital connection with our fatherland. For, together with a negligible handful of Galicians, Russian in spirit, how many Poles, Jews, and Ukrainized Uniates we would receive! The so-called Ukrainian, or Mazeppist, movement is not a menace to us at present, but we should not enable it to expand by increasing the number of turbulent Ukrainian elements, for in this movement there undoubtedly lies the seed of an extremely dangerous Little Russian separatism which, under favorable conditions, may assume quite unexpected proportions.

The obvious aim of our diplomacy in the rapprochement with England has been to open the Straits. But a war with Germany seems hardly necessary for the attainment of this object, for it was England, and not Germany at all, that closed our outlet from the Black Sea. Was it not because we made sure of the cooperation of the latter power, that we freed ourselves in 1871 from the humiliating restrictions imposed upon us by England under the Treaty of Paris?

Also, there is reason to believe that the Germans would agree sooner than the English to let us have the Straits, in which they have only a slight interest, and at the price of which they would gladly purchase our alliance.

Moreover, we should not cherish any exaggerated hopes from our occupation of the Straits. Their acquisition would be advantageous to us only as they served to close the Black Sea to others, making it an inland sea for us, safe from enemy attack.

The Straits would not give us an outlet to the open sea, however, since on the other side of them there lies a sea consisting almost wholly of territorial waters, a sea dotted with numerous islands where the British navy, for instance, would have no trouble whatever in closing to us every inlet and outlet, irrespective of the Straits. Therefore, Russia might safely welcome an arrangement which, while not turning the Straits over to our direct control, would safeguard us against a penetration of the Black Sea by an enemy fleet. Such an arrangement, attainable under favorable circumstances without any war, has the additional advantage that it would not violate the interests of the Balkan States, which would not regard our seizure of the Straits without alarm and quite natural jealousy.

In Trans-Caucasia we could, as a result of war, expand territorially only at the expense of regions inhabited by Armenians, a move which is hardly desirable in view of the revolutionary character of present Armenian sentiment, and of its dream of a greater Armenia; and in this region, Germany, were we allied to her, would certainly place even fewer obstacles in our way than England. Those territorial and economic acquisitions which might really prove useful to us are available only in places where our ambitions may meet opposition from England, but by no means from Germany. Persia, the Pamir, Kuldja, Kashgar, Dzungaria, Mongolia, and the Ulianghai territory—all these are regions where the interests of Russia and Germany do not conflict, whereas the interests of Russia and England have clashed there repeatedly.

And Germany is in exactly the same situation with respect to Russia. She could seize from us, in case of a successful war, only such territories as would be of slight value to her, and because of their population, would prove of little use for colonization; the Vistula territory, with a Polish-Lithuanian population, and the Baltic provinces, with a Lettish-Esthonian population, are all equally turbulent and anti-German.

Russia's Economic Advantages and Needs Do Not Conflict with Germany's. —It may be argued, however, that, under modern conditions in the various nations, territorial acquisitions are of secondary importance, while economic interests take first rank. But in this field again, Russia's advantages and needs do not conflict with Germany's as much as is believed. It is, of course, undeniable that the existing Russo-German trade agreements are disadvantageous to our agriculture and advantageous to Germany's, but it would be hardly fair to ascribe this circumstance to the treachery and unfriendliness of Germany.

It should not be forgotten that these agreements are in many of their sections advantageous to us. The Russian delegates who concluded these agreements were confirmed protagonists of a development of Russian industry at any cost, and they undoubtedly made a deliberate sacrifice, at least to some extent, of the interests of Russian agriculture to the interests of Russian industry. Furthermore we ought not to forget that Germany is far from being the direct consumer of the greater share of our agricultural exports abroad. For the greater share of our agricultural produce, Germany acts merely as middleman, and so it is for us and the consuming markets to establish direct relations and thus avoid the expensive German mediation. Lastly, we should keep in mind that the commercial relations of States depend on their political understandings, for no country finds advantage in the economic weakening of an ally but, conversely, profits by the ruin of a political foe. In short, even though it be obvious that the existing Russo-German commercial treaties are not to our advantage, and that Germany, in concluding them, availed herself of a situation that happened to be in her favor (commercial treaty of 1904, the time of the Japanese War)—in other words, forced us to the wall—this action should have been expected from Germany and thought of. It should not, however, be looked upon as a mark of hostility toward us, but rather as an expression of healthy national self-interest, worthy of our emulation. Aside from that, we observe, in the case of Austria-Hungary, an agricultural country that is in a far greater economic dependence upon Germany than ours, but nevertheless, is not prevented from attaining an agricultural development such as we may only dream of.

In view of what has been said, it would seem that the conclusion of a commercial treaty with Germany, entirely acceptable to Russia, by no means requires that Germany first be crushed. It will be quite sufficient to maintain neighborly relations with her, to make a careful estimate of our real interests in the various branches of national economy, and to engage in long, insistent bargaining with German delegates, who may be expected to protect the interests of their own fatherland and not ours.

But I would go still further and say that the ruin of Germany, from the viewpoint of our trade with her, would be disadvantageous to us. Her defeat would unquestionably end in a peace dictated from the viewpoint of England's economic interests. The latter will exploit to the farthest limit any success that falls to her lot, and we will only lose, in a ruined Germany without sea routes, a market which, after all, is valuable to us for our otherwise unmarketable products.

In respect to Germany's economic future, the interests of Russia and England are diametrically opposed. For England, it is profitable to kill Germany's maritime trade and industry, turning her into a poor and, if possible, agricultural country. For us, it is of advantage for Germany to develop her sea-going commerce and the industry which serves it, so as to supply the remotest world markets, and at the same time open her domestic market to our agricultural products, to supply her large working population.

But, aside from the commercial treaties, it has been customary to point out the oppressive character of German domination in Russian economic life, and the systematic penetration of German colonization into our country, as representing a manifest peril to the Russian State. We believe, however, that fears on these grounds are considerably exaggerated. The famous "Drang nach Osten" was in its own time natural and understandable, since Germany's land could not accommodate her increased population, and the surplus was driven in the direction of the least resistance, i.e., into a less densely populated neighboring country. The German Government was compelled to recognize the inevitability of this movement, but could hardly look upon it as to its own interests. For, after all, it was Germans who were being lost to the influence of the German State, thus reducing the man power of their country. Indeed, the German Government made such strenuous efforts to preserve the connection

between its emigrants and their old fatherland that it adopted even the unusual method of tolerating dual citizenship. It is certain, however, that a considerable proportion of German emigrants definitely and irrevocably settled in their new homes, and slowly broke their ties with the old country. This fact, obviously incompatible with Germany's State interests, seems to have been one of the incentives which started her upon a colonial policy and maritime commerce, previously so alien to her. And at present, as the German colonies increase and there is an attendant growth of German industry and naval commerce, the German colonization movement decreases, in a measure, and the day is not remote when the "Drang nach Osten" will become nothing more than a subject for history.

In any case, the German colonization, which undoubtedly conflicts with our State interests, must be stopped, and here, again, friendly relations with Germany cannot harm us. To express a preference for a German orientation does not imply the advocacy of Russian vassalage to Germany, and, while maintaining friendly and neighborly intercourse with her, we must not sacrifice our State interests to this object. But Germany herself will not object to measures against the continued flow of German colonists into Russia. To her, it is of greater benefit to turn the wave of emigration toward her own colonies. Moreover, even before Germany had colonies, when her industry was not yet sufficiently developed to employ the entire population, the German Government did not feel justified in protesting against the restrictive measures that were adopted against foreign colonization during the reign of Alexander III.

As regards the German domination in the field of our economic life, this phenomenon hardly justifies the complaints usually voiced against it. Russia is far too poor, both in capital and in industrial enterprise, to get along without a large import of foreign capital. A certain amount of dependence upon some kind of foreign capital is, therefore, unavoidable, until such time as the industrial enterprise and material resources of our population develop to a point where we may entirely forego the services of foreign investors and their money. But as long as we do require them, German capital is more advantageous to us than any other.

First and foremost, this capital is cheaper than any other, being satisfied with the lowest margin of profit. This, to a large extent, explains the relative cheapness of German products, and their gradual displacement of British products in the markets of the world. The lower demands of German capital, as regards returns, have for their consequence Germany's readiness to invest in enterprises which, because of their relatively small returns, are shunned by other foreign investors. Also, as a result of that relative cheapness of German capital, its influx into Russia is attended by a smaller outflow of investors' profits from Russia, as compared with French and English investments, and so a larger amount of rubles remain in Russia. Moreover, a considerable proportion of the profits made on German investments in Russian industry do not leave our country at all, but are spent in Russia.

Unlike the English or French, the German capitalists, in most cases, come to stay in Russia, themselves, with their money. It is this very German characteristic which explains in a considerable degree the amazing number of German industrialists, manufacturers, and mill owners in our midst, as compared with the British and French.

The latter live in their own countries, removing from Russia the profits pro-

duced by their enterprises, down to the last kopek. The German investors, on the contrary, live in Russia for long periods, and not infrequently settle down permanently. Whatever may be said to the contrary, the fact is that the Germans, unlike other foreigners, soon feel at home in Russia and rapidly become Russianized. Who has not seen Frenchmen and Englishmen, for example, who have spent almost their whole lives in Russia and yet do not speak a word of Russian? On the other hand, are there many Germans here who cannot make themselves understood in Russian, even though it be with a strong accent and in broken speech? Nay, more—who has not seen genuine Russians, Orthodox, loyal with all their hearts dedicated to the principles of the Russian State, and yet only one or two generations removed from their German emigrant ancestry? Lastly, we must not forget that Germany herself is, to a certain extent, interested in our economic well-being. In this regard, Germany differs, to our advantage, from other countries, which are interested exclusively in obtaining the largest possible returns from capital invested in Russia, even at the cost of the economic ruin of this country. Germany, however, in her capacity of permanent —although, of course, not unselfish— middleman for our foreign trade, has an interest in preserving the productive resources of our country, as a source of profitable intermediary operations for her.

Even a Victory over Germany Promises Russia an Exceedingly Unfavorable Prospect.—In any case, even if we were to admit the necessity for eradicating German domination in the field of our economic life, even at the price of a total banishment of German capital from Russian industry, appropriate measures could be taken, it would seem, without war against Germany. Such a war will demand such enormous expenditures that they will many times exceed the more than doubtful advantages to us in the abolition of the German [economic] domination. More than that, the result of such a war will be an economic situation compared with which the yoke of German capital will seem easy.

For there can be no doubt that the war will necessitate expenditures which are beyond Russia's limited financial means. We shall have to obtain credit from allied and neutral countries, but this will not be granted gratuitously. As to what will happen if the war should end disastrously for us, I do not wish to discuss now. The financial and economic consequences of defeat can be neither calculated nor foreseen, and will undoubtedly spell the total ruin of our entire national economy.

But even victory promises us extremely unfavorable financial prospects; a totally ruined Germany will not be in a position to compensate us for the cost involved. Dictated in the interest of England, the peace treaty will not afford Germany opportunity for sufficient economic recuperation to cover our war expenditures, even at a distant time. The little which we may perhaps succeed in extorting from her will have to be shared with our allies, and to our share there will fall but negligible crumbs, compared with the war cost. Meantime, we shall have to pay our war loans, not without pressure by the allies. For, after the destruction of German power, we shall no longer be necessary to them. Nay, more, our political might, enhanced by our victory, will induce them to weaken us, at least economically. And so it is inevitable that, even after a victorious conclusion of the war, we shall fall into the same sort of financial and economic dependence upon our creditors, compared with which our present dependence upon German capital will seem ideal.

However, no matter how sad may be the economic prospects which face us as a result of union with England, and, by that token, of war with Germany, they are still of secondary importance when we think of the political consequences of this fundamentally unnatural alliance. *A Struggle between Russia and Germany Is Profoundly Undesirable to Both Sides, as It Amounts to a Weakening of the Monarchist Principle.*—It should not be forgotten that Russia and Germany are the representatives of the conservative principle in the civilized world, as opposed to the democratic principle, incarnated in England and, to an infinitely lesser degree, in France. Strange as it may seem, England, monarchistic and conservative to the marrow at home, has in her foreign relations always acted as the protector of the most demagogical tendencies, invariably encouraging all popular movements aiming at the weakening of the monarchical principle.

From this point of view, a struggle between Germany and Russia, regardless of its issue, is profoundly undesirable to both sides, as undoubtedly involving the weakening of the conservative principle in the world of which the above-named two great powers are the only reliable bulwarks. More than that, one must realize that under the exceptional conditions which exist, a general European war is mortally dangerous both for Russia and Germany, no matter who wins. It is our firm conviction, based upon a long and careful study of all contemporary subversive tendencies, that there must inevitably break out in the defeated country a social revolution which, by the very nature of things, will spread to the country of the victor.

During the many years of peaceable neighborly existence, the two countries have become united by many ties, and a social upheaval in one is bound to affect the other. That these troubles will be of a social, and not a political, nature cannot be doubted, and this will hold true, not only as regards Russia, but for Germany as well. An especially favorable soil for social upheavals is found in Russia, where the masses undoubtedly profess, unconsciously, the principles of Socialism. In spite of the spirit of antagonism to the Government in Russian society, as unconscious as the Socialism of the broad masses of the people, a political revolution is not possible in Russia, and any revolutionary movement inevitably must degenerate into a Socialist movement. The opponents of the Government have no popular support. The people see no difference between a Government official and an intellectual. The Russian masses, whether workmen or peasants, are not looking for political rights, which they neither want nor comprehend.

The peasant dreams of obtaining a gratuitous share of somebody else's land; the workman, of getting hold of the entire capital and profits of the manufacturer. Beyond this, they have no aspirations. If these slogans are scattered far and wide among the populace, and the Government permits agitation along these lines, Russia will be flung into anarchy, such as she suffered in the ever-memorable period of troubles in 1905–6. War with Germany would create exceptionally favorable conditions for such agitation. As already stated, this war is pregnant with enormous difficulties for us, and cannot turn out to be a mere triumphal march to Berlin. Both military disasters—partial ones, let us hope—and all kinds of shortcomings in our supply are inevitable. In the excessive nervousness and spirit of opposition of our society, these events will be given an exaggerated importance,

and all the blame will be laid on the Government.

It will be well if the Government does not yield, but declares directly that in time of war no criticism of the governmental authority is to be tolerated, and resolutely suppresses all opposition. In the absence of any really strong hold on the people by the opposition, this would settle the affair. The people did not heed the writer of the Wiborg Manifesto, in its time, and they will not follow them now.

But a worse thing may happen: the Government authority may make concessions, may try to come to an agreement with the opposition, and thereby weaken itself just when the Socialist elements are ready for action. Even though it may sound like a paradox, the fact is that agreement with the opposition in Russia positively weakens the Government. The trouble is that our opposition refuses to reckon with the fact that it represents no real force. The Russian opposition is intellectual throughout, and this is its weakness, because between the intelligentsia and the people there is a profound gulf of mutual misunderstanding and distrust. We need an artificial election law, indeed, we require the direct influence of the governmental authority, to assure the election to the State Duma of even the most zealous champions of popular rights. Let the Government refuse to support the elections, leaving them to their natural course, and the legislative institutions would not see within their walls a single intellectual, outside of a few demagogic agitators. However insistent the members of our legislative institutions may be that the people confide in them, the peasant would rather believe the landless Government official than the Octobrist landlord in the Duma, while the workingman treats the wage-earning factory inspector with more confidence than the legislating manufacturer, even though the latter professes every principle of the Cadet Party.

It is more than strange, under these circumstances, that the governmental authority should be asked to reckon seriously with the opposition, that it should for this purpose renounce the role of impartial regulator of social relationships, and come out before the broad masses of the people as the obedient organ of the class aspirations of the intellectual and propertied minority of the population. The opposition demands that the Government should be responsible to it, representative of a class, and should obey the parliament which it artificially created. (Let us recall that famous expression of V. Nabokov: "Let the executive power submit to the legislative power!") In other words, the opposition demands that the Government should adopt the psychology of a savage, and worship the idol which he himself made.

Russia Will Be Flung into Hopeless Anarchy, the Issue of Which Will Be Hard To Foresee.—If the war ends in victory, the putting down of the Socialist movement will not offer any insurmountable obstacles. There will be agrarian troubles, as a result of agitation for compensating the soldiers with additional land allotments; there will be labor troubles during the transition from the probably increased wages of war time to normal schedules; and this, it is to be hoped, will be all, so long as the wave of the German social revolution has not reached us. But in the event of defeat, the possibility of which in a struggle with a foe like Germany cannot be overlooked, social revolution in its most extreme form is inevitable.

As has already been said, the trouble will start with the blaming of the Government for all disasters. In the legislative institutions a bitter campaign against the Government will begin, followed by revolutionary agitations throughout the country, with Socialist slogans, capable of arousing and rallying the masses, beginning with the division of the land and succeeded by a division of all valuables and property. The defeated army, having lost its most dependable men, and carried away by the tide of primitive peasant desire for land, will find itself too demoralized to serve as a bulwark of law and order. The legislative institutions and the intellectual opposition parties, lacking real authority in the eyes of the people, will be powerless to stem the popular tide, aroused by themselves, and Russia will be flung into hopeless anarchy, the issue of which cannot be foreseen. . . .

43

THE NATURE OF
IMPERIAL RUSSIAN SOCIETY

By Cyril Black; Hugh Seton-Watson

Professor Black, who teaches Russian history at Princeton, here summarizes some of the chief trends of Russian developments in the two centuries before the Revolution. Hugh Seton-Watson, professor of Russian history at the University of London, comments on these interpretations and makes some points of his own. For further literature on the many subjects discussed, see the footnotes. An alternative interpretation is available in Theodore Von Laue, "Of the Crises in the Russian Polity," *Essays in Russian and Soviet History*, edited by John S. Curtiss.

. . . A brief statement of the features that distinguished Russian imperial society must of necessity be highly selective and impressionistic, and it is proposed here to touch on only five characteristics: the physical setting, the autocratic state, the system of social stratification, the agrarian economy, and the multinational structure.

The most significant features of the physical setting of imperial Russia were its size, its location, and its poverty. The conquest of Siberia in the sixteenth and seventeenth centuries resulted in a vast increase in the territory under the rule of Moscow. This large territory inherited by Peter nevertheless lacked either well-defined frontiers or suitable maritime outlets for commerce, and at the same time was subject to many pressures on the long frontier with Europe and Western Asia. In the course

of the many wars of the eighteenth and nineteenth centuries the frontiers of the empire were further extended, and indeed throughout this period Russia was by all odds the largest country in the world in terms of territory. At the same time the number of inhabitants grew from 14 to 170 million, with the result that Russia was by 1917 inferior in population only to China and India. As significant as its size was its location, bordering as it did on Europe and on the broad sweep of Asia stretching from the Bosporus to the Kuril Islands. In earlier centuries Byzantine influences, and to a much lesser extent Mongol and Ottoman, had played a vital role in the culture of Muscovite Russia. To this

From *Slavic Review*, XX (1961), 565–88, 594–98. Footnotes have been edited and only English references retained. Used by permission of the managing editor of *Slavic Review*.

extent Russia, like Byzantium itself, could be said to have cultural roots in both Europe and Asia. In the period of the empire, which was one of almost exclusively European influences, the principal significance of geographical location lay in the realm of foreign policy. In an age in which Europe was embracing the world, a country of Russia's size and position could not well avoid being drawn into the affairs of the many countries on its borders and beyond.[1]

Economic poverty was also an important element in the Russian setting. The vast size of the country was to a considerable degree illusory, since only a small part of it was suitable for agriculture, and much of that had a poor soil or climate. It is now known to be rich in natural resources, but before the First World War only its petroleum and a few other minerals had been adequately developed. In per capita terms Russia was very poor by the standards of the European countries which were her principal competitors. Perhaps the best way of expressing the problem confronting the statesmen of the empire was that they had to find a means of converting her rather meager and scattered resources into effective national power. This is no doubt a rather abstract formulation, yet Peter the Great must have looked at things somewhat in this fashion when he undertook to strengthen the administrative apparatus of a state which already had a claim to autocratic power well established in theory if not in practice.

[1] George Vernadsky, "The Expansion of Russia," *Transactions of the Connecticut Academy of Arts and Sciences*, XXXI (July, 1933), 391–425, provides a succinct account. The very extensive development of the lands beyond the Urals after 1861 is described in Donald W. Treadgold, *The Great Siberian Migration: Government and Peasant in Resettlement from Emancipation to the First World War* (Princeton, 1957).

It would probably not be going too far to say that in no other major society in the eighteenth and nineteenth centuries did the sovereign and the state play as great a role as they did in Russia. Prussia in the eighteenth century and China and Turkey in earlier times are among the first examples that come to mind of centralized political systems which had a comparable role in the life of the country. In the nineteenth century, at any rate, the Russian empire stood alone as a society in which a great many aspects of human activity were to a large extent administered or at least regulated by the state. The Russian government was formally an autocracy in the sense that all political authority was vested in the autocrat. The theory of autocracy came from Byzantine political thought and, modified by adaptations from Tatar and Ottoman administrative practices, it became a reality in the course of the fifteenth and sixteenth centuries as the princes of Moscow succeeded in consolidating the political power which had been shared since the thirteenth century by the various principalities of northeastern Russia and their Tatar overlords. What was in theory an autocracy was often for all practical purposes an oligarchy, however, for the princes of Moscow had great difficulty in establishing effective and orderly control over the ruling families whose lands they successively incorporated into the new state. The reigns of the principal architects of the Muscovite political system—Vasilii II the Blind, Ivan III the Great, and Ivan IV the Terrible—were marked by continual internecine strife culminating in the Time of Troubles. After the establishment of the Romanov dynasty in 1613 it was half a century or more before the central administrative system was sufficiently effective to permit the sovereign to free himself from the assembly of notables which had established the dynasty and guided its early fortunes. It was this system which Peter the Great reshaped and rationalized on the basis of Swedish and other European models to form the "regulated state" which, with significant changes to be sure, lasted until 1917.

Under the system established by Peter, the Emperor was more of an autocrat than the tsars had even been, yet the oligarchy composed of high civilian and military officials and leading families of noble landowners continued to play an independent role throughout the eighteenth century during the reigns of eight rulers who were relatively weak for reasons of youth, sex, or mental disability. Paul, the last of these rulers, is generally portrayed as mad—but there was a method in his madness. He took the first measures in the direction of reaffirming the authority of the autocrat, and this authority was further consolidated by his successors. Despite the many political changes which occurred during the last century of the empire, the sovereign remained an autocrat in theory and to a considerable extent in practice, although only in the reign of Nicholas I did he in fact approximate the theoretical model.[2]

A more fundamental question than the relationship of the autocrat to the oligarchy is that of the role of the state in society. No less than two-fifths of the forty million peasants in European Russia were directly administered by the state before emancipation, as were many economic enterprises as well. Through its administration of the Holy Synod,

the Academy of Sciences, all higher education, and most primary and secondary education, and through the censorship, the state had a direct and permeating influence on the intellectual life of the country. The rapid economic and social changes which occurred after the emancipation of the serfs did not have the effect of reducing the role of the state. On the contrary, the state played a leading role in this process. There were a few phases of Russian life in which it was not directly interested, and over many of the most important it had a virtual monopoly through direct administration and a decisive influence in policy-making.

One of the most significant consequences of the "omnicompetence" of the Russian state, to borrow Sumner's felicitous term,[3] was its influence on the position of social strata. It was as though the autocrat could imagine no other way to assure the state of the support of its leading citizens and a regular income from the rather backward agrarian economy than by binding all individuals to its service. In a purely formal sense, all citizens of the empire were divided into three general categories: natives, non-natives, and Finns (who were a separate category by virtue of inhabiting an autonomous Grand Duchy). The native citizens in turn were divided by statute into four estates or strata—nobility, clergy, townsmen, and peasants—but these categories were not very meaningful. There were important differences between hereditary and personal nobles; townsmen were separated into four quite distinct categories —notable citizens, merchants, tradesmen and artisans; the clergy were an occupational group rather than a social stratum, for both those who left the clergy and children of clergymen in

[2] Nicholas V. Riasanovsky, *Nicholas I and Official Nationality in Russia, 1825–1855* (Berkeley, 1959), and Sidney Monas, *The Third Section: Police and Society in Russia under Nicholas I* (Cambridge, Mass., 1961) present in graphic detail the theory and practice of autocracy in the reign of Nicholas I, and offer a valuable guide to the large literature on this subject.

[3] Benedict H. Sumner, *A Short History of Russia* (New York, 1943), pp. 84–85.

general were legally regarded as towns-men of the rank of notable citizens; moreover a nobleman could also be a member of the clergy. Perhaps only the peasants were a legally homogeneous class, although there were significant differences between state peasants and serfs as well as those imposed by the widely varying customs of the diverse regions of Russia.

More fundamental than these formal distinctions was that which prevailed substantially until the revolution of 1905 between the privileged and the un-privileged. The privileged were not sub-ject to direct taxes or corporal punish-ment and could travel freely within the country. Only the nobles and townsmen of the rank of notable citizens, totaling between 1 and 2 per cent of the popula-tion, enjoyed these privileges. The nobles also had the privilege until 1861 of owning serfs. Moreover, the privi-leged had access to political power, if they did not actually share it, while the unprivileged bore the burden of sup-porting the privileged as well as the heavy superstructure of the state. The unprivileged were subjected to severe restrictions as to movement, along with other forms of personal and social disci-pline, and had virtually no access to the ranks of the privileged before the mid-dle of the nineteenth century. Indeed the gap between the two groups tended to widen during much of this period, as the privileged gained in education and influence while the position of the peas-ants in particular became more de-pressed. These hardships weighed even more heavily on the non-natives—the Jews, the Moslems, and the various in-digenous peoples of Siberia. The grosser inequities were relaxed in the latter part of the nineteenth century and were largely removed after 1905, but the gov-ernment yielded reluctantly and only under great pressure. The growth of civil liberties in the last decades of the

empire thus released accumulated ten-sions which could be contained only by a political system whose authority was not weakened by economic distress or foreign defeats.[4]

The system of social stratification also had the effect of inhibiting the de-velopment of a sense of political re-sponsibility. This was in part the result of the corporative organization of the social strata, which tended to isolate them from each other. Thus the heredi-tary nobles, three categories of towns-men (the merchants, the tradesmen, and the artisans), and the peasants were or-ganized in corporative associations by province, town, or village. These asso-ciations were collectively responsible for the conduct of their members, and in the case ot the townsmen and the peasants had important fiscal and disci-plinary functions. This form of social organization encouraged these groups, which formed the bulk of the popula-tion, to negotiate directly wtih the gov-ernment rather than to seek common cause against it. This attitude was fur-ther encouraged by contradictory pre-vailing trends of political thought which maintained either that the autocratic state was good, or that it must be elimi-nated, or that it should be ignored as a necessary evil. It was not until the end of the nineteenth century that the possi-bility of effective political action against the state within the framework of the empire was widely accepted.[5]

[4] The structure and functioning of the strati-fication system are discussed in Robert A. Feldmesser, "Social Classes and Political Struc-ture," *The Transformation of Russian Society: Aspects of Social Change since 1861*, ed. Cyril E. Black (Cambridge, Mass., 1960), pp. 235–52 (hereafter cited as *Transformation of Russian Society*) ; and Robert C. Tucker, "The Image of Dual Russia," *Transformation of Russian Society*, pp. 587–605.

[5] Leopold H. Haimson, "The Parties and the State: The Evolution of Political Attitudes," *Transformation of Russian Society*, pp. 110–45.

The system under which the peasants were bound to the soil and to the noble landowner is known as serfdom, and it existed in its most rigorous form between 1649 and 1861. Russian serfdom must be distinguished from feudalism as it existed in Western Europe. Feudalism was a political system characterized by a contractual relationship between lord and vassal, whereas in serfdom the relationship was primarily economic and was based not on contract but on the edict of the sovereign. There had been elements of the lord-vassal relationship earlier in Russian history, but these had disappeared with the rise of serfdom.[6] The state created serfdom as a means of assuring itself of a reliable source of revenue in a situation in which land was plentiful but labor was scarce, and agriculture was the principal source of income. The conditions of peasant life were so hard in Russia in the fifteenth and sixteenth centuries, because of the endemic civil strife and the increasing need of the state for revenue to meet the requirements of national defense, that the peasants tended constantly to escape to the south or east to avoid oppression. Various efforts were made to restrict the freedom of movement of the peasants, and these finally culminated in the middle of the seventeenth century in the imposition of a form of serfdom noted for its oppressiveness. . . .[7]

[6] For a discussion of this important question see Marc Szeftel, "Aspects of Feudalism in Russian History," *Feudalism in History*, ed. Rushton Coulborn (Princeton, 1956), pp. 167–82; and Rushton Coulborn, "Russia and Byzantium," *ibid.*, pp. 344–63. The extensive controversy in Russian historiography on this issue is reviewed by Marc Szeftel in *ibid.*, pp. 413–19. A similar conclusion is reached in George Vernadsky, "Feudalism in Russia," *Speculum*, XIV (July, 1939), 300–323.

[7] Jerome Blum, *Lord and Peasant in Russia from the Ninth to the Nineteenth Century* (Princeton, 1961), provides a comprehensive account of the origins and development of serfdom.

Serfdom had been established principally for the benefit of the state, and no doubt it provided the basis for a type of stable administrative and fiscal control over the peoples and the resources of the country which could not readily be achieved by other means. Stability was achieved at the price of stagnation, however, for there was no Russian counterpart of the rapid economic and social change which the societies of Western and Central Europe experienced during the period in which serfdom prevailed in Russia. Serfdom tended to discourage initiative on the part of peasant and noble landowner alike, and in a variety of ways inhibited the growth of industry. It may be argued that the real obstacle to social and economic change in Russia was in the minds of its leaders, and that much could have been done even within the framework of serfdom to stimulate technological improvements in agriculture and to encourage industry. In any event, as the conception of a modern society began to gain adherents among Russian leaders, a process in which the defeat in the Crimea appears to have had a large influence, serfdom was the first institution which they undertook to reform.[8]

The attempt to present a brief characterization of a complex society runs a particular danger in the case of Russia, since only 43.3 per cent of the population was Great Russian at the end of the nineteenth century, and the many minority peoples enjoyed a wide diversity of traditional institutions. What has been said about the decisively centralizing character of the administration must be modified to the extent that the Ukraine, the Baltic provinces, and Congress Poland all enjoyed a degree of

[8] G. Pavlovsky, *Agricultural Russia on the Eve of the Revolution* (London, 1930), and Geroid T. Robinson, *Rural Russia under the Old Regime* (New York, 1932).

autonomy during parts of the period under consideration, and the Grand Duchy of Finland had substantial privileges except for the short period between 1903 and 1905. Similarly as regards social stratification and the agrarian system, there were many differences in the position of the various minority peoples. Indeed, it was long the practice of the imperial government to respect the diverse institutions of the peoples annexed in the course of the expansion of the empire, and it was only toward the end of the nineteenth century that a rigorous policy of administrative and cultural Russification was attempted.[9]

The multinational character of imperial Russian society also had grave consequences in the realm of foreign policy. The chief concern of Russia in annexing these peoples, located almost entirely on her borders with Europe and Western and Central Asia, was for her own security. The territories they inhabited either blocked Russian access to the Baltic and Black seas; or, as was the case with Poland and Central Asia, might have come under the rule of other great powers to the detriment of Russia's interests; or again, as was the case with the Ukraine and Georgia, actually sought Russian protection against neighbors they feared more. It would doubtless be going too far to say that Russia had no imperialist ambitions, for numerous proposals for annexing noncontiguous territories can be found in her diplomatic records. The ambitions of Russia's statesmen were nevertheless limited, by the standards of the time, and were concerned principally with adjacent territories of strategic significance for commerce or defense. In this

sense Russian statesmen favored a continental policy, resembling perhaps that of China in earlier times and of the United States in the nineteenth century, and did not undertake to create an extensive overseas empire such as those carved out by the seafaring societies of Western Europe.

III

It has already been noted that the institutions of imperial Russian society underwent many changes in the course of two centuries, and indeed, the history of this period is punctuated with numerous reforms, revolts, assassinations, wars, territorial issues, and social conflicts reflecting the continuing readjustments in the structure of Russian society as well as the idiosyncrasies of its leaders. At the same time it was undergoing a more fundamental transformation, which was stimulated primarily by the example of the societies of Western and Central Europe. These societies were in the forefront of a revolutionary process intellectual in its origins and political in its initial impact, accompanied by economic growth and social change of unprecedented proportions. The levels of achievement attained in the course of this revolutionary transformation, which may be referred to in general terms as "modern" or at least "modernizing," were the prototypes of those which were eventually to become the goal of virtually all societies.

The initial reaction of Russia's political leaders to this momentous development was to adopt, or at least adapt, those modern institutions which seemed best suited to preserving the traditional Russian society from the increasingly threatening competition of its neighbors. This reaction is represented typically by the reforms of Peter the Great, which rationalized the civil and military structure of the central government and

[9] These developments are reviewed in L. I. Strakhovsky, "Constitutional Aspects of the Imperial Russian Government's Policy Toward National Minorities," *Journal of Modern History*, XIII (December, 1941), pp. 467–92.

tightened the control of the state over the noble landowners and the townsmen, and of the landowners over the peasants. No attempt was made, however, to adapt to Russian society the economic and social institutions which were being developed in the more modern societies. Peter's reforms were explicitly defensive in their motivation and implications, and they were successful in preserving the traditional social structure of the country with relatively few changes for a century and a half. In the course of time the gap between a relatively static Russia and an increasingly dynamic West grew to a point where it could not fail to cause concern to Russian leaders, and during the reigns of Alexander I and Nicholas I many plans and proposals for reform were considered and some actually undertaken. Nevertheless, human nature being what it is, they preferred the certainty of problems which they understood and felt confident in handling to the uncertainties of a thoroughgoing social transformation. It took the defeat in the Crimea to shift the balance of official opinion in favor of reform, and it has become customary to regard the emancipation of the serfs in 1861 as the turning point between the passive and the active phases of the attitude of Russia's political leaders toward modern ideas and institutions. It will of course be recognized that 1861 is in most respects simply a symbolic date, since some segments of Russian society felt the breath of reform a generation or more earlier, while others were relatively unaffected until a good deal later. Indeed, it was not until the end of the nineteenth century that Russian society as a whole was gripped by thoroughgoing change.

It has already been noted that the modern revolution was intellectual in its origins, resting as it did on the phenomenal expansion of knowledge which had its roots in the Middle Ages, and its initial impact on Russia was similarly intellectual. This impact may be traced back to the movements favoring the revision of religious texts and doctrine in the fifteenth and sixteenth centuries, and to the appearance in the seventeenth century of isolated nobles with a Western outlook.[10] It was nevertheless not until the eighteenth century that there was a general turning to the West on the part of the state and the nobility, and only in the nineteenth century did the problem of "Russia and Europe" come to absorb the full attention of Russian intellectuals. The diversity and brilliance of Russian political and literary thought concerning the relationship of traditional to modern values and institutions is probably matched only by that of China and Japan among non-European peoples. It produced a wide spectrum of interpretations, ranging from the strongest reaffirmation of the rightness and sanctity of the Russian way of doing things to the view that the imperial state was a form of "oriental despotism" which must be destroyed to make way for the socialist society toward which mankind was alleged to be moving ineluctably.

This rich body of thought moved in two currents, which were continually intermingling but which remained reasonably distinct. The first was represented by the political leaders and high officials, starting with Peter the Great and ending with Witte and Stolypin, who sought to adapt imperial Russian society in one degree or another to the requirements of the modern world. Their

[10] Dmitrij Cizevskij, *History of Russian Literature from the Eleventh Century to the End of the Baroque* (The Hague, 1960), chaps. vi and vii, provides a valuable discussion of early European influences.

views were set forth in speeches, reports, memoranda, and statutes, and perhaps in deeds more than in words. The second source of intellectual activity was that represented by the intelligentsia, who almost by definition were disassociated and not infrequently alienated from the governing circles. The intelligentsia left a fascinating heritage of speculation and interpretation which reflected a broad understanding of European society and a deep concern for the destiny of the Russian people. They had a profound influence on the development of Russian society during the period of the empire, since their works were read and discussed by all educated people. They nevertheless remained until the end alienated from official Russia, which bore the burden of responsibility and deserves much of the credit for the extent to which Russian society was transformed by the time of the First World War. The intelligentsia as a group did not gain access to political power until the fall of the empire, and this access was terminated for all but a few when the Bolsheviks began to suppress deviations from orthodoxy in the early 1920's. In the realm of scholarship Russia joined the world of modern knowledge in the course of the eighteenth and nineteenth centuries and made distinguished original contributions.

The history of Russian thought in the nineteenth century as a general phenomenon has yet to be written. Much able work has been done on individual writers and on the leading intellectual movements, such as the Decembrists, the Slavophiles, the Populists, and the Marxists. The thought of the reforming officials has not, however, received comparable attention. Neither the prerevolutionary intelligentsia nor the writers of the Soviet Union have been attracted to this subject, for reasons which are not hard to find, and Western scholars are only now beginning to explore it. Interest in intellectual history seems to have been concerned principally with a desire to study the background of the political revolution of 1917, and this has resulted in a serious neglect of the fundamental process of political, economic, and social change as a central issue in Russian thought.[11]

In the political sphere the adoption of modern institutions in Russia can be seen in the many reforms which had the purpose of rationalizing the system of law and administration, integrating the various territories and social strata, and establishing a closer rapport between state and society to the end that political decisions could be effectively formulated, communicated, and implemented. The reforms of the eighteenth century had performed a similar function for the state itself, and it was now a question of extending this process to the entire society. The codification of the laws by Speransky was the first significant step in this second phase, and it was followed in the 1860's by an extensive reform of the judiciary and local government and of the administrative system of the central government. As late as 1905, however, the state had relatively few direct administrative contacts with the peasants except for a rather scanty police force and the land captains established in 1889. Peasant affairs were handled largely by the peasants themselves. The administration

[11] The literature on this subject is virtually inexhaustible. Among recent American contributions, Theodore H. Von Laue, "The Industrialization of Russia in the Writings of Sergej Witte," *American Slavic and East European Review,* X (October, 1951), 177–90, and Marc Raeff, *Michael Speransky: Statesman of Imperial Russia, 1772–1839* (The Hague, 1957), are examples of a renewed interest in the thought of reforming bureaucrats.

of the Stolypin land settlement required the government for the first time in its history to establish organs for administering directly at the local level policies ultimately affecting a large proportion of the population and involving the co-ordination of several ministries. This was a very late development, however, and the weakness of the imperial bureaucracy was soon revealed in the harsh test of war.

The effort to transform the political system of imperial Russia along the lines pioneered by the societies of Western Europe provoked a struggle among several trends of thought. One was that of the supporters of the traditional system as it had been consolidated in the eighteenth and early nineteenth centuries. This was the view of the imperial family and its immediate entourage, and it had strong support in the army and bureaucracy and in the cabinet, even when that body was headed by a reforming minister. The reforms of the 1860's had indeed been launched by the emperor himself, but more in the Petrine spirit of trying to achieve a new conservative stability than with a view to a thoroughgoing social reconstruction. This approach continued to have strong official support until the end, and one may well attribute the catastrophic character of the fall of the empire to the stubbornness with which one group of its leaders resisted change.

Another main trend was the very large one represented by those both in the government and among the intelligentsia who favored fundamental change by evolutionary means and looked to models ranging from England and France to Prussia and Japan. The diversities of their various programs make it difficult to contain these many groups in a single category, but the Fundamental Laws of 1906 provided them with a more or less acceptable basis for action and there was a significant degree of continuity from the four successive Dumas to the Provisional Government. Included also in this category were the leaders of the national minorities who demanded a degree of self-government. Only the Poles insisted unconditionally on independence. This issue has been beclouded by war, revolution, and civil war, but it appears that under "normal" circumstances the leaders of the other minority peoples would in all likelihood have been satisfied on the eve of the First World War with some form of federalism.

A third trend was composed of those who had no faith in evolutionary changes within the framework of the empire. This was the view of the Bolsheviks and many Socialist Revolutionaries, who saw their political role principally as a destructive one so long as the empire survived. The final arbiter among these various approaches, as it turned out, was the First World War. The strains of the conflict eroded the political structure of the empire, and in so doing undermined the prospects for evolutionary change within its framework. The collapse of the empire opened the way for a revolutionary approach, and the revolutionaries were much more at home than the liberals in the ensuing chaos.[12]

Among the changes which occurred during the last half-century of the empire, those in the intellectual and political realm have attracted the most attention, but the remarkable economic

[12] The adaptation of Marxism to the Russian environment is a matter of particular interest. See especially Adam Ulam, "The Historical Role of Marxism and the Soviet System," *World Politics*, VIII (October, 1955), 371–401; and Karl A. Wittfogel, "The Marxist View of Russian Society and Revolution," *World Politics*, XII (July, 1960), 487–508.

growth in its later decades deserves equal emphasis. Agricultural production, which had not been able to keep up with the growth of the population during the first half of the century, increased much more rapidly, especially after the 1880's. Not only did agricultural production surpass the rate at which the population was growing, but it was also significantly diversified to include industrial crops and potatoes. The expansion of industrial production was of course much more rapid, with an annual average rate of growth of somewhat over 5 per cent for the period 1885–1913. The rate for the 1890's, the period of most rapid growth, was surpassed only by that of Japan, the United States, and Sweden. Underlying the increased rates of growth in agriculture and industry was the construction of an extensive railroad network, which grew from 1,000 miles in 1860 to 40,000 miles at the time of the First World War. In terms of national income, the Russian rate of growth for the period as a whole was higher than that of the United Kingdom, France and Italy, somewhat below that of Germany, and considerably below that of the United States and Japan. On a per capita basis Russia's position was of course less favorable, owing to the rapid growth of her population. By the time of the First World War real income per capita was about the same as that of Italy, which means that it was still a great deal lower than that of the advanced industrial societies.[13]

Although Russia had thus in no sense attained a leading position as an industrial society at the time of the First

World War, what is significant is that by the 1880's it was launched on a pattern of economic growth comparable in rate and dimensions to that of the more advanced societies. It should also be noted that this was very largely the achievement of the imperial government, which took the initiative and bore the main burden of building railroads and supplying capital to industry, and also provided the principal market for the output of heavy industry. No doubt the sovereign and the conservative-minded courtiers and ministers, like Peter the Great in his day, still thought of industrialization principally as a means of bolstering the autocratic system. The leading cabinet members and high officials, however, had a vision of a Russia transformed into a modern industrial society. Their goal may be said to have been of a West European character, but their methods were quite different. Little attention was devoted to agriculture, and such income as it normally provided was channeled into industry. Railroads and heavy industry were favored as against consumer goods. Modern technology was imported from the West to make up for deficiencies in skilled labor, and economies were made in management and supervision by concentrating production in large plants. A not inconsiderable role in this growth was played by private entrepreneurs and small businessmen, but the pace was set by the government and by the large enterprises which it controlled or patronized. Indeed, it was the role of the government as planner, investor, entrepreneur, and consumer which distinguished economic growth in Russia from that in the societies which started earlier.[14]

13 Alexander Gerschenkron, "The Rate of Industrial Growth of Russia since 1885," *Journal of Economic History*, VII, Supplement (1947), 144–74; and Raymond W. Goldsmith, "The Economic Growth of Tsarist Russia, 1860–1913," *Economic Development and Cultural Change*, IX (April, 1961), 441–75.

14 See Alexander Gerschenkron, "Problems and Patterns of Russian Economic Development," *Transformation of Russian Society*, esp. pp. 42–61, for a discussion of the underlying economic policies of the imperial government.

This economic growth was accomplished by fundamental social changes. The urban population grew from 7 to 20 million during the last fifty years of the empire, the rigid system of social stratification disintegrated rapidly, and the foundations were laid for a new stratum of professional people, businessmen, and officials. This "middle class" was drawn from all of the traditional strata. The nobles, clergy, and townsmen were naturally the principal sources of recruitment for this new stratum at the start, but the peasantry and workers were gradually drawn into it and represented in the long run its principal reserve of manpower. The nobles lost much of their distinctive position in the last decades of the empire and, with the exception of the relatively few families of great wealth, did not gain much advantage from their remaining formal privileges in the evolving industrial society. At the same time the industrial working class grew apace, and numbered some 3.5 million at the end of this period. In 1913, according to the official classification, 70.2 per cent of the population were farmers, 16.7 per cent were wage and salary workers, 7.2 per cent were craftsmen, 3.6 per cent were self-employed townsmen, and 2.3 per cent were military and others.[15]

The institutions of higher education were the chief training ground for this new class, and their enrollment in proportion to the population increased more than nine times between 1885 and 1914. The increase in secondary-school enrollment was even greater, and by the time of the First World War Russia had made substantial progress toward a system of universal elementary education. The social mobility accompanying the growth in higher education is reflected in the fact that the proportion of children of peasants, craftsmen, and workers enrolled in the universities grew from 15.7 per cent in 1880 to 38.8 per cent in 1914, and in the higher technical institutes was 54 per cent in the latter year.[16] The officer corps was no doubt the most conservative branch of the bureaucracy, but it appears that by the end of the empire a majority of the new officers came from non-noble families as did some of the leading generals in the First World War.[17] In recording these changes it should be noted that this rapid growth in educational opportunities and social mobility was not achieved without a momentous struggle. In the central government the reformers waged a constant battle with the traditionalists, and were strongly aided by the increasingly effective support which they received from the local government institutions, the municipalities, and the Duma. At the time of the First World War, Russia was still a country where 78 per cent of the population was agricultural and rural illiteracy was high. The changes of the last half century had been so rapid, however, that contemporary reforming statesmen could look forward with confidence to the day when the empire would attain the level

---

[15] Warren W. Eason, "Population Changes," *Transformation of Russian Society*, pp. 72–90, summarizes and interprets Russian statistical materials; Valentine T. Bill, *The Forgotten Class: The Russian Bourgeoisie from the Earliest Beginnings to 1900* (New York, 1959), has performed a useful service in calling attention to the role of the entrepreneur; Gaston V. Rimlinger, "Autocracy and the Factory Order in Early Russian Industrialization," *Journal of Economic History*, XX (March, 1960), 67–92, discusses the status of the workers in the last decades of the empire.

[16] Nicholas Hans, *History of Russian Educational Policy (1701–1917)* (London, 1931), pp. 229–42, provides a convenient summary of educational statistics.

[17] Raymond L. Garthoff, "The Military as a Social Force," *Transformation of Russian Society*, pp. 326–27, reviews the available evidence on the changing social status of the officer corps.

of achievement of Western societies.

Something should also be said about the personality changes which may have accompanied this general process. National character in the sense that it is used by the social psychologists is a controversial concept which is still in an early stage of formulation, and one hesitates to venture into a territory so ridden with pitfalls. Yet it is clear that the personality of the individual reflects the character of his upbringing in the family setting, which in turn depends on the larger social context. When the latter undergoes the drastic changes represented by urbanization, one would expect the family and its individual members to be vitally affected. In the case of the Great Russian people, for example, it has been maintained that the characteristically patriarchal peasant family tended to produce a personality which was markedly ambivalent. This is to say that the Great Russian personality contained simultaneously elements of great vitality and serious depression, which may be explained as resulting from a family setting in which an awesome father was both feared and resisted. As a peasant society with these characteristics is urbanized, with the mother as an urban worker gaining a position of authority more nearly equal to that of the father, an altered family setting is produced in which the children are exposed to somewhat different influences and will develop correspondingly different personalities. This example suggests what is meant by the effects of social change on personality, and it also reveals the difficulties which confront one in trying to deal with Russia in these terms. Russia was a vastly complex empire with many traditional cultures, of which the Great Russian was only one. Moreover, the available studies deal principally with the Soviet period, and there is little factual data

from earlier decades to draw on. One may argue that Chekhov, Gorky, and their literary colleagues did a pretty good job of reporting social change at the family level without benefit of professional training in the behavioral sciences, but it is difficult for a historian to generalize on the basis of their findings. It is also clear that the impact of social change on personality was at its very earliest stages in the last decades of the empire, and that one would not expect to find general manifestations of a transformation of national character in Russia until well into the twentieth century. Under the circumstances the best one can do is to call attention to this important aspect of social history and to regret that one cannot do it justice.[18]

IV

. . . The prevailing Western approach between the two world wars to Russian developments was to assume that the institutions characteristic of the more advanced societies of the West represented the model which other societies were destined to follow. There was therefore a tendency to judge the empire as well as its successors by the extent to which they adopted the Western pattern in such matters as civil liberties, representative government, education, and the role of the state in economic growth. By this standard the empire was reactionary, the Provisional Government had liberal aspirations, and the Soviet

18 A valuable introduction to this subject will be found in Clyde Kluckhohn, "Recent Studies of the National Character of Great Russians," *Human Development Bulletin* (February 5, 1955), pp. 39–60; Henry V. Dicks, "Some Notes on the Russian National Character," *Transformation of Russian Society*, pp. 636–52; and Alex Inkeles and Daniel J. Levinson, "National Character: The Study of Modal Personality and Socio-cultural Systems," *Handbook of Social Psychology*, ed. Gardner Lindzey (2 vols.; Cambridge, Mass., 1954), II, 977–1020.

Union represented a bewildering combination of modern and traditional elements. In the course of the past quarter of a century many other societies have entered and some have completed the experimental phase of adapting the traditional to the modern, and the process of transformation can now be seen as a much more complex matter than one of simply duplicating Western institutions. It seems clear that there are certain functions which all modern societies must perform—political decision-making effective for the entire population, sufficient savings to permit a reasonable rate of economic growth, education, social mobility, and so on—and perhaps most important of all, a value system compatible with the necessary institutional changes. It is also clear, however, that there is a wide degree of variety in the extent to which the diverse traditional institutional systems are adaptable to the functions of modern societies. No society can avoid very profound changes as it modernizes, but some traditional institutions are much more adaptable than others.

What is significant in the case of Russia is that its traditional institutional system was different from those of the societies of Western Europe, as indeed it was from those of non-European societies as well. In Western Europe modern political institutions, for example, evolved from those of feudalism into a characteristic form of liberal government in which political power was shared by elected representatives and a permanent civil service. In Russia, by contrast, the starting point was not a feudal system but an autocratic state which had characteristically exercised very extensive political functions. It was not difficult for this state, in the generation after the defeat in the Crimea, to initiate a very fundamental reorientation of national life. Between 1861 and

1917 the autocracy in Russia put into effect a series of reforms which resemble in many respects those achieved by very different methods in France between 1789 and 1848—if one may risk an historical analogy.[19] To extend the analogy a step further, one may suggest that the autocratic state in Russia played a role similar not only to that of the middle class and the Napoleonic empire in France but also to that of the samurai in Japan, the Young Turks in the Ottoman Empire, the army officers in Egypt, and the European-educated politicians in Africa today. Modernizing political leadership may take many forms, and the alternatives available to political leaders cannot fail to be profoundly affected by the traditional political institutions which a society has inherited from earlier centuries. This is not to assert an intitutional or a cultural determinism. It is rather to suggest that, however similar the ultimate functional goals, political leaders in different societies are likely to proceed by different routes.

It would be outside the limits set for this paper to venture beyond the fall of the empire in February/March, 1917, but it is relevant to discuss the bearing on subsequent developments of the changes which the empire was undergoing in its final decades. It is well enough to attribute the fall of the empire to the strains of the First World War, for the connection between the two is clear, but it is also necessary to note that the crisis was not so great that a more effective government might not have been able to cope with it. The vital struggle in the last decades of the empire was that which was going on within the government between those who sup-

[19] Isaac Deutscher, "The French Revolution and the Russian Revolution: Some Suggestive Analogies," *World Politics*, IV (April, 1952), 469–81.

ported the traditional autocracy to the bitter end, and those who favored the transformation of Russia into a modern bureaucratic and constitutional state. The Wittes and Stolypins were still separated by a wide gap from the liberals, but the gap was perhaps no wider than that which separated them from the emperor. The lines dividing the various conservative and liberal conceptions of an evolutionary constitutionalism were becoming increasingly blurred in the last years of the empire, and much would have depended on the leadership which might have emerged.

The war came at a time when these conflicts between the emperor and his critics within the government were still unresolved, and in fact it only served to make them more bitter. The fragmentation of Russian politics at this stage was such that the collapse of the autocracy in 1917 resulted in a situation in which no alternative had any wide support. There was of course a significant group of leaders favoring parliamentary democracy who had gained political experience in the Duma and in local government, but the political methods which they favored were not generally understood or accepted. Where parliamentary democracy has been successful it has in fact been a value system widely supported by many elements of a society rather than one reflecting the interests of a particular social stratum. The vast majority of Russians—whether peasants, workers, bureaucrats, officers, or professional people—were not generally familiar with the values and techniques of parliamentary democracy. To this extent the task of leaders favoring parliamentary methods in 1917 was infinitely more difficult than that of those prepared to rely on force. This does not necessarily mean that the empire might not under other circumstances have developed into a political democracy of the type familiar in the West, or even that something resembling such a system may not yet develop in Russia at some future time. It means only that, at the time the empire collapsed, the balance of domestic political experience weighed heavily in favor of those leaders who were prepared to employ authoritarian methods.

SETON-WATSON: RUSSIA AND MODERNIZATION

My own approach to this subject is very much the same as Professor Black's. Imperial Russia, it seems to me, was the prototype of the "underdeveloped society" whose problems are so familiar a theme in our own age. The study of nineteenth-century Russia is the study of a society in process of modernization, and probably the most useful service which non-Russian historians can render is to try to regard this process as a whole, and particularly to differentiate between those aspects of Russia's modernization process which are common to several known historical cases and those which are peculiar to Russia. The following comments on Professor Black's article are offered from this point of view.

The physical setting, rightly stressed by Professor Black at the outset, may be regarded as a peculiarly Russian aspect. Here human and physical geography are closely interrelated. Other nations besides the Russians have lived in forest areas where it was desperately hard to make a living. Some similarities could probably be found with the earlier history of the Germans, Poles, and Swedes, though the still greater severity of the Russian climate should be taken into account. But surely the case of the south Russian steppes is unique. Here is much of the most fertile grain land in the world, which for centuries was barely cultivated, being in fact *Durchmarschgebiet* for successive waves of nomadic invaders. Indeed it was only after the final subjugation of the Crimean Tatars by Russia in the late eighteenth century that its agricultural wealth began for the first time in history to be systematically exploited. In the previous centuries, Russia south of the forest zone had two "open frontiers," to the west and to the southeast. But whereas the "open frontier" in North America was a factor of opportunity, and so of liberty, in Russia it was a factor of insecurity, and so of despotism. The constant need of Russia for protection against enemies held back by no natural frontier—no Pyrenees, no English Channel —is surely a major factor in the development of autocracy. A strong central military command was indispensable. In fact Russian society as a whole became so militarized that—paradoxically—army officers as a separate category never acquired a special status, though the profession of arms of course had high prestige. It is true that the "open frontier" did offer opportunities to enterprising individuals, especially in Siberia. But the autocratic state caught up with them in time. Unlike the American pioneers, they had no ocean between them and their monarch. To sum up, the vastness, the absence of naturally defensible frontiers, and the vulnerability to incursions from west, east, and south for more than a thousand years constitute an exceptional, if not unique, environment.

Another factor, also to some extent peculiar to Russia, has barely been mentioned by Professor Black. This is the Orthodox Church. Orthodoxy came late to Russia, but Russia is the only Great Power since the great age of Byzantium which has been Orthodox. It is true that under the Tatar yoke the church suffered indirectly from the restrictions placed on the sovereignty of the Russian princes. But these were at no time comparable with the destruction of independent rulers in the Balkan Christian countries by the Ottoman Turks. (Incidentally, a comparison of the status of the Orthodox Church under the Tatars and the Turks, based on a detailed study of both with the use of Moslem documents, would be a task of great value.) In the period following the removal of the Tatar yoke the Church of course became extremely powerful, while from Peter the Great onwards it declined. Nevertheless, it seems to me that the role of the Orthodox Church even in nineteenth-century Russia has hitherto been grossly underrated. There is surely more to be said of it than is found in that fine example of anticlerical rhetoric, Belinsky's *Letter to Gogol*. One may sympathize with Belinsky in his particular argument with Gogol, and admit that the picture of obscurantism and superstition which he paints is an important part of reality. But it is only a part. Religion cannot be simply dismissed from modern Russian history, as has been the fashion for the last hundred years. This is true not only of Bolshevik historians, but of the radical *bien pensants* who dominated Russian historical literature long before 1917.

It seems to me that Professor Black somewhat overrates the power of the oligarchy, and underestimates that of the autocracy, in the period following the death of Peter the Great. It is true that the following rulers were weak. But the astonishing fact remains that none of the disputed successions, or reigns of foreign women, were used to establish any institutions that would give the nobility a regular share in central government. The failure of Golitsyn's project at the accession of Anna Ivanovna is the most striking example. The Guards officers objected to particular claimants to the throne, and particular favorites, but they never sought to limit the power of the autocracy as such. The tsars continued to wield arbitrary powers, though of course their practical ability to put them into practice depended on the strength of their characters and the ability of their advisers. The nobility were "independent" in the sense that they controlled the lives of their serfs. They were themselves pocket autocrats on their estates. But they left central power to the monarch. This situation is surely basically different from that in Europe. European "absolute monarchies" had arisen in the course of centuries of struggle between the monarchs and the nobility, which had its own corporate institutions and its own corporate consciousness. Even Louis XIV ruled through the regular channels. This was also the case in Prussia. It was not so in Russia. Surely this is what Speransky meant when he said that "monarchical government" did not exist in Russia.

I am also unable to agree with Professor Black's implication that there is any sense whatever in which Russian expansion was "less imperialistic" than that of any other Power. What is "imperialism" anyhow? Were the Arabs imperialists when they conquered Spain from the Visigoths, who had themselves conquered it from Rome three centuries earlier? Or the Christian princes when they drove the Arabs out of Toledo and Córdoba? Or the Tatars when they conquered southern Russia, or the Russians when they captured Kazan? The Volga is *russkaia reka* in the song, but from the early Middle Ages until the eighteenth century it was a Turkic river, and largely remained so even until the 1920's. Acquisition of border territories in the interest of security is how virtually all empires have arisen. British traders in India seized land in order to ensure their right to trade. They had got there in the first instance in the pursuit of trade, not conquest. Much the

same is true of Russian-protected Tatar traders in Central Asia and the conquest of Turkistan in the 1860's. Russian expansion seems to me to have exact parallels in the history of other nations, being morally neither better nor worse. It differs only in that it combines many different forms, roughly comparable with the expansion of the Île-de-France, the Spanish *reconquista*, French acquisition of Burgundy, North American conquest and extermination of the Red Indians, and British occupation of continental India.

The last problem raised by Professor Black which I should like to discuss, and at greatest length, is the problem of the middle classes. Here I do not think that I significantly disagree with Professor Black, but I should like to urge that definitions should be further developed, and to emphasize the complexity of the subject.

It seems to me that it is a mistake, in discussing nineteenth-century Russia, to speak of "a middle class." In Russia there were three separate "middle classes"—the businessmen, the government servants, and the intellectual elite. These three categories exist to some extent in almost any organized society. In traditional societies of course the intellectual elite is provided by a priesthood, while the category of government servants is not very well developed, and the businessmen are merchants with rather small capital. Modernization increases the importance of all three groups. This is characteristic of all underdeveloped societies, including post-Petrine Russia. What is not characteristic of all is a tendency for the three groups to become fused into a single "middle class," unified by a common ethos. This did in fact happen in post-Reformation Europe, and the process was accelerated by the industrial revolution. In the period after the Reformation the "bourgeois ethos"

—individualism, in matters of religion, of business enterprise, and later also of political opinion—became widespread. It was this bourgeoisie—a social and cultural category rather than an economic one—which carried out the industrial revolution. This bourgeoisie was especially strong in the Protestant countries —England, Scotland, Holland, and then the United States of America—but it was also to be found in France, northern Italy, western and southwestern Germany. In Russia, however, it did not exist. Russia had capitalists and bureaucrats (including professional army officers), and from the 1830's or so it acquired also a secular intellectual elite, the intelligentsia. But these categories remained clearly distinct from each other, and certainly none of the three had anything which can remotely be described as a bourgeois ethos. In all this, however, Russia was not exceptional but typical. This difference between three middle classes, and this absence of bourgeois ethos—and so, of a bourgeoisie—is typical of all the underdeveloped societies which have been modernized since the mid-nineteenth century in many parts of the world. It is northwest Europe and North America which have been exceptional.

The role of the intelligentsia in Russian political history is of course very well known. Even so, too little attention has been paid to the intelligentsia as a social group. Historians, whether Soviet or pre-Soviet, Russian or foreign, have studied their ideas in meticulous detail, but have on the whole neglected their emergence as a specific social group. Should one dare to brave Marxist and quasi-Marxist wrath by describing them as a "class"? Historians have also made too little effort to distinguish the general from the peculiarly Russian features of the intelligentsia. There is indeed a widespread tendency to consider the great

political role of the intelligentsia as a peculiarly Russian phenomenon. Yet it is nothing of the sort. The national and social revolutionary movements of the Christian peoples of the Ottoman Empire were created and led essentially by the intelligentsia. So also have been and are the similar movements in Asia and Africa. President Nasser is an example of this category (intelligentsia-in-uniform, as were the Russian Decembrists, but none the less intelligentsia for that). Again, though the intellectual qualities of the two men, if measured by traditional academic standards, are clearly very diverse, both Leopold Senghor and Patrice Lumumba must be regarded as examples of intelligentsia.

Even the "populist outlook"—the determination to "serve the people," to pay one's debt by devoting one's special skills and knowledge not to enriching oneself but to raising the masses up out of squalor and poverty—is not confined to Russian history. This outlook (as opposed to the particular political ideologies or political tactics adopted at particular periods in the face of particular needs) is shared, to take only some examples at random, by the Yugoslav Marxist students of the 1930's, the Rumanian Iron Guardist students of the same period, the early pioneers of *Aprismo* in Peru, and the early followers of Sun Yat-sen. The difference between the Russian intelligentsia and these later examples is a matter rather of nuance than of clear distinction. It seems to me that the Russian revolutionary intelligentsia, at least in the second half of the nineteenth century, was marked by an exceptional spirit of selfless devotion to the cause and of indifference to its own interests. Revolutionary fervor and heroism are of course to be found in all such movements, but the Russians had, I think, an overdose of idealism above and beyond the normal ration. It would be interesting to explore this question. I suspect that the explanation might be found in the direct and indirect influence of Orthodox Christianity on Russian thinking. The disproportionate number of *popovichi* among early Russian revolutionaries has often been noted. This was probably due to the fact that children of priests, being able to get a rudimentary education in seminaries, were more favorably placed for developing what talents they had than were other *raznochintsy*. But the *popovichi* may have introduced into the growing intellectual elite a peculiarly religious way of thinking. It would be interesting to know to what extent *popovichi* predominated among the Balkan revolutionaries. Professor Black, with his thorough knowledge of modern Bulgarian history, would be well placed to investigate, and draw conclusions from, this matter.

Modernization in Western Europe was a more or less spontaneous process, resulting from social development. It was accelerated or retarded by individual monarchs or cardinals, but it was not deliberately initiated by them. Modernization in Russia, Asia, and Africa has been deliberately initiated. Every government which sets out forcibly to modernize has to create a modern secular intellectual elite. It has to create a system of modern education. In the early stage of modernization, there is bound to be a profound gulf between the new intellectual elite and the majority of the nation. This "cultural gap" is inevitably a cause of frustration to the elite and a source of weakness to the state. This dangerous period of transition cannot be avoided unless the government and the society are willing to accept stagnation, leading to conquest by more progressive nations.

But if the problem of the "cultural gap" is common to all societies in which modernization is deliberately adopted and artificially pursued, the ways of handling the problem may and do vary. And here again there is an undoubted element of the unique in the Russian story.

Alexander I intended to create a system of education which would give every able child the chance to improve himself and to rise. But the absence of schools and teachers, and the poverty of the Russian state, greatly increased by the burden of the wars against Napoleon, prevented the achievement of his aims. In the following reign, under Count S. S. Uvarov, educational policy acquired a definite class bias. It was intended that higher education should be available only to the upper classes. However, the resources available were still so small, and the desire for education still comparatively so restricted, that even without Uvarov's class bias, it is clear that those who would have benefited from education would have been overwhelmingly the children of nobles and rich merchants. In fact the reign of Nicholas I was in a sense a period of genuine educational progress. The disastrous trend came in the second half of the century. The famous circular from the Minister of Education, recommending that children of "cooks, washerwomen, coachmen and suchlike people" should not be given an education above their station, was issued in 1887—nearly a century after Alexander I had created the Ministry of Education. Thus in Russia the "cultural gap" was kept artificially wide for an inordinately long time, in the belief that to educate the people was dangerous. The classical example of a contrary course is Japan, whose reformers decided that an educated people would be stronger than an uneducated people, and that mass education would not weaken but strengthen the regime. They accomplished their task in about thirty years, and the results justified their expectations. It is true that Japanese boys and girls were not brought up to be liberal democrats. But the "cultural gap" in Japan was narrowed, and this contributed enormously to the brilliant successes of Japan in the first four decades of the twentieth century. In Russia, on the other hand, the gap remained wide open, and contributed greatly to the continued alienation, not only of the intelligentsia in the narrower sense, but of the whole public (*obshchestvo*) from the regime, and so to the breakdown not only of tsardom but of the Russian state.

No other modernizing state has ever made such a bad job of national education as imperial Russia, nor such a good job as Japan. Their examples are still far too little known by the "educationalists" of the West or of the Asian and African nations, who are lavish in the use of rhetoric about education but might well find that study of Russian and Japanese experience would be more beneficial to them than the ritual invocation of "Asianism" or *négritude*.

These scattered comments were intended as a contribution to discussion on a number of interesting problems and as a tribute to Professor Black's admirable and stimulating survey of this great subject.

BLACK: REPLY

II

Professor Seton-Watson's comments are concerned in particular with the role of the Orthodox Church, the nature of the autocracy, the Russian form of imperialism, and the composition of the middle class. His comments also have some implications of a general theoretical character about which I would like to make some remarks.

As concerns the Orthodox Church, what strikes me as being of relatively little importance in imperial Russia, by contrast with the Muscovite period, is its formal theology, structure, and political role. The church was thoroughly subordinated to the state in an administrative sense, and in its official capacity it was not a particularly fertile source of ideas or inspiration. What seems to me of much greater importance is what might be called the value system or "ideology"—to use a much abused term —of the Orthodox faith. This was no doubt only a part of a more general value system characteristic of imperial Russian society which included important secular elements, but Orthodoxy probably accounted for some of its most significant features. This unofficial Orthodoxy was expressed at a sophisticated level by leading thinkers such as Soloviev, Dostoevsky, and Berdiaev, among others. At a more popular level it took the form of the beliefs and attitudes of the common people, for whom religion provided much of the vocabulary and symbolism for the expression of thought. It is a difficult matter, however, to define just what these values were. It may well be, as is often asserted, that this value system stressed otherworldliness, encouraged passivity in regard to the political authorities, emphasized the importance of the group at the expense of the individual, deprecated the accumulation of private property, and advanced the view that the Russians are the only "God-bearing" people. To the extent that one can see important reflections of such attitudes in contemporary Soviet society, it may well be that these were in fact important elements of the prerevolutionary value system and that they have now assumed a Marxist aspect. My own feeling is that not enough is known about the value system of imperial Russia or about its Orthodox component, and that this is among the significant questions that deserve further study.

As regards the autocracy and the oligarchy, there may have been some misunderstanding of the way in which I used the terms. I defined the oligarchy to include the "higher civilian and military officials and leading families of noble landowners," and thought of the autocracy much more narrowly as the autocrat himself. For Professor Seton-Watson the autocracy comprises the autocrat together with the bureaucratic apparatus, and the oligarchy consists of the leading noble families and the Guards officers who led their regiments into action at critical moments. His definitions may well correspond more accurately to current usage, and in that event I am inclined to agree with the substance of his remarks. I have been impressed by the fact that more often than not between 1725 and 1917 the initiative in the great decisions of state came not from the autocrat but from the leading bureaucrats. This is particularly true of the dramatic reforms in the reign of Alexander II. The circumstance that all decrees were issued in the name of the emperor obscures this somewhat, but the fact remains that Peter alone among the rulers of the empire had the ability and imagination to offer outstanding personal leadership.

It seems that the problem of Russian expansionism offers a more lively source of controversy, although here again it may be more a question of terminology than a fundamental difference in interpretation. On rereading my remarks on this subject I was relieved to find that the "less imperialistic" which Professor Seton-Watson puts in quotation marks does not come from my paper, although my use of the term "imperialist" was perhaps ambiguous. The distinction I had in mind was between a continental and an overseas expansionism. In this case it amounts also to a distinction be-

tween a policy inspired by a bureaucratic government and one inspired by chartered trading companies, or between motives of security and of commerce. Apart from nebulous schemes involving India and parts of Africa, and rather minor financial investments and technical assistance missions in Persia and Mongolia, characteristically commercial expansionism in the period of the empire was limited essentially to Alaska and Manchuria. As an exporter almost exclusively of agricultural products and natural resources, Russian commerce was with the developed societies rather than with the undeveloped, with countries where the flag could not follow trade. The sale of Alaska after the discovery of gold is a classic example of a government sacrificing economic gains in the interest of security. In the case of Manchuria and the associated treaty ports, the reverse was true. The distinction between continental and overseas expansionism strikes me as particularly important in the modern age, when political leaders are confronted by the powerful but antagonistic trends favoring administrative and economic integration on the one hand and nationalistic separatism on the other. In the case of an overseas empire, which characteristically embraces a wide diversity of cultures, the nationalist trend tends to gain the upper hand. In a continental empire, on the other hand, administrative and economic integration have a good chance of success if the nationalities problem can be worked out. In any event, it does not seem to me that moral judgments are involved in this distinction. Morality in these matters concerns the way peoples are ruled rather than the motives underlying the creation of an empire.

I find Professor Seton-Watson's comments about the middle class particularly valuable. The sources and character of the modernizing leadership are perhaps the key to an understanding of the process of change characteristic of the modern age, and scholars trained in the Western tradition have to be constantly on guard against applying concepts valid in their own culture—and the "middle class" is typical of such concepts—to societies with a somewhat different background. I would not go so far as Professor Seton-Watson, however, in his use of the term "intelligentsia" to describe a variety of modernizing leaders around the world. In Russia the intelligentsia certainly formed an important group, distinct both from the bureaucrats—many of whom were well-educated intellectuals—and from the merchants. What is significant about the Russian situation, however, is less the distinction and influence of this group than the fact that so many able and well-educated individuals should have been alienated from public service to the extent that their principal contribution was one of comment and criticism. The difference between the Russian intelligentsia and the leaders of the new states in Asia and Africa seems to be more than a nuance, as Professor Seton-Watson asserts. Sun Yat-sen and Fidel Castro may perhaps be considered as members of an intelligentsia in the Russian sense, but Kemal in Turkey, Chiang in China, and Nasser in Egypt were military bureaucrats well along in their professional careers before they seized power, and the leaders of modern Japan were likewise predominantly bureaucrats. If one is going to make a distinction between an intelligentsia and a bureaucracy, I would hazard a guess that persons trained for the civilian and military bureaucracy have contributed more modernizing leaders in the new states than have members of an intelligentsia. As I suggested in my paper, I believe that the role of the modernizing

bureaucrats in imperial Russia also has been greatly underrated.

The comparative study of modernizing leadership is related to a question of a more general theoretical character which seems to me relevant at this point. In his opening paragraph Professor Seton-Watson refers to imperial Russia as "the prototype of 'the underdeveloped society' whose problems are so familiar a theme in our own age." Later on, in discussing the question of the middle class, he appears to regard imperial Russia and all of the underdeveloped societies as a single general category distinct from the societies of "northwest Europe and North America." This strikes me as much too sweeping a generalization, with one that tends to blur the distinctive character of the various societies concerned. I would prefer an approach that places greater emphasis on the diversities among the traditional societies that form the base from which modernization has proceeded. One example from Professor Seton-Watson's argument will illustrate my point. He compares the educational policies of Russia and Japan in the nineteenth century, much to the advantage of the latter. I take no exception to what he says in this regard, but he neglects to point out the very significant difference in their point of departure. By the end of the seventeenth century Japan had a relatively high rate of literacy. Not only were bureaucrats, merchants, and townspeople in general comparatively well educated, but there was also a significant degree of literacy in the villages and a brisk trade in books in the market places. In seventeenth-century Russia, by contrast, literacy was very limited even in the towns. I do not know what difference this made in the educational policies of these countries a century or two later, but I suspect that it was considerable. In brief, I do not think the Russia in the sixteenth, seventeenth, and eighteenth centuries was particularly typical of traditional societies in general—whether the comparison is with a contemporary African society, or with China, Japan, or India two or three centuries ago, or with England and France in the later Middle Ages. I would be inclined to emphasize not only the fundamental diversities among traditional societies but also the essentially different institutional structures that modern societies are likely to possess even when they perform essentially similar functions. Consequently, I am more impressed with the uniqueness of Russian institutions than with the features it shares in common with other developing societies. There are "many roads to modernization," to paraphrase Khrushchev, and that of imperial Russia is only one of them.

CHRONOLOGY VOLUME II

1730	Struggle over the terms of the succession
1730–40	Reign of Anna
1741	Lomonosov appointed to the Academy of Sciences
1741–62	Reign of Elizabeth
1746	Ban on purchase of serfs by non-nobles
1750's	First regular Russian theatre founded in Yaroslavl by the merchant Volkov
1753	Decree abolishing internal customs
1754–62	Rastrelli builds the Winter Palace
1755	Foundation of Moscow University
1760's	Fonvizin's comedies *The Brigadier-General* and *The Minor*
1760	Landowners granted right to exile serfs to Siberia
1762	Peter III issues Manifesto on the Rights of the Nobility—they are freed from service Peter III murdered
1762	CATHERINE II, THE GREAT, 1762–96
1764	Final secularization of church lands
1765	Establishment of the Free Economic Society
1767	Peasants forbidden to submit complaints against their landowners
1767–68	Legislative Commission
1769–74	Catherine publishes satirical journals; Novikov's journals *The Drone* and *The Painter*
1772	First partition of Poland—parts of Belorussia annexed to Russia
1773–75	Revolt of Pugachev
1774	Treaty of Kuchunk-Kainardji: acquisition of Black Sea steppes from Turkey
1775	Liquidation of the Zaporozhian Cossacks
1780's	Englishman Cameron builds at Tsarskoe Selo
1781–86	Full absorption of Little Russia into Russian Empire
1782–85	Italian Quarenghi builds the Hermitage
1783	Incorporation of the Crimea Private printing presses permitted
1783–84	Taurida Palace built by the Russian Starov
1785	Charter constituting the nobility and gentry an estate
1790	Radishchev's *Journey from St. Petersburg to Moscow*
1793	Second Partition of Poland
1794	Founding of Odessa
1795	Third Partition of Poland
1796	Death of Catherine the Great

1796	PAUL I, 1796–1801
1797	Establishment of "three-day barshchina"
1799	Russo-American Trading Company formed
	Suvorov's campaign in northern Italy and Switzerland
1801	Murder of Paul I
1801	ALEXANDER I, 1801–25
	Acquisition of eastern Georgia
	Sale of serfs without land prohibited
1802	Formation of ministries
1806	Conquest of Daghestan and Baku
1806–15	The new admiralty built by Zakharov
1807–11	Reforms of Speransky
1809	Krylov's *Fables*
	Annexation of Finland
1812	Napoleon's invasion of Russia; burning of Moscow
1815–25	Ascendancy of Arakcheev
1816–19	Abolition of serfdom in Baltic provinces
1817	Transfer of the Makariev fair to Nizhnii Novgorod
1817–57	The Frenchman Montferrand builds St. Isaac's Cathedral
1818	Karamzin's *History of the Russian State*
1819	University of St. Petersburg founded
1819–29	The Italian Rossi builds the General Staff Building on Palace Square
1825	The death of Alexander I
1825	NICHOLAS I, 1825–55
	Decembrist revolt
	Griboedov's comedy *Woe from Wit*
1830	Briullov's painting *Last Day of Pompeii*
	Pushkin completes *Evgenii Onegin*
	Mathematician Lobachevsky publishes first works
1830–31	Polish rebellion
1832	Uvarov's three principles enunciated: autocracy, orthodoxy, nationality
	Alexandriiskii Theatre in St. Petersburg opened
1833	Code of Laws
1834	Kiev University founded
1836	Glinka's opera *Life for the Tsar* (*Ivan Susanin*)
	Gogol's *Inspector General*
	Chadaaev's *Philosophical Letters*
1838	First Russian railroad—St. Petersburg to Tsarskoe Selo
1839–47	Belinsky works on the *Notes of the Fatherland*
1840	Lermontov's *Hero of Our Time*
1841	Ban against the sale of peasants individually

1842	Glinka's opera *Ruslan and Ludmila*
	Gogol's *Dead Souls*
1846	Abolition of Corn Laws in England: increase of Russian grain exports
1847	Herzen leaves Russia forever
	Belinsky's *Letter to Gogol*
1849	Dostoevsky sentenced to forced labor in Siberia
	Russian intervention in Hungary
1851	St. Petersburg–Moscow railway opened
1852	Turgenev's *Sportsman's Notebook*
1853	Ostrovsky's first play produced
1853–56	Crimean War
1855	Death of Nicholas I
1855	ALEXANDER II, 1855–81
1857	First issue of Herzen's *Kolokol* (*The Bell*)
	Alexander Ivanov's painting, "Christ's First Appearance to the People"
1858–60	Acquisition from China of Amur and Maritime provinces
1859	Surrender of Shamil; conquest of Caucasus completed
	Goncharov's *Oblomov*
1860	Founding of Vladivostok
1860–73	First railway boom
1861	Emancipation of the serfs
1862	St. Petersburg Conservatory founded; Anton Rubinstein, director
	The Five (Balakierev, Cui, Borodin, Rimsky-Korsakov, Mussorgsky) announce their intention to create a school of "true Russian music"
	Turgenev's *Fathers and Sons*
1863	Polish rebellion
	Artists Co-operative Society founded
	Chernyshevsky's *What Is To Be Done?*
1863–65	Law (courts) and education reform
	Zemstvo instituted
	Censorship relaxed
1864–85	Conquest of central Asia
1865	Capture of Tashkent
1866	Moscow Conservatory founded: Tchaikovsky professor
1867	Alaska sold to the United States of America
1868	Capture of Samarkand and Bukhara
1869	Tolstoy's *War and Peace*
1870	Society for Traveling Art Exhibitions
	Mendeleyev's *Principles of Chemistry*
1872	Russian translation of Marx's *Capital*

1873	Capture of Khiva Beginning of the movement "To the People" (*V narod*) Repin's painting "The Bargemen"
1874	Compulsory military service Mussorgsky's opera *Boris Godunov*
1876	Land and Freedom Party Conquest of Kokand khanate (Fergana)
1877	Tchaikovsky's *Swan Lake*
1877–78	War with Turkey
1878	Tchaikovsky's *First Piano Concerto* takes Paris by storm His opera *Eugene Onegin* Tolstoy's *Anna Karenina*
1879	People's Will Party, and Black Partition
1880	*Brothers Karamazov*
1881	Assassination of Alexander II

1881	ALEXANDER III, 1881–94
1882	Establishment of factory inspection system
1884	Reactionary regulations for universities
1888	Rimsky-Korsakov's *Scheherazade*
1890	Borodin's opera *Prince Igor* Tchaikovsky's *Sleeping Beauty* Shchukin Museum, Moscow Reactionary statute on zemstvos and cities
1891	Tchaikovsky conducts at Carnegie Hall Beginning of Trans-Siberian railway Famine in twenty-one provinces of European Russia
1891–93	Making of Franco-Russian alliance
1892	Tretiakov donates his art collection to the city of Moscow
1892–1903	Witte as minister of communications, finance, and commerce

1894	NICHOLAS II, 1894–1917
1897	First general population census in Russia
1898	Moscow Art Theatre founded, produces Chekhov's *Sea Gull* First Congress of the Russian Social Democratic party Occupation of Port Arthur
1900	Boxer rebellion; Russia occupies Manchuria
1902	Gorky's *Lower Depths*
1903	Split into Mensheviks and Bolsheviks
1904	General strike in Tiflis and Baku
1904–5	Russo-Japanese War
1905	Revolution: General Strike, October Manifesto, Moscow rising
1906	First Duma

1906–11	Stolypin: agrarian legislation
1909	Diaghilev ballet, yearly tours to western Europe
1912	Mayakovsky's "A Slap in the Face of Public Taste"
1914 (August)	World War I
1917 (March)	**REVOLUTION**
	Abdication of Nicholas II
	Provisional Government

CORRELATION *of* READINGS IN RUSSIAN CIVILIZATION

Vols. I, II, and III with Representative Texts

CLARKSON, JESSE D., *A History of Russia*, Random House, 1964

Chapter Nos.	Related Selections in READINGS IN RUSSIAN CIVILIZATION	Chapter Nos.	Related Selections in READINGS IN RUSSIAN CIVILIZATION
1	I: 16	19	II: 36, 37
2	I: 1	20	II: 35
3	I: 2	21	II: 39–41
4	I: 3–5	22	II: 38
5	I: 6, 10, 15	23	II: 42, 43
6		24	III: 44
7	I: 7–9	25	III: 45
8		26	III: 46
9	I: 11–13	27	
10	I: 14, 17	28	III: 47
11		29	III: 48
12	II: 18	30	III: 49–51
13	II: 19	31	III: 55, 56
14	II: 20–22	32	III: 52–54
15	II: 23–27	33	
16		34	III: 57, 58
17	II: 28, 30	35	III: 59–62
18	II: 29, 31–34	36	III: 63–69
		37	III: 70–72

DMYTRYSHYN, BASIL, *USSR: A Concise History*, Scribners, 1965

Chapter Nos.	Related Selections in READINGS IN RUSSIAN CIVILIZATION	Chapter Nos.	Related Selections in READINGS IN RUSSIAN CIVILIZATION
1		5	III: 47, 48
2	III: 44, 45	6	III: 49–56
3	III: 46	7	III: 57–62
4		8	
		9	III: 63–72

ELLISON, HERBERT J., *History of Russia*, Holt, Rinehart, and Winston, 1964

Chapter Nos.	Related Selections in READINGS IN RUSSIAN CIVILIZATION	Chapter Nos.	Related Selections in READINGS IN RUSSIAN CIVILIZATION
1	I: 16	13	III: 44–45
2	I: 1–5	14	III: 46
3	I: 6–10, 15	15	III: 47
4	I: 11–14, 17	16	III: 48
5	II: 18	17	
6	II: 19–22	18	III: 49–56
7	II: 23	19	
8	II: 24–27	20	III: 57, 58
9	II: 28–31	21	III: 59–62
10	II: 32–37	22	
11	II: 38–41	23	III: 63–70
12	II: 42–43	24	III: 71, 72

FLORINSKY, MICHAEL T., *Russia: A History and an Interpretation*, 2 vols., Macmillan, 1953

Chapter Nos.	Related Selections in READINGS IN RUSSIAN CIVILIZATION	Chapter Nos.	Related Selections in READINGS IN RUSSIAN CIVILIZATION
1	I: 1, 2	25	
2		26	
3	I: 15	27	II: 23
4	I: 6	28	II: 24
5	I: 3, 4	29	
6	I: 5, 10	30	
7		31	II: 25–27
8	I: 7–9	32	
9		33	
10	I: 13	34	
11	I: 11, 12, 14, 16, 17	35	
12		36	II: 33
13	II: 18	37	II: 28–32
14		38	II: 34, 36, 37
15		39	II: 35
16		40	II: 38–41
17		41	II: 43
18	II: 19	42	II: 42
19		43	
20		44	
21	II: 20, 21	45	III: 44
22		46	III: 45
23	II: 22	47	
24		48	III: 46

FLORINSKY, MICHAEL T., *Russia: A Short History*, Macmillan, 1964

Chapter Nos.	Related Selections in READINGS IN RUSSIAN CIVILIZATION	Chapter Nos.	Related Selections in READINGS IN RUSSIAN CIVILIZATION
1	I: 1, 2, 16	15	II: 28–33
2	I: 3–5	16	II: 34–42
3	I: 15	17	
4	I: 10	18	II: 43
5	I: 6	19	III: 44, 45
6	I: 7–9	20	III: 46–48
7		21	III: 52–56
8	I: 13	22	III: 49–51
9	I: 11, 12, 14, 17	23	
10	II: 18	24	III: 57, 58
11	II: 19	25	III: 59–62
12	II: 20–22	26	III: 63–72
13	II: 23, 24	27	
14	II: 25–27		

HARCAVE, SIDNEY, *Russia: A History*, 6th ed., Lippincott, 1968

Chapter Nos.	Related Selections in READINGS IN RUSSIAN CIVILIZATION	Chapter Nos.	Related Selections in READINGS IN RUSSIAN CIVILIZATION
1	I: 16	17	II: 36, 37
2	I: 1–5, 15	18	II: 33
3	I: 6–10	19	II: 31
4	I: 11–14, 17	20	II: 39–41
5	II: 18	21	II: 42
6	II: 19	22	II: 43
7	II: 20–21	23	III: 44, 45
8		24	III: 46
9	II: 22	25	III: 47

HARCAVE, SIDNEY, *Russia: A History*, 6th ed., Lippincott, 1968

Chapter Nos.	Related Selections in READINGS IN RUSSIAN CIVILIZATION	Chapter Nos.	Related Selections in READINGS IN RUSSIAN CIVILIZATION
10		26	III: 48
11	II: 23	27	III: 49–51
12	II: 24	28	III: 52–56
13	II: 25–27	29	III: 57, 58
14		30	III: 59–62
15	II: 28–30	31	III: 63–72
16	II: 34, 38		

MAZOUR, ANATOLE G., *Russia: Tsarist and Communist*, Van Nostrand, 1962

Chapter Nos.	Related Selections in READINGS IN RUSSIAN CIVILIZATION	Chapter Nos.	Related Selections in READINGS IN RUSSIAN CIVILIZATION
1	I: 16	19	II: 37
2	I: 1, 2	20	II: 35, 38
3	I: 15	21	II: 39–41
4	I: 3–5, 10	22	
5	I: 7–9	23	II: 25–28
6	I: 6	24	
7		25	
8	I: 11–14, 17	26	
9	II: 18	27	II: 42–43
10		28	III: 44, 45
11		29	III: 46
12	II: 19	30	III: 47, 48
13	II: 20–22	31	
14		32	III: 49–51
15	II: 23	33	III: 52–56
16	II: 24	34	
17	II: 29–31	35	III: 57
18	II: 32–34, 36	36	III: 58
		37	III: 59–62
		38	III: 63–72

PARES, BERNARD, *A History of Russia*, Vintage Books, 1965

Chapter Nos.	Related Selections in READINGS IN RUSSIAN CIVILIZATION	Chapter Nos.	Related Selections in READINGS IN RUSSIAN CIVILIZATION
1	I: 16	15	II: 22
2	I: 1, 2	16	II: 23
3	I: 15	17	II: 24
4	I: 3, 4	18	II: 25–27
5	I: 5, 10	19	II: 28
6	I: 7–9	20	II: 29–33
7	I: 6	21	II: 34–37
8		22	II: 38
9	I: 11–13	23	II: 39–41
10	I: 14, 17	24	II: 42, 43
11		25	III: 44–48
12	II: 18	26	III: 49–56
13	II: 19	27	III: 57–72
14	II: 20, 21		

PUSHKAREV, SERGEI, *The Emergence of Modern Russia, 1801–1917*, Holt, Rinehart, and Winston, 1963

Chapter Nos.	Related Selections in READINGS IN RUSSIAN CIVILIZATION	Chapter Nos.	Related Selections in READINGS IN RUSSIAN CIVILIZATION
1	II: 23	7	II: 36, 37
2		8	II: 35, 39–41
3	II: 24–27	9	
4		10	II: 38, 42
5	II: 28	11	II: 43
6	II: 29–34		

RAUCH, GEORG VON, *A History of Soviet Russia*, 5th rev. ed., Praeger, 1967

Chapter Nos.	Related Selections in READINGS IN RUSSIAN CIVILIZATION	Chapter Nos.	Related Selections in READINGS IN RUSSIAN CIVILIZATION
1	III: 44–46	6	III: 52–56
2		7	
3		8	III: 57, 58
4	III: 47–51	9	III: 59–62
5		10	III: 63–72

RIASANOVSKY, NICHOLAS V., *A History of Russia*, Oxford University Press, 1963

Chapter Nos.	Related Selections in READINGS IN RUSSIAN CIVILIZATION	Chapter Nos.	Related Selections in READINGS IN RUSSIAN CIVILIZATION
1	I: 16	22	II: 20, 21
2		23	
3	I: 1	24	II: 22
4		25	II: 23
5	I: 2	26	II: 24
6		27	
7		28	II: 25–27
8	I: 15	29	II: 29, 31
9	I: 3, 4	30	II: 34
10		31	II: 35, 39–42
11		32	II: 30, 36–38
12		33	II: 28, 32, 33, 43
13	I: 5, 10	34	III: 44, 45
14		35	
15	I: 7–9	36	III: 46–48
16		37	III: 49–56
17		38	III: 57–58
18	I: 6, 13, 14	39	III: 59–62
19	I: 11, 12, 17	40	III: 63–66
20	II: 18	41	III: 67–71
21	II: 19	42	III: 72

Seton-Watson, Hugh, *The Russian Empire, 1801–1917*, Oxford, 1967

Chapter Nos.	Related Selections in READINGS IN RUSSIAN CIVILIZATION	Chapter Nos.	Related Selections in READINGS IN RUSSIAN CIVILIZATION
1	II: 18–22	11	II: 29–31
2		12	
3	II: 23	13	II: 32–34
4		14	II: 36, 37
5	II: 24	15	II: 35
6		16	
7		17	II: 39–41
8	II: 25–27	18	II: 38
9		19	II: 42
10	II: 28	20	II: 43

Treadgold, Donald W., *Twentieth Century Russia*, 2d ed., Rand McNally, 1964

Chapter Nos.	Related Selections in READINGS IN RUSSIAN CIVILIZATION	Chapter Nos.	Related Selections in READINGS IN RUSSIAN CIVILIZATION
1		16	
2	II: 22–29, 31–33	17	III: 49–51
3		18	III: 52–56
4	II: 35	19	
5	II: 34, 39–41	20	
6		21	
7	II: 30, 36, 37	22	
8	II: 38, 42, 43	23	III: 57
9	III: 44, 45	24	III: 58
10	III: 46	25	
11		26	
12		27	III: 59–62
13	III: 47, 48	28	III: 63–66
14		29	III: 67–72
15			

Vernadsky, George, *A History of Russia*, 5th ed., Yale University Press, 1961

Chapter Nos.	Related Selections in READINGS IN RUSSIAN CIVILIZATION	Chapter Nos.	Related Selections in READINGS IN RUSSIAN CIVILIZATION
1	I: 1, 16	10	II: 28–34
2	I: 2	11	II: 36–38
3	I: 3–5, 15	12	II: 35, 39–41
4	I: 7–9	13	II, III: 42–46
5	I: 6, 10–14, 17	14	III: 47–51
6	II: 18–21	15	III: 52–56
7	II: 22, 23	16	III: 59–62
8	II: 25–27	17	III: 57, 58
9	II: 24	18	III: 63–72

WREN, MELVIN C., *The Course of Russian History*, 3d ed., Macmillan, 1968

Chapter Nos.	Related Selections in READINGS IN RUSSIAN CIVILIZATION	Chapter Nos.	Related Selections in READINGS IN RUSSIAN CIVILIZATION
1	I: 16	12	II: 28–33
2	I: 1	13	II: 34–38
3	I: 2, 5	14	II: 39–43
4	I: 3, 4	15	III: 44–46
5	I: 6, 10	16	III: 47, 48, 52–56
6	I: 7–9	17	III: 49–51, 64, 66, 67, 70
7	I: 11–17	18	III: 59–62
8	II: 18	19	
9	II: 19–22	20	III: 57, 58, 65, 71
10	II: 23	21	III: 63, 68, 69, 72
11	II: 24–27		

WALSH, WARREN B., *Russia and the Soviet Union*, University of Michigan Press, 1958

Chapter Nos.	Related Selections in READINGS IN RUSSIAN CIVILIZATION	Chapter Nos.	Related Selections in READINGS IN RUSSIAN CIVILIZATION
1	I: 16	16	II: 32–34, 36–37
2	I: 1, 3, 4	17	II: 35
3	I: 2, 5	18	II: 39–41
4	I: 15	19	II: 38, 42, 43
5	I: 7, 8, 9	20	III: 44–45
6	I: 6, 10–14, 17	21	III: 46
7	II: 18	22	
8	II: 19	23	III: 47, 48
9	II: 20, 21, 22	24	III: 49–56
10	II: 23	25	
11	II: 24	26	III: 57, 58
12		27	III: 59–62
13	II: 25, 26, 27	28	
14	II: 28–31	29	III: 63–72
15			

INDEX VOLUME II